CONTEMPORARY ISSUES
IN CURRICULUM

CONTEMPORARY ISSUES IN CURRICULUM

SIXTH EDITION

ALLAN C. ORNSTEIN

St. John's University

EDWARD F. PAJAK

Johns Hopkins University

STACEY B. ORNSTEIN

New York University

PEARSON

Boston   Columbus   Indianapolis   New York   San Francisco   Upper Saddle River
Amsterdam   Cape Town   Dubai   London   Madrid   Milan   Munich   Paris   Montreal   Toronto
Delhi   Mexico City   São Paulo   Sydney   Hong Kong   Seoul   Singapore   Taipei   Tokyo

Vice President and Editorial Director: Jeffery W. Johnston
Senior Acquisitions Editor: Meredith Fossel
Editorial Assistant: Janelle Criner
Vice President, Director of Marketing: Margaret Waples
Senior Marketing Manager: Darcy Betts
Production Project Manager: Jenny Gessner
Procurement Specialist: Pat Tonneman
Senior Art Director: Jayne Conte
Cover Designer: Suzanne Behnke
Cover Photo: © kras99, Fotolia
Media Project Manager: Noelle Chun
Development Project Management: Aptara®, Inc.
Full-Service Project Management: Niraj Bhatt, Aptara®, Inc.
Composition: Aptara®, Inc
Printer/Binder: Courier/Westford
Cover Printer: Moore Langen
Text Font: Palatino LT Std 10/12

Credits and acknowledgments for material borrowed from other sources and reproduced, with permission, in this textbook appear on the appropriate page within the text.

Every effort has been made to provide accurate and current Internet information in this book. However, the Internet and information posted on it are constantly changing, so it is inevitable that some of the Internet addresses listed in this textbook will change.

Library of Congress Cataloging-in-Publication Data

Contemporary issues in curriculum/Allan C. Ornstein, Edward F. Pajak,
    Stacey B. Ornstein.—Sixth edition.
        p. cm.
    Includes index.
    ISBN-13: 978-0-13-325997-1
    ISBN-10: 0-13-325997-8
    1. Education—Curricula—United States.   2. Curriculum planning—United States.
I. Ornstein, Allan C.   II. Pajak, Edward   III. Ornstein, Stacey B.
    LB1570.C813 2015
    375'.001—dc23

2013029293

10 9 8 7 6 5 4 3 2 1

ISBN 10:   0-13-325997-8
ISBN 13: 978-0-13-325997-1

Contributors

Ronald S. Brandt, Association for Supervision and Curriculum Development
Ted Britton, WestEd's National Center for Improving Science Education
Arthur L. Costa, Emeritus, California State University, Sacramento
Larry Cuban, Emeritus, Stanford University
Linda Darling-Hammond, Stanford University
Daniel L. Duke, University of Virginia
Elliot Eisner, Stanford University
Norman Eng, Brooklyn College
Chester E. Finn, Jr., Thomas B. Fordham Institute
Howard Gardner, Harvard Graduate School of Education
Tom Gasner, University of Wisconsin, Whitewater
Geneva Gay, University of Washington
Carl D. Glickman, Emeritus, University of Georgia
Maxine Greene, Emeritus, Teachers College, Columbia University
Andy Hargreaves, Lynch School of Education, Boston College
Edwin Lou Javius, EDEquity Inc.
Lawrence Kohlberg, Emeritus, Harvard University
Todd I. Lubart, Yale University
Veronica Boix Mansilla, Harvard Graduate School of Education
Frank Masci, Johns Hopkins University
Laura McCloskey, Stanford University
Nel Noddings, Stanford University
Allan C. Ornstein, St. John's University
Edward F. Pajak, Johns Hopkins University
Parker J. Palmer, American Association for Higher Education
David Perkins, Harvard Graduate School of Education
James Popham, Emeritus, University of California, Los Angeles
Robert Rothman, Alliance for Excellent Education
Thomas J. Sergiovanni, Trinity University
Dennis Shirley, Lynch School of Education, Boston College
Nancy Faust Sizer, Francis W. Parker Charter School, Massachusetts
Theodore R. Sizer, Coalition of Essential Schools, California
Robert J. Sternberg, Yale University
Elaine Stotko, Johns Hopkins University
Carol Ann Tomlinson, University of Virginia
Ralph W. Tyler, Center for Advanced Study in the Behavioral Sciences, California
Herbert J. Walberg, Emeritus, University of Illinois, Chicago and Hoover Institute, Palo Alto
Grant Wiggins, Authentic Education
Harry K. Wong, Author and Lecturer on Teacher Success and Retention
Yong Zhao, University of Oregon

Preface

This sixth edition of *Contemporary Issues in Curriculum* is a text for students or school leaders studying the disciplines of curriculum, instruction, supervision, administration, and teacher education. It is written for those who are exploring the issues that have the potential to influence the planning, implementation, and evaluation of curriculum at all levels of teaching and learning. The articles reflect emergent trends in the field of curriculum and instruction.

NEW TO THIS EDITION

In an effort to improve the quality and relevance of the new edition, the editors have added 10 new chapters. As in earlier editions, the overall intent of the editors was to focus on well-known contributors in the field of curriculum and to select articles that were easy to read and that simultaneously offered an in-depth perspective on a subject or issue important to curriculum. In deciding to delete or add chapters, the editors considered two factors: (1) Whether the original article had become dated or less relevant to the changing trends in schools and/or society and (2) whether the original piece was either too lengthy or difficult to fully understand. Then, the purpose was to incorporate new chapters that students and instructors would find relevant to the field of curriculum and their own personal situations. The criteria for selection of the new chapters were as follows:

- The new articles are meant to interest those who are preparing for a teaching career as well as experienced educators concerned with issues and policies that influence education.
- The chapters are valuable for use in introductory courses in curriculum and in a variety of upper-level and graduate education courses and address relevant topics such as the Common Core Standards and aiming higher with expectations for student performance.
- The new authors (as in the case of previous editions) are well known in the field of curriculum and/or related domains—philosophy, teaching, learning, instruction, supervision, and policy. To be sure, the best authors in all fields of social science and education have a distinctive message.
- The new authors chosen include a wide range of philosophical viewpoints, but always represent contemporary and emerging issues such as changing societal demographics, pre-K education, and teacher induction and retention.
- The story and issues in the new chapters are well defined and coherent and offer a comprehensive body of information on various educational trends and curriculum issues. They are written in a way that engages readers or takes sides in some political or philosophical struggle.
- The articles selected are intended to be controversial and encourage critical thinking as well as to give the reader ready access to important ideas and issues that affect education in general and curriculum, including new topics related to international comparisons and competitiveness, as well as how one can truly judge the success of a school and the value of an education.
- Although the notions of currency and relevancy filtered through the selection process, it is essential to understand that our pasts blend with our present, and there are no single timelines, no specific historical periods, separate from another time period. Another factor was

duration, that the articles selected would have a time value of at least 5 years into the future.

- The editors are particularly concerned about traditional issues related to teaching and learning, as well as contemporary issues such as global, multicultural, and egalitarian perspectives. Given this bias, the greatest amount of change took place in the sections on curriculum and philosophy, curriculum and learning, curriculum and instruction, and curriculum and policy.

- Finally, it is naïve to believe that more education stories on the front page of any newspaper or news media will change the course of schools or radically alter the curriculum. Nevertheless, the authors chosen tend to have the wind behind their backs and a broad frame of reference for understanding the important problems and trends affecting the present and future in education, as well as the field of curriculum.

ORGANIZATION OF THE TEXT

This text is divided into six parts: philosophy, teaching, learning, instruction, supervision, and policy. Each part consists of five or six chapters and is preceded by an introduction that provides a brief overview of the articles and focuses the reader's attention on the issues to be discussed. Each chapter begins with a set of focusing questions and ends with several discussion questions. A pro–con chart that explores views on both sides of a current controversial curricular concern and a case study problem appear at the end of each part. These instructional features help the reader integrate the content and the issues of the text. Instructors may wish to use these features as the bases for class discussion or essay assignments.

To ensure that the breadth and depth of viewpoints in the field are represented, we have included articles that portray current trends and illustrate the dynamism within the field. The readings present views that reflect traditionally held beliefs as well as other perspectives that might be considered more controversial in nature. Students and practitioners should have an opportunity to investigate the breadth of issues that are affecting curriculum and be able to access such information in a single source. Readers are encouraged to examine and debate these issues, formulate their own ideas regarding the issues affecting the field of curriculum, and decide what direction that field should take.

In Part I, the Eisner and Rothman chapters are new. No additions were made for Part II. The Finn and Eng pieces were added for Part III. In the next part, the Zhao, Tomlinson and Javius, and Wiggins chapters are new. There is one new piece in Part V, by Ingersoll. As for the sixth part, two new chapters were added by Odden and Ornstein.

Acknowledgments

We acknowledge with gratitude the many authors who granted us permission to reprint their work. Allan Ornstein expresses love for Esther, his wife, and especially his children, Joel, Stacey, and Jason, and advises them to always take the high road in life. Edward Pajak thanks Diane, his wife, and his children, Alexandra and Zachary, for their unflagging encouragement. Stacey Ornstein dedicates this book to her husband David, and her son Adrian, and thanks them for their continuous support in all her endeavors.

We thank the following reviewers for their helpful suggestions: Savilla Banister, Bowling Green State University; Timothy G. Cashman, University of Texas at El Paso; and Jo Ann Sumbry, University of Montevallo.

CONTENTS

PART ONE

Curriculum and Philosophy

How does philosophy influence the curriculum? To what extent does the curriculum reflect personal beliefs and societal ways? How do different conceptions of curriculum affect schooling and student achievement? In what way has curriculum been a catalyst in empowering certain segments of society while disenfranchising others?

In Chapter 1, Allan Ornstein considers how philosophy guides the organization of the curriculum. He explores how beliefs about the purposes of education are reflected in the subject matter and the process of teaching and learning. In Chapter 2, Ronald Brandt and Ralph Tyler present a rationale for establishing educational goals. They identify the sources that they believe should be considered before articulating goals, as well as how goals should be used in planning learning activities.

In Chapter 3, Elliot Eisner warns that leadership in education requires more than just accepting the limited measures now used for determining how well schools are doing and describes some features of a more human vision of schooling. The true measure of educational attainment, he tells us, is what students do with what they learn and when they can do what they want to do. Next, Maxine Greene reminds us in Chapter 4 of the essential role that arts experiences play in helping students develop esthetic awareness. She explains why encounters with the arts are likely to enrich students' learning experiences. She also discusses why experience with the arts is critical to combating the delivery of prescriptive curricula and developing students' metacognitive strategies. In Chapter 5, Robert Rothman argues for the importance of adopting the Common Core Curriculum Standards, such as the need for highly skilled workers in the midst of rapidly changing technology and the inadequacy of state standards for global competitiveness and for comparing student performance across state lines. He describes the content of the Common Core for reading, writing, and mathematics as well as next steps to be taken toward implementation.

1

Philosophy as a Basis for Curriculum Decisions

ALLAN C. ORNSTEIN

FOCUSING QUESTIONS

1. How does philosophy guide the organization and implementation of curriculum?
2. What are the sources of knowledge that shape a person's philosophy of curriculum?
3. What are the sources of knowledge that shape your philosophical view of curriculum?
4. How do the aims, means, and ends of education differ?
5. What is the major philosophical issue that must be determined before we can define a philosophy of curriculum?
6. What are the four major educational philosophies that have influenced curriculum in the United States?
7. What is your philosophy of curriculum?

Philosophic issues always have had and still do have an impact on schools and society. Contemporary society and its schools are changing fundamentally and rapidly, much more so than in the past. There is a special urgency that dictates continuous appraisal and reappraisal of the role of schools, and calls for a philosophy of education. Without philosophy, educators are directionless in the whats and hows of organizing and implementing what we are trying to achieve. In short, our philosophy of education influences, and to a large extent determines, our educational decisions, choices, and alternatives.

PHILOSOPHY AND CURRICULUM

Philosophy provides educators, especially curriculum specialists, with a framework for organizing schools and classrooms. It helps them answer questions about what the school's purpose is, what subjects are of value, how students learn, and what methods and materials to use. Philosophy provides them with a framework for broad issues and tasks, such as determining the goals of education, subject content and its organization, the process of teaching and learning, and, in general, what experiences and activities to stress in schools and classrooms. It also provides educators with a basis for making such decisions as what workbooks, textbooks, or other cognitive and noncognitive activities to utilize and how to utilize them, what and how much homework to assign, how to test students and how to use the test results, and what courses or subject matter to emphasize.

The importance of philosophy in determining curriculum decisions is expressed well by the classic statement of Thomas Hopkins (1941): "Philosophy has entered into every important decision that has ever been made about curriculum and teaching in the past and will continue to be the basis of every important decision in the future. . . . There is rarely a moment in a school day when a teacher is not confronted with occasions where philosophy is a vital part of action." Hopkins' statement reminds us of how important philosophy is to all aspects of curriculum decisions, whether it operates overtly or covertly. Indeed, almost all elements of curriculum are based on philosophy. As John Goodlad (1979b) points out, philosophy is the beginning point in curriculum decision making and is the basis for all subsequent decisions regarding curriculum. Philosophy becomes the criterion for determining the aims, means, and ends of curriculum. The aims are statements of value, based on philosophical beliefs; the means represent processes and methods, which reflect philosophical choices; and the ends connote the facts, concepts, and principles of the knowledge or behavior learned—what is felt to be important to learning.

Smith, Stanley, and Shores (1957) also put great emphasis on the role of philosophy in developing curriculum, asserting that it is essential when formulating and justifying educational purposes, selecting and organizing knowledge, formulating basic procedures and activities, and dealing with verbal traps (what we see versus what is read). Curriculum theorists, they point out, often fail to recognize both how important philosophy is to developing curriculum and how it influences aspects of curriculum.

Philosophy and the Curriculum Specialist

The philosophy of curriculum specialists reflects their life experiences, common sense, social and economic background, education, and general beliefs about people. An individual's philosophy evolves and continues to evolve as long as there is personal growth, development, and learning from experience. Philosophy is a description, explanation, and evaluation of the world as seen from personal perspective, or through what some social scientists call "social lenses."

Curriculum specialists can turn to many sources of knowledge, but no matter how many sources they draw on or how many authorities they listen to, their decisions are shaped by all the experiences that have affected them and the social groups with which they identify. These decisions are based on values, attitudes, and beliefs that they have developed, involving their knowledge and interpretation of causes, events, and their consequences. Philosophy determines principles for guiding action.

No one can be totally objective in a cultural or social setting, but curriculum specialists can broaden their base of knowledge and experiences by trying to understand other people's sense of values and by analyzing problems from various perspectives. They can also try to modify their own critical analyses and points of view by learning from their experiences and those of others. Curriculum specialists who are unwilling to modify their points of view, or to compromise philosophical positions when school officials or their colleagues espouse another philosophy, are at risk of causing conflict and disrupting the school. Ronald Doll (1986) puts it this way: "Conflict among curriculum planners occurs when persons . . . hold positions along a continuum of [different] beliefs and . . . persuasions." The conflict may become so intense that "curriculum study grinds to a halt." Most of the time, the differences can be reconciled "temporarily in deference to the demands of a temporary, immediate task." However, Doll further explains that "teachers and administrators who are clearly divided in philosophy can seldom work together in close proximity for long periods of time."

The more mature and understanding and the less personally threatened and ego-involved individuals are, the more capable they are of reexamining or modifying their philosophy, or at least of being willing to appreciate other points of view. It is important for curriculum specialists to regard their attitudes and beliefs as tentative—as subject to reexamination whenever facts or trends challenge them. Equally dangerous for curriculum specialists is the opposite—indecision or lack of any philosophy, which can be reflected in attempts to avoid commitment to a set of values. A measure of positive conviction is essential to prudent action. Having a personal philosophy that is tentative or subject to modification, however, does not lead to lack of conviction or disorganized behavior. Curriculum specialists can arrive at their conclusions on the best evidence available, and they then can change when better evidence surfaces.

Philosophy as a Curriculum Source

The function of philosophy can be conceived as either the base for the starting point in curriculum development or an interdependent function of other functions in curriculum development. John Dewey (1916) represents the first school of thought by contending that "philosophy may . . . be defined as the general theory of education," and that "the business of philosophy is to provide [the framework] for the aims and methods" of schools. For Dewey, philosophy provides a generalized meaning to our lives and a way of thinking, "an explicit formulation of the . . . mental and moral attitudes in respect to the difficulties of contemporary social life." Philosophy is not only a starting point for schools; it is also crucial for all curriculum activities. For as Dewey adds, "Education is the laboratory in which philosophic distinctions become concrete and are tested."

Highly influenced by Dewey, Ralph Tyler's (1949) framework of curriculum includes philosophy as only one of five criteria commonly used for selecting educational purposes. The relationship between philosophy and the other criteria—studies of learners, studies of contemporary life, suggestions from subject specialists, and the psychology of learning—is the basis for determining the school's purposes. Although philosophy is not the starting point in Tyler's curriculum, but rather interacts on an equal basis with the other criteria, he does seem to place more importance on philosophy for developing educational purposes. Tyler (1949) writes, "The educational and social philosophy to which the school is committed can serve as the first screen for developing the social program." He concludes that "philosophy attempts to define the nature of the good life and a good society," and that the "educational philosophies in a democratic society are likely to emphasize strongly democratic values in schools."

There can be no serious discussion about philosophy until we embrace the question of what is education. When we agree on what education is, we can ask what the school's purpose is. We can then pursue philosophy, aims, and goals of curriculum. According to Goodlad (1979b), the school's first responsibility is to the social order, what he calls the "nation-state," but in our society the sense of individual growth and potential is paramount. This duality—society versus the individual—has been a major philosophical issue in Western society for centuries and was a very important issue in Dewey's works. As Dewey (1916) claimed, we not only wish "to make [good] citizens and workers" but also ultimately want "to make human beings who will live life to the fullest."

The compromise of the duality between national allegiance and individual fulfillment is a noble aim that should guide all curriculum specialists—from the means to the ends. When many individuals grow and prosper, then society flourishes. The original question set forth by Goodlad can be answered: Education is growth and the focal point for the individual as well as society; it is a never-ending process of life, and the more refined the guiding philosophy, the better the quality of the educational process.

In considering the influence of philosophic thought on curriculum, several classification schemes are possible; therefore, no superiority is claimed for the categories used in the tables here. The clusters of ideas are those that often evolve openly or unwittingly during curriculum planning.

Four major educational philosophies have influenced curriculum in the United States: Perennialism, Essentialism, Progressivism, and Reconstructionism. Table 1.1 provides an overview of these education philosophies and how they affect curriculum, instruction, and teaching. Teachers and administrators should compare the content of the categories with their own philosophical "lens" in terms of how they view curriculum and how other views of curriculum and related instructional and teaching issues may disagree.

Another way of interpreting philosophy and its effect on curriculum is to analyze philosophy in terms of polarity. The danger of this method is that it may simplify philosophies in terms of a dichotomy, and not recognize that there are overlaps and shifts. Table 1.2 illustrates philosophy in terms of traditional and contemporary categories. The traditional philosophy, as shown, tends to

overlap with Perennialism and Essentialism. Contemporary philosophy tends to coincide with Progressivism and Reconstructionism.

Table 1.2 shows that traditional philosophy focuses on the past, emphasizes fixed and absolute values, and glorifies our cultural heritage. Contemporary philosophy emphasizes the present and future and views events as changeable and relative; for the latter, nothing can be preserved forever, for despite any attempt, change is inevitable. The traditionalists wish to train the mind, emphasize subject matter, and fill the learner with knowledge and information. Those who subscribe to contemporary philosophies are more concerned with problem solving and emphasize student interests and needs. Whereas subject matter is considered important for its own sake, according to traditionalists, certain subjects are more important than others. For contemporary educators, subject matter is considered a medium for teaching skills and attitudes, and most subjects have similar value. According to the traditionalists, the teacher is an authority in subject matter, who dominates the lesson with explanations and lectures. For the contemporary proponent, the teacher is a guide for learning, as well as an agent for change; students and teachers often are engaged in dialogue.

In terms of social issues and society, traditionalists view education as a means of providing direction, control, and restraint, while their counterparts focus on individual expression and freedom from authority. Citizenship is linked to cognitive development for the traditional educator, and it is linked to moral and social development for the contemporary educator. Knowledge and the disciplines prepare students for freedom, according to the traditional view, but it is direct experience in democratic living and political/social action that prepares students for freedom, according to the contemporary ideal. Traditionalists believe in excellence, and contemporary educators favor equality.

TABLE 1.1 Overview of Educational Philosophies

	Philosophical Base	Instructional Objective	Knowledge	Role of Teacher	Curriculum Focus	Related Curriculum Trends
Perennialism	Realism	To educate the rational person; to cultivate the intellect	Focus on past and permanent studies; mastery of facts and timeless knowledge	Teacher helps students think rationally; based on Socratic method and oral exposition; explicit teaching of traditional values	Classical subjects; literary analysis; constant curriculum	Great books; *Paideia* proposal
Essentialism	Idealism, Realism	To promote the intellectual growth of the individual; to educate the competent person	Essential skills and academic subjects; mastery of concepts and principles of subject matter	Teacher is authority in his or her field; explicit teaching of traditional values	Essential skills (three Rs) and essential subjects (English, arithmetic, science, history, and foreign language)	Back to basics; excellence in education
Progressivism	Pragmatism	To promote democratic, social living	Knowledge leads to growth and development; a living-learning process; focus on active and interesting learning	Teacher is a guide for problem solving and scientific inquiry	Based on students' interests; involves the application of human problems and affairs; inter-disciplinary subject matter; activities, and projects	Relevant curriculum; humanistic education; alternative and free schooling
Reconstructionism	Pragmatism	To improve and reconstruct society; education for change and social reform	Skills and subjects needed to identify and ameliorate problems of society; learning is active and concerned with contemporary and future society	Teacher serves as an agent of change and reform; acts as a project director and research leader; helps students become aware of problems confronting humankind	Emphasis on social sciences and social research methods; examination of social, economic, and political problems; focus on present and future trends as well as national and international issues	Equality of education; cultural pluralism; international education; futurism

Source: Allan C. Ornstein and Francis P. Hunkins, *Curriculum: Foundations, Principles, and Theory,* 3rd ed. (Boston: Allyn and Bacon, 1998), p. 56.

TABLE 1.2 Overview of Traditional and Contemporary Philosophies

Philosophical Consideration	Traditional Philosophy	Contemporary Philosophy
Educational philosophy	Perennialism, Essentialism	Progressivism, Reconstructionism
Direction in time	Superiority of past; education for preserving past	Education is growth; reconstruction of present experiences; changing society; concern for future and shaping it
Values	Fixed, absolute, objective, and/or universal	Changeable, subjective, and/or relative
Educational process	Education is viewed as instruction; mind is disciplined and filled with knowledge	Education is viewed as creative self-learning; active process in which learner reconstructs knowledge
Intellectual emphasis	To train or discipline the mind; emphasis on subject matter	To engage in problem-solving activities and social activities; emphasis on student interests and needs
Worth of subject matter	Subject matter for its own importance; certain subjects are better than others for training the mind	Subject matter is a medium for teaching skills, attitudes, and intellectual processes; all subjects have similar value for problem-solving activities
Curriculum content	Curriculum is composed of three Rs, as well as liberal studies or essential academic subjects	Curriculum is composed of three Rs, as well as skills and concepts in arts, sciences, and vocational studies
Learning	Emphasis on cognitive learning; learning is acquiring knowledge and/or competency in disciplines	Emphasis on whole child; learning is giving meaning to experiences and/or active involvement in reform
Grouping	Homogeneous grouping and teaching of students by ability	Heterogeneous grouping and integration of students by ability (as well as race, sex, and class)
Teacher	Teacher is an authority on subject matter; teacher plans activities; teacher supplies knowledge to student; teacher talks, dominates lesson; Socratic method	Teacher is a guide for inquiry and change agent; teacher and students plan activities; students learn on their own independent of the teacher; teacher-student dialogue; student initiates much of the discussion and activities
Social roles	Education involves direction, control, and restraint; group (family, community, church, nation, etc.) always comes first	Education involves individual expression; individual comes first
Citizenship	Cognitive and moral development leads to good citizenship	Personal and social development leads to good citizenship
Freedom and democracy	Acceptance of one's fate, conformity, and compliance with authority; knowledge and discipline prepare students for freedom	Emphasis on creativeness, nonconformity, and self-actualization; direct experiences in democratic living and political/social action prepare students for freedom
Excellence vs. equality	Excellence in education; education as far as human potential permits; academic rewards and jobs based on merit	Equality of education; education that permits more than one chance and more than an equal chance to disadvantaged groups; education and employment sectors consider unequal abilities of individuals and put some restraints on achieving individuals so that different outcomes and group scores, if any, are reduced
Society	Emphasis on group values; acceptance of norms of and roles in society; cooperative and conforming behavior; importance of society; individual restricted by customs and traditions of society	Emphasis on individual growth and development; belief in individual with ability to modify, even reconstruct, the social environment; independent and self-realizing, fully functioning behavior; importance of person; full opportunity to develop one's own potential

The traditional view of education maintains that group values come first, where cooperative and conforming behaviors are important for the good of society. Contemporary educators assert that what is good for the individual should come first, and they believe in the individual modifying and perhaps reconstructing society.

The Curriculum Specialist at Work

Philosophy gives meaning to our decisions and actions. In the absence of a philosophy, educators are vulnerable to externally imposed prescriptions, to fads and frills, to authoritarian schemes, and to other "isms." Dewey (1916) was so convinced of the importance of philosophy that he viewed it as the all-encompassing aspect of the educational process—as necessary for "forming fundamental dispositions, intellectual and emotional, toward nature and fellow man." If this conclusion is accepted, it becomes evident that many aspects of a curriculum, if not most of the educational processes in school, are developed from a philosophy. Even if it is believed that Dewey's point is an overstatement, the pervasiveness of philosophy in determining views of reality, the values and knowledge that are worthwhile, and the decisions to be made about education and curriculum should still be recognized.

Very few schools adopt a single philosophy; in practice, most schools combine various philosophies. Moreover, the author's position is that no single philosophy, old or new, should serve as the exclusive guide for making decisions about schools or about the curriculum. All philosophical groups want the same things of education—that is, they wish to improve the educational process, to enhance the achievement of the learner, to produce better and more productive citizens, and to improve society. Because of their different views of reality, values, and knowledge, however, they find it difficult to agree on how to achieve these ends.

What we need to do, as curricularists, is to search for the middle ground, a highly elusive and abstract concept, in which there is no extreme emphasis on subject matter or student, cognitive development or sociopsychological development, excellence or equality. What we need is a prudent school philosophy, one that is politically and economically feasible, that serves the needs of students and society. Implicit in this view of education is that too much emphasis on any one philosophy may do harm and cause conflict. How much one philosophy is emphasized, under the guise of reform (or for whatever reason), is critical because no one society can give itself over to extreme "isms" or political views and still remain a democracy. The kind of society that evolves is in part reflected in the education system, which is influenced by the philosophy that is eventually defined and developed.

CONCLUSION

In the final analysis, curriculum specialists must understand that they are continuously faced with curriculum decisions, and that philosophy is important in determining these decisions. Unfortunately, few school people test their notions of curriculum against their school's statement of philosophy. According to Brandt and Tyler (1983), it is not uncommon to find teachers and administrators developing elaborate lists of behavioral objectives with little or no consideration to the overall philosophy of the school. Curriculum workers need to provide assistance in developing and designing school practices that coincide with the philosophy of the school and community. Teaching, learning, and curriculum are all interwoven in school practices and should reflect a school's and a community's philosophy.

REFERENCES

Brandt, R. S., & Tyler, R. W. (1983). Goals and objectives. In F. W. English (Ed.), *Fundamental curriculum decisions.* Alexandria, VA: Association for Supervision and Curriculum Development.

Dewey, J. (1916). *Democracy and education.* New York, NY: Macmillan, pp. 383–384.

Doll, R. C. (1986). *Curriculum improvement: Decision-making and process,* 6th ed. Boston, MA: Allyn & Bacon, p. 30.

Goodlad, J. I. (1979b). *What schools are for.* Bloomington, IN: Phi Delta Kappa Educational Foundation.

Hopkins, L. T. (1941). *Interaction: The democratic process.* Boston, MA: D. C. Heath, pp. 198–200.

Smith, B. O., Stanley, W. O., & Shores, J. H. (1957). *Fundamentals of curriculum development,* rev. ed. New York, NY: Worldbook.

Tyler, R. W. (1949). *Basic principles of curriculum and instruction.* Chicago, IL: University of Chicago Press, pp. 33–34.

DISCUSSION QUESTIONS

1. Which philosophical approach reflects your beliefs about (a) the school's purpose, (b) what subjects are of value, (c) how students learn, and (d) the process of teaching and learning?
2. What curriculum focus would the perennialists and essentialists recommend for our increasingly diverse school-age population?
3. What curriculum would the progressivists and reconstructionists select for a multicultural student population?
4. Should curriculum workers adopt a single philosophy to guide their practices? Why? Why not?
5. Which philosophy is most relevant to contemporary education? Why?

2

Goals and Objectives

RONALD S. BRANDT
RALPH W. TYLER

FOCUSING QUESTIONS

1. Why is it important to establish goals for student learning?
2. How do goals and objectives differ?
3. What are three types of goals?
4. What are the factors that should be considered in developing educational goals?
5. What is the relationship between goals and learning activities?
6. In what ways are curriculum goals integral to the process of evaluation?
7. What types of goals should be addressed by schools?

Whether planning for one classroom or many, curriculum developers must have a clear idea of what they expect students to learn. Establishing goals is an important and necessary step because there are many desirable things students could learn—more than schools have time to teach them—so schools should spend valuable instructional time only on high-priority learnings.

Another reason for clarifying goals is that schools must be able to resist pressures from various sources. Some of the things schools are asked to teach are untrue, would hinder students' development, or would help make them narrow, bigoted persons. Some would focus students' learning so narrowly it would reduce, rather than increase, their life options.

FORMS OF GOALS AND OBJECTIVES

Statements of intent appear in different forms, and words such as goals, objectives, aims, ends, outcomes, and purposes are often used interchangeably. Some people find it useful to think of goals as long-term aims to be achieved eventually and objectives as specific learning that students are to acquire as a result of current instruction.

Planners in the Portland, Oregon, area schools say these distinctions are not clear enough to meet organizational planning requirements. They use "goal" to mean any desired outcome of a program, regardless of its specificity, and "objective" only in connection with *program change objectives,* which are defined as statements of intent to change program elements in specified ways. Doherty and Peters (1981) say this distinction avoids confusion and is consistent with the philosophy of "management by objectives."

They refer to three types of goals: instructional, support, and management. Educational goals are defined as learnings to be acquired; support goals as services to be rendered; and management goals as functions of management, such as planning, operating, and evaluating. Such a goal structure permits evaluation to focus on measures of learning acquired (educational outcomes), measures of quantity and quality of service delivery (support outcomes), and measures of quality and effectiveness of management functions (management outcomes).

The Tri-County Goal Development Project, which has published 14 volumes containing over 25,000 goal statements,[1] is concerned only with *educational goals.* For these collections, the following distinctions are made within the general category of "goals":

System level goals (set for the school district by the board of education)
Program level goals (set by curriculum personnel in each subject field)
Course level goals (set by groups of teachers for each subject or unit of instruction)
Instructional level goals (set by individual teachers for daily planning)

Examples of this outcome hierarchy are shown in Figure 2.1.

What distinguishes this system of terminology from others is its recognition that a learning outcome has the same essential character at all levels of planning (hence the appropriateness of a single term, goal, to describe it) and that the level of generality used to represent learning varies with the planning requirements at each level of school organization. The degree of generality chosen for planning at each level is, of course, a matter of judgment; there is no "correct" level but only a sense of appropriateness to purpose.

Teachers, curriculum specialists, and university consultants who write and review course goals use the following guidelines (Doherty & Peters, 1980, pp. 26–27):

1. Is the stated educational outcome potentially significant?
2. Does the goal begin with "The student knows . . ." if it is a knowledge goal and "The student is able to . . ." if it is a process goal?
3. Is the goal stated in language that is sufficiently clear, concise, and appropriate? (Can it be stated in simpler language and/or fewer words?)
4. Can learning experiences be thought of that would lead to the goal's achievement?
5. Do curricular options exist for the goal's achievement? (Methodology should not be a part of the learning outcome statement.)

System Goal:	The student knows and is able to apply basic scientific and technological processes.
Program Goal:	The student is able to use the conventional language, instruments, and operations of science.
Course Goal:	The student is able to classify organisms according to their conventional taxonomic categories.
Instructional Goal:	The student is able to correctly classify cuttings from the following trees as needle-leaf, hemlock, pine, spruce, fir, larch, cypress, redwood, and cedar.

FIGURE 2.1   Examples of Goals at Each Level of Planning

6. Does the goal clearly contribute to the attainment of one or more of the program goals in its subject area?
7. Can the goal be identified with the approximate level of student development?
8. Can criteria for evaluating the goal be identified?

Curriculum developers need to decide the types and definitions of goals most useful to them and to users of their materials. Some authors advise avoiding vagueness by using highly specific language.[2] Mager (1962) and other writers insist that words denoting observable behaviors, such as "construct" and "identify," should be used in place of words like "understand" and "appreciate." Others reject this approach, claiming that behavioral objectives "are in no way adequate for conceptualizing most of our most cherished educational aspirations" (Eisner, 1979, p. 101). Unfortunately this dispute has developed into a debate about behavioral objectives rather than dialogue over the kinds of behavior appropriate for a humane and civilized person.

The debate is partly semantic and partly conceptual. To some persons the word "behavior" carries the meaning of an observable act, like the movement of the fingers in typing. To them, behavioral objectives refer only to overt behavior. Others use the term "behavior" to emphasize the active nature of the learner. They want to emphasize that learners are not passive receptacles but living, reasoning persons. In this sense, behavior refers to all kinds of human reactions.

For example, a detailed set of "behavioral goals" was prepared by French and others (1957). Organized under the major headings of "self-realization," "face-to-face relationships," and "membership in large organizations," *Behavioral Goals of General Education in High School* includes aims such as "Shows growing ability to appreciate and apply good standards of performance and artistic principles." These are expanded by illustrative behaviors such as "Appreciates good workmanship and design in commercial products."

The other aspect of the debate over behavioral objectives arises from focusing on limited kinds of learning, such as training factory workers to perform specific tasks. The term "conditioning" is commonly used for the learning of behaviors initiated by clear stimuli and calling for automatic, fixed responses. Most driving behavior, for example, consists of conditioned responses to traffic lights, to the approach of other cars and pedestrians, and to the sensations a driver receives from the car's movements. Conditioning is a necessary and important type of learning.

In some situations, though, an automatic response is inappropriate. A more complex model of learning compatible with development of responsible persons in a changing society conceives of the learner as actively seeking meaning. This implies understanding and conscious pursuit of one's goals. The rewards of such learning include the satisfaction of coping with problems successfully.

Planning curriculum for self-directed learning requires goals that are not directly observable: ways of thinking, understanding of concepts and principles, broadening and deepening of interests, changing of attitudes, developing satisfying emotional responses to aesthetic experiences, and the like.

Even these goals, however, should use terms with clearly defined meanings. Saying that a student should "understand the concept of freedom" is far too broad and ambiguous, both because the meaning of the term "concept" is not sufficiently agreed on among educators and because concept words such as "freedom" have too great a range of possible informational loadings to ensure similar interpretation from teacher to teacher. If used at all, such a statement would be at the program level and would require increasingly specific elaboration at the course and lesson plan levels.

Some educators find it useful to refer to a particular type of goal as a *competency*. Used in the early 1970s in connection with Oregon's effort to relate high school instruction to daily life (Oregon State Board of Education, 1972), the term "minimum competency" has become identified with state and district testing programs designed to ensure that students have a minimum level of basic skills before being promoted or graduated. Spady (1978) and other advocates of performance-based education point out that competency involves more than "capacities" such as the ability to read and calculate; it should refer to *application* of school-learned skills in situations outside of school.

One definition of competency is the ability to perform a set of related tasks with a high degree of skill. The concept is especially useful in vocational education, where a particular competency can be broken down through task analysis into its component skills so that teachers and curriculum planners have both a broad statement of expected performance and an array of skills specific enough to be taught and measured (Chalupsky, Phillips-Jones, & Danoff, 1981).

CONSIDERATIONS IN CHOOSING GOALS

Educational goals should reflect three important factors: the nature of organized knowledge, the nature of society, and the nature of learners (Tyler, 1949). An obvious source is the nature of organized fields of study. Schools teach music, chemistry, and algebra because these fields have been developed through centuries of painstaking inquiry. Each academic discipline has its own concepts, principles, and processes. It would be unthinkable to neglect passing on to future generations this priceless heritage and these tools for continued learning.

Another factor affecting school goals is the nature of society. For example, the goals of education in the United States are quite different from those in Russia. In the United States,

we stress individuality, competition, creativity, and freedom to choose government officials. Russian schools teach loyalty to the state and subordination of one's individuality to the welfare of the collective. One result is that most U.S. schools offer a great many electives, while the curriculum in Russian schools consists mostly of required subjects. For example, all students in Russia must study advanced mathematics and science to serve their technologically advanced nation (Wirszup, 1981).

U.S. schools have assumed, explicitly or implicitly, many goals related to the nature of society. For example, schools offer drug education, sex education, driver education, and other programs because of concerns about the values and behavior of youth and adults. Schools teach visual literacy because of the influence of television, consumer education because our economic system offers so many choices, and energy education because of the shortage of natural resources.

A goal statement by Ehrenberg and Ehrenberg (1978) specifically recognizes the expectations of society. Their model for curriculum development begins with a statement of "ends sought": "It is intended that as a result of participating in the K–12 educational program students will consistently and effectively take *intelligent, ethical action:* (1) to accomplish the tasks society legitimately expects of all its members, and (2) to establish and pursue worthwhile goals of their own choosing."

The curriculum development process outlined by the Ehrenbergs involves preparing a complete rationale for the ends-sought statement and then defining, for example, areas of societal expectations. The work of the curriculum developer consists of defining a framework of "criterion tasks," all either derived from expectations of society or necessary to pursue individual goals. These tasks, at various levels of pupil development, become the focus of day-to-day instruction. In this way, all curriculum is directly related to school system goals.

A third consideration in choosing goals, sometimes overlooked, is the nature of learners. For example, because Lawrence Kohlberg (1980) found that children pass through a series of stages in their moral development, he believes schools should adopt the goal of raising students' levels of moral reasoning. Sternberg (1981) and other "information processing" psychologists believe that intelligence is, partly at least, a set of strategies and skills that can be learned. Their research suggests, according to Sternberg, that schools can and should set a goal of improving students' intellectual performance.

Recognizing that students often have little interest in knowledge for its own sake or in adult applications of that knowledge, some educators believe goals not only should be based on what we know about students, but should come from students themselves. Many alternative schools emphasize this source of goals more than conventional schools typically do (Raywid, 1981).

While knowledge, society, and learners are all legitimate considerations, the three are sometimes in conflict. For example, many of the products of the curriculum reform movement of the 1960s had goals based almost exclusively on the nature of knowledge. The emphasis of curriculum developers was on the "structure of the disciplines" (Bruner, 1960). Goals of some curriculums failed to fully reflect the nature of society and students, so teachers either refused to use them or gave up after trying them for a year or two (Stake & Easley, 1978).

In the 1970s, educators and the general public reacted against this discipline-centered emphasis by stressing practical activities drawn from daily life. Schools were urged to teach students how to balance a checkbook, how to choose economical purchases, how to complete a job application, and how to read a traffic ticket. Career education enthusiasts, not content with the reasonable idea that education should help prepare students for satisfying careers,

claimed that *all* education should be career-related in some way.

Conflicts of this sort between the academic and the practical are persistent and unavoidable, but curriculum developers err if they emphasize only one source of goals and ignore the others. If noneducators are preoccupied with only one factor, educational leaders have a responsibility to stress the importance of the others and to insist on balance.

SCOPE OF THE SCHOOL'S RESPONSIBILITY

There have been many attempts to define the general aims of schools and school programs, including the well-known Cardinal Principles listed by a national commission in 1918 (Commission on the Reorganization of Secondary Education, U.S. Office of Education, 1918). The seven goals in that report—health, fundamental processes, worthy home membership, vocation, civic education, worthy use of leisure, and ethical character—encompass nearly every aspect of human existence, and most goal statements written since that time have been equally comprehensive.

Some authors contend that schools are mistaken to assume such broad aims. Martin (1980) argued that intellectual development and citizenship are the only goals for which schools should have primary responsibility and that other institutions should be mainly responsible for such goals as worthy home membership. He proposed that schools undertake a new role of coordinating educational efforts of all community agencies.

Paul (1982) reported that in three different communities large numbers of teachers, students, and parents agreed on a limited set of goals confined mostly to basic skills. Paul contended that schools often confuse the issue when involving citizens in setting goals because they ask what students should learn rather than what schools should teach. Goal surveys conducted by her organization showed, she said, that adults want young people to develop many qualities for which they do not expect schools to be responsible.

Undeniably, the aims and activities of U.S. schools are multiple and diverse. They not only teach toothbrushing, crafts, religion, care of animals, advertising, cooking, automobile repair, philosophy, hunting, and chess; they also provide health and food services to children, conduct parent education classes, and offer a variety of programs for the elderly. Periodic review of these obligations is clearly in order. However, in trying to delimit their mission, schools must not minimize concern for qualities that, though hard to define and develop, distinguish educated persons from the less educated.

A carefully refined statement of goals of schooling in the United States was developed by Goodlad (1979) and his colleagues in connection with their Study of Schooling. Deliberately derived from an analysis of hundreds of goal statements adopted by school districts and state departments of education so as to reflect accurately the currently declared aims of U.S. education, the list comprises 65 goals in 12 categories, including "intellectual development," "self-concept," and "moral and ethical character."

An equally broad set of goals is used in Pennsylvania's Educational Quality Assessment, which includes questions intended to measure such elusive aims as "understanding others" and "self-esteem." School districts must give the tests at least once every five years as part of a plan to make schools accountable for the 12 state-adopted goals (Seiverling, 1980). An adaptation of the Pennsylvania goals was used by the ASCD Committee on Research and Theory (1980) in connection with their plan for *Measuring and Attaining the Goals of Education.*

In many cases, schools contribute modestly or not at all to helping students become loving parents and considerate neighbors. In other cases, school experiences may have lasting effects on values, attitudes, and behavior. We believe school goals should include such aims as "interpersonal relations" and "autonomy," as well as "intellectual development" and "basic skills" (Goodlad, 1979), although the goal statement should specifically recognize that most goals are not the exclusive domain of schools but are a shared responsibility with other institutions.

ESTABLISHING LOCAL GOALS

It is usually helpful to begin identification of goals by listing all the promising possibilities from various sources. Consider contemporary *society.* What things could one's students learn that would help them meet current demands and take advantage of future opportunities? General data about modern society may be found in studies of economic, political, and social conditions. Data directly relevant to the lives of one's students will usually require local studies, which can be made by older students, parents, and other local people.

Consider the *background of the students:* their previous experiences, things they have already learned, their interests and needs—that is, the gaps between desired ways of thinking, feeling, and acting and their present ways. This information should be specific to one's own students, although generalized studies of the development of children and youth in our culture will suggest what to look for.

Consider the potential of the various *subject fields.* What things could one's students learn about their world and themselves from the sciences, history, literature, and so on? What can mathematics provide as a resource for their lives? Visual arts? Music? Each new generation is likely to find new possibilities in these growing fields of knowledge and human expression.

In the effort to identify possible goals, don't be unduly concerned about the form in which you state these "things to be learned." For example, you may find a possibility in "Learn new ways of expressing emotions through various experiences provided in literature," and another in "Understand how animal ecologies are disturbed and the consequences of the disturbance." These are in different forms and at different levels of generality, but at this stage the purpose is only to consider carefully all the promising possibilities. Later, those selected as most important and appropriate for one's students can be refined and restated in common form so as to guide curriculum developers in designing learning experiences. At that point, it will probably be helpful to standardize terms and definitions. At early stages, however, curriculum developers should use terminology familiar and understandable to teachers, principals, parents, and citizens rather than insisting on distinctions that others may have difficulty remembering and using.

The comprehensive list of possible outcomes should be carefully scrutinized to sift out those that appear to be of minor importance or in conflict with the school's educational philosophy. The list should also be examined in the light of the apparent prospects for one's students being able to learn these things in school. For example, we know that things once learned are usually forgotten unless there are continuing opportunities to use them. So one criterion for retaining a goal is that students will have opportunities in and out of school to think, feel, and act as expected. We also know that learning of habits requires continuous practice with few errors, so work and study habits should be selected as goals only if they are to be emphasized consistently in school work.

This procedure for identifying what students are to be helped to learn is designed to prevent a common weakness in curriculum development: selection of goals that are obsolete or irrelevant, inappropriate for students' current levels of development, not in keeping with sound scholarship, not in harmony with America's democratic philosophy, or for which the school cannot provide the necessary learning conditions.

A common practice when planning curriculum is to refer to published taxonomies (Bloom, 1956; Krathwohl et al., 1964). Taxonomies can be useful for their original purpose—classifying goals already formulated—but they do not resolve the issue of the relevance of any particular goal to contemporary society or to one's own students. The Bloom and Krathwohl taxonomies are organized in terms of what the authors conceive to be higher or lower levels, but higher ones are not always more important or even necessary. In typewriting, for example, so-called higher mental processes interfere with the speed and accuracy of typing.

A similar caution applies to uncritically taking goals from curriculum materials of other school systems. The fact that educators in Scarsdale or some other district chose certain goals is not in itself evidence that they are appropriate for your students.

Development of general goals for a school system should be a lengthy process with opportunities for students, parents, and others to participate. This can be done, for example, by sponsoring "town meetings," by publishing draft statements of goals in local newspapers with an invitation to respond, and by holding and publicizing hearings on goals sponsored by the board of education.

A factor that complicates the matter is that some sources of goals are simply not subject to a majority vote. Knowledge—whether about physics, poetry, or welding—is the province of specialists. Educators sometimes know more about the nature of children and the learning process than many other adults in the community. Nevertheless, in a democracy there is no higher authority than the people, so the people must be involved in deciding what public schools are to teach.

Most general goals, because they are so broad and because they deal with major categories of human experience, are acceptable to most people. Few will quarrel with a goal such as "Know about human beings, their environments and their achievements, past and present." The problem in developing a general goal statement is usually not to decide which goals are proper and which are not, but to select among many possibilities the ones that are most important, are at the proper level of generality, and are at least partially the responsibility of schools.

While general goals are not usually controversial, more specific ones can be. For example, parents might not quarrel with "Understand and follow practices associated with good health," but some would reject "Describe two effective and two ineffective methods of birth control." Thus, parents and other citizens should be involved in formulating course and program goals as well as general system goals.

USING GOALS TO PLAN LEARNING ACTIVITIES

To some extent, well-stated goals imply the kinds of learning activities that would be appropriate for achieving them. For example, if an instructional goal is "Solve word problems requiring estimation involving use of simple fractions such as 1/2, 1/4, 2/3," students would have to practice estimating solutions to practical problems as well as learning to calculate using fractions. In many instances, however, knowing the goal does not automatically help an educator know how to teach it. For example, to enable students to "understand and appreciate significant human achievements," one teacher might have students read about outstanding scientists of the nineteenth century, supplement the readings with several lectures, and give a multiple-choice examination. Another teacher might decide to divide students into groups and have each group prepare a presentation to the class about a great scientist using demonstrations, dramatic skits, and so on. Forging the link between goals and other steps in curriculum development requires professional knowledge, experience, and imagination.

A factor that distorts what might appear to be a straightforward relationship between goals and activities is that every instructional activity has multiple goals. The goal-setting process is sometimes seen as a one-to-one relationship between various levels of goals and levels of school activity. For example, the mission of a local school system might be to "Offer all students equitable opportunities for a basic education plus some opportunities to develop individual talents and interests." "Basic education" would be defined to include "Communicate effectively by reading, writing, speaking, observing, and listening." A middle school in that district might have a goal such as "Read and understand nonfiction at a level of the average article in *Reader's Digest*" or, more specifically, "Students will be able to distinguish between expressions of fact and opinion in writing."

While similar chains of related goals are basic to sound curriculum planning, developers should never assume that such simplicity fully represents the reality of schools. When a teacher is engaged in teaching reading, he or she must also be conscious of and teach toward other goals: thinking ability, knowledge of human achievements, relationships with others, positive self-concept, and so on.

Not only must teachers address several officially adopted "outside" goals all at once; they must cope with "inside" goals as well. Although Goodlad (1979) uses declared goals to remind educators and the public what schools are said to be for, he cautions that the ends-means model doesn't do justice to the educational process and offers, as an alternative, an ecological perspective. Insisting that school activities should "be viewed for their intrinsic value, quite apart from their linkage or lack of linkage to stated ends" (p. 76), he points out that in addition to "goals that have been set outside of the system for the system" there are also goals inside the system—"students' goals, teachers' goals, principals' goals, and so on—and . . . these goals are not necessarily compatible" (p. 77).

The message to curriculum developers is that although "outside" goals and objectives are fundamental to educational planning, the relationship between purposes and practices is more complex than it may seem.

USING GOALS IN CURRICULUM EVALUATION

Some writers argue that specific objectives are essential in order to design suitable evaluation plans and write valid test items. The work of the National Assessment of Educational Progress shows, however, that even evaluators may not require objectives written in highly technical language.[3] National Assessment objectives do not contain stipulations of conditions or performance standards; in fact, they are expected to meet just two criteria: clarity and importance. The educators, citizens, and subject matter experts who review the objectives are asked, "Do you understand what this objective means? How important is it that students learn this in school?" Objectives are often considered clear and important even though they are stated briefly and simply. When the objectives have been identified, National Assessment staff members or consultants develop exercises designed to be operational definitions of the intended outcomes. Conditions, standards of performance, and so on are specified for the exercises, not for the objectives.

Setting goals is difficult because it requires assembling and weighing all the factors to be considered in selecting the relatively few but important goals that can be attained with the limited time and resources available to schools. The demands and opportunities of society, the needs of students, the resources of scholarship, the values of democracy, and the conditions needed for effective learning must all be considered.

A common error is the failure to distinguish purposes appropriate for the school from those attainable largely through experiences in the home and community. The school can reinforce the family in helping children develop punctuality, dependability, self-discipline, and other important habits. The school can be and usually is a community in which children and adults respect each other, treat each other fairly, and cooperate. But the primary task for which public schools were established is to enlarge students' vision and experience by helping them learn to draw upon the resources of scholarship, thus overcoming the limitations of direct experience and the narrow confines of a local environment. Students can learn to use sources of knowledge that are more accurate and reliable than folklore and superstition. They can participate vicariously through literature and the arts with peoples whose lives are both similar to and different from those they have known. The school is the only institution whose primary purpose is enabling students to explore these scholarly fields and to learn to use them as resources in their own lives. Great emphasis should be given to goals of this sort.

Goals are frequently not stated at the appropriate degree of generality–specificity for each level of educational responsibility. Goals promulgated by state education authorities should not be too specific because of the wide variation in conditions among districts in the state. State goals should furnish general guidance for the kinds and areas of learning for which schools are responsible in that state. The school district should furnish more detailed guidance by identifying goals that fall between the general aims listed by the state and those appropriate to the local school. School goals should be adapted to the background of students and the needs and resources of the neighborhood, especially the educational role the parents can assume. The goals of each teacher should be designed to attain the goals of the school.

The test of whether a goal is stated at the appropriate degree of generality–specificity is its clarity and helpfulness in guiding the educational activities necessary at that level of responsibility.

CONCLUSION

When states list specific skills as goals and develop statewide testing programs to measure them, they may overlook a significant part of what schools should teach: understanding, analysis, and problem solving. If students are taught only to follow prescribed rules, they will be unable to deal with varied situations. Another common limitation of such lists is their neglect of affective components, such as finding satisfaction in reading and developing the habit of reading to learn.

The form and wording of goals and objectives should be appropriate for the way they are to be used. For clarity, we have generally used the term "goal" for all statements of intended learning outcomes regardless of their degree of specificity, but we recognize that no one formula is best for all situations. The criteria for judging goals and objectives are their usefulness in communicating educational purposes and their helpfulness to teachers in planning educational activities.

ENDNOTES

1. Available from Commercial-Educational Distributing Service, P.O. Box 4791, Portland, OR 97208.
2. Collections of "measurable objectives" may be purchased from Instructional Objectives Exchange, Box 24095-M, Los Angeles, CA 90024-0095.
3. National Assessment has developed objectives for a number of subject areas, including art, citizenship, career and occupational development, literature, mathematics, music, reading, science, social studies, and writing. Because they have been carefully written and thoroughly reviewed, the objectives and accompanying exercises are a helpful resource for local curriculum developers, although they are designed only for assessment, not for curriculum planning.

REFERENCES

ASCD Committee on Research and Theory, Wilbur B. Brookover, Chairman. (1980). *Measuring and attaining the goals of education.* Alexandria, VA: Association for Supervision and Curriculum Development.

Bloom, Benjamin S. (Ed.). (1956). *Taxonomy of educational objectives: The classification of educational goals. Handbook I: Cognitive domain.* New York, NY: David McKay.

Bruner, Jerome. (1960). *The process of education.* Cambridge, MA: Harvard University.

Chalupsky, Albert B., Phillips-Jones, Linda, & Danoff, Malcolm N. (1981). Competency measurement in vocational education: A review of the state of the art. Prepared by American Institute for Research. Washington, DC: Office of Vocational and Adult Education, U.S. Department of Education.

Commission on the Reorganization of Secondary Education, U.S. Office of Education. (1918). *Cardinal principles of secondary education.* Washington, DC: Government Printing Office.

Doherty, Victor W., & Peters, Linda B. (1980). *Introduction to K–12 course goals for educational planning and evaluation,* 3rd ed. Portland, OR: Commercial-Educational Distributing Services.

Doherty, Victor W., & Peters, Linda B. (1981, May). Goals and objectives in educational planning and evaluation. *Educational Leadership, 38,* 606.

Ehrenberg, Sydelle D., & Ehrenberg, Lyle M. (1978). *A strategy for curriculum design—the ICI model.* Miami, FL: Institute for Curriculum and Instruction.

Eisner, Eliot W. (1979). *The educational imagination.* New York, NY: Macmillan.

French, Will. (1957). *Behavioral goals of general education in high school.* New York, NY: Russell Sage Foundation.

Goodlad, John I. (1979). *What schools are for?* Bloomington, IN: Phi Delta Kappa.

Kohlberg, Lawrence. (1980, October). Moral education: A response to Thomas Sobol. *Educational Leadership, 38,* 19–23.

Krathwohl, David R., Bloom, Benjamin S., & Masia, Bertram B. (1964). *Taxonomy of educational objectives: The classification of educational goals, handbook II: Affective domain.* New York, NY: David McKay Company, Inc.

Mager, R. F. (1962). *Preparing instructional objectives.* Palo Alto, CA: Fearon Publishers.

Martin, John Henry. (1980, January). Reconsidering the goals of high school education. *Educational Leadership, 37,* 278–285.

Oregon State Board of Education. (1972). Minimum state requirements standards for graduation from high school. Salem, OR.

Paul, Regina. (1982, January). Are you out on a limb? *Educational Leadership, 39,* 260–264.

Raywid, Mary Anne. (1981, April). The first decade of public school alternatives. *Phi Delta Kappan, 62,* 551–554.

Seiverling, Richard F. (Ed.). (1980). *Educational quality assessment: Getting out the EQA results.* Harrisburg, PA: Pennsylvania Department of Education.

Spady, William G. (1978, October). The concept and implications of competency-based education. *Educational Leadership, 36,* 16–22.

Stake, R. E., & Easley, J. A., Jr. (1978). *Case studies in science education.* 2 vols. Washington, DC: U.S. Government Printing Office.

Sternberg, Robert J. (1981, October). Intelligence as thinking and learning skills. *Educational Leadership, 39,* 18–20.

Tyler, Ralph W. (1949). *Basic principles of curriculum and instruction* (1974 ed.). Chicago, IL: University of Chicago Press.

Wirszup, Izaak. (1981, February). The Soviet challenge. *Educational Leadership, 38,* 358–360.

DISCUSSION QUESTIONS

1. What should the goals of contemporary education be?
2. Should the goals of education be the same for all students?
3. What is the best method for defining goals: by behavioral objectives or by competencies?
4. Who should assume responsibility for determining educational goals: the federal government, the state board of education, local school districts, building principals, or the faculty at each school? Why?
5. What is the best criterion for judging goals and objectives?

3

What Does It Mean to Say a School Is Doing Well?

ELLIOT W. EISNER

FOCUSING QUESTIONS

1. What kinds of decisions about education should made at the national level? At the state level? At the local level?

2. How much freedom should students have in deciding what they want to learn, when, and how much?

3. Might it be possible for education policy to promote creativity, spontaneity, surprise, and discovery as educational outcomes?

4. Can schools pursue both quality and equality without sacrificing one or the other?

Driven by discontent with the performance of our schools, we are, once again, in the midst of education reform, as we were in 1983 with *A Nation at Risk*, in 1987 with *America 2000*, and a few years later with *Goals 2000*. Each of these reform efforts was intended to rationalize the practice and performance of our schools. Each was designed to work out and install a system of measurable goals and evaluation practices that would ensure that our nation would be first in science and mathematics by the year 2000, that all our children would come to school ready to learn, and that each school would be drug-free, safe, and nonviolent.

The formulation of standards and the measurement of performance were intended to tidy up a messy system and to make teachers and school administrators truly accountable. The aim was then, and is today, to systematize and standardize so that the public will know which schools are performing well and which are not. There were to be then, and there are today, payments and penalties for performance.

America is one of the few nations in which responsibility for schools is not under the aegis of a national ministry of education. Although we have a federal agency, the U.S. Department of Education, the Tenth Amendment to the U.S. Constitution indicates that those responsibilities that the Constitution does not assign explicitly to the federal government belong to the states (or to the people). And because the Constitution makes no mention of education, it is a responsibility of the states.

As a result, we have 50 departments of education, one for each state, overseeing some 16,000 school districts that serve 52 million students in more than 100,000 schools. In addition, each school district has latitude for shaping education policy. Given the complexity of the way education is organized in the United States, it is understandable that from one perspective the view looks pretty messy and not altogether rational. Furthermore, more than a few believe that we have a national problem in American education and that national problems require national solutions. The use of highly rationalized procedures for improving schools is a part of the solution.

I mention the concept of rationalization because I am trying to describe the ethos being created in our schools. I am trying to reveal a world view that shapes our conception of education and the direction we take for making our schools better.

Rationalization as a concept has a number of features. First, it depends on a clear specification of intended outcomes. That is what standards and rubrics are supposed to do. We are supposed to know what the outcomes of educational practice are to be, and rubrics are to exemplify those outcomes. Standards are more general statements intended to proclaim our values. One argument for the use of standards and rubrics is that they are necessary if we are to function rationally. As the saying goes, if you don't know where you're headed, you will not know where you have arrived. In fact, it's more than knowing where you're headed; it's also knowing the precise destination. Thus the specification of intended outcomes has become one of the primary practices in the process of rationalizing school reform efforts. Holding people accountable for the results is another.

Second, rationalization typically uses measurement as a means through which the quality of a product or performance is assessed and represented. Measurement, of course, is one way to describe the world. Measurement has to do with determining matters of magnitude, and it deals with matters of magnitude through the specification of units. In the United States, the unit for weight is pounds. In Sweden or the Netherlands, it is kilograms. It's kilometers in Europe; it's miles in the United States. It really doesn't matter what unit you use, as long as everyone agrees what the unit is.

Quantification is believed to be a way to increase objectivity, secure rigor, and advance precision in assessment. For describing some features of the world, including the educational world, it is indispensable. But it is not good for everything, and the limitations of quantification are increasingly being recognized. For example, although initial discussions about standards emphasized the need for them to be measurable, as standards have become increasingly general and ideological, measurability has become less salient.

Third, the rationalization of practice is predicated on the ability to control and predict. We assume that we can know the specific effects of our interventions, an assumption that is questionable.

Fourth, rationalization downplays interactions. Interactions take into account not simply the conditions that are to be introduced in classrooms or schools but also the kinds of personal qualities, expectations, orientations, ideas, and temperaments that interact with those conditions. Philosophical constructivists have pointed out that what something means comes both from the features of the phenomenon to be addressed and from the way those features are interpreted or experienced by individuals. Such idiosyncratic considerations always complicate assessment. They complicate efforts to rationalize education as well. Prediction is not easy when what the outcome is going to be is a function not only of what is introduced in the situation but also of what a student makes of what has been introduced.

Fifth, rationalization promotes comparison, and comparison requires what is called "commensurability." Commensurability is possible only if you know what the programs were in which the youngsters participated in the schools being compared. If youngsters are in schools that have different curricula or that allocate differing amounts of time to different areas of the curriculum, comparing the outcomes of those schools without taking into account their differences is extremely questionable. Making comparisons between the math performance of youngsters in Japan and those in the United States without taking into account cultural differences, different allocations of time for instruction, or different approaches to teaching makes it impossible to account for differences in student performance or to consider the side-effects or opportunity costs associated with different programs in different cultures. The same principle holds in comparing student performance across school districts in the United States.

Sixth, rationalization relies upon extrinsic incentives to motivate action; that's what vouchers are intended to do. Schools are likened to businesses, and the survival of the fittest is the principle that determines which ones survive. If schools don't produce effective results on tests, they go out of business.

In California and in some other parts of the country, principals and superintendents are often paid a bonus if their students perform well on standardized tests: payment by results. And, of course, such a reward system has consequences for a school's priorities. Are test scores the criteria that we want to use to reward professional performance?

The features that I have just described are a legacy of the Enlightenment. We believe that our rational abilities can be used to discover the regularities of the universe and, once we've found them, to implement, as my colleague David Tyack titled his book, "the one best system." We have a faith in our ability to discover what the U.S. Department of Education once described as "what works."

The result is an approach to reform that leaves little room for surprise, for imagination, for improvisation, or for the cultivation of productive idiosyncrasy. Our reform efforts are closer in spirit to the ideas of René Descartes and Auguste Comte than to those of William Blake. They are efforts that use league tables to compare schools and that regard test scores as valid proxies for the quality of education our children receive. And they constitute an approach to reform that has given us three major educationally feckless reform efforts in the past 20 years. Are we going to have another?

What are the consequences of the approach to reform that we have taken and that should we pay attention to in order to tell when a school is doing well? First, one of the consequences of our approach to reform is that the curriculum gets narrowed as school district policies make it clear that what is to be tested is what is to be taught. Tests come to define our priorities, and now we have legitimated those priorities by talking about "core subjects." The introduction of the concept of core subjects explicitly marginalizes subjects that are not part of the core. One of the areas that we marginalize is the arts, an area that when well taught offers substantial benefits to students. Our idea of core subjects is related to our assessment practices and the tests we use to determine whether or not schools are doing well.

Because we who are in education take test scores seriously, the public is reinforced in its view that test scores are good proxies for the quality of education a school provides. Yet what test scores predict best are other test scores. If we are going to use proxies that have predictive validity, we need proxies that predict performances that matter outside the context of school. The function of schooling is not to enable students to do better in school. The function of schooling is to enable students to do better in life. What students learn in school ought to exceed in relevance the limits of the school's program.

As we focus on standards, rubrics, and measurement, the deeper problems of schooling go unattended. What are some of the deeper problems of schooling? One has to do with the quality of conversation in classrooms. We need to provide opportunities for youngsters and adolescents to engage in challenging kinds of conversation, and we need to help them learn how to do so. Such conversation is all too rare in schools. I use the term "conversation" seriously, for challenging conversation is an intellectual affair. It has to do with thinking about what people have said and responding reflectively, analytically, and imaginatively to that process. The practice of conversation is almost a lost art. We turn to talk shows to experience what we cannot do very well or very often.

The deeper problems of schooling have to do with teacher isolation and the fact that teachers don't often have access to other people who know what they're doing when they teach and who can help them do it better. Although there are many issues that need attention in schooling, we search for the silver bullet and believe that, if we get our standards straight and our rubrics right and make our tests tough enough, we will have an improved school system. I am not so sure.

The message that we send to students is that what really matters in their education are their test scores. As a result, students in high-stakes testing programs find ways to cut corners—and so do some teachers. We read increasingly often not only about students who are cheating but also about teachers who are unfairly helping students get higher scores on the tests. It's a pressure that undermines the kind of experience that students ought to have in schools.

Perhaps the major consequence of the approach we have taken to rationalize our schools is that it ineluctably colors the school climate. It promotes an orientation to practice that emphasizes extrinsically defined attainment targets that have a specified quantitative value. This, in turn, leads students to want to know just what it is they need to do to earn a particular grade. Even at Stanford, I sometimes get requests from graduate students who want to know precisely, or as precisely as I can put it, what they need to do in order to get an A in the class.

Now from one angle such a request sounds reasonable. After all, it is a means/ends approach to educational planning. Students are, it can be said, rationally planning their education. But such planning has very little to do with intellectual life, where risk-taking, exploration, uncertainty, and speculation are what it's about. And if you create a culture of schooling in which a narrow means/ends orientation is promoted, that culture can undermine the development of intellectual dispositions. By intellectual dispositions I mean a curiosity and interest in engaging and challenging ideas.

What the field has not provided is an efficient alternative to the testing procedures we now use. And for good reason. The good reason is that there are no efficient alternatives. Educationally useful evaluation takes time, it's labor intensive and complex, and it's subtle, particularly if evaluation is used not simply to score children or adults but to provide information to improve the process of teaching and learning.

The price one pays for providing many ways for students to demonstrate what has been learned is a reduction of commensurability. Commensurability decreases when attention to individuality increases. John Dewey commented about comparisons in a book that he wrote in 1934 when he was 76 years old. The book is *Art as Experience*. He observed that nothing is more odious than comparisons in the arts. What he was getting at was that attention to or appreciation of an art form requires attention to and appreciation of its distinctive features. It was individuality that Dewey was emphasizing, and it is the description of individuality we would do well to think about in our assessment practices. We should be trying to discover where a youngster is, where his strengths are, where additional work is warranted. Commensurability is possible when everybody is on the same track, when there are common assessment practices, and when there is a common curriculum. But when students work on different kinds of problems, and when there is concern with the development of an individual's thumbprint, so to speak, commensurability is an inappropriate aim.

What have been the consequences of the rationalized approach to education reform that we have embraced? Only this: In our desire to improve our schools, education has become a casualty. That is, in the process of rationalization, education—always a delicate, complex, and subtle process having to do with both cultural transmission and self-actualization—has become a commodity. Education has evolved from a form of human development serving personal and civic needs into a product our nation produces to compete in a global economy. Schools have become places to mass produce this product.

Let us assume that we impose a moratorium on standardized testing for a five-year period. What might we pay attention to in schools in order to say that a school is doing well? If it is not higher test scores that we are looking for, what is it? Let me suggest the kind of data we might seek by raising some questions that might guide our search.

What kinds of problems and activities do students engage in? What kind of thinking do these activities invite? Are students encouraged to wonder and to raise questions about what they have studied? Perhaps we should be less concerned with whether they can answer our questions than with whether they can ask their own. The most significant intellectual achievement is not so much in problem solving, but in question posing. What if we took that idea seriously and concluded units of study by looking for the sorts of questions that youngsters are able to raise as a result of being immersed in a domain of study? What would that practice teach youngsters about inquiry?

What is the intellectual significance of the ideas that youngsters encounter? (I have a maxim that I work with: If it's not worth teaching, it's not worth teaching well.) Are the ideas they encounter important? Are they ideas that have legs? Do they go someplace?

Are students introduced to multiple perspectives? Are they asked to provide multiple perspectives on an issue or a set of ideas? The implications of such an expectation for curriculum development are extraordinary. To develop such an ability and habit of mind, we would need to invent activities that encourage students to practice, refine, and develop certain modes of thought. Taking multiple perspectives is just one such mode.

In 1950 the American psychologist J. P. Guilford developed what he called "the structure of intellect," in which 130 different kinds of cognitive processes were identified. What if we used that kind of structure to promote various forms of thinking? My point is that the activities in which youngsters participate in classes are the means through which their thinking is promoted. When youngsters have no reason to raise questions, the processes that enable them to learn how to discover intellectual problems go undeveloped.

The ability to raise telling questions is not an automatic consequence of maturation. Do you know the biggest problem that Stanford students have in the course of their doctoral work? It is not getting good grades in courses; they all get good grades in courses. Their biggest obstacle is in framing a dissertation problem. We can do something about that before students get to the doctoral level. In a school that is doing well, opportunities for the kind of thinking that yields good questions would be promoted.

What connections are students helped to make between what they study in class and the world outside of school? A major aim of education has to do with what psychologists refer to as "transfer of learning." Can students apply what they have learned or what they have learned how to learn? Can they engage in the kind of learning they will need in order to deal with problems and issues outside the classroom? If what students are learning is simply used as a means to increase their scores on the next test, we may win the battle and lose the war. In such a context, school learning becomes a hurdle to jump over. We need to determine whether students can use what they have learned. But even being able to use what has been learned is no indication that it will be used. There is a difference between what a student can do and what a student will do.

The really important dependent variables in education are not located in classrooms. Nor are they located in schools. The really important dependent variables are located outside schools. Our assessment practices haven't even begun to scratch that surface. It's what students do with what they learn when they can do what they want to do that is the real measure of educational achievement.

What opportunities do youngsters have to become literate in the use of different representational forms? By representational forms, I mean the various symbol systems through which humans shape experience and give it meaning. Different forms of human meaning are expressed in different forms of representation. The kinds of meaning one secures from poetry are not the kinds of meaning one secures from propositional signs. The kinds of meanings expressed in music are not the meanings experienced in the visual arts. To be able to secure any of those meanings, you have to know how to "read" them. Seeing is a reading. Hearing is a reading. They are the processes of interpreting and construing meaning from the material encountered; reading text is not only a process of decoding, it is also a process of encoding. We make sense of what we read.

What opportunities do students have to formulate their own purposes and to design ways to achieve them? Can a school provide the conditions for youngsters, as they mature, to have increased opportunity to set their own goals and to design ways to realize them? Plato once defined a slave as someone who executes the purposes of another. I would say that, in a free democratic state, at least a part of the role of education is to help youngsters learn how to define their own purposes.

What opportunities do students have to work cooperatively to address problems that they believe to be important? Can we design schools so that we create communities of learners who know how to work with one another? Can we design schools and classrooms in which cooperating with others is part of what it means to be a student?

Do students have the opportunity to serve the community in ways that are not limited to their own personal interests? Can we define a part of the school's role as establishing or helping students establish projects in which they do something beyond their own self-interest? We want to know that in order to know how well a school is doing.

To what extent are students given the opportunity to work in depth in domains that relate to their aptitudes? Is personal talent cultivated? Can we arrange the time for youngsters to work together on the basis of interest rather than on the basis of age grading? Youngsters who are interested in ceramics might work in depth in ceramics; those interested in science might work in depth in science. To make these possibilities a reality, we would need, of course, to address the practical problems of allocating time and responsibility. But without a conception of what is important, we will never even ask questions about allocating time. A vision of what is educationally important must come first.

Do students participate in the assessment of their own work? If so, how? It is important for teachers to understand what students themselves think of their own work. Can we design assessment practices in which students can help us?

To what degree are students genuinely engaged in what they do in school? Do they find satisfaction in the intellectual journey? How many students come to school early and how many would like to stay late? The motives for such choices have to do with the "locus of satisfactions." Satisfactions generate reasons for doing something. Basically, there are three reasons for doing anything. One reason for doing something is that you like what it feels like and you like who you are when you do it. Sex, play, and art fall into this category. They are intrinsically satisfying activities.

A second reason for doing something is not because you like doing it, but because you like the results of having done it. You might like a clean kitchen, but you might not enjoy cleaning your kitchen. The process is not a source of enjoyment, but the outcome is.

A third reason for doing something is not because you like the process or even the outcome, but because you like the rewards. You like the grades you earn. You like the paycheck you receive. That's what Hannah Arendt described as labor. There is too much labor in our schools— and not enough work. Work is effort from which you derive satisfaction. We ought to be paying attention to the joy of the journey. This is easy to say but difficult and challenging to do. Nevertheless, we ought to keep our minds focused on it as a goal.

Are teachers given the time to observe and work with one another? To what degree is professional discourse an important aspect of what being a teacher means in the school? Is the school a resource, a center for the teacher's own development? Is the school a center for teacher education? The center for teacher education is not the university; it is the school in which the teacher works. Professional growth should be promoted during the 25 years that a teacher works in a school—

not just during the year and a half that he or she spends in a teacher education program. Can we create schools that take the professional development of teachers seriously? And what would they look like? Schools will not be better for students than they are for the professionals who work in them.

All of us who teach develop repertoires. We all have routines. We all get by. We get by without serious problems, but getting by is not good enough. We need to get better. And to get better, we have to think about school in ways that address teachers' real needs. And when I say, "address teachers' real needs," I don't mean sending them out every 6,000 miles to get "inserviced" by a stranger.

Are parents helped to understand what their child has accomplished in class? Do they come to understand the educational import of what is going on? Very often children's artwork is displayed in the school, with the only information provided being the student's name, the grade, and the teacher's name, all in the lower right-hand corner. Then the best student work is posted more formally. What we do, in effect, is use a gallery model of exhibition. We take the best work, and we display it. What we need to create is an educationally interpretive exhibition that explains to viewers what problems the youngsters were addressing and how they resolved them. This can be done by looking at prior work and comparing it with present work—that is, by looking at what students have accomplished over time. I am talking about interpretation. I am talking about getting people to focus not so much on what the grade is, but on what process led to the outcome.

What is my point? All my arguments have had to do with creating an educationally informed community. We need to ask better questions.

Can we widen what parents and others believe to be important in judging the quality of our schools? Can we widen and diversify what they think matters? Can those of us who teach think about public education not only as the education of the public in the schools (i.e., our students), but also as the education of the public outside our schools (i.e., parents and community members)? Can a more substantial and complex understanding of what constitutes good schooling contribute to better, more enlightened support for our schools?

Can a more informed conception of what constitutes quality in education lead to greater equity for students and ultimately for the culture? Educational equity is much more than just allowing students to cross the threshold of the school. It has to do with what students find after they do so. We ought to be providing environments that enable each youngster in our schools to find a place in the educational sun. But when we narrow the program so that there is only a limited array of areas in which assessment occurs and performance is honored, youngsters whose aptitudes and interests lie elsewhere are going to be marginalized in our schools. The more we diversify those opportunities, the more equity we are going to have because we are going to provide wider opportunities for youngsters to find what it is that they are good at.

And that leads me to the observation that, in our push for attaining standards, we have tended to focus on outcomes that are standard for all youngsters. We want youngsters to arrive at the same place at about the same time. I would argue that really good schools increase variance in student performance. Really good schools increase the variance and raise the mean. The reason I say that is because, when youngsters can play to their strengths, those whose aptitudes are in, say, mathematics are going to go faster and further in that area than youngsters whose aptitudes are in other fields. But in those other fields, those youngsters would go faster and further than those whose aptitudes are in math. Merely by con-

ceiving of a system of educational organization that regards productive variance as something to be valued and pursued, we undermine the expectation that everybody should be moving in lockstep through a series of 10-month years in a standardized system and coming out at pretty much the same place by age 18.

Part of our press toward standardization has to do with what is inherent in our age-graded schools system. Age-graded systems work on the assumption that children remain more alike than different over time and that we should be teaching within the general expectations for any particular grade. Yet, if you examine reading performance, for example, the average range of reading ability in an ordinary classroom approximates the grade level. Thus at the second grade, there is a two-year spread; at the third grade, a three-year range; at the fourth grade, a four-year range. Consider how varied the picture would be if performance in four or five different fields were examined. Children become more different as they get older, and we ought to be promoting those differences and at the same time working to escalate the mean.

Does a more enlightened grasp of what matters in schools put us in a better position to improve them? I hope so. What I have argued here is intended to divert our focus away from what we normally use to make judgments about the quality of schools and redirect it instead toward the processes, conditions, and culture that are closer to the heart of education. I am unabashedly endorsing the promotion of improvisation, surprise, and diversity of outcomes as educational virtues that we ought to try to realize through our teaching.

The point of the questions I have raised is to provide something better than the blinkered vision of school quality that now gets front-page coverage in our newspapers. Perhaps this vision serves best those in positions of privilege. Perhaps our society needs losers so that it can have winners. Whatever the case, I believe that those of us who wish to exercise leadership in education must do more than simply accept the inadequate criteria that are now used to determine how well our schools are doing.

We need a fresh and humane vision of what schools might become because what our schools become has everything to do with what our children and our culture will become. I have suggested some of the features and some of the questions that I believe matter educationally. We need reform efforts that are better than those we now have. The vision of education implicit in what I have described here is just a beginning.

DISCUSSION QUESTIONS

1. How does Eisner's vision for education differ from what most policy makers advocate?
2. Do you agree that a sole focus on the measurable outcomes of education blinds us to what are the true measures of quality?
3. What does Eisner suggest is the relationship between rationalization and quantification? Do these processes serve any useful purposes?
4. How would schools have to be organized and operate differently if student interests were the starting point for learning?

4 Art and Imagination: Overcoming a Desperate Stasis

MAXINE GREENE

FOCUSING QUESTIONS

1. What are the existential contexts of education?
2. How do encounters with the arts influence student engagement in learning?
3. How might experience with the arts affect student (a) imagination, (b) construction of reality, and (c) depth of perspective?
4. What is the relationship between individual freedom and learning?
5. What are the contradictory goals of education?
6. What is the relationship between encounters with the arts and the goals of education?

The existential contexts of education reach far beyond what is conceived of in Goals 2000. They have to do with the human condition in these often desolate days, and in some ways they make the notions of world-class achievement, benchmarks, and the rest seem superficial and limited, if not absurd. They extend beyond the appalling actualities of family breakdown, homelessness, violence, and the "savage inequalities" described by Jonathan Kozol, although social injustice has an existential dimension.

Like their elders, children and young persons inhabit a world of fearful moral uncertainty—a world in which it appears that almost nothing can be done to reduce suffering, contain massacres, and protect human rights. The faces of refugee children in search of their mothers, of teenage girls repeatedly raped by soldiers, of rootless people staring at the charred remains of churches and libraries may strike some of us as little more than a "virtual reality." Those who persist in looking feel numbed and, reminded over and over of helplessness, are persuaded to look away.

It has been said that Pablo Picasso's paintings of "weeping women" have become the icons of our time.[1] They have replaced the statues of men on horseback and men in battle; they overshadow the emblems of what once seemed worth fighting for, perhaps dying for. When even the young confront images of loss and death, as most of us are bound to do today, "it is important that everything we love be summed up into something unforgettably beautiful."[2] This suggests one of the roles of the arts. To see sketch after sketch of women holding dead babies, as Picasso has forced us to do, is to become aware of a tragic deficiency in the fabric of life. If we know enough to make those paintings the objects of our experience, to encounter them against the background of our lives, we are likely to strain toward conceptions of a better order of things, in which there will be no more wars that make women weep like that, no more bombs to murder innocent children. We are likely, in rebelling against such horror, to summon up images of smiling mothers and lovely children, metaphors for what *ought* to be.

Clearly, this is not the only role of the arts, although encounters with them frequently do move us to want to restore some kind of order, to repair, and to heal. Participatory involvement with the many forms of art does enable us, at the very least, to *see* more in our experience, to *hear* more on normally unheard frequencies, to *become conscious* of what daily routines, habits, and conventions have obscured.

We might think of what Pecola Breedlove in *The Bluest Eye* has made us realize about the metanarrative implicit in the Dick and Jane basal readers or in the cultural artifact called Shirley Temple, who made so many invisible children yearn desperately to have blue eyes.[3] We might recall the revelations discovered by so many through an involvement with *Schindler's List*. We might try to retrieve the physical consciousness of unutterable grief aroused in us by Martha Graham's dance "Lamentation," with only feet and hands visible outside draped fabric—and agony expressed through stress lines on the cloth. To see more, to hear more. By such experiences, we are not only wrenched out of the familiar and the taken-for-granted, but we may also discover new avenues for action. We may experience a sudden sense of new possibilities and thus new beginnings.

The prevailing cynicism with regard to values and the feelings of resignation it breeds cannot help but create an atmosphere in the schools that is at odds with the unpredictability associated with the experience of art. The neglect of the arts by those who identified the goals of Goals 2000 was consistent with the focus on the manageable, the predictable, and the measurable. There have been efforts to include the arts in the official statements of goals, but the arguments mustered in their favor are of a piece with the arguments for education geared toward economic competitiveness, technological mastery, and the rest. They have also helped support the dominant arguments for the development of "higher-level skills," academic achievement, standards, and preparation for the workplace.

The danger afflicting both teachers and students because of such emphases is, in part, the danger of feeling locked into existing circumstances defined by others. Young people find themselves described as "human resources," rather than as persons who are centers of choice and evaluation. It is suggested that young people are to be molded in the service of technology and the market, no matter who they are. Yet, as many are now realizing, great numbers of our young people will find themselves unable to locate satisfying jobs, and the very notion of "all the children" and even of human resources carries with it deceptions of all kinds. Perhaps it is no wonder that the dominant mood in many classrooms is one of passive reception.

Umberto Eco, the Italian critic of popular culture, writes about the desperate need to introduce a critical dimension into such reception. Where media and messages are concerned, it is far more important, he says, to focus on the point of reception than on the point of transmission. Finding a threat in "the universal of technological communication" and in situations where "the medium is the message," he calls seriously for a return to individual resistance. "To the anonymous divinity of Technological Communication, our answer could be: 'Not thy, but *our* will be done.'"[4]

The kind of resistance Eco has in mind can best be evoked when imagination is released. But, as we well know, the bombardment of images identified with "Technological Communication" frequently has the effect of freezing imaginative thinking. Instead of freeing audiences to look at things as if they could be otherwise, present-day media impose predigested frameworks on their audiences. Dreams are caught in the meshes of the salable; the alternative to gloom or feelings of pointlessness is consumerist acquisition. For Mary Warnock, imagination is identified with the belief that "there is more in our experience of the world than can possibly meet the unreflecting eye."[5] It tells us that experience always holds more than we can predict. But Warnock knows that acknowledging the existence of undiscovered vistas and perspectives requires reflectiveness. The passive, apathetic person is all too likely to be unresponsive to ideas of the unreal, as if, the merely possible. He or she becomes the one who bars the arts as frivolous, mere frills, irrelevant to learning in the postindustrial world.

It is my conviction that informed engagements with the several arts would be the most likely way to release the imaginative capacity and give it play. However, this does not happen automatically or "naturally." We have all witnessed the surface contacts with paintings when groups of tourists hasten through museums. Without time spent, without tutoring, and without dialogue regarding the arts, people merely seek the right labels. They look for the artists' names. There are those who watch a ballet for the story, not for the movement or the music; they wait for Giselle to go mad or for Sleeping Beauty to be awakened or for the white swan to return.

Mere exposure to a work of art is not sufficient to occasion an aesthetic experience. There must be conscious participation in a

work, a going out of energy, an ability to notice what is there to be noticed in the play, the poem, the quartet. "Knowing about," even in the most formal, academic manner, is entirely different from creating an unreal world imaginatively and entering it perceptually, affectively, and cognitively. To introduce people to such engagement is to strike a delicate balance between helping learners to pay heed—to attend to shapes, patterns, sounds, rhythms, figures of speech, contours, lines, and so on—and freeing them to perceive particular works as meaningful. Indeed, the inability to control what is discovered as meaningful makes many traditional educators uneasy and strikes them as being at odds with conceptions of a norm, even with notions of appropriate "cultural literacy." This uneasiness may well be at the root of certain administrators' current preoccupation with national standards.

However, if we are to provide occasions for significant encounters with works of art, we have to combat standardization and what Hannah Arendt called "thoughtlessness" on the part of all those involved. What she meant by thoughtlessness was "the heedless recklessness or hopeless confusion or complacent repetition of 'truths' which have become trivial and empty."[6] There is something in that statement that recalls what John Dewey described as a "social pathology"—a condition that still seems to afflict us today. Dewey wrote that it manifests itself "in querulousness, in impotent drifting, in uneasy snatching at distractions, in idealization of the long established, in a facile optimism assumed as a cloak."[7] Concerned about "sloppiness, superficiality, and recourse to sensations as a substitute for ideas," Dewey made the point that "thinking deprived of its normal course takes refuge in academic specialism."[8]

For Arendt, the remedy for this condition is "to think what we are doing." She had in mind developing a self-reflectiveness that originates in situated life, the life of persons open to one another in their distinctive locations and engaging one another in dialogue. Provoked by the spectacle of the Nazi Adolf Eichmann, Arendt warned against "clichés, stock phrases, adherence to conventional, standardized codes of expression and conduct," which have, she said, "the socially recognized function of protecting us against reality, that is, against the claim on our thinking attention that all events and facts make by virtue of their existence."[9] She was not calling for a new intellectualism or for a new concentration on "higher-order skills." She was asking for a way of seeking clarity and authenticity in the face of thoughtlessness, and it seems to me that we might ask much the same thing if we are committed to the release of the imagination and truly wish to open the young to the arts.

Thoughtfulness in this sense is necessary if we are to resist the messages of the media in the fashion Eco suggests, and it is difficult to think of young imaginations being freed without learners finding out how to take a critical and thoughtful approach to the illusory or fabricated "realities" presented to them by the media. To be thoughtful about what we are doing is to be conscious of ourselves struggling to make meanings, to make critical sense of what authoritative others are offering as objectively "real."

I find a metaphor for the reification of experience in the plague as it is confronted in Albert Camus' novel. The pestilence that struck the town of Oran (submerged as it was in habit and "doing business") thrust most of the inhabitants into resignation, isolation, or despair. Gradually revealing itself as inexorable and incurable, the plague froze people in place; it was simply *there*. At first Dr. Rieux fights the plague for the most abstract of reasons: because it is his job. Only later, when the unspeakable tragedies he witnesses make him actually think about what he is doing, does he reconceive his practice and his struggle and talk about not wanting to be complicit with the pestilence. By then he has met Tarrou, who is trying to be a "saint without God" and who has the wit and, yes, the imagination to organize people into sanitary squads to fight the plague and make it the moral concern of all.

Tarrou has the imagination too to find in the plague a metaphor for indifference or distancing or (we might say) thoughtlessness. Everyone carries the microbe, he tells his friend; it is only natural. He means what Hannah Arendt meant—and Dewey and Eco and all the others who resist a lack of concern. He has in mind evasions of complex problems, the embrace of facile formulations of the human predicament, the reliance on conventional solutions—all those factors I would say stand in the way of imaginative thinking and engagement with the arts. "All the rest," says Tarrou, "health, integrity, purity (if you like)—is a product of the human will, of a vigilance that must never falter." He means, of course, that we (and those who are our students) must be given opportunities to choose to be persons of integrity, persons who care.

Tarrou has a deep suspicion of turgid language that obscures the actualities of things, that too often substitutes abstract constructions for concrete particulars. This is one of the modes of the thoughtlessness Arendt was urging us to fight. She, too, wanted to use "plain, clear-cut language." She wanted to urge people, as does Tarrou, to attend to what is around them, "to stop and think." I am trying to affirm that this kind of awareness, this openness to the world, is what allows for the consciousness of alternative possibilities and thus for a willingness to risk encounters with the "weeping women," with Euripides' *Medea*, with *Moby Dick*, with Balanchine's (and, yes, the Scripture's) *Prodigal Son*, with Mahler's *Songs of the Earth*.

Another novel that enables its readers to envisage what stands in the way of imagination is Christa Wolf's *Accident: A Day's News*. It moves me to clarify my own response to the technical and the abstract. I turn to it not in order to add to my knowledge or to find some buried truth, but because it makes me see, over the course of time, what I might never have seen in my own lived world.

The power the book holds for me may be because it has to do with the accident at Chernobyl, as experienced by a woman writer, who is also a mother and grandmother. She is preoccupied by her brother's brain surgery, taking place on the same day, and by the consequences of the nuclear accident for her grandchildren and for children around the world. She spends no time wondering about her own response to such a crisis; her preoccupation is with others—those she loves and the unknown ones whom she cannot for a moment forget. It is particularly interesting, within the context of an ethic of care, to contain for a moment within our own experience the thoughts of a frightened young mother, the narrator's daughter, picturing what it means to pour away thousands of liters of milk for fear of poisoning children while "children on the other side of the earth are perishing for lack of those foods."

The narrator wants to change the conversation and asks her daughter to "tell me something else, preferably about the children." Whereupon she hears that "the little one had pranced about the kitchen, a wing nut on his thumb, his hand held high. Me Punch. Me Punch. I was thrilled by the image."[10] Only a moment before, another sequence of pictures had come into her mind and caused her to

> admire the way in which everything fits together with a sleepwalker's precision: the desire of most people for a comfortable life, their tendency to believe the speakers on raised platforms and the men in white coats; the addiction to harmony and the fear of contradiction of the many seem to correspond to the arrogance and hunger for power, the dedication to profit, unscrupulous inquisitiveness, and self-infatuation of the few. So what was it that didn't add up in this equation?[11]

This passage seems to me to suggest the kind of questioning and, yes, the kind of picturing that may well be barred by the preoccupation with "world-class achievement" and by the focus on human resources that permeate Goals 2000.

But it does not have to be so. Cognitive adventuring and inquiry are much more likely to be provoked by the narrator's question about "this equation" than by the best of curriculum frameworks or by the most responsible and "authentic" assessment. To set the imagination moving in response to a text such as Wolf's may well be to confront learners with a demand to choose in a fundamental way between a desire for harmony with its easy answers and a commitment to the risky search for alternative possibilities.

Wolf's narrator, almost as if she were one of Picasso's weeping women, looks at the blue sky and, quoting some nameless source, says, "Aghast, the mothers search the sky for the inventions of learned men."[12] Like others to whom I have referred, she begins pondering the language and the difficulty of breaking through such terms as "half-life," "cesium," and "cloud" when "polluted rain" is so much more direct. Once again, the experience of the literary work may help us feel the need to break through the mystification of technology and the language to which it has given rise.

The narrator feels the need to battle the disengagement that often goes with knowing and speaking. When she ponders the motives of those who thought up the procedures for the "peaceful utilization of nuclear energy," she recalls a youthful protest against a power plant and the rebukes and reprimands directed at the protesters for their skepticism with regard to a scientific utopia. And then she lists the activities that the men of science and technology presumably do not pursue and would probably consider a waste of time if they were forced to:

> Changing a baby's diapers. Cooking, shopping with a child on one's arm or in the baby carriage. Doing the laundry, hanging it up to dry, taking it down, folding it, ironing it, darning it. Sweeping the floor, mopping it,

polishing it, vacuuming it. Dusting. Sewing. Knitting. Crocheting. Embroidering. Doing the dishes. Taking care of a sick child. Thinking up stories to tell. Singing songs. And how many of these activities do I myself consider a waste of time?[13]

Reading this passage and posing a new set of questions, we cannot but consider the role of such concrete images in classroom conversation and in our efforts to awaken persons to talk about what ought to be. The narrator believes that the "expanding monstrous technological creation" may be a substitute for life for many people. She is quite aware of the benevolent aspects of technology: her brother, after all, is having advanced neurosurgery (which he does survive). But she is thinking, as we might well do in the schools, about the consequences of technological expansion for the ones we love. Her thinking may remind us of how important it is to keep alive images of "everything we love." I want to believe that by doing so we may be able to create classroom atmospheres that once again encourage individuals to have hope.

This brings me back to my argument for the arts, so unconscionably neglected in the talk swirling around Goals 2000. It is important to make the point that the events that make up aesthetic experiences are events that occur within and by means of the transactions with our environment that situate us in time and space. Some say that participatory encounters with paintings, dances, stories, and the rest enable us to recapture a lost spontaneity. By breaking through the frames of presuppositions and conventions, we may be enabled to reconnect ourselves with the processes of becoming who we are. By reflecting on our life histories, we may be able to gain some perspective on the men in white coats, even on our own desires to withdraw from complexity and to embrace a predictable harmony. By becoming aware of ourselves as questioners, as makers of meaning, as persons engaged in constructing and

reconstructing realities with those around us, we may be able to communicate to students the notion that reality depends on perspective, that its construction is never complete, and that there is always more. I am reminded of Paul Cézanne's several renderings of Mont St. Victoire and of his way of suggesting that it must be viewed from several angles if its reality is to be apprehended.

Cézanne made much of the insertion of the body into his landscapes, and that itself may suggest a dimension of experience with which to ground our thinking and the thinking of those we teach. There are some who suggest that, of all the arts, dance confronts most directly the question of what it means to be human. Arnold Berleant writes that

> in establishing a human realm through movement, the dancer, with the participating audience, engages in the basic act out of which arise both all experience and our human constructions of the world. . . . [That basic act] stands as the direct denial of that most pernicious of all dualisms, the division of body and consciousness. In dance, thought is primed at the point of action. This is not the reflection of the contemplative mind but rather intellect poised in the body, not the deliberate consideration of alternative courses but thought in process, intimately responding to and guiding the actively engaged body.[14]

The focus is on process and practice; the skill in the making is embodied in the object made. In addition, dance provides occasions for the emergence of the integrated self. Surely, this ought to be taken into account in our peculiarly technical and academic time.

Some of what Berleant says relates as well to painting, if painting is viewed as an orientation in time and space of the physical body—of both perceiver and creator. If we take a participatory stance, we may enter a landscape or a room or an open street. Different modes of perception are asked of us, of course, by different artists, but that ought to mean a widening of sensitivity with regard to perceived form, color, and space. Jean-Paul Sartre, writing about painting, made a point that is significant for anyone concerned about the role of art and the awakening of imagination:

> The work is never limited to the painted, sculpted or narrated object. Just as one perceives things only against the background of the world, so the objects represented by art appear against the background of the universe. . . . [T]he creative act aims at a total renewal of the world. Each painting, each book, is a recovery of the totality of being. Each of them presents this totality to the freedom of the spectator. For this is quite the final goal of art: to recover this world by giving it to be seen as it is, but as if it had its source in human freedom.[15]

In this passage Sartre suggests the many ways in which classroom encounters with the arts can move the young to imagine, to extend, and to renew. And surely nothing can be more important than finding the source of learning not in extrinsic demands, but in human freedom.

All this is directly related to developing what is today described as the active learner, here conceived as one awakened to pursue meaning. There are, of course, two contradictory tendencies in education today: One has to do with shaping malleable young people to serve the needs of technology in a postindustrial society; the other has to do with educating young people to grow and to become different, to find their individual voices, and to participate in a community in the making. Encounters with the arts nurture and sometimes provoke the growth of individuals who reach out to one another as they seek clearings in their experience and try to live more ardently in the world. If the significance of the arts for growth, inventiveness, and problem solving is recognized at last, a desperate stasis may be overcome, and people may come to recognize the need for new raids on what T. S. Eliot called the "inarticulate."

I choose to end this extended reflection on art and imagination with some words from "Elegy in Joy," by Muriel Rukeyser:

> Out of our life the living eyes
> See peace in our own image made,
> Able to give only what we can give:
> Bearing two days like midnight. "Live,"
> The moment offers: the night requires
> Promise effort love and praise.
>
> Now there are no maps and no magicians.
> No prophets but the young prophet, the sense
>   of the world.
> The gift of our time, the world to be discovered.
> All the continents giving off their several lights,
> the one sea, and the air. And all things glow.[16]

These words offer life; they offer hope; they offer the prospect of discovery; they offer light. By resisting the tyranny of the technical, we may yet make them our pedagogic creed.

ENDNOTES

1. Judi Freeman, *Picasso and the Weeping Women* (Los Angeles: Los Angeles Museum of Art, 1994).
2. Michel Leiris. "Faire-part," in E. C. Oppler, ed., *Picasso's Guernica* (New York: Norton, 1988), p. 201.
3. Toni Morrison, *The Bluest Eye* (New York: Washington Square Press, 1970), p. 19.
4. Richard Kearney, *The Wake of Imagination* (Minneapolis: University of Minnesota Press, 1988), p. 382.
5. Mary Warnock, *Imagination* (Berkeley: University of California Press, 1978), p. 202.
6. Hannah Arendt, *The Human Condition* (Chicago: University of Chicago Press, 1958), p. 5.
7. John Dewey, *The Public and Its Problems* (Athens, OH: Swallow Press, 1954), p. 170.
8. Ibid., p. 168.
9. Hannah Arendt, *Thinking: Vol. II, The Life of the Mind* (New York: Harcourt Brace Jovanovich, 1978), p. 4.
10. Christa Wolf, *Accident: A Day's News* (New York: Farrar, Straus & Giroux, 1989), p. 17.
11. Ibid.
12. Ibid., p. 27.

13. Ibid., p. 31.
14. Arnold Berleant, *Art and Engagement* (Philadelphia: Temple University Press, 1991), p. 167.
15. Jean-Paul Sartre, *Literature and Existentialism* (New York: Citadel Press, 1949), p. 57.

16. Muriel Rukeyser, "Tenth Elegy: An Elegy in Joy," in idem. *Out in Silence: Selected Poems* (Evanston, IL: TriQuarterly Books, 1992), p. 104.

DISCUSSION QUESTIONS

1. What are the implications of understanding the existential contexts of education and educational goals?
2. Why does inclusion of the arts in the school curriculum continue to be a topic of debate among many educators?
3. Why is mere exposure to a work of art insufficient for stimulating an aesthetic experience?
4. How does a neglect of the arts in school experiences affect students?
5. How might repeated significant encounters with the arts be used to combat standardization?

5   A Common Core of Readiness

ROBERT ROTHMAN

FOCUSING QUESTIONS

1. Why is postsecondary education increasingly important?
2. How does the Common Core ensure college and career readiness for all students?
3. Explain why college-completion rates are lower among younger people in the United States?
4. What is the problem with state standards?
5. Describe how student reading and writing will change under the Common Core.
6. How will the Common Core affect high school math?

The common core state standards, which have now been adopted by 46 states and the District of Columbia, differ from most previous state standards in many ways. Perhaps the most significant difference, however, is that the new standards were explicitly designed around the goal of ensuring college and career readiness for all students. How likely are the common core state standards to achieve this goal?

READY OR (MOSTLY) NOT

In the past decade, a growing body of research has shown the increased importance of postsecondary education. A 2004 study by labor economists Frank Levy and Richard Murnane, for example, found that technology is transforming the workplace by reducing the need for routine skills and placing a premium on problem-solving and communication skills. Carnevale, Smith, and Strohl (2010) quantified this workplace shift. They projected that 62 percent of U.S. jobs in 2018 (compared with just 28 percent in 1973) will require education beyond high school.

The resulting shortage of college-educated workers has driven up the wage premium for postsecondary education: Workers with bachelor's degrees earned 74 percent more than those with high school diplomas in 2010, compared with 40 percent more in 1980. If current trends continue, college-educated workers will earn twice as much as high school graduates by 2025 (Carnevale & Rose, 2011).

Unfortunately, the proportion of U.S. students with college degrees is not rising fast enough to meet the demand. Although the U.S. college graduation rate increased from 42 percent in 2000 to 49 percent in 2009, the rate increased much faster in other countries. As a result, in 2011, the United States ranked 15th among 20 major industrialized countries in the number of adults ages 25–34 with bachelor's degrees. In fact, the United States is the only country in the Organisation for Economic Co-operation and Development in which the college-completion rate is lower among younger people than it is among older workers (Organisation for Economic Co-operation and Development, 2011).

One likely reason for the shortfall in postsecondary success is the inadequate preparation of students in high school. ACT has conducted research for years to determine the level of performance a student would have to achieve on its widely used college admissions test to have a 50 percent chance of earning a grade of B or higher, or a 75 percent chance of earning a C or higher, in an entry-level college class. In 2011, just one in four students who took the ACT test met the benchmark scores in all four subjects: English, mathematics, reading, and science (ACT, 2011). And because these data were based on scores for students who had taken the test—that is, students who had indicated their intentions to go to college—we can assume that the preparation of high school students overall is lower.

The ACT findings are consistent with the relatively high remediation rates in colleges and universities. Nationwide, about 40 percent of entering college students are required to take at least one remedial course before enrolling in credit-bearing coursework, and the rates are much higher for students of color.[1] Students who enroll in remedial courses are more likely than those who do not to drop out of college before earning a degree.

Businesses, college professors, and students themselves agree that there are gaps in student preparation for the postsecondary world. In a 2005 survey, U.S. employers stated that 39 percent of high school graduates were unprepared for entry-level work and 45 percent of graduates were inadequately prepared for jobs beyond the entry level. Only 18 percent of college instructors said that students came to their classes extremely or very well prepared. And 39 percent of graduates themselves said that they were unprepared for college or the workplace (Peter D. Hart Research Associates, 2005).

THE TROUBLE WITH STATE STANDARDS

What has caused this mismatch between student preparation and the needs of college and career? A growing number of educators believe the answer might be inadequate curriculum standards. If standards are too low, K–12 students may do everything we expect them to do but still come up short when they get to college or begin a career.

Standards-based reform has been the de facto national education reform strategy for more than two decades. Spurred by federal legislation, states have placed standards—statements of the content and skills all students should learn—at the center of their improvement efforts. By the end of the 1990s, all states had adopted standards for student learning, assessments aligned to the standards, and accountability systems that measured school performance on the basis of student attainment of the standards.

But gradually, educators and policymakers have realized that many state standards were set too low and that these standards varied widely from state to state. A 2008 study conducted by researchers at the University of Pennsylvania compared state content standards in mathematics and found very little commonality among the states (National Research Council, 2008).

The most glaring evidence of the variation in state standards came from the results of the National Assessment of Educational Progress (NAEP). No Child Left Behind requires every state to administer the NAEP in reading and mathematics every two years, and the data appear to show some wide differences between NAEP results and the results on state tests. For example, in 2005, 87 percent of fourth graders in Tennessee were proficient on the state test in mathematics, but only 28 percent were proficient on the NAEP. In contrast, in Massachusetts, 40 percent of fourth graders were proficient on the state test in mathematics and almost the same proportion (41 percent) were proficient on the NAEP. These discrepancies have raised concerns that some states' standards set expectations below what students need to succeed in college and careers.

NEW STANDARDS FOCUSED ON READINESS

Faced with such data, state leaders in 2006 began to consider developing standards that would be common among states, not only to reduce variability but also to ensure that the expectations matched the requirements of postsecondary education. The Council of Chief State School Officers and the National Governors Association led the effort, which became known as the Common Core State Standards Initiative (CCSS).

The project, launched in April 2009, was divided into two parts. First, teams would develop anchor standards for college and career readiness in English language arts and mathematics, which would indicate the knowledge and skills students needed at the end of high school. Then a separate team would design grade-by-grade standards in those two subjects that would lead students to the anchor standards. The final set of standards was released in June 2010.

From the outset, CCSS leaders designed the effort to differ from the process most

states had used to set their standards. Many state standards were developed by teams of educators and community members, using a variety of criteria. In many cases, the process involved logrolling to gain political support; the result was a long list of standards that might or might not have anything to do with college and career readiness.

CCSS leaders, in contrast, established clear criteria for the standards; one of the most important was that the standards reflect research on college and career readiness. Topics that might be interesting but that were not essential for postsecondary success would be thrown out. The research did not have to be ironclad; it just had to represent the best available knowledge. This criterion guided the standards writers' work and minimized some of the ideological battles that had plagued standards setting in the past.

In addition, the CCSS leaders asked representatives from Achieve, ACT, and the College Board to craft the anchor standards. These organizations had considerable expertise in the area of college and career readiness, and they could enlist business and higher education partners to verify their judgments about what might be necessary for employment or postsecondary education.

In developing the college and career readiness standards, the standards writers defined readiness as the ability to succeed in entry-level, credit-bearing, academic college courses and in workforce training programs. That is, students who met the standards should be able to enroll in postsecondary education without needing remediation. For college, that meant enrolling in either a two-year or four-year institution; for workforce training, it meant enrolling in programs that prepare students for careers that offer competitive, livable salaries and opportunities for career advancement in a growing or sustainable industry.

To develop the standards for college and career readiness, the standards writers started with evidence from postsecondary education and the workplace. They also conducted their own research by buying introductory college textbooks and studying the kinds of reading and mathematics that students would be expected to do in their first year of college. And they asked teachers of first-year college courses to confirm their judgments about what students should know and be able to do.

WHAT'S NEW IN THE NEW STANDARDS?

Will the common core state standards succeed in their ultimate aim of improving the college and career readiness of U.S. students? We won't have the definitive answer to that question until states have implemented the standards and collected evidence to determine whether students who meet them can function successfully in postsecondary education and in the workplace.

Preliminary reviews indicate, however, that the standards at least reflect the expectations of colleges. For example, in a survey by the Education Policy Improvement Center (EPIC) at the University of Oregon, professors of first-year college courses agreed that the standards reflect the knowledge and skills students need to have in their courses (Conley, Drummond, deGonzalez, Rooseboom, & Stout, 2011a). And a separate EPIC study found that the standards match well with the expectations students encounter in such highly regarded programs as the International Baccalaureate (Conley et al., 2011b).

In the end, the standards define some clear expectations for what students should know and be able to do. And these expectations are more closely aligned in several important ways with what students need to succeed in college and careers.

Reading. In reading, the standards place a heavy emphasis on the ability to comprehend complex texts. This emphasis stems from research that shows that students who can comprehend complex texts are more likely to be successful after high school (ACT, 2006).

Many students currently lack this ability. The complexity of workplace materials and college textbooks has held steady or increased over the past 50 years (Council of Chief State School Officers & National Governors Association Center on Best Practices, 2010); meanwhile, the level of text complexity in high schools has actually declined over time (Chall, Conard, & Harris, 1977; Hayes, Wolfer, & Wolfe, 1996). And in many high schools, teachers often don't even require students to read or comprehend these easier texts. Instead, many teachers attempt to make comprehension simpler for students by presenting material via PowerPoint or reading aloud.

Writing. In writing, the common core state standards reflect college and career readiness by reducing the traditional emphasis on narrative writing and placing a greater emphasis on informational and explanatory writing. Personal narratives are a staple of schooling ("How I Spent My Summer Vacation"), but except for college application essays, students will seldom be required to write personal narratives in college or the workplace. Informational writing, in which the author attempts to explain something or to inform others about a topic, is a much more important skill in these settings.

Mathematics. The high school mathematics standards are intended for all students and represent the threshold level necessary for college and career readiness. In fact, as the standards document notes, research on college and career readiness suggests that much of the mathematics necessary for postsecondary success is taught in grades 6–8. This includes applying ratio reasoning in solving problems; computing fluently with fractions and decimals; and solving problems involving angle measure, surface area, and volume. However, the standards also include content that students would need to know if they pursue higher-level mathematics, such as calculus, discrete mathematics, or advanced statistics. This content is designated with a special symbol (+).

NEXT STEPS

Even the most fervent advocate of the common core state standards would acknowledge that the standards themselves will not ensure that students graduate from high school ready for college and careers. A lot more has to happen to bring that about.

The first big step is underway: Two consortia of states are developing assessments to measure student attainment of the standards. The consortia's plans state that the results from the assessments will indicate whether students are on track for college and career readiness. But for those plans to be realized, higher education institutions must be engaged to validate that the assessments actually measure readiness. If these institutions agree to use the assessment scores for placement in first-year college courses, it will send a clear signal to students that passing the exams means they are ready for postsecondary education.

More significant, teachers must be prepared to teach the new standards. The standards call for some major changes in classroom practice to enable students to meet higher expectations, such as the greater level of text complexity in reading and challenging math expectations for all. Many teachers are not prepared for these shifts. Teacher preparation institutions must embrace the standards to ensure that those entering the profession are ready to teach what students are expected to learn.

The United States, since its inception, has acted on the belief that all students deserve a basic education. The common core state standards define a basic education in a new way: readiness for college and careers. And for the first time, the expectations are the same for almost all students, regardless of where they live. These standards represent a great opportunity to advance equity and excellence.

ENDNOTE

1. Computed February 9, 2011, using NCES PowerStats, U.S. Department of Education, National Center for Education Statistics, 2007–08 National Postsecondary Student Aid Study (NPSAS:08).

REFERENCES

ACT. (2006). *Reading between the lines: What the ACT reveals about college readiness in reading.* Iowa City, IA: Author.

ACT. (2011). *The condition of college and career readiness, 2011.* Iowa City, IA: Author. Retrieved from http://www.act.org/research/policymakers/cccr11/pdf/ConditionofCollegeandCareerReadiness2011.pdf

Carnevale, A., & Rose, S. J. (2011). *The undereducated American.* Washington, DC: Georgetown University Center on Education and the Workforce.

Carnevale, A., Smith, N., & Strohl, J. (2010). *Help wanted: Projections of jobs and education requirements through 2018.* Washington, DC: Georgetown University Center on Education and the Workforce.

Chall, J., Conard, S., & Harris, S. (1977). *An analysis of textbooks in relationship to declining SAT scores.* New York: College Entrance Examination Board.

Conley, D., Drummond, K., de Gonzalez, A., Rooseboom, J., & Stout, O. (2011a). *Reaching the goal: The applicability and importance of the common core state standards to college and career readiness.* Eugene, OR: Educational Policy Improvement Center.

Conley, D., Drummond, K., de Gonzalez, A., Seburn, M., Stout, O., & Rooseboom, J. (2011b). *Lining up: The relationship between the common core state standards and five sets of companion standards.* Eugene, OR: Educational Policy Improvement Center.

Council of Chief State School Officers & National Governors Association Center on Best Practices. (2010). *Common core state standards for English language arts and literacy in history/social science, science, and technical subjects (Appendix A).* Washington, DC: Authors. Retrieved from the Common Core State Standards Initiative at http://www.corestandards.org/assets/Appendix_A.pdf

Hayes, D. P., Wolfer, L. T., & Wolfe, M. F. (1996). Sourcebook simplification and its relation to the decline in SAT-verbal scores. *American Educational Research Journal, 33,* 498–508.

Levy, F., & Murnane, R. J. (2004). *The new division of labor: How computers are creating the next job market.* Princeton, NJ: Princeton University Press.

National Research Council. (2008). *Common standards for K–12 education? Considering the evidence.* Washington, DC: National Academies Press.

Organisation for Economic Co-operation and Development. (2011). *Education at a glance, 2011.* Paris: Author.

Peter D. Hart Research Associates. (2005). *Rising to the challenge: Are high school graduates prepared for college and work?* Washington, DC: Achieve. Retrieved from http://www.achieve.org/files/pollreport_0.pdf

DISCUSSION QUESTIONS

1. How would you define college and career readiness?
2. Are there any disadvantages to implementing Common Core standards?
3. Why might states set their expectations and standards too low?
4. How can teachers be better prepared for the Common Core standards?
5. How important might it be to have Common Core standards for science or social studies?

Should the schools introduce a values-centered curriculum for all students?

PRO	CON
1. There are certain basic core values that educators involved in curriculum development should be able to agree on.	1. Values are not objective or neutral. Therefore, educators involved in curriculum development cannot easily agree on them.
2. The classroom is a place in which students can define what values are and share a diversity of viewpoints.	2. Engaging students in discussion will lead to peer pressure and indoctrination.
3. Students should be able to explore their values in a classroom setting.	3. Unstated teacher attitudes may impinge upon students' ability to identify their own preferences.
4. Valuing is part of citizenship education, and therefore, schools have a responsibility to teach valuing.	4. Values are not part of civic education. Moreover, values education is the responsibility of the home, not the school.
5. Students need to learn to express themselves forthrightly and to make choices without fear of condemnation.	5. There is no assurance that the teacher can model values, much less provide appropriate instructional activities that will promote these behaviors.

A Clash Concerning the Arts Curriculum

Andrea Brown had recently been hired as the assistant principal in charge of curriculum at the Newberry Elementary School. Brown, an advocate for arts education, had a humanistic orientation to curriculum. The principal, Al Sigel, had an essentialist view of the curriculum. Adhering to a back-to-basics focus, Sigel felt that math, science, and computer education should be emphasized and that arts courses were frivolous.

The state code and the school's educational manuals indicated that all students were required to receive 40 minutes of music, art, and dance per week. Without discussing his intentions with Brown or eliciting faculty reactions, Sigel distributed a memo to the staff at the first faculty meeting of the school year indicating that music, art, and dance courses were to be eliminated from the academic schedule as specific courses and that teachers should integrate these subjects into social studies and English. The extra class time was to be equally distributed to provide additional math, science, and computer education classes.

Upon learning about this decision, several parents approached Brown and asked that she assist them in getting the arts classes placed back into the schedule. Brown felt an ethical and educational obligation to address the parents' concern. While cognizant of the legal implications, she also believed the arts were an essential curriculum component. She pondered how she might approach this situation.

Assume that you are the assistant principal. Consider the circumstances described in the case. How would you propose to handle the parents' concerns?

Consider also the implications of taking one of the following actions in response to the parents' request:

1. Confront the principal and cite the state- and school-mandated requirements concerning course time allocations.
2. Resign from the position and state that she and Sigel had irresolvable differences regarding their philosophical orientation to curriculum.
3. Take the curriculum-related concerns to the district superintendent in charge of instruction.
4. Present an inservice workshop to the teaching staff about the intrinsic and utilitarian values of an arts education.
5. Lead a coalition of concerned parents and ask for a meeting with the principal.

PART TWO

Curriculum and Teaching

What are the trends that influence student success and teachers' selection of instructional approaches? What methods are most appropriate for teaching a diverse population of learners? How do teachers' identities, teacher thinking, practical knowledge, and teacher effectiveness affect the ways in which teachers deliver the curriculum?

In Chapter 6, Nel Noddings explains why caring for oneself and others is an important outcome of education and how curriculum can be chosen to develop the inner growth of students. She proposes that schools should become communities of caring, where care becomes a major purpose that guides school policy, as well as the individual and collective practices of teachers. Next, Parker Palmer in Chapter 7 describes three origins of difficulties that teachers face: the enormous scope and ever-changing nature of subject matter, the complexity of students as real human beings, and the fact that the best teaching emerges from who the teacher is as a person. Taking time to listen to the teacher who resides within oneself, he proposes, is a better guide to practice than the latest instructional techniques.

In Chapter 8, Allan Ornstein raises the question of whether teaching should be considered an art or a science. His discussion of this issue provides a framework for a proposal to reconceptualize teaching and its study in a way that would place greater emphasis on matters of moral and humanistic importance. Next, Herbert Walberg in Chapter 9 provides a comprehensive review of research on the effects of various methods of teaching. He summarizes what is known about the psychological elements of teaching, the various patterns that individual teachers can implement in their classrooms, the more complex systems of instruction that require special planning and resources, and effective instructional methods for specific content areas and populations of students.

In Chapter 10, Edward Pajak, Elaine Stotko, and Frank Masci suggest that support for new teachers should respect and nurture and build on their preferred styles of teaching. Four styles are identified—knowing, caring, inspiring, and inventing—and suggestions for a new and powerful way to differentiate support for beginning teachers are offered. In Chapter 11, Linda Darling-Hammond documents the importance of qualified teachers for student achievement and describes four factors that research has shown help to reduce teacher attrition. A number of practical steps that leaders can take to retain good teachers are described.

6

Teaching Themes of Care

NEL NODDINGS

FOCUSING QUESTIONS

1. How is caring an essential part of teaching?
2. Why is it important to teach children to care?
3. How can caring be incorporated into the curriculum?
4. Are some subject areas more suited for teaching themes of care?
5. What might a curriculum that included themes of caring look like and how would it be implemented?

Some educators today—and I include myself among them—would like to see a complete reorganization of the school curriculum. We would like to give a central place to the questions and issues that lie at the core of human existence. One possibility would be to organize the curriculum around themes of care—caring for self, for intimate others, for strangers and global others, for the natural world and its nonhuman creatures, for the human-made world, and for ideas.[1]

A realistic assessment of schooling in the present political climate makes it clear that such a plan is not likely to be implemented. However, we can use the rich vocabulary of care in educational planning and introduce themes of care into regular subject-matter classes. Here, I will first give a brief rationale for teaching themes of care; second, I will suggest ways of choosing and organizing such themes; and, finally, I'll say a bit about the structures required to support such teaching.

WHY TEACH CARING?

In an age when violence among schoolchildren is at an unprecedented level, when children are bearing children with little knowledge of how to care for them, when the society and even the schools often concentrate on materialistic messages, it may be unnecessary to argue that we should care more genuinely for our children and teach them to care. However, many otherwise reasonable people seem to believe that our educational problems consist largely of low scores on achievement tests. My contention is, first, that we should want more from our educational efforts than adequate academic achievement and, second, that we will not achieve even that meager success unless our children believe that they themselves are cared for and learn to care for others.

There is much to be gained, both academically and humanly, by including themes of care in our curriculum. First, such inclusion may well expand our students' cultural literacy. For example, as we discuss in math classes the attempts of great mathematicians to prove the existence of God or to reconcile a God who is all good with the reality of evil in the world, students will hear names, ideas, and words that are not part of the standard curriculum. Although such incidental learning cannot replace the systematic and sequential learning required by those who plan careers in mathematically oriented fields, it can be powerful in expanding students' cultural horizons and in inspiring further study.

Second, themes of care help us to connect the standard subjects. The use of literature in mathematics classes, of history in science classes, and of art and music in all classes can give students a feeling of the wholeness in their education. After all, why should they seriously study five different subjects if their teachers, who are educated people, only seem to know and appreciate one?

Third, themes of care connect our students and our subjects to great existential questions. What is the meaning of life? Are there gods? How should I live?

Fourth, sharing such themes can connect us person-to-person. When teachers discuss themes of care, they may become real persons to their students and so enable them to construct new knowledge. Martin Buber put it this way:

> Trust, trust in the world, because this human being exists—that is the most inward achievement of the relation in education. Because this human being exists, meaninglessness, however hard pressed you are by it, cannot be the real truth. Because this human being exists, in the darkness the light lies hidden, in fear salvation, and in the callousness of one's fellowman the great love.[2]

Finally, I should emphasize that caring is not just a warm, fuzzy feeling that makes people kind and likable. Caring implies a continuous search for competence. When we care, we want to do our very best for the objects of our care. To have as our educational goal the production of caring, competent, loving, and lovable people is not anti-intellectual. Rather, it demonstrates respect for the full range of human talents. Not all human beings are good at or interested in mathematics, science, or British literature. But all humans can be helped to lead lives of deep concern for others, for the natural world and its creatures, and for the preservation of the human-made world. They can be led to develop the skills and knowledge necessary to make positive contributions, regardless of the occupation they may choose.

CHOOSING AND ORGANIZING THEMES OF CARE

Care is conveyed in many ways. At the institutional level, schools can be organized to provide continuity and support for relationships of care and trust.[3] At the individual level, parents and teachers show their caring through characteristic forms of attention: by cooperating in children's activities, by sharing their own dreams and doubts, and by providing carefully for the steady growth of the children in their charge. Personal manifestations of care are probably more important in children's lives than any particular curriculum or pattern of pedagogy.

However, curriculum can be selected with caring in mind. That is, educators can manifest their care in the choice of curriculum, and appropriately chosen curriculum can contribute to the growth of children as carers. Within each large domain of care, many topics are suitable for thematic units: In the domain of "caring for self," for example, we might consider life stages, spiritual growth, and what it means to develop an admirable character; in exploring the topic of caring for intimate others, we might include units on love, friendship, and parenting; under the theme of caring for strangers and global others, we might study war, poverty, and tolerance; in addressing the idea of caring for the human-made world, we might encourage competence with the machines that surround us and a real appreciation for the marvels of technology. Many other examples exist. Furthermore, there are at least two different ways to approach the development of such themes: Units can be constructed by interdisciplinary teams, or themes can be identified by individual teachers and addressed periodically throughout a year's or semester's work.

The interdisciplinary approach is familiar in core programs, and such programs are becoming more and more popular at the middle school level. One key to a successful interdisciplinary unit is the degree of genuinely enthusiastic support it receives from the teachers involved. Too often, arbitrary or artificial groupings are formed, and teachers are forced to make contributions that they themselves do not value highly. For example, math and science teachers are sometimes automatically lumped together, and rich humanistic possibilities may be lost. If I, as a math teacher, want to include historical, biographical, and literary topics in my math lessons, I might prefer to work with English and social studies teachers. Thus, it is important to involve teachers in the initial selection of broad areas for themes, as well as in their implementation.

Such interdisciplinary arrangements also work well at the college level. I recently received a copy of the syllabus for a college course titled "The Search for Meaning," which was co-taught by an economist, a university chaplain, and a psychiatrist.[4] The course is interdisciplinary, intellectually rich, and aimed squarely at the central questions of life.

At the high school level, where students desperately need to engage in the study and practice of caring, it is harder to form interdisciplinary teams. A conflict arises as teachers acknowledge the intensity of the subject-matter preparation their students need for further education. Good teachers often wish there were time in the day to co-teach unconventional topics of great importance, and they even admit that their students are not getting what they need for full personal development. But they feel constrained by the requirements of a highly competitive world and the structures of schooling established by that world.

Is there a way out of this conflict? Imaginative, like-minded teachers might agree to emphasize a particular theme in their separate classes. Such themes as war, poverty, crime, racism, or sexism can be addressed in almost every subject area. The teachers should agree on some core ideas related to caring that will be discussed in all classes, but beyond the central commitment to address themes of care, the topics can be handled in whatever way seems suitable in a given subject.

Consider, for example, what a mathematics class might contribute to a unit on crime. Statistical information might be gathered on the location and number of crimes, on rates for various kinds of crime, on the ages of offenders, and on the cost to society; graphs and charts could be constructed. Data on changes in crime rates could be assembled. Intriguing questions could be asked: Were property crime rates lower when penalties were more severe—when, for example, even children were hanged as thieves? What does an average criminal case cost by way of lawyers' fees, police investigation, and court processing? Does it cost more to house a youth in a detention center or in an elite private school?

None of this would have to occupy a full period every day. The regular sequential work of the math class could go on at a slightly reduced rate (e.g., fewer textbook exercises as homework), and the work on crime could proceed in the form of interdisciplinary projects over a considerable period of time. Most important would be the continual reminder in all classes that the topic is part of a larger theme of caring for strangers and fellow citizens. It takes only a few minutes to talk about what it means to live in safety, to trust one's neighbors, to feel secure in greeting strangers. Students should be told that metal detectors and security guards were not part of their parents' school lives, and they should be encouraged to hope for a safer and more open future. Notice the words I've used in this paragraph: caring, trust, safety, strangers, hope. Each could be used as an organizing theme for another unit of study.

English and social studies teachers would obviously have much to contribute to a unit on crime. For example, students might read *Oliver Twist,* and they might also study and discuss the social conditions that seemed to promote crime in nineteenth-century England. Do similar conditions exist in our country today? The selection of materials could include both classic works and modern stories and films. Students might even be introduced to some of the mystery stories that adults read so avidly on airplanes and beaches, and teachers should be engaged in lively discussion about the comparative value of the various stories.

Science teachers might find that a unit on crime would enrich their teaching of evolution. They could bring up the topic of social Darwinism, which played such a strong role in social policy during the late nineteenth and early twentieth centuries. To what degree are criminal tendencies inherited? Should children be tested for the genetic defects that are suspected of predisposing some people to crime? Are females less competent than males in moral reasoning? (Why

did some scientists and philosophers think this was true?) Why do males commit so many more violent acts than do females?

Teachers of the arts could also be involved. A unit on crime might provide a wonderful opportunity to critique "gangsta rap" and other currently popular forms of music. Students might profitably learn how the control of art contributed to national criminality during the Nazi era. These are ideas that pop into my mind. Far more various and far richer ideas will come from teachers who specialize in these subjects.

There are risks, of course, in undertaking any unit of study that focuses on matters of controversy or deep existential concern, and teachers should anticipate these risks. What if students want to compare the incomes of teachers and cocaine dealers? What if they point to contemporary personalities from politics, entertainment, business, or sports who seem to escape the law and profit from what seems to be criminal behavior? My own inclination would be to allow free discussion of these cases and to be prepared to counteract them with powerful stories of honesty, compassion, moderation, and charity.

An even more difficult problem may arise. Suppose a student discloses his or her own criminal activities? Fear of this sort of occurrence may send teachers scurrying for safer topics. But, in fact, any instructional method that uses narrative forms or encourages personal expression runs this risk. For example, students of English as a second language who write proudly about their own hard lives and new hopes may disclose that their parents are illegal immigrants. A girl may write passages that lead her teacher to suspect sexual abuse. A boy may brag about objects he has "ripped off." Clearly, as we use these powerful methods that encourage students to initiate discussion and share their experiences, we must reflect on the ethical issues involved, consider appropriate responses to such issues, and prepare teachers to handle them responsibly.

Caring teachers must help students make wise decisions about what information they will share about themselves. On the one hand, teachers want their students to express themselves, and they want their students to trust in and consult them. On the other hand, teachers have an obligation to protect immature students from making disclosures that they might later regret. There is a deep ethical problem here. Too often educators assume that only religious fundamentalists and right-wing extremists object to the discussion of emotionally and morally charged issues. In reality, there is a real danger of intrusiveness and lack of respect in methods that fail to recognize the vulnerability of students. Therefore, as teachers plan units and lessons on moral issues, they should anticipate the tough problems that may arise. I am arguing here that it is morally irresponsible to simply ignore existential questions and themes of care; we must attend to them. But it is equally irresponsible to approach these deep concerns without caution and careful preparation.

So far, I have discussed two ways of organizing interdisciplinary units on themes of care. In one, teachers actually teach together in teams; in the other, teachers agree on a theme and a central focus on care, but they do what they can, when they can, in their own classrooms. A variation on this second way—which is also open to teachers who have to work alone—is to choose several themes and weave them into regular course material over an entire semester or year. The particular themes will depend on the interests and preparation of each teacher.

For example, if I were teaching high school mathematics today, I would use religious/existential questions as a pervasive theme because the biographies of mathematicians are filled with accounts of their speculations on matters of God, other dimensions, and the infinite—and because these topics fascinate me. There are so many wonderful stories to be told: Descartes' proof of the existence of God, Pascal's famous wager, Plato's world of forms, Newton's attempt to verify biblical chronology, Leibniz's detailed theodicy, current attempts to describe a divine domain in terms of metasystems, and mystical speculations on the infinite.[5] Some of these stories can be told as rich "asides" in five minutes or less. Others might occupy the better part of several class periods.

Other mathematics teachers might use an interest in architecture and design, art, music, or machinery as continuing themes in the domain of "caring for the human-made world." Still others might introduce the mathematics of living things. The possibilities are endless. In choosing and pursuing these themes, teachers should be aware that they are both helping their students learn to care and demonstrating their own caring by sharing interests that go well beyond the demands of textbook pedagogy.

Still another way to introduce themes of care into regular classrooms is to be prepared to respond spontaneously to events that occur in the school or in the neighborhood. Older teachers have one advantage in this area: They probably have a greater store of experience and stories on which to draw. However, younger teachers have the advantage of being closer to their students' lives and experiences; they are more likely to be familiar with the music, films, and sports figures that interest their students. All teachers should be prepared to respond to the needs of students who are suffering from the death of friends, conflicts between groups of students, pressure to use drugs or to engage in sex, and other troubles so rampant in the lives of today's children. Too often schools rely on experts—"grief counselors" and the like—when what children really need is the continuing compassion and presence of adults who represent constancy and care in their lives. Artificially separating the emotional, academic, and moral care of children into tasks for specially designated experts contributes to the fragmentation of life in schools.

Of course, I do not mean to imply that experts are unnecessary, nor do I mean to suggest that some matters should not be reserved for parents or psychologists. But our society has gone too far in compartmentalizing the care of its children. When we ask whose job it is to teach children how to care, an appropriate initial response is "Everyone's." Having accepted universal responsibility, we can then ask about the special contributions and limitations of various individuals and groups.

SUPPORTING STRUCTURES

What kind of schools and teacher preparation are required, if themes of care are to be taught effectively? First, and most important, care must be taken seriously as a major purpose of schools; that is, educators must recognize that caring for students is fundamental in teaching and that developing people with a strong capacity for care is a major objective of responsible education. Schools properly pursue many other objectives—developing artistic talent, promoting multicultural understanding, diversifying curriculum to meet the academic and vocational needs of all students, forging connections with community agencies and parents, and so on. Schools cannot be single-purpose institutions. Indeed, many of us would argue that it is logically and practically impossible to achieve that single academic purpose if other purposes are not recognized and accepted. This contention is confirmed in the success stories of several inner-city schools.[6]

Once it is recognized that school is a place in which students are cared for and learn to care, that recognition should be powerful in guiding policy. In the late 1950s, schools in the United States, under the guidance of James Conant and others, placed the curriculum at the top of the educational priority list. Because the nation's leaders wanted schools to provide high-powered courses in mathematics and science, it was recommended that small high schools be replaced by efficient larger structures complete with sophisticated laboratories and specialist teachers. Economies of scale were anticipated, but the main argument for consolidation and regionalization centered on the curriculum. All over the country, small schools were closed, and students were herded into larger facilities with "more offerings." We did not think carefully about schools as communities and about what might be lost as we pursued a curriculum-driven ideal.

Today many educators are calling for smaller schools and more family-like groupings. These are good proposals, but teachers, parents, and students should be engaged in continuing discussion about what they are trying to achieve through the new arrangements. For example, if test scores do not immediately rise, participants should be courageous in explaining that test scores were not the main object of the changes. Most of us who argue for caring in schools are intuitively quite sure that children in such settings will in fact become more competent learners. But, if they cannot prove their academic competence in a prescribed period of time, should we give up on caring and on teaching them to care? That would be foolish. There is more to life and learning than the academic proficiency demonstrated by test scores.

In addition to steadfastness of purpose, schools must consider continuity of people and place. If we are concerned with caring and community, then we must make it possible for students and teachers to stay together for several years so that mutual trust can develop and students can feel a sense of belonging in their "schoolhome."[7]

More than one scheme of organization can satisfy the need for continuity. Elementary school children can stay with the same teacher for several years, or they can work with a stable team of specialist teachers for several years. In the latter arrangement, there may be program advantages; that is, children taught by subject-matter experts who get to know them well over an extended period of time may learn more about the particular subjects. At the high school level, the same specialist teachers might work with students throughout their years in high school. Or, as Theodore Sizer has suggested, one teacher might teach two subjects to a group of 30 students rather than one subject to 60 students, thereby reducing the number of different adults with whom students interact each day.[8] In all the suggested arrangements, placements should be made by mutual consent whenever possible. Teachers and students who hate or distrust one another should not be forced to stay together.

A policy of keeping students and teachers together for several years supports caring in two essential ways: It provides time for the development of caring relations, and it makes teaching themes of care more feasible. When trust has been established, teachers and students can discuss matters that would be hard for a group of strangers to approach, and classmates learn to support one another in sensitive situations.

The structural changes suggested here are not expensive. If a high school teacher must teach five classes a day, it costs no more for three of these classes to be composed of continuing students than for all five classes to comprise new students (i.e., strangers). The recommended changes come directly out of a clear-headed assessment of our major aims and purposes. We failed to suggest them earlier because we had other, too limited, goals in mind.

I have made one set of structural changes sound easy, and I do believe that they are easily made. But the curricular and pedagogical changes that are required may be more difficult. High school textbooks rarely contain the kinds of supplementary material I have described, and teachers are not formally prepared to incorporate such material. Too often, even the people we regard as strongly prepared in a liberal arts major are unprepared to discuss the history of their subject, its relation to other subjects, the biographies of its great figures, its connections to the great existential questions, and the ethical responsibilities of those who work in that discipline. To teach themes of care in an academically effective way, teachers will have to engage in projects of self-education.

At present, neither liberal arts departments nor schools of education pay much attention to connecting academic subjects with themes of care. For example, biology students may learn something of the anatomy and physiology of mammals but nothing at all about the care of living animals; they may never be asked to consider the moral issues involved in the annual euthanasia of millions of pets. Mathematics students may learn to solve quadratic equations but never study what it means to live in a mathematicized world. In enlightened history classes, students may learn something about the problems of racism and colonialism but never hear anything about the evolution of childhood, the contributions of women in both domestic and public caregiving, or the connection between the feminization of caregiving and public policy. A liberal education that neglects matters that are central to a fully human life hardly warrants the name,[9] and a professional education that confines itself to technique does nothing to close the gaps in liberal education.

The greatest structural obstacle, however, may simply be legitimizing the inclusion of themes of care in the curriculum. Teachers in the early grades have long included such themes as a regular part of their work, and middle school educators are becoming more sensitive to developmental needs involving care. But secondary schools, where violence, apathy, and alienation are most evident, do little to develop the capacity to care. Today, even elementary teachers complain that the pressure to produce high test scores inhibits the work they regard as central to their mission: the development of caring and competent people. Therefore, it would seem that the most fundamental change required is one of attitude. Teachers can be very special people in the lives of children, and it should be legitimate for them to spend time developing relations of trust, talking with students about problems that are central to their lives, and guiding them toward greater sensitivity and competence across all the domains of care.

ENDNOTES

1. For the theoretical argument, see Nel Noddings, *The Challenge to Care in Schools* (New York: Teachers College Press, 1992); for a practical example and rich documentation, see Sharon Quint, *Schooling Homeless Children* (New York: Teachers College Press, 1994).

2. Martin Buber, *Between Man and Man* (New York: Macmillan, 1965), p. 98.

3. Noddings, *The Challenge to Care in Schools.*

4. See Thomas H. Naylor, William H. Willimon, and Magdalena R. Naylor, *The Search for Meaning* (Nashville, TN: Abingdon Press, 1994).

5. Nel Noddings, *Educating for Intelligent Belief and Unbelief* (New York: Teachers College Press, 1993).

6. See Deborah Meier, "How Our Schools Could Be," *Phi Delta Kappan*, January 1995, pp. 369–373; Quint, *Schooling Homeless Children.*

7. See Jane Roland Martin, *The Schoolhome: Rethinking Schools for Changing Families* (Cambridge, MA: Harvard University Press, 1992).

8. Theodore Sizer, *Horace's Compromise: The Dilemma of the American High School* (Boston: Houghton Mifflin, 1984).

9. See Bruce Wilshire, *The Moral Collapse of the University* (Albany: State University of New York Press, 1990).

DISCUSSION QUESTIONS

1. Is teaching themes of care a legitimate responsibility for schools?
2. What are some advantages of an interdisciplinary unit on caring?
3. What might be some obstacles to implementing a curriculum that included themes of care?
4. What arguments would be useful for convincing a school board that themes of caring should be included in the curriculum?
5. What steps would you take as curriculum director to implement themes of caring in classrooms districtwide?

The Heart of a Teacher

PARKER J. PALMER

FOCUSING QUESTIONS

1. Is teaching an occupation or is it a vocation?
2. Does it matter who a teacher is as a person? Why?
3. What are the qualities of a great teacher?
4. Why do some teachers eventually become disillusioned and cynical?
5. How might teacher colleagues support each other's efforts to become great teachers?

WE TEACH WHO WE ARE

I am a teacher at heart, and there are moments in the classroom when I can hardly hold the joy. When my students and I discover uncharted territory to explore, when the pathway out of a thicket opens up before us, when our experience is illumined by the lightning-life of the mind—then teaching is the finest work I know.

But at other moments, the classroom is so lifeless or painful or confused—and I am so powerless to do anything about it—that my claim to be a teacher seems a transparent sham. Then the enemy is everywhere: in those students from some alien planet, in that subject I thought I knew, and in the personal pathology that keeps me earning my living this way. What a fool I was to imagine that I had mastered this occult art—harder to divine than tea leaves and impossible for mortals to do even passably well!

The tangles of teaching have three important sources. The first two are commonplace, but the third, and most fundamental, is rarely given its due. First, the subjects we teach are as large and complex as life, so our knowledge of them is always flawed and partial. No matter how we devote ourselves to reading and research, teaching requires a command of content that always eludes our grasp. Second, the students we teach are larger than life and even more complex. To see them clearly and see them whole, and respond to them wisely in the moment, requires a fusion of Freud and Solomon that few of us achieve.

If students and subjects accounted for all the complexities of teaching, our standard ways of coping would do—keep up with our fields as best we can, and learn enough techniques to stay ahead of the student psyche. But there is another reason for these complexities: We teach who we are.

Teaching, like any truly human activity, emerges from one's inwardness, for better or worse. As I teach, I project the condition of my soul onto my students, my subject, and our way of being together. The entanglements I experience in the classroom are often no more or less than the convolutions of my inner life. Viewed from this angle, teaching holds a mirror to the soul. If I am willing to look in that mirror, and not run from what I see, I have a chance to gain self-knowledge—and knowing myself is as crucial to good teaching as knowing my students and my subject.

In fact, knowing my students and my subject depends heavily on self-knowledge. When I do not know myself, I cannot know who my students are. I will see them through a glass darkly, in the shadows of my unexamined life—and when I cannot see them clearly, I cannot teach them well. When I do not know myself, I cannot know my subject—not at the deepest levels of embodied, personal meaning. I will know it only abstractly, from a distance, a congeries of concepts as far removed from the world as I am from personal truth.

We need to open a new frontier in our exploration of good teaching: the inner landscape of a teacher's life. To chart that landscape fully, three important paths must be taken—intellectual, emotional, and spiritual—and none can be ignored. Reduce teaching to intellect and it becomes a cold abstraction; reduce it to emotions and it becomes narcissistic; reduce it to the spiritual and it loses its anchor to the world. Intellect, emotion, and spirit depend on each other for wholeness. They are interwoven in the human self and in education at its best, and we need to interweave them in our pedagogical discourse as well.

By intellectual I mean the way we think about teaching and learning—the form and content of our concepts of how people know and learn, of the nature of our students and our subjects. By emotional, I mean the way we and our students feel as we teach and learn—feelings that can either enlarge or diminish the exchange between us. By spiritual, I mean the diverse ways we answer the heart's longing to be connected with the largeness of life—a longing that animates love and work, especially the work called teaching.

TEACHING BEYOND TECHNIQUE

After three decades of trying to learn my craft, every class comes down to this: my students and I, face to face, engaged in an ancient and exacting exchange called education. The techniques I have mastered do not disappear, but neither do they suffice. Face to face with my students, only one resource is at my immediate command: my identity, my selfhood, my sense of this "I" who teaches—without which I have no sense of the "Thou" who learns.

Here is a secret hidden in plain sight: Good teaching cannot be reduced to technique; good teaching comes from the identity and integrity of the teacher. In every class I teach, my ability to connect with my students, and to connect them with the subject, depends less on the methods I use than on the degree to which I know and trust my selfhood—and am willing to make it available and vulnerable in the service of learning.

My evidence for this claim comes, in part, from years of asking students to tell me about their good teachers. As I listen to those stories, it becomes impossible to claim that all good teachers use similar techniques: Some lecture nonstop and others speak very little; some stay close to their material and others set loose the imagination; some teach with the carrot and others with the stick.

But in every story I have heard, good teachers share one trait: A strong sense of personal identity infuses their work. "Dr. A is really there when she teaches," a student tells me, or "Mr. B has such enthusiasm for his subject," or "You can tell that this is really Prof. C's life."

One student I heard about said she could not describe her good teachers because they were so different from each other. But she could describe her bad teachers because they were all the same: "Their words float somewhere in front of their faces, like the balloon speech in cartoons." With one remarkable image she said it all. Bad teachers distance themselves from the subject they are teaching—and, in the process, from their students.

Good teachers join self, subject, and students in the fabric of life because they teach from an integral and undivided self; they manifest in their own lives, and evoke in their students, a "capacity for connectedness." They are able to weave a complex web of connections between themselves, their subjects, and their students, so that students can learn to weave a world for themselves. The methods used by these weavers vary widely: lectures, Socratic dialogues, laboratory experiments, collaborative problem-solving, creative chaos. The connections made by good teachers are held not in their methods but in their hearts—meaning heart in its ancient sense, the place where intellect and emotion and spirit and will converge in the human self.

If good teaching cannot be reduced to technique, I no longer need to suffer the pain of having my peculiar gift as a teacher crammed into the Procrustean bed of someone else's method and the standards prescribed by it. That pain is felt throughout education today as we insist upon the method *du jour*—leaving people who teach differently feeling devalued, forcing them to measure up to norms not their own.

I will never forget one professor who, moments before I was to start a workshop on teaching, unloaded years of pent-up workshop animus on me: "I am an organic chemist. Are you going to spend the next two days

telling me that I am supposed to teach organic chemistry through role-playing?" His wry question was related not only to his distinctive discipline but also to his distinctive self: We must find an approach to teaching that respects the diversity of teachers as well as disciplines, which methodological reductionism fails to do.

The capacity for connectedness manifests itself in diverse and wondrous ways—as many ways as there are forms of personal identity. Two great teachers stand out from my own undergraduate experience. They differed radically from each other in technique, but both were gifted at connecting students, teacher, and subject in a community of learning.

One of those teachers assigned a lot of reading in her course on methods of social research and, when we gathered around the seminar table on the first day, said, "Any comments or questions?" She had the courage to wait out our stupefied (and stupefying) silence, minute after minute after minute, gazing around the table with a benign look on her face—and then, after the passage of a small eternity, to rise, pick up her books, and say, as she walked toward the door, "Class dismissed."

This scenario more or less repeated itself a second time, but by the third time we met, our high SAT scores had kicked in, and we realized that the big dollars we were paying for this education would be wasted if we did not get with the program. So we started doing the reading, making comments, asking questions—and our teacher proved herself to be a brilliant interlocutor, co-researcher, and guide in the midst of confusions, a "weaver" of connectedness in her own interactive and inimitable way.

My other great mentor taught the history of social thought. He did not know the meaning of silence and he was awkward at interaction; he lectured incessantly while we sat in rows and took notes. Indeed, he became so engaged with his material that he was often impatient with our questions. But his classes were nonetheless permeated with a sense of connectedness and community.

How did he manage this alchemy? Partly by giving lectures that went far beyond presenting the data of social theory into staging the drama of social thought. He told stories from the lives of great thinkers as well as explaining their ideas; we could almost see Karl Marx, sitting alone in the British Museum Library, writing *Das Kapital*. Through active imagination we were brought into community with the thinker himself, and with the personal and social conditions that stimulated his thought.

But the drama of my mentor's lectures went farther still. He would make a strong Marxist statement, and we would transcribe it in our notebooks as if it were holy writ. Then a puzzled look would pass over his face. He would pause, step to one side, turn, and look back at the space he had just exited—and argue with his own statement from a Hegelian point of view! This was not an artificial device but a genuine expression of the intellectual drama that continually occupied this teacher's mind and heart.

"Drama" does not mean histrionics, of course, and remembering that fact can help us name a form of connectedness that is palpable and powerful without being overtly interactive, or even face to face. When I go to the theater, I sometimes feel strongly connected to the action, as if my own life were being portrayed on stage. But I have no desire to raise my hand and respond to the line just spoken, or run up the aisle, jump onto the stage, and join in the action. Sitting in the audience, I am already on stage "in person," connected in an inward and invisible way that we rarely credit as the powerful form of community that it is. With a good drama, I do not need overt interaction to be "in community" with those characters and their lives.

I used to wonder how my mentor, who was so awkward in his face-to-face relations

with students, managed to simulate community so well. Now I understand: He was in community without us! Who needs 20-year-olds from the suburbs when you are hanging out constantly with the likes of Marx and Hegel, Durkheim, Weber, and Troeltsch? This is "community" of the highest sort— this capacity for connectedness that allows one to converse with the dead, to speak and listen in an invisible network of relationships that enlarges one's world and enriches one's life. (We should praise, not deride, First Ladies who "talk" with Eleanor Roosevelt; the ability to learn from wise but long-gone souls is nothing less than a classic mark of a liberal education!)

Yet my great professor, though he communed more intimately with the great figures of social thought than with the people close at hand, cared deeply about his students. The passion with which he lectured was not only for his subject, but for us to know his subject. He wanted us to meet and learn from the constant companions of his intellect and imagination, and he made those introductions in a way that was deeply integral to his own nature. He brought us into a form of community that did not require small numbers of students sitting in a circle and learning through dialogue.

These two great teachers were polar opposites in substance and in style. But both created the connectedness, the community, that is essential to teaching and learning. They did so by trusting and teaching from true self, from the identity and integrity that is the source of all good work—and by employing quite different techniques that allowed them to reveal rather than conceal who they were.

Their genius as teachers, and their profound gifts to me, would have been diminished and destroyed had their practice been forced into the Procrustean bed of the method of the moment. The proper place for technique is not to subdue subjectivity, not to mask and distance the self from the work, but—as one grows in self-knowledge—to help bring forth and amplify the gifts of self on which good work depends.

TEACHING AND TRUE SELF

The claim that good teaching comes from the identity and integrity of the teacher might sound like a truism, and a pious one at that: Good teaching comes from good people. But by "identity" and "integrity" I do not mean only our noble features, or the good deeds we do, or the brave faces we wear to conceal our confusions and complexities. Identity and integrity have as much to do with our shadows and limits, our wounds and fears, as with our strengths and potentials.

By identity I mean an evolving nexus where all the forces that constitute my life converge in the mystery of self: my genetic makeup, the nature of the man and woman who gave me life, the culture in which I was raised, people who have sustained me and people who have done me harm, the good and ill I have done to others and to myself, the experience of love and suffering—and much, much more. In the midst of that complex field, identity is a moving intersection of the inner and outer forces that make me who I am, converging in the irreducible mystery of being human.

By integrity I mean whatever wholeness I am able to find within that nexus as its vectors form and re-form the pattern of my life. Integrity requires that I discern what is integral to my selfhood, what fits and what does not—and that I choose life-giving ways of relating to the forces that converge within me: Do I welcome them or fear them, embrace them or reject them, move with them or against them? By choosing integrity, I become more whole, but wholeness does not mean perfection. It means becoming more real by acknowledging the whole of who I am.

Identity and integrity are not the granite from which fictional heroes are hewn. They are subtle dimensions of the complex, demanding, and lifelong process of self-discovery. Identity lies in the intersection of the diverse forces that make up my life, and integrity lies in relating to those forces in ways that bring me wholeness and life rather than fragmentation and death.

Those are my definitions—but try as I may to refine them, they always come out too pat. Identity and integrity can never be fully named or known by anyone, including the person who bears them. They constitute that familiar strangeness we take with us to the grave, elusive realities that can be caught only occasionally out of the corner of the eye.

Stories are the best way to portray realities of this sort, so here is a tale of two teachers—a tale based on people I have known, whose lives tell me more about the subtleties of identity and integrity than any theory could.

Alan and Eric were born into two different families of skilled craftspeople, rural folk with little formal schooling but gifted in the manual arts. Both boys evinced this gift from childhood onward, and as each grew in skill at working with his hands, each developed a sense of self in which the pride of craft was key.

The two shared another gift as well: Both excelled in school and became the first in their working-class families to go to college. Both did well as undergraduates, both were admitted to graduate school, both earned doctorates, and both chose academic careers.

But here their paths diverged. Though the gift of craft was central in both men's sense of self, Alan was able to weave that gift into his academic vocation, while the fabric of Eric's life unraveled early on.

Catapulted from his rural community into an elite private college at age 18, Eric suffered severe culture shock—and never overcame it. He was insecure with fellow students and, later, with academic colleagues who came from backgrounds he saw as more "cultured" than his own. He learned to speak and act like an intellectual, but he always felt fraudulent among people who were, in his eyes, to the manor born.

But insecurity neither altered Eric's course nor drew him into self-reflection. Instead, he bullied his way into professional life on the theory that the best defense is a good offense. He made pronouncements rather than probes. He listened for weaknesses rather than strengths in what other people said. He argued with anyone about anything—and responded with veiled contempt to whatever was said in return.

In the classroom, Eric was critical and judgmental, quick to put down the "stupid question," adept at trapping students with trick questions of his own, then merciless in mocking wrong answers. He seemed driven by a need to inflict upon his students the same wound that academic life had inflicted upon him—the wound of being embarrassed by some essential part of one's self.

But when Eric went home to his workbench and lost himself in craft, he found himself as well. He became warm and welcoming, at home in the world and glad to extend hospitality to others. Reconnected with his roots, centered in his true self, he was able to reclaim a quiet and confident core—which he quickly lost as soon as he returned to campus.

Alan's is a different story. His leap from countryside to campus did not induce culture shock, in part because he attended a land-grant university where many students had backgrounds much like his own. He was not driven to hide his gift, but was able to honor and transform it by turning it toward things academic: He brought to his study, and later to his teaching and research, the same sense of craft that his ancestors had brought to their work with metal and wood.

Watching Alan teach, you felt that you were watching a craftsman at work—and if you knew his history, you understood that this feeling was more than metaphor. In his lectures, every move Alan made was informed by attention to detail and respect for the materials at hand; he connected ideas with the precision of dovetail joinery and finished the job with a polished summary.

But the power of Alan's teaching went well beyond crafted performance. His students knew that Alan would extend himself with great generosity to any of them who wanted to become an apprentice in his field, just as the elders in his own family had extended themselves to help young Alan grow in his original craft.

Alan taught from an undivided self—the integral state of being that is central to good teaching. In the undivided self, every major thread of one's life experience is honored, creating a weave of such coherence and strength that it can hold students and subject as well as self. Such a self, inwardly integrated, is able to make the outward connections on which good teaching depends.

But Eric failed to weave the central strand of his identity into his academic vocation. His was a self divided, engaged in a civil war. He projected that inner warfare onto the outer world, and his teaching devolved into combat instead of craft. The divided self will always distance itself from others, and may even try to destroy them, to defend its fragile identity.

If Eric had not been alienated as an undergraduate—or if his alienation had led to self-reflection instead of self-defense—it is possible that he, like Alan, could have found integrity in his academic vocation, could have woven the major strands of his identity into his work. But part of the mystery of selfhood is the fact that one size does not fit all: What is integral to one person lacks integrity for another. Throughout his life, there were persistent clues that academia was not a life-giving choice for Eric, not a context in which his true self could emerge healthy and whole, not a vocation integral to his unique nature.

The self is not infinitely elastic—it has potentials and it has limits. If the work we do lacks integrity for us, then we, the work, and the people we do it with will suffer. Alan's self was enlarged by his academic vocation, and the work he did was a joy to behold. Eric's self was diminished by his encounter with academia, and choosing a different vocation might have been his only way to recover integrity lost.

WHEN TEACHERS LOSE HEART

As good teachers weave the fabric that joins them with students and subjects, the heart is the loom on which the threads are tied: The tension is held, the shuttle flies, and the fabric is stretched tight. Small wonder, then, that teaching tugs at the heart, opens the heart, even breaks the heart—and the more one loves teaching, the more heartbreaking it can be.

We became teachers for reasons of the heart, animated by a passion for some subject and for helping people to learn. But many of us lose heart as the years of teaching go by. How can we take heart in teaching once more, so that we can do what good teachers always do—give heart to our students? The courage to teach is the courage to keep one's heart open in those very moments when the heart is asked to hold more than it is able, so that teacher and students and subject can be woven into the fabric of community that learning and living require.

There are no techniques for reclaiming our hearts, for keeping our hearts open. Indeed, the heart does not seek "fixes" but insight and understanding. When we lose heart, we need an understanding of our condition that will liberate us from that condition, a diagnosis that will lead us toward new ways of being in the classroom simply by telling the truth about who, and how, we are. Truth, not technique, is what heals and empowers the heart.

We lose heart, in part, because teaching is a daily exercise in vulnerability. I need not reveal personal secrets to feel naked in front of a class. I need only parse a sentence or work a proof on the board while my students doze off or pass notes. No matter how technical or abstract my subject may be, the things I teach are things I care about—and what I care about helps define my selfhood.

Unlike many professions, teaching is always done at the dangerous intersection of personal and public life. A good therapist must work in a personal way, but never publicly: The therapist who reveals as much as a client's name is derelict. A good trial lawyer must work in a public forum, but unswayed by personal opinion: The lawyer who allows his or her feelings about a client's guilt to weaken the client's defense is guilty of malpractice.

But a good teacher must stand where personal and public meet, dealing with the thundering flow of traffic at an intersection where "weaving a web of connectedness" feels more like crossing a freeway on foot. As we try to connect ourselves and our subjects with our students, we make ourselves, as well as our subjects, vulnerable to indifference, judgment, ridicule.

To reduce our vulnerability, we disconnect from students, from subjects, and even from ourselves. We build a wall between inner truth and outer performance, and we play-act the teacher's part. Our words, spoken at a remove from our hearts, become "the balloon speech in cartoons," and we become caricatures of ourselves. We distance ourselves from students and subject to minimize the danger—forgetting that distance makes life more dangerous still by isolating the self.

This self-protective split of personhood from practice is encouraged by an academic culture that distrusts personal truth. Though the academy claims to value multiple modes of knowing, it honors only one—an "objective" way of knowing that takes us into the "real" world by taking us "out of ourselves."

In this culture, objective facts are regarded as pure while subjective feelings are suspect and sullied. In this culture, the self is not a source to be tapped but a danger to be suppressed, not a potential to be fulfilled but an obstacle to be overcome. In this culture, the pathology of speech disconnected from self is regarded, and rewarded, as a virtue.

If my sketch of the academic bias against selfhood seems overdone, here is a story from my own teaching experience. I assigned my students a series of brief analytical essays involving themes in the texts we were going to be reading. Then I assigned a parallel series of autobiographical sketches, related to those themes, so my students could see connections between the textbook concepts and their own lives.

After the first class, a student spoke to me: "In those autobiographical essays you asked us to write, is it okay to use the word 'I'?"

I did not know whether to laugh or cry—but I knew that my response would have considerable impact on a young man who had just opened himself to ridicule. I told him that not only could he use the word "I," but I hoped he would use it freely and often. Then I asked what had led to his question.

"I'm a history major," he said, "and each time I use 'I' in a paper, they knock off half a grade."

The academic bias against subjectivity not only forces our students to write poorly ("It is believed . . ." instead of "I believe . . ."); it deforms their thinking about themselves and their world. In a single stroke, we delude our students into believing that bad prose turns opinions into facts and we alienate them from their own inner lives.

Faculty often complain that students have no regard for the gifts of insight and understanding that are the true payoff of education—they care only about short-term outcomes in the "real" world: "Will this major get me a job?" "How will this assignment be useful in 'real' life?"

But those are not the questions deep in our students' hearts. They are merely the questions they have been taught to ask, not

only by tuition-paying parents who want their children to be employable, but by an academic culture that distrusts and devalues inner reality. Of course our students are cynical about the inner outcomes of education: We teach them that the subjective self is irrelevant and even unreal.

The foundation of any culture lies in the way it answers the question "Where do reality and power reside?" For some cultures the answer is the gods; for some it is nature; for some it is tradition. In our culture, the answer is clear: Reality and power reside in the external world of objects and events, and in the sciences that study that world, while the inner realm of "heart" is a romantic fantasy—an escape from harsh realities perhaps, but surely not a source of leverage over "the real world."

We are obsessed with manipulating externals because we believe that they will give us some power over reality and win us some freedom from its constraints. Mesmerized by a technology that seems to do just that, we dismiss the inner world. We turn every question we face into an objective problem to be solved—and we believe that for every objective problem there is some sort of technical fix.

That is why, we train doctors to repair the body but not to honor the spirit; clergy to be CEOs but not spiritual guides; teachers to master techniques but not to engage their students' hearts—or their own. That is why our students are cynical about the efficacy of an education that transforms the inner landscape of their lives: When academic culture dismisses inner truth and pays homage only to the objective world, students as well as teachers lose heart.

LISTENING TO THE TEACHER WITHIN

Recovering the heart to teach requires us to reclaim our relationship with the teacher within. This teacher is one whom we knew when we were children but lost touch with as we grew into adulthood, a teacher who continually invites me to honor my true self—not my ego or expectations or image or role, but the self I am when all the externals are stripped away.

By inner teacher, I do not mean "conscience" or "superego," moral arbiter or internalized judge. In fact, conscience, as it is commonly understood, can get us into deep vocational trouble. When we listen primarily for what we "ought" to be doing with our lives, we may find ourselves hounded by external expectations that can distort our identity and integrity. There is much that I "ought" to be doing by some abstract moral calculus. But is it my vocation? Am I gifted and called to do it? Is this particular "ought" a place of intersection between my inner self and the outer world, or is it someone else's image of how my life should look?

When I follow only the "oughts," I may find myself doing work that is ethically laudable but that is not mine to do. A vocation that is not mine, no matter how externally valued, does violence to the self—in the precise sense that it violates my identity and integrity on behalf of some abstract norm. When I violate myself, I invariably end up violating the people I work with. How many teachers inflict their own pain on their students—the pain that comes from doing a work that never was, or no longer is, their true work?

The teacher within is not the voice of conscience but of identity and integrity. It speaks not of what ought to be, but of what is real for us, of what is true. It says things like, "This is what fits you and this is what doesn't." "This is who you are and this is who you are not." "This is what gives you life and this is what kills your spirit—or makes you wish you were dead." The teacher within stands guard at the gate of selfhood, warding off whatever insults our integrity and welcoming whatever affirms it. The voice of the inward teacher reminds me of my potentials and limits as I negotiate the force field of my life.

I realize that the idea of a "teacher within" strikes some academics as a romantic fantasy, but I cannot fathom why. If there is no such reality in our lives, centuries of Western discourse about the aims of education become so much lip-flapping. In classical understanding, education is the attempt to "lead out" from within the self a core of wisdom that has the power to resist falsehood and live in the light of truth, not by external norms but by reasoned and reflective self-determination. The inward teacher is the living core of our lives that is addressed and evoked by any education worthy of the name.

Perhaps the idea is unpopular because it compels us to look at two of the most difficult truths about teaching. The first is that what we teach will never "take" unless it connects with the inward, living core of our students' lives, with our students' inward teachers.

We can, and do, make education an exclusively outward enterprise, forcing students to memorize and repeat facts without ever appealing to their inner truth—and we get predictable results: many students never want to read a challenging book or think a creative thought once they get out of school. The kind of teaching that transforms people does not happen if the student's inward teacher is ignored.

The second truth is even more daunting: We can speak to the teacher within our students only when we are on speaking terms with the teacher within ourselves.

The student who said that her bad teachers spoke like cartoon characters was describing teachers who have grown deaf to their inner guide, who have so thoroughly separated inner truth from outer actions that they have lost touch with a sense of self. "Deep speaks to deep," and when we have not sounded our own depths, we cannot sound the depths of our students' lives.

How does one attend to the voice of the teacher within? I have no particular methods to suggest, other than the familiar ones: solitude and silence, meditative reading and walking in the woods, keeping a journal, finding a friend who will simply listen. I merely propose that we need to learn as many ways as we can of "talking to ourselves."

That phrase, of course, is one we normally use to name a symptom of mental imbalance—a clear sign of how our culture regards the idea of an inner voice! But people who learn to talk to themselves may soon delight in the discovery that the teacher within is the sanest conversation partner they have ever had.

We need to find every possible way to listen to that voice and take its counsel seriously, not only for the sake of our work, but for the sake of our own health. If someone in the outer world is trying to tell us something important and we ignore his or her presence, that person either gives up and stops speaking or becomes more and more violent in attempting to get our attention.

Similarly, if we do not respond to the voice of the inward teacher, it will either stop speaking or become violent: I am convinced that some forms of depression, of which I have personal experience, are induced by a long-ignored inner teacher trying desperately to get us to listen by threatening to destroy us. When we honor that voice with simple attention, it responds by speaking more gently and engaging us in a life-giving conversation of the soul.

That conversation does not have to reach conclusions in order to be of value: We do not need to emerge from "talking to ourselves" with clear goals, objectives, and plans. Measuring the value of inner dialogue by its practical outcomes is like measuring the value of a friendship by the number of problems that are solved when friends get together.

Conversation among friends has its own rewards: In the presence of our friends we have the simple joy of feeling at ease, at home, trusted and able to trust. We attend to the inner teacher not to get fixed but to befriend the deeper self, to cultivate a sense of identity and integrity that allows us to feel at home wherever we are.

Listening to the inner teacher also offers an answer to one of the most basic questions teachers face: How can I develop the authority to teach, the capacity to stand my ground in the midst of the complex forces of both the classroom and my own life?

In a culture of objectification and technique we often confuse authority with power, but the two are not the same. Power works from the outside in, but authority works from the inside out. We are mistaken when we seek "authority" outside ourselves, in sources ranging from the subtle skills of group process to that less-than-subtle method of social control called grading. This view of teaching turns the teacher into the cop on the corner, trying to keep things moving amicably and by consent, but always having recourse to the coercive power of the law.

External tools of power have occasional utility in teaching, but they are no substitute for authority, the authority that comes from the teacher's inner life. The clue is in the word itself, which has "author" at its core. Authority is granted to people who are perceived as "authoring" their own words, their own actions, their own lives, rather than playing a scripted role at great remove from their own hearts. When teachers depend on the coercive powers of law or technique, they have no authority at all.

I am painfully aware of the times in my own teaching when I lose touch with my inner teacher, and therefore, with my own authority. In those times, I try to gain power by barricading myself behind the podium and my status while wielding the threat of grades. But when my teaching is authorized by the teacher within me, I need neither weapons nor armor to teach.

Authority comes as I reclaim my identity and integrity, remembering my selfhood and my sense of vocation. Then teaching can come from the depths of my own truth—and the truth that is within my students has a chance to respond in kind.

INSTITUTIONS AND THE HUMAN HEART

My concern for the "inner landscape" of teaching may seem indulgent, even irrelevant, at a time when many teachers are struggling simply to survive. Wouldn't it be more practical, I am sometimes asked, to offer tips, tricks, and techniques for staying alive in the classroom, things that ordinary teachers can use in everyday life?

I have worked with countless teachers, and many of them have confirmed my own experience: As important as methods may be, the most practical thing we can achieve in any kind of work is insight into what is happening inside us as we do it. The more familiar we are with our inner terrain, the more surefooted our teaching—and living—becomes.

I have heard that in the training of therapists, which involves much practical technique, there is a saying: "Technique is what you use until the therapist arrives." Good methods can help a therapist find a way into the client's dilemma, but good therapy does not begin until the real-life therapist joins with the real life of the client.

Technique is what teachers use until the real teacher arrives, and we need to find as many ways as possible to help that teacher show up. But if we want to develop the identity and integrity that good teaching requires, we must do something alien to academic culture: We must talk to each other about our inner lives—risky stuff in a profession that fears the personal and seeks safety in the technical, the distant, the abstract.

I was reminded of that fear recently as I listened to a group of faculty argue about what to do when students share personal experiences in class—experiences that are related to the themes of the course, but that some professors regard as "more suited to a therapy session than to a college classroom."

The house soon divided along predictable lines. On one side were the scholars, insisting that the subject is primary and must never be compromised for the sake of the students' lives. On the other side were the student-centered folks, insisting that the lives of students must always come first even if it means that the subject gets short-changed. The more vigorously these camps promoted their polarized ideas, the more antagonistic they became—and the less they learned about pedagogy or about themselves.

The gap between these views seems unbridgeable—until we understand what creates it. At bottom, these professors were not debating teaching techniques. They were revealing the diversity of identity and integrity among themselves, saying, in various ways, "Here are my own limits and potentials when it comes to dealing with the relation between the subject and my students' lives."

If we stopped lobbing pedagogical points at each other and spoke about who we are as teachers, a remarkable thing might happen: Identity and integrity might grow within us and among us, instead of hardening as they do when we defend our fixed positions from the foxholes of the pedagogy wars.

But telling the truth about ourselves with colleagues in the workplace is an enterprise fraught with danger, against which we have erected formidable taboos. We fear making ourselves vulnerable in the midst of competitive people and politics that could easily turn against us, and we claim the inalienable right to separate the "personal" and the "professional" into airtight compartments (even though everyone knows the two are inseparably intertwined). So we keep the workplace conversation objective and external, finding it safer to talk about technique than about selfhood.

Indeed, the story I most often hear from faculty (and other professionals) is that the institutions in which they work are the heart's worst enemy. In this story, institutions continually try to diminish the human heart in order to consolidate their own power, and the individual is left with a discouraging choice: to distance one's self from the institution and its mission and sink into deepening cynicism (an occupational hazard of academic life) or to maintain eternal vigilance against institutional invasion and fight for one's life when it comes.

Taking the conversation of colleagues into the deep places where we might grow in self-knowledge for the sake of our professional practice will not be an easy, or popular, task. But it is a task that leaders of every educational institution must take up if they wish to strengthen their institution's capacity to pursue the educational mission. How can schools educate students if they fail to support the teacher's inner life? To educate is to guide students on an inner journey toward more truthful ways of seeing and being in the world. How can schools perform their mission without encouraging the guides to scout out that inner terrain?

Now that this century of objectification and manipulation by technique has drawn to a close, we are experiencing an exhaustion of institutional resourcefulness at the very time when the problems that our institutions must address grow deeper and more demanding. Just as twentieth-century medicine, famous for its externalized fixes for disease, has found itself required to reach deeper for the psychological and spiritual dimensions of healing, so twentieth-century education must open up a new frontier in teaching and learning—the frontier of the teacher's inner life.

How this might be done is a subject I have explored in earlier essays,[1,2] so I will not repeat myself here. In "Good Talk about Good Teaching," I examined some of the key elements necessary for an institution to host noncompulsory, noninvasive opportunities for faculty to help themselves and each other grow inwardly as teachers. In "Divided No More," I explored things we can do on our own when institutions are resistant or hostile to the inner agenda.

Our task is to create enough safe spaces and trusting relationships within the academic workplace—hedged about by appropriate structural protections—that more of us will be able to tell the truth about our own struggles and joys as teachers in ways that befriend the soul and give it room to grow. Not all spaces can be safe, not all relationships trustworthy, but we can surely develop more of them than we now have so that an increase of honesty and healing can happen within us and among us—for our own sake, the sake of our teaching, and the sake of our students.

Honesty and healing sometimes happen quite simply, thanks to the alchemical powers of the human soul. When I, with 30 years of teaching experience, speak openly about the fact that I still approach each new class with trepidation, younger faculty tell me that this makes their own fears seem more natural—and thus easier to transcend—and a rich dialogue about the teacher's selfhood often ensues. We do not discuss techniques for "fear management," if such exist. Instead, we meet as fellow travelers and offer encouragement to each other in this demanding but deeply rewarding journey across the inner landscape of education—calling each other back to the identity and integrity that animate all good work, not least the work called teaching.

ENDNOTES

1. Parker J. Palmer, "Good Talk about Good Teaching: Improving Teaching Through Conversation and Community," *Change Magazine*, November/December, 1993, pp. 8–13. A revised version appears as Chapter VI in *The Courage to Teach.*
2. Parker J. Palmer, "Divided No More: A Movement Approach to Educational Reform," Change Magazine, March/April, 1992, pp. 10–17. A revised version appears as Chapter VII in *The Courage to Teach.*

REFERENCE

Palmer, P. J. (1998). *The courage to teach: Exploring the inner landscape of a teacher's life*. San Francisco: Jossey-Bass.

DISCUSSION QUESTIONS

1. Have you ever personally known any great teachers? What made them great teachers?
2. In what ways have you been profoundly influenced by teachers you have encountered?
3. Do all great teachers have certain qualities in common?
4. What does Palmer mean when he talks about listening to the "inner teacher"?
5. What are some implications of Palmer's ideas for curriculum? For professional development?

8 Critical Issues in Teaching

ALLAN C. ORNSTEIN

FOCUSING QUESTIONS

1. In what ways may teaching be considered to be a science?
2. In what ways may teaching be considered to be an art?
3. How are teachers portrayed in the popular media?
4. How much influence do teachers have in making the world a better place?
5. How should schools and teachers address the horrors of twentieth-century violence?

This chapter will briefly examine the issue of whether teaching is a science or an art; it is an issue that has gained attention among teachers of teachers and their students. This issue is also used as a springboard to introduce the second part of the piece: how we can improve teaching by emphasizing humanistic and moral issues, as well as the need for reconceptualizing the nature of teaching. In the second part of the chapter, the discussion will extend beyond the traditional themes of teaching. The content will most likely upset some readers, and still others may find it far too emotional or argumentative. I do believe, however, that when a critic or commentator attempts to rethink, reevaluate, or reconceptualize a field of study, a subject, or a domain that is rooted in tradition, a certain amount of resistance and criticism will surface and reflect the reader's thoughts.

THE SCIENCE VERSUS THE ART OF TEACHING

We cannot agree on whether teaching is a science or an art. Some readers may say that this is a hopeless dichotomy, similar to that of theory versus practice, because the real world rarely consists of neat packages and either–or situations. N. L. Gage uses this

This chapter is based on portions of the author's book *Teaching and Schooling in America: Prior and Post 9-11* (Boston: Allyn and Bacon, 2003). The book is concerned with life and death, good and evil, peace and war, education and miseducation, traditional and progressive education, equality and inequality. It starts with the ancient Greeks and Romans and ends with post 9-11 society, including American, Chinese, Indian, and Arabic cultures.

distinction between *teaching as a science* and *as an art* to describe the elements of predictability in teaching and what constitutes good teaching. A science of teaching, he contends, "implies that good teaching will some day be attainable by closely following vigorous laws that yield high predictability and control." Teaching is more than a science, he observes, because it also involves "artistic judgment about the best ways to teach." When teaching leaves the laboratory or textbook and goes face to face with students, "the opportunity for artistry expands enormously."[1] No science can prescribe successfully at all the twists and turns as teaching unfolds or as teachers respond with judgment, insight, or sensitivity to promote learning. These are expressions of art that depart from the rules and principles of science.

Is such a limited scientific basis of teaching even worthwhile to consider? Yes, but the practitioner must learn as a teacher to draw not only from his or her professional knowledge (which is grounded in *scientific principles*), but also from a set of personal experiences and resources (sometimes called *craft knowledge*) that is uniquely defined and exhibited by the teacher's own personality and "gut" reaction to classroom events that unfold (which form the basis for the *art* of teaching). For Philip Jackson, the hunches, judgments, and insights of the teacher, as he or she responds spontaneously to events in the classroom, are as important as, and perhaps even more important than, the science of teaching.[2] The routine activities of the classroom, the social patterns and dynamics among students, and the accommodations and compromises between students and teachers are much more important than any theory about teaching, because it is the everyday routines and relationships that determine the processes and outcomes of teaching.

To some extent, the act of teaching must be considered intuitive and interactive, not prescriptive or predictable. According to Elliot Eisner, teaching is based primarily on feelings and artistry, not scientific rules. In an age of science and technology, there is a special need to consider teaching as an art and craft. Eisner condemns the scientific movement in psychology, especially behaviorism, and the scientific movement in education, especially school management, as reducing the teaching act to trivial specifications. He regards teaching as a "poetic metaphor" more suited to satisfying the soul than to informing the head, more concerned with the whole than with a set of discrete skills or stimuli. Our role as teachers, he claims, should not be that of a "puppeteer," an "engineer," or a manager; rather, it is "to orchestrate the dialogue [as the conductor of a symphony] moving from one side of the room to the other."[3]

The idea is to perceive patterns in motion, to improvise within the classroom, and to avoid the mechanical or prescribed rules. The need is to act human, to display feelings to affirm and value our students. The idea is to be able to smile, clap, and laugh with your students while you teach them. Sadly, many teachers lack the self-confidence to openly express their emotions, feelings, or real personality.

Louis Rubin has a similar view of teaching: that effectiveness and artistry go hand in hand. The interplay of students and teacher is crucial and cannot be predetermined with carefully devised strategies. Confronted with everyday problems that cannot be easily predicted, the teacher must rely on intuition and on "insight acquired through long experience."[4] Rubin refers to such terms as "with-it-ness," "instructional judgments," "quick cognitive leaps," and "informal guesses" to explain the difference between the effective teacher and the ineffective teacher. Recognizing the limits to rationality, he claims that for the artistic teacher a "feel for what is right often is more productive than prolonged analysis." In the final analysis, Rubin compares the teacher's pedagogy with the "artist's colors, poet's words, sculptor's clay, and musician's notes,"[5] all of which, in my view, need a certain amount of artistic judgment to get the right mix, medium, or blend.

Other researchers are more extreme in their analysis of teaching solely as an art, providing romantic accounts and tales of successful teaching and teaching strategies, described in language that could hardly be taken for social science research. They consider the act of teaching akin to drama, an esthetic and kinesthetic endeavor, and feel that those who wish to teach should audition in a teaching studio and be trained as performing artists. Good teaching is likened to good theater, and a good teacher is likened to a good actor.[6]

Seymour Sarason describes the teacher as a performing artist. Like an actor, conductor, or artist, the teacher attempts to *instruct* and *move* the audience.[7] More significantly, this author maintains that the actor, artist, or teacher attempts to *transform* the audience in terms of thinking and instilling new ideas. By transforming the audience, we alter the person's outlook toward objects or ideas. Revolutionary thought, I maintain, is built on poetry, music, art, movies, and speeches. And, ultimately, it is the esthetics, ideas, and values (the art, music, food, customs, laws, and thoughts) that define who we are. Hence, it is teachers in the broadest sense, including actors, artists, poets, writers, and, of course, parents, who make the difference for society.

Given the metaphor of the *performing artist,* a certain amount of talent or innate ability is needed to be effective, along with sufficient rehearsal and caring behavior. But knowledge or understanding of the audience is also needed. *Mr. Holland's Opus* makes the point. The teacher was unsuccessful in the beginning of the movie, despite his knowledge of music, compassion, and desire to give the students his "all." In the remaining part of the movie, however, through some "magical" awakening, he redefined his methods (science of teaching) and acting (art of teaching), with the result that the audience

(students) became interested and learned to appreciate good music. Mr. Holland originally thought the problem was in the minds of the audience. Not until he realized that it was the other way around, that it was his attitude that needed to be improved, was he successful.[8]

In *The King and I,* the British teacher, Anna, was successful from the outset, despite cultural differences and the gender inequalities of the society (Siam). Not only was she caring and compassionate, but she also understood her students. She was able to adapt to their needs, interests, and abilities—and affirm their individuality. The song "Getting to Know You" makes the point. She reminded some of us of the school teachers we knew when we were kids—the loving and joyful teacher in Sylvia Ashton-Warner's *Teacher,* written some 40 years ago, or a combination of the author's two favorite elementary school teachers whom he remembers fondly and dedicated one of his books to: Mrs. Katz, "a warm, friendly, and understanding teacher," and Mrs. Schwartz, "a tough, nurturing school marm who drilled the facts and enforced the rules."[9]

Both movies underscore the need for teachers to understand students and for good teachers to connect with the audience. Through either previous learning (*pedagogical knowledge*) or practical experience (*craft knowledge*), the teacher must know how students think and feel. A certain amount of training helps one to understand students, but it is only a starting point. A successful teacher first understands and accepts himself or herself, then understands and accepts others. Arthur Jersild summed it up some 50 years ago: "self understanding requires something quite different from the methods . . . and skills of know-how . . . emphasized in education [courses]." Planning, role playing, and all the other methods and techniques—what we call scientific principles—are helpful, but what is also needed "is a more personal kind of searching, which will enable the teacher to identify his own concerns and to share the concerns of his students."[10] Thus, teaching is not just an academic or cognitive enterprise; it involves people and an affective (feelings, attitudes, and emotions) or artistic component that has little to do with pedagogical or scientific knowledge.

The more we consider teaching as an art, packed with emotions, feelings, and excitement, the more difficult it is to derive rules or generalizations. If teaching is more an art than a science, then principles and practices cannot be easily codified or developed in the classroom or easily learned by others. Hence, there is little reason to offer instructional method courses in education. If, however, teaching is more of a science, or at least partly a science, then pedagogy is predictable to that extent; it can be observed and measured with some accuracy, and the research can be applied to the practice of teaching (as a physician applies scientific knowledge to the practice of medicine) and also learned in a college classroom or on the job.

But a word of caution is needed. The more we rely on artistic interpretations or on old stories and accounts about teachers, the more we fall victim to fantasy, wit, and romantic rhetoric, and the more we depend on hearsay and conjecture, rather than on social science or objective data, in evaluating teacher competency. On the other hand, the more we rely on the scientific interpretations of teaching, the more we overlook those commonsense and spontaneous processes of teaching, and the sounds, smells, and visual flavor of the classroom. The more scientific we are in our approach to teaching, the more we ignore what we cannot accommodate to our empirical assumptions or principles. What sometimes occurs, according to Eisner, is that the educationally significant but difficult to measure or observe is replaced by what is insignificant but comparatively easy to measure or observe.[11]

It is necessary to blend artistic impressions and relevant stories about teaching, because good teaching involves emotions and feeling, with the objectivity of observations and measurements and the precision of language. There is nothing wrong with considering good teaching to be an art, but we must also consider it to lend itself to a prescriptive science or practice. If it does not, then there is little assurance that prospective teachers can be trained to be teachers—told what to do, how to instruct students, how to manage students, and so forth—and educators will be extremely vulnerable to public criticism and to people outside the profession telling them how and what to teach.

True knowledge of teaching is achieved by practice and experience in the classroom. According to some observers, the beliefs, values, and norms—that is, the knowledge—that teachers come to have the most faith in and use most frequently to guide their teaching are those consistent with traditions that have "worked" in the classroom. Although it seems to be more everyday and common sense–based than highly specialized and theoretical, the process still includes the receiving and using of data that can be partially planned and scientifically analyzed. But we assume that there are still professional and technical skills that can be taught to teachers and designed and developed in advance with underlying scientific principles and research-based data. Some of us would refer to this as *pedagogical knowledge* or *craft knowledge* as opposed to subject-matter or content-based knowledge.

Indeed, the real value of scientific procedures may not be realized in terms of research or theoretical generalizations that can be translated into practice. Research may have limited potential for teachers, but it can help them to become aware of the problems and needs of students. Scientific generalizations and theories may not always be applicable to specific teaching situations, but such propositions can help in the formulation of a reliable and valid base for teaching in classrooms. Scientific ideas can serve as a starting point for the discussion and analysis of the art of teaching.

RECONCEPTUALIZING TEACHING

To argue that good teaching boils down to a set of prescriptive behaviors, methods, or proficiency levels, that teachers must follow a "new" research-based teaching plan or evaluation system, or that decisions about teacher accountability can be assessed in terms of students passing a multiple-choice test is to miss the human aspect of teaching, the real *stuff* of what teaching is all about.

Stress on assessment and evaluation systems illustrates that behaviorism has won at the expense of humanistic psychology. Put in different terms, the ideas of Thorndike and Watson have prevailed over the ideas of Dewey and Kilpatrick. It also suggests that school administrators, policy makers, and researchers would rather focus on the *science* of teaching—behaviors and outcomes that can be observed, counted, or measured—than on the *art* of teaching with its humanistic and hard-to-measure variables.

Robert Linn contends that assessments of teachers and students can be easily mandated, implemented, and reported and thus have wide appeal under the guise of "reform." Although these assessment systems are supposed to improve education, they don't necessarily do so.[12] Real reform is complex and costly (for example, reducing class size, raising teacher salaries, introducing special reading programs, extending the school day and year), and it takes time before the results are evident. People such as politicians and business leaders, who seem to be leading this latest wave of reform, want a quick, easy, and cheap fix. Thus, they will always opt for assessment because it is simple and inexpensive to implement. It creates heightened media visibility, the feeling that something is being done, and the Hawthorne effect or novelty tends to elevate short-term gains. This assessment focus (which is a form of behaviorism) also provides a rationale for teacher education programs, because it suggests that we can identify good teaching. Yet it is questionable, given our current knowledge of teaching and teacher education and the importance of personality, whether new teachers can be properly prepared in terms of both academic rigor and practical reality.

For those in the business of preparing teachers, there is the need to provide a research base and rationale showing that teachers who enroll and complete a teacher education program are more likely to be effective teachers than those who lack such training. The fact that there are several alternative certification programs for teachers in more than 40 states, through which nearly 5 percent (as high as 16 percent in Texas and 22 percent in New Jersey) of the nationwide teaching force entered teaching,[13] makes teachers of teachers (professors of education) take notice and try to demonstrate that their teacher preparation programs work and that they can prepare effective teachers. Indeed, there is a need to identify teacher behaviors and methods that work under certain conditions, leading many educators to favor behaviorism (or prescriptive ideas and specific tasks) and assessment systems (closed-ended, tiny, measurable variables) that correlate teaching and learning.

Being able to describe detailed methods of teaching and how and why teachers do what they do should improve the performance of teachers. But all the new research hardly tells the whole story of teaching— what leads to teacher effectiveness and student learning. Being able to describe teachers' thinking or decision making and analyzing their stories and reflective practices suggest that we understand and can improve teaching. The new research on teaching, with its stories, biographies, reflective practices, and qualitative methods, provides a platform and publication outlet for researchers. It promotes their expertise (which in turn continues to separate them from practitioners) and permits them to continue to subordinate teaching to research. It also provides a new paradigm for analyzing teaching, because the old models (teacher styles, teacher characteristics, teacher effectiveness, etc.) have become exhausted and repetitive. The issues and questions related to the new paradigm create new educational wars and controversy between traditional and nontraditional researchers, between quantitative and qualitative advocates. It is questionable, however, whether this new knowledge base about teaching really improves teaching and learning or leads to substantial and sustained improvement.

The Need for Humanistic Teaching

The focus of teacher research should be on the learner, not on the teacher; on the feelings and attitudes of the student, not on knowledge and information (because feelings and attitudes will eventually determine what knowledge and information are sought after and acquired); and on the long-term development and growth of the students, not on short-term objectives or specific teacher tasks. But if teachers spend more time with the learners' feelings and attitudes, as well as on social and personal growth, teachers may be penalized when cognitive student outcomes (little pieces of information) on high-stake tests are correlated with their behaviors and methods in class.

Students need to be encouraged and nurtured by their teachers, especially when they are young. They are too dependent on approval from significant adults—first their parents, then their teachers. Parents and teachers need to help young children and adolescents to establish a source for self-esteem by focusing on their strengths, supporting them, discouraging negative self-talk, and helping them to take control of their lives with their own culture and values.

People (including young people) with high self-esteem achieve at high levels, and the more one achieves, the better one feels about oneself. The opposite is also true: Students who fail to master the subject matter get down on themselves and eventually give up. Students with low self-esteem give up quickly. In short, student self-esteem and achievement are directly related. If we can nurture students' self-esteem, almost everything else will fall into place, including achievement scores and academic outcomes. Regardless of how smart or talented a child, if he or she has personal problems, cognition will be detrimentally affected.

This builds a strong argument for creating successful experiences for students to help them to feel good about themselves. The long-term benefits are obvious: The more students learn to like themselves, the more they will achieve; and the more they achieve, the more they will like themselves. But this takes time, involves a lot of nurturing, and does not show up on a standardized test within a semester or school year; moreover, it does not help the teacher who is being evaluated by a content- or test-driven school administrator who is looking for results now. It certainly does not benefit the teacher who is being evaluated for how many times he or she attended departmental meetings, whether the shades in the classroom were even, or whether his or her instructional objectives were clearly stated.

It is obvious that certain behaviors contribute to good teaching. The trouble is that there is little agreement on exactly what behaviors or methods are most important. There are some teachers who gain theoretical knowledge of "what works," but are unable to put the ideas into practice. Some teachers with similar preparation act effortlessly in the classroom and others consider teaching a chore. All this suggests that teaching cannot be described in terms of a checklist or a precise model. It also suggests that teaching is a humanistic activity that deals with people (not tiny behaviors or competencies) and how people (teachers and students) develop and behave in a variety of classroom and school settings.

Although the research on teacher effectiveness provides a vocabulary and system for improving our insight into good teaching, there is a danger that this research may lead to some of us becoming too rigid in our view of teaching. Following only one teacher model or evaluation system can lead to too much emphasis on specific behaviors that can be easily measured or prescribed in advance, at the expense of ignoring humanistic behaviors, such as esthetic appreciation, emotions, values, and moral responsibility, that cannot be easily measured or prescribed in advance.

Although some educators recognize that humanistic factors influence teaching, we continue to define most teacher behaviors in terms of behaviorist and cognitive factors. Most teacher evaluation instruments tend to de-emphasize the human side of teaching because it is difficult to measure. In an attempt to be scientific, to predict and control behavior and to assess group patterns, we sometimes lose sight of the attitudes of teachers and their relations with students.

In providing feedback and evaluation for teachers, many factors need to be considered so that the advice or information does not fall on deaf ears. Teachers appreciate feedback processes whereby they can improve their teaching as long as the processes are honest and professionally planned and administered, as long as teachers are permitted to make mistakes, and as long as more than one model of effectiveness is considered so that they can adapt recommended behaviors and methods to fit their own personality and philosophy of teaching.

Teachers must be permitted to incorporate specific teacher behaviors and methods according to their own unique personalities and philosophies, to pick and choose from a wide range of research and theory, and to discard other teacher behaviors that conflict with their own style without the fear of being considered ineffective. Many school districts, and even state departments of education, have developed evaluation instruments and salary plans based exclusively on prescriptive and product-oriented behaviors. Even worse, teachers who do not exhibit these behaviors are often penalized or labeled as "marginal" or "incompetent."[14] There is danger that many more school districts and states will continue to jump on this bandwagon and make decisions based on prescriptive teacher research, without recognizing or giving credibility to other teacher behaviors or methods that might be humanistic because they deal with feelings, emotions, and personal connections with people—what some educators label as fuzzy or vague criteria.

Humanistic Teaching

In the early twentieth century, humanistic principles of teaching and learning were envisioned in the theories of progressive education: in the *child-centered* lab school directed by John Dewey at the University of Chicago from 1896 to 1904; the *play-centered* methods and materials introduced by Maria Montessori, which were designed to develop the practical, sensor, and formal skills of prekindergarten and kindergarten slum children of Italy starting in 1908; and the *activity-centered* practices of William Kilpatrick, who in the 1920s and 1930s urged that elementary teachers organize classrooms around social activities, group enterprises, and group projects and allow children to say what they think.

All these progressive theories were highly humanistic and stressed the child's interests, individuality, and creativity—in short, the child's freedom to develop naturally, free from teacher domination and the weight of rote learning. But progressivism failed because, in the view of Lawrence Cremin, there were not enough good teachers to implement progressive thought in classrooms and schools.[15] To be sure, it is much easier to stress knowledge, rote learning, and right answers than it is to teach about ideas, to consider the interests and needs of students, and to give them freedom to explore and interact with each other without teacher constraints.

By the end of the twentieth century, the humanistic teacher was depicted by William Glasser's "positive" and "supportive" teacher who could manage students without coercion and teach without failure.[16] It was also illustrated by Robert Fried's "passionate" teacher and Vito Perrone's "teacher with a heart"—teachers who live to teach young children and refuse to submit to apathy or criticism that may infect the school in which they work.[17] These teachers are dedicated and caring, they actively engage students in their classrooms, and they affirm their identities. The students do not have to ask whether their teacher is interested in them, thinks of them, or knows their interests or concerns. The answer is definitely yes.

The humanistic teacher is also portrayed by Theodore Sizer's mythical teacher called "Horace," who is dedicated and enjoys teaching, treats learning as a humane enterprise, inspires his students to learn, and encourages them to develop their powers of thought, taste, and character.[18] Yet the system forces Horace to make a number of compromises in planning, teaching, and grading, which he knows that, if we lived in an ideal world (with more than 24 hours in a day), he would not make. Horace is a trooper; he hides his frustration. Critics of teachers don't really want to hear him or face facts; they don't even know what it is like to teach. Sizer simply states, "Most jobs in the real world have a gap between what would be nice and what is possible. One adjusts."[19] Hence, most caring, dedicated teachers are forced to make some compromises, take some shortcuts, and make some accommodations. As long as no one gets upset and no one complains, the system permits a chasm between rhetoric (the rosy picture) and reality (slow burnout).

There is also the humanistic element in Nel Noddings' ideal teacher, who focuses on

the nurturing of "competent, caring, loving, and lovable persons." To that end, she describes teaching as a caring profession in which teachers should convey to students the caring way of thinking about one's self, siblings, strangers, animals, plants, and the physical environment. She stresses the affective aspect of teaching: the need to focus on the child's strengths and interests, the need for an individualized curriculum built around the child's abilities and needs.[20] Caring, according to Noddings, cannot be achieved by a formula or checklist. It calls for different behaviors for different situations, from tenderness to tough love. Good teaching, like good parenting, requires continuous effort, trusting relationships, and continuity of purpose—the purpose of caring, appreciating human connections, and respecting people and ideas from a historical, multicultural, and diverse perspective.[21]

Actually, the humanistic teacher is someone who highlights the personal and social dimension in teaching and learning, as opposed to the behavioral, scientific, or technological aspects. We might argue that everything that the teacher does is "human" and the expression "humanistic teaching" is a cliché. However, I would use the term in a loose sense to describe the teacher who emphasizes the arts as opposed to the sciences and people instead of numbers. Although the teacher understands the value of many subjects, including the sciences and social sciences, he or she feels that there is the need for students to understand certain *ideas* and *values,* some rooted in 3,000 years or more of philosophy, literature, art, music, theater, and the like. Without certain agreed-on content, our heritage would crumble and we would be at the mercy of chance and ignorance; moreover, our education enterprise would be subject to the whim and fancy of local fringe groups.

Humanistic education, according to Jacques Barzun, the elegant and eloquent writer on history and humanism, leads to a form of knowledge that helps us to deal with the nature of life, but it does not guarantee a more gracious or noble life:

> The humanities will not sort out the world's evils and were never meant to cure [our] troubles. . . . They will not heal diseased minds or broken hearts any more than they will foster political democracy or settle international disputes.

The humanities (and, if I may add, the humanistic teacher) "have meaning," according to Barzun, "because of the inhumanity of life; what they depict is strife and disaster"[22]; and, if I may add, by example, they help us to deal with the human condition and provide guidelines for moral behavior, good taste, and the improvement of civilization.

On a schoolwide level, the author would argue that humanism (what Fried calls "passion," Perrone calls "heart," Sizer calls "dedication," Noddings calls "caring," and Barzun calls "the well-rounded person") means eliminating homogeneous grouping and the labeling and tracking of students and reducing competitive grading. It means that we eliminate the notion that everyone should go to college since it creates frustration, anger, and unrealistic expectations among large numbers of children and youth. According to Paul Goodman, it requires that society find viable occupational options for noncollege graduates and jobs that have decent salaries, respect, and social status.[23] It suggests, according to John Gardner, that we recognize various forms of excellence—the excellent teacher, the excellent artist, the excellent plumber, and the excellent bus driver; otherwise, we create a myopic view of talent and a subsequent tension that will threaten a democratic society.[24] It also means that we appreciate and nurture different student abilities, aptitudes, and skills, what Howard Gardner calls "multiple intelligences."[25]

Humanistic versus Nonhumanistic Thought

If we fail to adapt a more caring and compassionate view of teaching and schooling, then we fall victim to excessive competiveness and materialism—and eventually to class differences that will divide society into dominant and subordinate groups. Pursuant to neo-Marxist and radical postmodern thinking, we create a permanent underclass who live in "squalid" (Kozol's word), "dehumanizing" (Freire's word), and "colonialized" (Giroux's and McClain's word) conditions. The outcome is a society in which a disproportionate number of low-achieving students and poor, minority, and special needs children are locked into future low-end jobs, unemployment, or what Oscar Lewis, some 40 years ago, referred to as the "culture of poverty," whereby poverty is transferred from generation to generation.[26] In short, a new subordinate group, the have-nots, is construed as dumb, lazy, and de-skilled by a school system and society that encourage competitiveness and judge people on different characteristics and different outcomes.

This human situation is tolerated by the majority of the populace because egalitarianism, social justice, and human dignity are wrongly conceived or ignored. Our prejudices become ingrained in our thinking because they become institutionalized by society. Moreover, we come to rely on "scientific objectivity" to excuse or defend educational and social practices that generate and then perpetuate these dominant–subordinate conditions. There should be no room in this country, or in any society that claims to be civilized, for second-class citizenship, or even for people who think of themselves as second-class citizens. There have been enough second-class citizens in the world.

Down through the ages, the vast majority of humans have been barbarians, slaves, serfs, peasants, and extremely poor and uneducated. Almost one half to one percent of the population—the monarchs and nobility, popes and cardinals, military leaders and generals, czars, capitalists, and the like—have possessed more than 50 percent of the wealth and resources existing within their particular period of history. Even today, 1.2 billion people (or 20 percent of the world's population) live on less than one dollar a day, and 50 percent of the developing countries' 4.5 billion population live on less than two dollars a day, the greatest percentages being in South Asia, sub-Saharan Africa, and Latin America.[27] These poor people live under squalid conditions that very few of us, except for a few scholars and human rights workers, fully comprehend or care to know about. But it is this poverty and hopelessness in developing countries, and the resulting difference in quality of life and culture, that leads to deep and lasting hatred toward the more prosperous Western World and a form of madness in which people don't care if they die or are blown to pieces.

Too many people in this country and other countries have been forced to give up their identities, to move from their world to another world, to assimilate: to pass for white, Christian, or "straight." No one should have to pretend her or his whole life; to live in a closet; to disown her or his family, ethnic group, or religion—never to return to her or his people. Of course, we can argue that ethnocentrism and religious zeal are also sources of the worst atrocities. True believers come in all shapes, stripes, and ideologies, and there has been a steady oversupply of lawless opportunists and willing executioners, no matter how low their position in the chain of command may be, who take pleasure in the destruction and annihilation of other people.

Some readers may consider the above interpretation as an attempt to instill neo-Marxist, postmodern, or illusory rhetoric in the discussion, but the author contends that lack of humanism and moral teaching has resulted in lack of conscience and caring throughout the ages and throughout the globe. The outcomes are similar for all time: human suffering, oppression, fanaticism, and wholesale slaughter of human life under a political or religious ideology that mocks the individual and is suffused with hatred, brute force, and terrorism. It represents the exploitive and dark side of the human psyche, inflicted on humans by humans for centuries, from the treatment of Roman gladiators, African slaves, and European peasantry to the burning of witches and hanging of blacks and gays in the United States. Of course, the Japanese atrocities in Nanking, the Holocaust in Europe, the purges of Stalin and Mao, and the killing fields of Pol Pot are the darkest pages of history, totally irrational and extreme forms of evil that cannot be fully understood with only words. Narratives from victims, photographs, and films must become part of the discourse for us to fully comprehend the extent of this rampant barbarism and blasphemy. Blaming today's generation for another generation's sins is not the answer, but learning from old injustices and immorality is valuable so that we do not repeat history, so that we become a more civil and compassionate society.

Remembering the Dead

All of us have lived most of our lives in the twentieth century, and all the lost souls who no longer exist because of mankind's cruelty and hatred must be remembered. Most of the voices and faces we never knew; therefore, it is easy to become detached from their demise and to treat them as an abstract statistic. In fact, the larger the number of dead, thousands or millions, the easier it is to become detached by adding zeros (because the mind is unable to fathom the reality and enormity of the deed) unless the individual or his or her loved ones were part of the cruel nature of history. Among the dead, some were famous for something and are in our encyclopedias, but the vast majority have been forgotten and funneled into anonymity and nothingness. All they can hope is for the poet, painter, or musician to make use of them through pen, canvas, or lyrics in order for the living to gain understanding. In this connection, it is for the teacher to educate the next generation—to make use of these forgotten and transitory people, to help them to return among the living just for a brief moment, to explain the order of magnitude of lost lives and a counting system that involves five, six, or seven zeros.

As educators who grew up in the twentieth century, we must now educate students of the twenty-first century that the most cruel and vile acts against humanity were committed in the twentieth century, much worse than the attacks on the World Trade Center, which I mention because some of us have lost loved ones or known people who died. Despite its educated populace, the most heinous deeds were committed in the last century, which produced the most efficient machines to kill the most people. And, after being surrounded by mass murder, rape, and pillage, we become detached from these violent and deathward-leaning acts; we deal with these encounters by abstracting and anatomizing them through a variety of academic subjects and topics. We keep them under lock and key so that our young children and students have almost no real knowledge of Nanking, the Holocaust, Stalin's or Mao's purges, the killing fields, or more recently Kosovo and Rwanda. Even at home—Antietam (4,000+ dead), Gettysburg (50,000+), Pearl Harbor (2,300), and now the World Trade Center (2,900)—the dead are forgotten, as if they never existed, except by some individual who buried a loved one.

As teachers, we must make sense of our past through our philosophy, history, literature, art, poetry, and music. We are required to ask our students to think about the true believers and zealots and the willing oppressors and opportunists who have ravaged the earth. We must pay homage to the millions who perished in the wars and witch hunts, the purges and extermination camps of the twentieth century. We must hear their voices, see their faces, and understand their final thoughts of life in the midst of background screams, muzzled groans, and sad good-byes—and then the stench of death—to fully comprehend the barbaric deeds of humanity, and how many more times throughout all time that evil has prevailed over good.

Indeed, I am reminded of an old soldier, a World War II veteran, discussing the Battle of the Bulge (275,000 dead). He could not remember how he celebrated his last birthday or why he just opened the refrigerator, but he could vividly recount the conditions of the battlefield as if it had been yesterday: gray foreboding clouds, the snow-covered grass, the cold nipping at his toes and fingers, the rubble of the dead around him, the eyes of the enemy and the tatter of machine guns in front, the smell of fuel oil and ashes of annihilation mixed in the countryside air.

In detail, he could still recall the names of the fallen dead on his left side and right side, the last words and groans of his doomed comrades; but soon the old soldier would die along with his memories. For that moment, there was nothing impersonal or abstract about the slaughter—the excruciating combat, the lost voices and faces, the sense of madness around him.

We must try to provide, as part of the teaching role, some reassurance to our students that good can prevail over evil, that morality can topple immorality. Although we should not be weighed down by the past, we must remember all the nameless and voiceless people who suffered and died a senseless or terrible death before their time and keep the specter and memory of the nations, tribes, and political and religious zealots that committed the acts of violence against these victims. We must fight off fading memories and amnesia so that we have a chance to prevent, or at least reduce, the worst natures in us, the resulting blasphemy and evil that have characterized so many of the inhabitants of the last century.

As teachers, we should inspire our students and help them to deal with the nature of life and society; this is one of our most important professional roles. Yet it ought to come as no surprise that we rarely connect with our students in this way. Is it because we lack passion, a sense of history or loyalty to an ideal, or merely shy from moral messages? I think that it is all these, and thus we fail the memory of the people of the last century and previous centuries who died unjustly.

As teachers, we often fail in our role to elaborate on the agony of our history, that the need to reduce the ruthlessness and atrocities of humans rests with us. All the people who are alive today are connected to the past like a cloud that sweeps through the constellations and eventually disappears. Among the thinkers of society, and especially among our writers, poets, and artists, as well as our teachers, there should be a thirst for knowledge that remembers the dead and then goes beyond the borders of the dead to elaborate on life and improve society.

Students' Learning Opportunities

Edward Pajak questions whether teaching children about evil is likely to make them virtuous. Introducing students to this kind of "content" before they are emotionally mature and intellectually sophisticated may have exactly the opposite effect of what is intended.[28] There is a human tendency to identify with the aggressor and those in power, to laugh at or ridicule the victim. Like many adults, young children may not have the intellectual or emotional capacity to process horrifying information in a clear and sophisticated manner. Premature and excessive emphasis on the dark side of history and society informs unsophisticated students about which groups represent "legitimate" targets for hate.

But we cannot protect the new generation from the chambers of horrors that have characterized most of our history. We cannot continue to allow only a little darkness to spill out in our classrooms, to keep the horrors hemmed in by limiting the dark side of human behavior to a few sentences or paragraphs in a textbook or a few comments in class. However, I would rely on Piaget's principles of cognition, that the child's formal mental operations (or advanced stage of cognition) develop between ages 11 and 15, whereby the adolescent is capable of analyzing ideas, engaging in abstract operations, and clarifying values. Even before the age of 11, the concepts of right and wrong, fairness, and basic democratic laws and principles are understood. Similarly, Piaget's theory of moral development, along with Kohlberg's notion of moral reasoning and moral ideology, suggests that teens can understand the principles of ethics, contractual obligations, conscience, and justice. There is some variation, of course, which has to do with the student's family, religion, and cultural background, due to biases and prejudices that develop outside the school. But this is exactly what the teacher has to overcome; it is part of the teacher's role.

Let me put it in a different way: Blind hatred, erroneous claims of superiority, and ideological fanaticism, by which the individual is drowned out by the mass, made impotent, then dehumanized and/or slaughtered, represent the ugly side of humanity. They can be depicted as the opposite of the music of Bach; the art of Michelangelo; the stories of Cervantes and Shakespeare; the philosophy of Kant, Locke, and Rousseau; the poems of Robert Frost, Emily Dickinson, and Lao-Tzu; and the spiritual messages of Muhammad, Buddha, and Gandhi. Teachers, in the past, have emphasized the good side of humanity. I urge that both sides need to be explored. By ignoring the ugly side of civilization, teachers unwittingly create a void among future generations—a lack of humanity, compassion, and moral constraint.

The ideals of right and wrong, justice and goodness are rooted in Western morality,

Greek and Judeo-Christian ideas, as well as Eastern philosophy and religious thought, and should be incorporated into the curriculum. Education without concern for certain universal and humanistic truths, values, and ways of behaving hinders the moral fiber of society. Taken to the next step, it leads to man's natural aggression, based on biological and animal instincts. Freud would say this means that the *id* has gained the upper hand over the *superego* (personal and social conscience). In the worst case scenario, it suggests the rise of Nieztche's "superman" complex and the subsequent rationale for racism, imperialism, colonialism, religious fanaticism, and militarism, accompanied by the death of hundreds of millions of people (50 million people alone in World War II) and the destruction of hundreds of nation-states and racial, ethnic, or religious groups, since Rome was built and Christ preached the gospel. With moral constraints, man's aggressive instincts are played out in boardrooms and on Wall Street, as well as on high school, college, and professional football fields and wrestling arenas; on Saturday and Sunday mornings on suburban pee-wee soccer fields and on big-city asphalt basketball courts; and daily among us older "folks" (Bush's term) who commit road rage on American highways and byways—what most of us would call socially acceptable behavior or wink at and write off as a little extreme.

But the teaching of knowledge without morality leads to extreme competitiveness, human stratification, and survival of the fittest. Put in different words, unchecked emphasis on performance through which the same students always "win" and another group always "loses"; or the elitist notion that the right of a student to an education persists only as far as his or her intellectual capabilities; or the labeling, categorizing, and tracking of students and noting of differences among people (smart, dumb; superior, inferior) suggest a school system and a society

that encourage, and even foster, all the wrong "isms"—colonialism, imperialism, fascism, and racism. In fact, almost all militant and imperialist societies stress their own efficiency and superiority over other societies—nothing more than excuses and theories for explaining man's inhumanity to man. Even worse, this type of thinking and behavior is often derived from and supported by "scientific explanations," laws, religious theology, or political ideology—doctrines created by people to suppress other people.

Moral and Civic Virtues

Teaching and schooling should be committed to a higher purpose, a humanistic–moral purpose designed not only to enhance academic grades but also for personal and social responsibility. It should be built around people and community, around respecting, caring for, and having compassion toward others. It means that teachers in the classroom deal with social and moral issues, with the human condition and good and evil. It means that students be encouraged to ask "why," as opposed to being encouraged to give the "right" answer. The question should start with family conversation, but must be nurtured in school during the formative years of learning so that a sense of social and moral consciousness is developed. But precisely on this score, our teachers and schools register a disturbing deficit, originally because it was thought to tread on the spiritual domain and now because there is little time to inquire about and discuss important ideas and issues, because the curriculum is test driven by trivia items of knowledge and short-answer outcomes.

According to one social critic, "why?" is the existential question that every individual must be permitted to ask and must receive an appropriate and meaningful answer to from those in power or who mete out justice. If the question is denied, then the individual has no basic rights.[29] It is the purest form of totalitarianism in which the individual is trivialized, as in the Roman empire, where the ruling classes' main amusement was watching humans being eaten by animals or fighting each other to the death; in the cattle cars to the concentration camps of Auschwitz and Maidenek, where the individual was reduced to a serial number and human remains were often retrofitted into soap products, lamp shades, and gold rings; and in the Serbian ethnic cleansing and rape of Bosnia and Kosovo and the cleansing and rape of Rwanda.

How many of us can locate Rwanda on the map? Does anyone among us know where Auschwitz and Maidenek are located? How many among us, except for a few elderly statesmen, scholars, and descendants of the victims, care? Given the "luxury of late birth" and "geographical distance," who among us are expected to do more than cite a few numbers or statements to put the horrors of humanity into some context or understanding? Who cares about the sufferings of all the folk groups, tribes, and nations since we came out of the caves? How many of us know the names of one or two people who died in Nanking, at Pearl Harbor, in the Holocaust, at Juno or Utah beach, in the killing fields of Cambodia, or in Croatia or Kosovo? Can we cite one name that appears on the Arch of Triumph or the Vietnam Memorial? Who can recall or ever knew the name of the pilot (Paul Tibbots) who dropped the A-bomb on Hiroshima—what his thoughts were as he approached the target or after the carnage and cloud of dust? Who among us care to know or can explain what happened or why it happened that more than 100 million soldiers and civilians died in war (or related civilian activities) in what I would call the most ruthless century—consisting of the most vile deeds and crimes against people? How do we weigh the smug claims of Western technology and industry with the millions who died beside railroad tracks and in battle trenches?

Well, we all die—no kidding—but many of us die when we are not ready to die, without any maps or charts of the journey. Modern philosophy, history, and literature have sanitized these deaths. We have more details (dates, names, and places) than we can process, so those who were murdered, raped, gassed, and executed have been generalized into nonindividuals. The lucky ones were cared for by people who rarely knew anything about their history, knew nothing about who they were, and sometimes did not even know their names. It is an old story, repeated several times in different places and periods of history, yet it must be examined by teachers and students so that there is a better chance of preventing, or at least reducing, this common madness in society.

And Americans are not innocent, given our inhuman and criminal treatment of Native Americans and black Americans—that is, the near extermination and remaining dismemberment of an entire Indian civilization over a 50-year period under the banner of westward expansion and the subhuman treatment of blacks during 100 years of slavery, followed by the exclusion of blacks from American society during the Post-Reconstruction and Jim Crow era (keenly illustrated by white and black toilets and segregated schools and housing and other public facilities).

We all know when injustices are being perpetrated, but we often do not act or want to deal with them. Throughout the ages, man has deceived himself by remaining indifferent or looking the other way in the midst of the worst atrocities and crimes, connoting a human flaw or moral fault in our character. Periodically, a nation or ethnic group has to pay a heavy price and be held accountable for its actions or inactions. Although the past has taught us how not to act, we periodically fall from civilized to uncivilized practices because our dark side checkmates our good side (the music of Bach, the plays of Shakespeare), because of our aggressive and competitive nature to beat the next person. As long as we have bread on our table and sufficient clothes on our back, we often remain silent, look the other way, or become true believers—in effect, blinded by our own inaction to the vile deeds of others.

Moral practices start with the family and continue with the church and community, but teachers must play an active role if ours is to be a more compassionate, caring, and just society. As teachers, we need to encourage open debate concerning the thorniest issues of the present and past, welcome discussions without *ad hominem* attacks or stereotypes, and build a sense of community (what the French call *civisme*) and character. We are forced to flee from our comfortable classroom niches, go beyond facts, raise thoughtful questions that stem from meaningful readings, and transcend the cognitive domain into the moral universe. We must promote this type of teaching for all grade levels.

Our readings in school should have a moral flavor to encourage discussion, thinking, and ultimately the transformation of the learner. Even at the primary grade level, reading must not be wasted by assigning "See Spot Run" or "A Sunday Trip to Granny"; rather the emphasis should be on folktales and stories, such as "Jack and the Beanstalk," "Rumpelstiltskin," "Seasons," and "The Mouse and the Wizard," from all parts of the world.

The relationships among history, literary criticism, and philosophy raise many questions about human conditions and civilizations. These ideas express the nature of humanity and society, considered by some to be part of the Great Books, Junior Great Books, or Great Ideas programs. Call it what you want, these readings deal with moral conscience and historical consciousness, and this is what students should be reading.

The idea is for the teacher to capture the students' imaginations, to have them explore ideas and issues, support arguments, and draw conclusions—what some of us might call *critical thinking*. At the same time, students need to examine, analyze, and interpret morally laden books to help them understand the evil or dark side of humans—what happens when morality is dethroned for greed, hatred, or some god or ideology; when excellence or efficiency is pushed to an extreme in which *all* trains are expected to run on time and all soldiers are expected to follow orders and die for the glory of some god, the nation, or the ego of old politicians.

There is need to balance the scales of justice and face the truth when history is rewritten for religious or nationalistic reasons or for apologies and excuses that what happened was historically inevitable or historically justifiable; or when "those people" were different from us, backward and uneducated; or when "they" had too much power and money—whatever hocus-pocus rationale is used to distort the truth and alter beliefs. Teachers must decide what is important in the curriculum, what has been omitted and what has been included for discussion. Often big-city teachers are rendered impotent in this professional role, and the curriculum is imposed on them from the central office by a few bureaucrats (former teachers and principals) who eventually lose touch with the community, classroom reality, and the needs of students. Regardless of our politics and idiosyncratic judgments, as professionals we need to become more involved in curriculum development and decide how the content in class achieves a balanced portrait of the past and present, of other people and nations. We need to take positions—moral positions appropriate for a changing society and diverse society, a society that is willing to face and deal with its problems. Students must be encouraged by their teachers to raise questions, take positions, and act morally responsible. To some extent, it is a position set forth by old reconstructionists such as John Dewey, George Counts, and Ted Brameld.

The writer, poet, musician, and teacher need to summon the shades of the past to fight off anonymity and amnesia. Through selected readings or even through film (for students who are unable to read fluently), we need to restore our fading and faltering memories, to show that the dead who were taken before it was their time to die did not die in vain. A war memorial is not the answer. It may serve political or nationalistic interests and raise the specter (genre) of jingoism, but it cannot convey the moral lessons of the past. It can evoke tears and stimulate pride, but it cannot lead to critical and analytical thought to clarify arguments, to explain and defend concepts and ideas, and to maintain purposeful and critical discussion.

The writer, poet, musician, and teacher must remember the people who lived and died. As teachers, we must capture the agony and lessons of history as well as the goodness of humanity through our philosophy, history, literature, music, and art. We must retain the vestiges of the lost world, where people died a terrible death as victims of war, poverty, nationalism, racism, or religious fanaticism, and try to make sense of all the senseless crimes that people are capable of committing.

The people who shaped my world and your world, for the greater part, no longer exist. We have twenty-five or thirty years as teachers to make an imprint on the next generation, to remember the millions who are not in the encyclopedias and who no longer exist, to pass on their thoughts and deeds to the next generations. As teachers, the necessity of our work requires that we understand what is at stake: improving and enriching society by making the next generation care about what is morally right and motivating students to accomplish great things that exhibit the good side of what is human.

Moving from literature and philosophy to active teaching and learning means that students be encouraged and rewarded for moral and community action, for helping others and volunteering their time and service. It means that character development and civic service receive the same attention and recognition that we give to A students and star quarterbacks. It calls for special assemblies, special scholarships, and special staff development programs that promote character development, the desire to help others, and the expectation of social and civic involvement. It means that we give character development—helping and caring for others, contributing and giving back to the school and community—as much attention as we give academics and sports in school.

I am not talking about a special course or program to meet some "service-learning" requirement, but rather a school ethos or a common philosophy that teachers and administrators support. The idea must permeate the entire school and be expected and required for all students. One or two teachers attempting to teach moral responsibility or civic participation cannot effect long-term change; it takes a team effort and schoolwide policy. It demands nothing less than a reconceptualization of the roles, expectations, and activities of students and teachers involved in the life of schools and communities. The idea flows back to the early philosophy and cardinal principles of progressive education of the 1910s and 1920s and the old core curriculum of the 1930s and 1940s, which promoted the study of moral and social issues, social responsibility, and civic education and youth service for the community and nation.

It also means that we consider the basic elementary school, conceived by Ernest Boyer and the Carnegie Foundation, that focuses on the child and community, where schools are kept small so that people work together and feel connected and empowered; it means that the school provides emotional and social support for children, beyond academics, to focus on the whole child and to teach the importance of values, ethics, and moral responsibility.[30] It suggests that a moral and civil society is a requirement for democracy to work, as so keenly described 150 years ago in Alexis de Tocqueville's classic treatise *Democracy in America;* it means that we teach the importance of connecting with nature and the ecology of our planet, to preserve our resources and ensure our future. It requires that we bring competitiveness and social cohesion, excellence and equality, as well as material wealth and poverty, into harmony—not an easy task, like squaring a circle. Finally, we need to look into the future: The bomb is an eclipse, but the products of technology and the biological sciences—from medicines and foods to better babies (altering the DNA of generations to come) and extending life (by eliminating or adding genes or inserting computer chips)—offer new ways to play god and leave us with many moral issues to ponder.

FINAL WORDS

A few final and personal notes to the reader. We have shared some reflective moments together, maybe as long as an hour, and perhaps some of these thoughts will last. All of us are filled with memories of people who lived and died, and all of us can personally identify with our own racial, ethnic, or religious group that has suffered from the ruthless behavior of others. All of us who perceive ourselves as members of a minority group understand the notions of subordination and suffering. We experience our own transitoriness and mortality every day as we read in the news or see on television the acts of violence committed by people toward other people.

The wisdom of the Bible and the virtues of religious leaders provide me with little comfort or hope, because the people who should know better and preach hope are often burdened by their own biases, prejudices, and ill-feelings toward other people who summon up different interpretations of the past and present. Although the clergy can be construed as teachers, their mission and agenda center around ideology, and their methods historically have been used to promote this way of thinking. The sword and fire, or worse, are the same methods adopted by modern-day totalitarian nations.

As I take hold of my pen and describe a cruel and sad world—flawed by its own stupidity, hatred, and crimes, a host of isms—I provide the idea for teachers to speculate about their own roles and what education is all about or should be about. I hope that a deep sense of human guilt and teacher triumph of consciousness of humanity will help future citizens of the world be more responsible in terms of character and compassion. Indeed, it is the teacher's role to keep revisiting history, to fight off amnesia and to become a spokesperson for the dead, and thus to improve the human condition. It is a professional role rarely, if ever, described in the education literature in such a blunt way; it is an idea worth considering, in a world where the United States is at the zenith of its power, but would rather hide from the evils of the world.

Finally, I am reminded of an old saying that was popular when, in the words of Billy Joel, "I wore a younger man's clothes" (in my case, cutoff shorts and roman sandals): "We don't know what World War III will be fought with, but World War IV will be fought with rocks."[31] I am reminded of the mundane words of last goodbyes—"I love you," "I will wait for you in heaven," "Tell her I will forever miss her." I am reminded of Carl Sandburg's *Grass*—all the wars, all the dead, and all the grass that keeps growing; then I think of James Joyce's *The Dead,* describing the demise of the ordinary people, "falling faintly through the universe."

On a more personal level, I am reminded of Yevgeni Yevtushenko, who saw himself and his ancestors "persecuted, spat on, and slandered" for centuries in Europe. It culminated in his homeland, Mother Russia, with the death of tens of thousands in Belostok (the most violent pogrom) and hundreds of thousands at Babi Yar (a mass murder, mass grave). "Like one long soundless scream . . . I'm every old man executed here/As I am every child murdered./Rest the victims' bones." So few people seem to care, so few seem to remember. Yet, because of the long roads and caravans traveled by my ancestors, I recall that so many people in so many lands, since ancient Egypt and Rome, have been thrown back by the boot, the sword, and the law—by a soldier, crusader, king, or despot. I have no need to hear false excuses or false proclamations in the name of hatred, stupidity, or herd behavior. I have no patience or pity for fools, zealots, and tyrants who strip people of their dignity and then put them to death. Even worse, I fear those in power who are given to genocidal impulses and are bent on reducing whole villages to rubble and destroying whole cultures and civilizations to nothing more than a line or two in some morally toned poems like "The Waste Land" or "Babi Yar." I can only take some limited comfort in John Donne's holy sonnet "Death, be not proud": "we wake eternally, and Death shall be no more."

I am reminded of all the English teachers trying to teach these poems, and also trying to teach the *Iliad, King Lear, Gulliver's Travels,* and *The Death of Ivan Illych,* the best that has been thought and said in our culture. Then I am reminded of all the bored students, squirming and sweating in their seats, dozing and doodling, watching the clock tick by tick, and missing the bittersweet phrases and opportunity to reflect on ways ordinary and tragic.

I long for a simpler day: *Little House on the Prairie, Leave It to Beaver, Gilligan's Island,* and *Ozzie and Harriet.* But the clock cannot be turned back. In another instant, I recall Mickey and Minnie and Uncle Miltie; Huey, Louie, and Dewey; Captain Video, Captain Kangaroo, and Howdy Doody; "Here's to You, Mrs. Robinson"; Marilyn and Jolt'n Joe. Has anyone seen my childhood heroes—Jackie, Pee Wee, and Duke? Can you tell me

where? They're all gone, especially John, Bobby, and Martin, but remembered in history books.

I can also recall playing catch with Dad and stickball in the schoolyard with Jack and Larry. Then there were Mrs. Katz, Mrs. Schwartz, and Miss Hess from P.S. 42 Queens; Mr. Faulkner, Mr. Tietz, and Miss Gussow from Far Rockaway High School. All my favorite teachers are gone, too, but I thought it would be the right thing to do, in the dearness of remembering a simpler period and vanishing era, to recall the names of teachers, largely forgotten, who taught for 25 to 30 years and made a difference to thousands of kids from my generation. All of you can cherish the names of other teachers who made a difference in your lives—and all of you can ponder the larger role of teaching in the changing world that we live in.

ENDNOTES

1. N. L. Gage, *The Scientific Basis of the Art of Teaching* (New York: Teachers College Press, Columbia University, 1978), pp. 15, 17.
2. Philip Jackson, *Life in Classrooms,* 2nd ed. (New York: Teachers College Press, 1990).
3. Elliot W. Eisner, "The Art and Craft of Teachers," *Educational Researcher* (April 1983), p. 8. Also see Elliot W. Eisner, *The Kind of Schools We Need* (Portsmouth, NH: Heinemann, 1998).
4. Louis J. Rubin, *Artistry of Teaching* (New York: Random House, 1985), p. 61.
5. Ibid., pp. 60, 69.
6. Jonathan Cohen, *Educating Minds and Hearts* (New York: Teachers College Press, Columbia University, 1999); Robert Fried, *The Passionate Teacher* (Boston: Beacon Press, 1995).
7. Seymore B. Sarason, *Teaching as a Performing Art* (New York: Teachers College Press, Columbia University, 1999).
8. Ibid.
9. Sylvia Ashton-Warner, *Teacher* (New York: Simon and Schuster, 1964); Allan C. Ornstein, *Strategies for Effective Teaching,* 2nd ed. (Dubuque, IA: Brown and Benchmark, 1995), dedication page.

10. Arthur Jersild, *When Teachers Face Themselves* (New York: Teachers College Press, Columbia University, 1955), p. 3.

11. Elliot W. Eisner, "The Promise and Perils of Alternative Forms of Data Representation," *Educational Researcher* (August–September 1997), pp. 4–11.

12. Robert L. Linn, "Assessment and Accountability," *Educational Researcher* (March 2000), pp. 4–15.

13. Abbey Goodnough, "Regents Create a New Path to Teaching," *New York Times*, July 15, 2000, pp. B4, B7.

14. Allan C. Ornstein, "Beyond Effective Teaching," in A. C. Ornstein, ed., *Teaching: Theory into Practice* (Boston: Allyn and Bacon, 1995), pp. 273–291.

15. Lawrence A. Cremin, *The Transformation of the School* (New York: Random House, 1961).

16. William Glasser, *Schools Without Failure* (New York: Harper & Row, 1969); Glasser, *The Quality School* (New York: HarperCollins, 1990).

17. Robert Fried, *The Passionate Teacher*; Vito Perrone, *Teacher with a Heart* (New York: Teachers College Press, 1998).

18. Theodore R. Sizer, *Horace's Compromise* (Boston: Houghton Mifflin, 1985).

19. Ibid., p. 20.

20. Nel Noddings, *The Challenge to Care in Schools* (New York: Teachers College Press, Columbia University, 1992).

21. Ibid.

22. Jacques Barzun, *Teachers in America*, rev. ed. (Lanham, MD: University Press of America, 1972).

23. Paul Goodman, *Compulsory Mis-Education* (New York: Horizon Press, 1964).

24. John Gardner, *Excellence: Can We Be Equal Too?* (New York: Harper & Row, 1962).

25. Howard Gardner, *Frames of Mind: The Theory of Multiple Intelligences* (New York: Basic Books, 1983).

26. Oscar Lewis, "The Culture of Poverty," *Scientific American* (October 1996), pp. 19–25.

27. "Poverty and Globalization," Center for Global Studies Conference, St. John's University, April 26, 2001. Based on 1998 World Bank Data.

28. Comments made by Edward Pajak to the author, September 6, 2001.

29. Fritz Stern, "The Importance of 'Why'," *World Policy Journal* (Spring 2000), pp. 1–8.

30. Ernest L. Boyer, "The Basic School: Focusing on the Child," *Elementary Principal* (January 1994), pp. 29–32.

31. Francis X. Clines, "A New Form of Grieving," *New York Times*, September 16, 2001, Sect. 4, p. 3.

DISCUSSION QUESTIONS

1. How would you defend the claim that teaching should be considered an art?

2. How would you defend the claim that teaching should be considered a science?

3. What qualities does the author think are most important for a teacher to possess?

4. What are the benefits of having teachers focus their instruction on the dark side of human nature? What are the drawbacks?

5. Who should decide which topics are legitimate for students to learn about? How should such decisions be made?

9 Productive Teachers: Assessing the Knowledge Base

Herbert J. Walberg

FOCUSING QUESTIONS

1. What are the components of teaching that emphasize what teachers do?

2. What does the behavioral model emphasize concerning cues, engagement, correctives, and reinforcement?

3. How do explicit teaching and comprehension teaching differ?

4. What is open education?

5. How do programmed instruction, mastery learning, adaptive instruction, and computer-assisted instruction differ in terms of planning and instructional components?

6. How do the aims of accelerated programs, ability grouping, whole-group instruction, and cooperative learning programs differ?

7. What approaches and goals are emphasized by microteaching and in-service education?

Some teaching techniques have remarkable effects on learning, while others confer only trivial advantages or even hinder the learning process. Over the past decade, there has been an explosion of research activity centering on the question of what constitutes effective teaching. Ten years ago, several psychologists observed signs of a "quiet revolution" in educational research. Five years later, nearly 3,000 studies of effective teaching techniques existed. By 1987, an Australian/U.S. team was able to assess 134 reviews of 7,827 field studies and several large-scale U.S. and international surveys of learning.[1]

Here, I will give an overview of the findings to date on elementary and secondary school students and will evaluate the more recent and definitive reviews of research on teaching and instruction. Surveying the vast literature on the effects of various instructional methods allows us to consider the advantages and disadvantages of different techniques—including some effective ones that are no longer popular.

I will begin by considering the effects of the psychological elements of teaching, and I will discuss methods and patterns of teaching that a single teacher can accomplish without unusual arrangements or equipment. Then I will turn to systems of instruction that require special planning, student grouping, and materials. Next I will describe effects that are unique to particular methods of teaching reading, writing, science, and mathematics. Finally, I will discuss special students and techniques for dealing with them and the effects of particular types of training on teachers. It is important to bear in mind that, when we try to apply in our own classrooms the methods we have read about, we may attain results that are half—or twice—as good as the average estimates reported below. Our success will depend not only on careful implementation but also on our purposes. The best saw swung as a hammer does little good.

PSYCHOLOGICAL ELEMENTS

A little history will help us understand the evolution of psychological research on teaching. Even though educators require balance, psychologists have often emphasized thought, feeling, or behavior at the expense of the other two components of the psyche. Today, thinking or cognition is sovereign in psychology, but half a century ago behaviorists insisted on specific operational definitions (and they continue to do so). In particular, Yale psychologists John Dollard and Neal Miller, stimulated by E. L. Thorndike and B. F. Skinner, wrote about cues, responses, and positive reinforcement, especially in psychotherapy. Later Miller and Dollard isolated three components of teaching—cues, engagement, and reinforcement—that are similar to the elements of input, process, and output in physiology.[2] Their influential work led researchers to consider what teachers *do* rather than focus on their age, experience, certification, college degrees, or other factors not directly connected to what their students learn.[3]

The behavioral model emphasized (1) the quality of the instructional cues impinging on the learner, (2) the learner's active engagement, and (3) the reinforcements or rewards that encourage continuing effort over time. Benjamin Bloom recognized, however, that in cycles of cues and effort learners may fail the first time or even repeatedly. Thus they may practice incorrect behavior, and so they cannot be reinforced. Therefore, he emphasized feedback to correct errors and frequent testing to check progress. Inspired by John Carroll's model of school learning, Bloom also emphasized engaged learning time and stressed that some learners require much more time than others.[4]

The effects of cues, engagement, reinforcement, and corrective feedback on student learning are enormous.[5] The research demonstrating these effects has been unusually rigorous and well-controlled. Even though the research was conducted in school classes, the investigators helped to ensure precise timing and deployment of the elements and relied on short-term studies, which usually lasted less than a month. Similar effects are difficult to sustain for long time periods.

Cues

As operationalized, cues show students what is to be learned and explain how to learn it. Their quality depends on the clarity, salience, and meaningfulness of explanations and directions provided by the teacher, the instructional materials, or both. Ideally, as the learners gain confidence, the salience and number of cues can be reduced.

Engagement

The extent to which students actively and persistently participate in learning until appropriate responses are firmly entrenched in their repertoires is known as engagement. Such participation can be indexed by the extent to which the teacher engages students in overt or covert activity. A high degree of engagement is indicated by an absence of irrelevant behavior and by concentration on tasks, enthusiastic contributions to group discussion, and lengthy study.

Corrective Feedback

Corrective feedback remedies errors in oral or written responses. Ideally, students should waste little time on incorrect responses, and teachers should detect difficulties rapidly and then remedy them by reteaching or using alternative methods. When necessary, teachers should also provide students with additional time for practice.

Reinforcement

The immense effort elicited by athletics, games, and other cooperative and competitive activities illustrates the power of immediate and direct reinforcement and shows that some endeavors are intrinsically rewarding. By comparison, classroom reinforcement may seem crass or jejune. The usual classroom reinforcers are acknowledgment of correctness and social approval, typically expressed by praise or a smile. More unusual reinforcers include providing contingent activity—for example, initiating a music lesson or other enjoyable activity as a reward for 90 percent correctness on a math test. Other reinforcers are tokens or check marks that are accumulated for discrete accomplishments and that can be exchanged for tangible reinforcers such as cookies, trinkets, or toys.

In special education programs, students have been reinforced not only for academic achievement but also for minutes spent on reading, for attempts to learn, and for the accuracy with which they perform tasks. Margo Mastropieri and Thomas Scruggs

have shown that results can be impressive when the environment can be rigorously controlled and when teachers can accurately gear reinforcement to performance, as in programs for unruly or emotionally disturbed students. Improved behavior and achievement, however, may fail to extend past the period of reinforcement or beyond the special environment.[6]

Educators ordinarily confine reinforcement to marks, grades, and awards because they must assume that students work for such intangible, long-term goals as pleasing parents, furthering their education, achieving success in later life, and the intrinsic satisfaction of learning itself. Even so, when corrective feedback and reinforcement are clear, rapid, and appropriate, they can powerfully affect learning by efficiently signaling students what to do next. In ordinary classrooms, then, the chief value of reinforcement is informational rather than motivational.

METHODS OF TEACHING

The psychological elements just discussed undergird many teaching methods and the design of most instructional media. Techniques to improve the affective or informational content of cues, engagement, correctives, and reinforcement have shown a wide range of effects.

Cues

Advance organizers are brief overviews that relate new concepts or terms to previous learning. They are effective if they connect new learning and old. Those delivered by the teacher or graphically illustrated in texts work best.

Adjunct questions alert students to key questions that should be answered—particularly in texts. They work best when questions are repeated on posttests, and they work moderately well when posttest questions are similar or related to the adjuncts. As we might expect, however, adjunct questions divert attention from incidental material that might otherwise be learned.

Goal setting suggests specific objectives, guidelines, methods, or standards for learning that can be spelled out explicitly. Like the use of adjunct questions, goal setting sacrifices incidental for intended learning.

Learning hierarchies assume that instruction can be made more efficient if the facts, skills, or ideas that logically or psychologically precede others are presented first. Teaching and instructional media sequenced in this way appear to be slightly more effective. However, learners may adapt themselves to apparently ill-sequenced material, and it may even be advantageous to learn to do so, since human life, as Franz Kafka showed, may depart from logic.

Pretests are benchmarks for determining how much students learn under various methods of teaching. Psychologists have found, however, that pretests can have positive cuing effects if they show students what will be emphasized in instruction and on posttests.

Several principles follow from surveying the effects of these methods. To concentrate learning on essential points and to save time (as would be appropriate in training), remove elaborations and extraneous oral and written prose. To focus learners on selected questions or to teach them to find answers in elaborated prose, use adjunct questions and goal setting. To encourage the acquisition of as much undifferentiated material as possible, as in college lecture courses, assign big blocks of text and test students on randomly selected points.

Although the means of producing certain results may seem clear, reaching a consensus on educational purposes may be difficult. Clarity at the start saves time and helps learners to see things the teacher's way, but it limits individual autonomy and deep personal insights. Zen masters ask novices about the sound of one hand clapping and wait a decade or two for an answer.

Hiroshi Azuma and Robert Hess find that Japanese mothers use more indirection and vagueness in teaching their young children than do assertive American mothers, and I have observed Japanese science teachers asking questions and leaving them long unresolved. Do the Japanese cultivate initiative and perseverance by these methods?

Engagement

High expectations transmit teachers' standards of learning and performance. They may function both as cues and as incentives for students to put extended effort and perseverance into learning.

Frequent tests increase learning by stimulating greater effort and providing intermittent feedback. However, the effects of tests on performance are larger for quizzes than for final examinations.

Questioning also appears to work by promoting engagement and may encourage deeper thinking—as in Plato's accounts of Socrates. Questioning has bigger effects in science than in other subjects. Mary Budd Rowe and Kenneth Tobin have shown that *wait time*—allowing students several seconds to reflect rather than the usual .9 of a second—leads to longer and better answers.

Correctives and Reinforcement

Corrective feedback remedies errors by reteaching, either with the same or with a different method. This practice has moderate effects that are somewhat higher in science—perhaps because learning science often involves more conceptualizing while learning other subjects may allow more memorizing.

Homework by itself constructively extends engaged learning time. Correctives and reinforcement in the form of grades and comments on homework raise its effects dramatically.

Praise has a small positive effect. For young or disturbed children, praise may lack the power of the tangible reinforcers used in psychological experiments. For students who are able to see ahead, grades and personal standards may be more powerful reinforcers than momentary encouragement. Moreover, praise may be under- or oversupplied; it may appear demeaning or sardonic; and it may pale in comparison with the disincentives to academic achievement afforded by youth culture in the form of cars, clothing, dating, and athletics.

None of this is to say that encouragement, incentives, and good classroom morale should be abandoned; honey may indeed be better than vinegar. Yet, as cognitive psychologists point out, the main classroom value of reinforcement may lie in its capacity to inform the student about progress rather than in its power to reward.

PATTERNS OF TEACHING

As explained above, methods of teaching enact or combine more fundamental psychological elements. By further extension, *patterns* of teaching integrate elements and methods of teaching. The process of determining these more inclusive formulations was another step in the evolution of psychological research on education. Behavioral research evolved in the 1950s from psychological laboratories to short-term, controlled classroom experiments on one element at a time. In the 1970s, educational researchers tried to find patterns of effective practices from observations of ordinary teaching.

Thus behaviorists traded educational realism for theoretical parsimony and scientific rigor; later psychologists preferred realism until their insights could be experimentally confirmed. Fortunately, the results of both approaches appear to converge. Moreover, it seems possible to incorporate the work of cognitive psychologists of the

1980s into an enlarged understanding of teaching.

Explicit Teaching

Explicit teaching can be viewed as traditional or conventional whole-group teaching done well. Since most teaching has changed little in the last three-quarters of a century and may not change substantially in the near future,[7] it is worth knowing how to make the usual practice most productive. Since it has evolved from ordinary practice, explicit teaching seems natural to carry out and does not disrupt conventional institutions and expectations. Furthermore, it can incorporate many previously discussed elements and methods.

Systematic research was initiated in the early 1960s by N. L. Gage, Donald Medley, and others who employed "process–product" investigations of the association between what teachers do and how much their students learn. Jere Brophy, Carolyn Evertson, Thomas Good, and Jane Stallings later contributed substantially to this effort. Walter Doyle, Penelope Peterson, and Lee Shulman put the results into a psychological context. Barak Rosenshine has periodically reviewed the research, and Gage and Margaret Needels recently measured the results and pointed out their implications.

The various contributors to the knowledge base do not completely agree about the essential components of explicit teaching, and they refer to it by different names, such as process–product, direct, active, and effective teaching. The researchers weigh their own results heavily, but Rosenshine, a longstanding and comprehensive reviewer, has taken an eagle's-eye view of the results.[8]

In his early reviews of the correlational studies, Rosenshine discussed the traits of effective teachers, including clarity, task orientation, enthusiasm, and flexibility, as well as their tendency to structure their presentations and occasionally to use student ideas.

From later observational and control-group research, Rosenshine identified six phased functions of explicit teaching: (1) daily review, checking of homework, and reteaching if necessary; (2) rapid presentation of new content and skills in small steps; (3) guided student practice with close monitoring by teachers; (4) corrective feedback and instructional reinforcement; (5) independent practice in seatwork and homework, with a success rate of more than 90 percent; and (6) weekly and monthly review.

Comprehension Teaching

The heirs of Aristotle and of the Anglo-American tradition of Bacon, Locke, Thorndike, and Skinner objected to philosophical "armchair" opinions; mid-century behaviorists, particularly John Watson, constructively insisted on hard empirical data about learning. But they also saw the child's mind as a blank tablet and seemed to encourage active teaching and passive acquisition of isolated facts. Reacting to such atomism and to William James' "bucket" metaphor, cognitive psychologists in the early 1980s revived research on student-centered learning and "higher mental processes," in the tradition of Plato, Socrates, Kant, Rousseau, Dewey, Freud, and Piaget. In American hands, however, this European tradition has sometimes led to vacuity and permissiveness, as in the extremes of the "progressive education" movement of the 1930s.

Oddly, the Russian psychologist Lev Vygotsky hit on an influential compromise: emphasizing the two-way nature of teaching, he identified a "zone of proximal development," which extends from what learners can do independently to the maximum that they can do with the teacher's help.[9] Accordingly, teachers should set up "scaffolding" for building knowledge and then remove it when it becomes unnecessary. In mathematics, for example, the teacher can give prompts and examples, foster independent use, and then withdraw support. This approach is similar to the "prompting" and "fading" of the behavioral cues, and it seems common-sensical. It has revived interest in granting some autonomy to students.

During the 1980s, cognitive research on teaching sought ways to encourage self-monitoring, self-teaching, or "metacognition" to foster independence. Skills were seen as important, but the learner's monitoring and management of them had priority, as though the explicit teaching functions of planning, allocating time, and reviewing were partly transferred to the learner.

For example, David Pearson outlined three phases: (1) modeling, in which the teacher exhibits the desired behavior; (2) guided practice, in which students perform with help from the teacher; and (3) application, in which students perform independently of the teacher—steps that correspond to explicit teaching functions. Anne Marie Palincsar and Anne Brown described a program of "reciprocal teaching" that fosters comprehension by having students take turns in leading dialogues on pertinent features of a text. By assuming the kind of planning and executive control ordinarily exercised by teachers, students learn planning, structuring, and self-management. Perhaps that is why tutors learn from teaching and why we say that to learn something well, one should teach it.

Comprehension teaching encourages students to measure their progress toward explicit goals. If necessary, they can reallocate their time to different activities. In this way, self-awareness, personal control, and positive self-evaluation can be increased.[10]

LEARNER AUTONOMY IN SCIENCE

The National Science Foundation sponsored many studies of student inquiry and autonomy that showed that giving students opportunities to manipulate science materials, to contract with teachers about what to learn, to inquire on their own, and to engage in activity-based curricula all had substantial positive effects. Group- and self-direction, however, had smaller positive effects, and pass/fail and self-grading had small negative effects. Methods of providing greater learner autonomy may also work well in subjects other than science, as in the more radical approach that I discuss next.

OPEN EDUCATION

In the late 1960s, open educators expanded autonomy in the primary grades by enabling students to join teachers in planning educational purposes, means, and evaluation. In contrast to teacher- and textbook-centered education, open education gave students a voice in deciding what to learn—even to the point of writing their own texts to share with one another. Open educators tried to foster cooperation, critical thinking, constructive attitudes, and self-directed lifelong learning. They revived the spirit of the New England town meeting, Thoreau's self-reliance, Emerson's transcendentalism, and Dewey's progressivism. Their ideas also resonate with the "client-centered" psychotherapy of Carl Rogers, which emphasizes the "unconditional worth" of the person.

Rose Giaconia and Larry Hedges' synthesis of 153 studies showed that open education had worthwhile effects on creativity, independence, cooperation, attitudes toward teachers and schools, mental ability, psychological adjustment, and curiosity. Students in open programs had less motivation for grade grubbing, but they differed little from other students in actual achievement, self-concept, and anxiety.

However, Giaconia and Hedges also found that the open programs that were more effective in producing the positive outcomes with regard to attitudes, creativity, and self-concept sacrificed some academic achievement on standardized tests. These programs emphasized the role of the child in learning and the use of individualized instruction, manipulative materials, and diagnostic rather than norm-referenced evaluation. However, they did not include three other components thought by some to be essential to open programs: multi-age grouping, open space, and team teaching.

Giaconia and Hedges speculated that children in the most extreme open programs may do somewhat less well on conventional achievement tests because they have little experience with them. At any rate, it appears that open classrooms enhance several nonstandard outcomes without detracting from academic achievement unless they are radically extreme.[11]

INSTRUCTIONAL SYSTEMS

All the techniques discussed thus far can be planned and executed by a single teacher. They may entail some extra effort, encouragement, or training, but they do not call for unusual preparation or materials. In contrast, instructional systems require special arrangements and planning, and they often combine several components of instruction. Moreover, they tend to emphasize the adaptation of instruction to individual students rather than the adaptation of students to a fixed pattern of teaching. A little history will aid our understanding of current instructional systems.

Programmed Instruction

Developed in the 1950s, programmed instruction presents a series of "frames," each one of which conveys an item of information and requires a student response. *Linear programs* present a graduated series of frames that require such small increments in knowledge that learning steps may be nearly errorless and may be continuously reinforced by progression to the next frame. Able students proceed quickly under these conditions. *Branched programs* direct students back for reteaching when necessary, to the side for correctives, and ahead when they already know parts of the material. The ideas of continuous progress and branching influenced later developers, who tried to optimize learning by individualization, mastery learning, and adaptive instruction.

Individualization adapts instruction to individual needs by applying variations in speed or branching and by using booklets, worksheets, coaching, and the like. Perhaps because they have been vaguely defined and poorly operationalized, individualized programs have had small effects. Other systems (discussed below) appear more effective for adapting instruction to the needs of individual learners.

Mastery Learning

Combining the psychological elements of instruction with suitable amounts of time, mastery learning employs formative tests to allocate time and to guide reinforcement and corrective feedback. In the most definitive synthesis of research on mastery learning, James Kulik and Chen-Lin Kulik reported substantial positive effects. Mastery programs that yielded larger effects established a criterion of 95 percent to 100 percent mastery and required repeated testing to mastery before allowing students to proceed to additional units (which yielded gigantic effects of one standard deviation). Mastery learning yielded larger effects with less-able students and reduced the difference between their performance and that of abler groups.

The success of mastery learning is attributable to several factors. The Kuliks, for example, found that when control groups were provided feedback from quizzes, the mastery groups' advantage was smaller. As Bloom pointed out, mastery learning takes additional time; the Kuliks found that mastery learning required a median of 16 percent (and up to 97 percent) more time than conventional instruction. The seven studies that

provided equal time for mastery and control groups showed only a small advantage for mastery learning on standardized tests. However, the advantage was moderate on experimenter-made, criterion-referenced tests for nine equal-time studies. These results illustrate the separate contributions to mastery learning of cuing, feedback, and time.

Mastery learning yielded larger effects in studies of less than a month's duration than in those lasting more than four months. Retention probably declines sharply no matter what the educational method, but the decline can be more confidently noted with regard to mastery learning since it has been more extensively studied than other methods.

Bloom and his students have reported larger effects than has Robert Slavin, who reviewed their work. Thomas Guskey and S. L. Gates, for example, reported an average effect size of .78 estimated from 38 studies of elementary and secondary students. In response to Slavin, Lorin Anderson and Robert Burns pointed out two reasons for larger effects in some studies, especially those under Bloom's supervision. Bloom has been more interested in what is possible than in what is likely; he has sought to find the limits of learning. His students, moreover, have conducted tightly controlled experiments over time periods of less than a semester or less than a year.[12]

Adaptive Instruction

Developed by Margaret Wang and others, adaptive instruction combines elements of mastery learning, cooperative learning, open education, tutoring, computer-assisted instruction, and comprehension teaching into a complex system whose aim is to tailor instruction to the needs of individuals and small groups. Managerial functions—including such activities as planning, allocating time, delegating tasks to aides and students, and quality control—are carried out by a master teacher. Adaptive instruction is a comprehensive program for the whole school day rather than a single method that requires simple integration into one subject or into a single teacher's repertoire. Its effects on achievement are substantial, but its broader effects are probably underestimated, since adaptive instruction aims at diverse ends—including student autonomy, intrinsic motivation, and teacher and student choice—which are poorly reflected by the usual outcome measures.

COMPUTER-ASSISTED INSTRUCTION

Ours is an electronic age, and computers have already had a substantial impact on learning. With the costs of hardware declining and with software becoming increasingly sophisticated, we may hope for still greater effects as computers are better integrated into school programs.

Computers show the greatest advantage for handicapped students—probably because they are more adaptive to their special needs than teachers might be. Computers may also be more patient, discreet, nonjudgmental, or even encouraging about progress. Perhaps for the same reasons, computers generally have bigger effects in elementary schools than in high schools or colleges.

Another explanation for the disparate results is also plausible. Elementary schools provide less tracking and fewer differentiated courses for homogeneous groups. Computers may be better adapted to larger within-class differences among elementary students because they allow them to proceed at their own pace without engaging in invidious comparisons.

Simulations and games, with or without computer implementation, require active, specific responses from learners and may strike a balance between vicarious book learning and the dynamic, complicated, and competitive "real world." The interactiveness, speed, intensity, movement, color, and sound of computers add interest and information to academic learning. Unless geared to educational purposes, however, computer games can also waste time.

STUDENT GROUPING

Teaching students what they already know and teaching them what they are yet incapable of learning are equally wasteful practices and may even be harmful to motivation. For this reason, traditional whole-class teaching of heterogeneous groups can present serious difficulties—a problem that is often unacknowledged in our egalitarian age. Outside of universities, however, most educators recognize that it is difficult to teach arithmetic and trigonometry at the same time. (Even some English professors might balk at teaching phonics and deconstructionism simultaneously.) If we want to teach students as much as possible rather than to make them all alike, we need to consider how they are grouped and try to help the full range of students.

Acceleration

Accelerated programs identify talented youth (often in mathematics and science) and group them together or with older students. Such programs provide counseling, encouragement, contact with accomplished adults, grade skipping, summer school, and the compression of the standard curriculum into fewer years. The effects are huge in elementary schools, substantial in junior high schools, and moderate in senior high schools. The smaller effects at more advanced levels may be attributable to the smaller advantage of acceleration over the tracking and differentiated course selection practiced in high schools.

The effects of acceleration on educational attitudes, vocational plans, participation in school activities, popularity, psychological adjustment, and character ratings have been mixed and often insignificant. These outcomes may not be systematically affected in either direction.

Ability Grouping

Students are placed in ability groups according to achievement, intelligence test scores, personal insights, and subjective opinions. In high school, ability grouping leaves deficient and average students unaffected, but it has beneficial effects on talented students and on attitudes toward the subject matter. In elementary school, the grouping of students with similar reading achievement but from different grades yields substantial effects. Within-class grouping in mathematics yields worthwhile effects, but generalized ability grouping does not.

Tutoring

Because it gears instruction to individual or small-group needs, tutoring is highly beneficial to both tutors and tutees. It yields particularly large effects in mathematics—perhaps because of the subject's well-defined scope and organization.

In whole-group instruction, teachers may ordinarily focus on average or deficient students to ensure that they master the lessons. When talented students are freed from repetition and slow progression, they can proceed quickly. Grouping may work best when students are accurately grouped according to their specific subject-matter needs rather than according to I.Q., demeanor, or other irrelevant characteristics.

Well-defined subject matter and student grouping may be among the chief reasons why Japanese students lead the world in academic achievement: The curriculum is explicit, rigorous, and nationally uniform. In primary schools, weaker students, with maternal help, study harder and longer to keep up with these explicit requirements. Subject-matter tests are administered to screen students for "lower" and "upper" secondary schools and for universities of various gradations of rigor and prestige. Each such screening determines occupational, marital, and other adult prospects; long-term adult rewards thus reinforce educational effort.[13]

SOCIAL ENVIRONMENT

Cooperative learning programs delegate some control of the pacing and methods of learning to groups of between two and six students, who work together and sometimes compete with other groups within classes. Such programs are successful for several reasons. They provide relief from the excessive teacher/student interaction of whole-group teaching, they free time for the interactive engagement of students, and they present opportunities for targeted cues, engagement, correctives, and reinforcement. As in comprehension teaching, the acts of tutoring and teaching may encourage students to think for themselves about the organization of subject matter and the productive allocation of time.

Many correlational studies suggest that *classroom morale* is associated with achievement gains, with greater interest in subject matter, and with the worthy outcome of voluntary participation in nonrequired subject-related activities. Morale is assessed by asking students to agree or disagree with such statements as "Most of the students know one another well" and "The class members know the purpose of the lessons."

Students who perceive the atmosphere as friendly, satisfying, focused on goals, and challenging and who feel that the classroom has the required materials tend to learn more. Those who perceive the atmosphere as fostering student cliques, disorganization, apathy, favoritism, and friction learn less. The research on morale, though plausible, lacks the specificity and causal confidence of the controlled experiments on directly alterable methods.

READING EFFECTS

Comprehension teaching, because it may extend to several subjects in elementary school, has already been discussed as a pattern of teaching. Several other methods have substantial effects on reading achievement.

Adaptive speed training involves principles that are similar to those of comprehension training. Students learn to vary their pace and the depth of their reflection according to the difficulty of the material and their reading purposes.

Reading methods vary widely, but their largest effects seem to occur when teachers are systematically trained, almost irrespective of particularities of method. Phonics or "word-attack" approaches, however, have a moderate advantage over guessing and "whole-word" approaches in the teaching of beginning reading—perhaps because early misconceptions are avoided. Phonics may also reduce the need for excessive reteaching and correctives.

Pictures in the text can be very helpful, although they add to the cost of a book and occupy space that could otherwise be used for prose. In order of their effectiveness, several types of pictures can be distinguished. Transformative pictures recode information into concrete and memorable form, relate information in a well-organized context, and provide links for systematic retrieval. Interpretive pictures, like advance organizers, make the text comprehensible by relating abstract terms to concrete ones and by connecting the unfamiliar and difficult to previously acquired knowledge. Organizational pictures, including maps and diagrams, show the coherence of objects or events in space and time. Representational pictures are photos or other concrete representations of what is discussed in the text. Decorative

pictures present (possibly irrelevant or conflicting) information that is incidental to intended learning (although decoration may add interest if not information).

Pictures can provide vivid imagery and metaphors that facilitate memory, show what is important to learn, and intensify the effects of prose. Pictures may sometimes allow students to bypass the text, but memorable, well-written prose may obviate pictures.[14]

WRITING EFFECTS

Sixty well-designed studies of methods of teaching writing compared 72 experimental groups with control groups. The methods below are presented in the order of their effectiveness.

The *inquiry method* requires students to find and state specific details that convey personal experience vividly, to examine sets of data to develop and support explanatory generalizations, or to analyze situations that present ethical problems and arguments.

Scales are criteria or specific questions that students can apply to their own and others' writing to improve it.

Sentence combining shows students how to build complex sentences from simpler ones.

Models are presentations of good pieces of writing to serve as exemplars for students.

Free writing allows students to write about whatever occurs to them.

Grammar and mechanics include sentence parsing and the analysis of parts of speech.

SCIENCE EFFECTS

Introduced in response to the launch of *Sputnik I*, the "new" science curricula, sponsored by the National Science Foundation, yielded substantial effects on learning. They efficiently added value by producing superior learning on tests of their intended outcomes and on tests of general subject-matter goals. The new curricula also yielded effects ranging from small to substantial on such often-unmeasured outcomes as creativity, problem solving, scientific attitudes and skills, logical thinking, and achievement in nonscience subject matter.

Perhaps these advantages are attributable to the combined efforts of teachers, psychologists, and scientists, who collaborated to ensure that the curricula would be based on modern content and would foster effective teaching practices. The scientists may have been able to generate enthusiasm for teaching scientific methods, for laboratory work, and for other reforms.

The new science curricula worked well in improving achievement and other outcomes. Ironically, they are often forgotten today, despite the fact that, by international standards, U.S. students score poorly in mathematics and science.

Inquiry Teaching.   Often practiced in Japan, this method requires students to formulate hypotheses, reason about their credibility, and design experiments to test their validity. Inquiry teaching yields substantial effects, particularly on the understanding of scientific processes.

Audiotutorials.   These are tape-recorded instructions for using laboratory equipment, manipulatives, and readings for topical lessons or whole courses. This simple approach yields somewhat better results than conventional instruction, allows independent learning, and has the further advantage of individual pacing—allowing students to pursue special topics or to take courses on their own.

Original Source Papers.   This method derives from the Great Books approach of the late Robert Maynard Hutchins, former president of the University of Chicago, and his colleague Mortimer Adler. They saw more value in reading Plato or Newton than in resorting to predigested textbook accounts. The use of original sources in teaching trades

breadth for depth in the belief that it is better to know a few ideas of transcending importance than to learn many unconnected bits of soon-forgotten information. Advocates of this approach have shown that such knowledge can be acquired by studying and discussing original scientific papers of historical or scientific significance.

Other methods of teaching science have effects that are near zero—that is, close to the effects of traditional methods of teaching. They include team teaching, departmentalized elementary programs, and media-based instruction. The equal results for media methods, however, suggest that choices can be based on cost and convenience. Because television programs and films can be broadcast, they can provide equally effective education in different and widespread locations (even in different parts of the world by satellite). Moreover, students today can interact online with teachers and fellow students who are far away.

There are some successful precedents for the use of media-based instruction. For a decade, the Chicago community colleges provided dozens of mainly one-way television courses to hundreds of thousands of students, who did most of their studying at home but participated in discussion and testing sessions at several sites in the metropolitan area. The best lecturers, media specialists, and test constructors could be employed, and tapes of the courses could be rebroadcast repeatedly.

In several Third World countries that are gaining in achievement and school enrollments, ministries of education make efficient and successful use of such low-cost, effective "distance education" for remote elementary and secondary schools.

The Oklahoma and Minnesota state departments of education apparently lead the nation in providing small high schools in rural areas with specialized television teachers and interactive courses in advanced science, mathematics, foreign languages, and other subjects.

MATHEMATICS EFFECTS

In the heyday of its Education Directorate, the National Science Foundation sponsored considerable research not only on science but also on mathematics. Some worthwhile effects were found.

Manipulative Materials

The use of Cuisenaire rods, balance beams, counting sticks, and measuring scales allows students to engage directly in learning instead of passively following abstract presentations by the teacher. Students can handle the materials, see the relation of abstract ideas and concrete embodiments, and check hypothesized answers by quick empirical testing without having to wait for quiz results or feedback from the teacher. This method apparently results in enormous effects.

Problem Solving

In mathematics teaching, a focus on problem solving yields worthwhile effects. Such an approach requires comprehension of terms and their application to varied examples. It may motivate students by showing them the application of mathematical ideas to "real-world" questions.

New Math

The so-called new math produced beneficial results, although it was not as successful as the new science curricula. Both reforms probably gained their learning advantages partly by testing what they taught.

SPECIAL POPULATIONS AND TECHNIQUES

We can also gain insights from programs that lie outside the usual scope of elementary and secondary classrooms.

Early Intervention

Programs of early intervention include educational, psychological, and therapeutic components for handicapped, at-risk, and disadvantaged children from the ages of one month to 5½ years. Studies of these programs found that the large, immediate effects of these programs declined rapidly and disappeared after three years.

Preschool Programs

Preschool programs also showed initial learning effects that were not sustained. It appears that young children can learn more than is normally assumed, but, like other learners, they can also forget. The key to sustained gains may be sustained programs and effective families—not one-shot approaches.

Programs for the Handicapped

Students classified as mentally retarded, emotionally disturbed, or learning disabled have been subjects in research that has several important implications. When they serve as tutors of one another and of younger students, handicapped students can learn well—a finding similar to those in comprehension-monitoring and tutoring studies of nonhandicapped children. Moreover, handicapped students are often spuriously classified, and we may underestimate their capacities.

Mainstreaming

Studies show that mildly to moderately handicapped students can prosper in regular classes and thereby avoid the invidious "labeling" that is often based on misclassification.

Psycholinguistic Training

Providing psycholinguistic training to special needs students yields positive effects.

This approach consists of testing and remedying specific deficits in language skills.

Patient Education

Educating patients about diseases and treatments can affect mortality, morbidity, and lengths of illness and hospitalization. In studies of the acquisition of knowledge regarding drug usage for hypertension, diabetes, and other chronic conditions, one-to-one and group counseling (with or without instructional material) produced greater effects than providing instruction through labels on bottles or package inserts for patients.

Labels, special containers, memory aids, and behavior modification were successful in minimizing later errors in drug usage. The most efficacious educational principles were specification of intentions, relevance to the needs of the learner, provision of personal answers to questions, reinforcement and feedback on progress, facilitation of correct dosage (e.g., the use of unit-dose containers), and instructional and treatment regimens suited to personal convenience (e.g., prescribing drugs for administration at mealtimes).

In-Service Training of Physicians

Such training shows large effects on doctors' knowledge and on their classroom or laboratory performance but only moderate effects on the outcomes of treating actual patients. Knowledge and performance, even in practical training, may help, but they hardly guarantee successful application in practice. Can an accomplished mathematician handle the intricacies of federal income tax?

Panaceas and Shortcuts

At the request of the U.S. Army, the National Academy of Sciences evaluated exotic techniques for enhancing learning and performance that are described in popular psychology (and presumably are being exploited in Cali-

fornia and Russia).[15] However, little or no evidence was found for the efficacy of learning during sleep; for mental practice of motor skills; for "integration" of left and right hemispheres of the brain; for parapsychological techniques; for biofeedback; for extrasensory perception, mental telepathy, and "mind over matter" exercises; or for "neurolinguistic programming," in which instructors identify the students' modes of learning and mimic the students' behaviors as they teach.

The Greeks found no royal road to geometry; even kings, if they desired mastery, had to sweat over Euclid's elements. Perhaps brain research will eventually yield a magic elixir or a panacea, but for proof of its existence educators should insist on hard data in refereed scientific journals.

EFFECTS ON TEACHERS

Programs to help teachers in their work have had substantial effects—notwithstanding complaints about typical in-service training sessions. Do physicians complain about the medical care they get?

Microteaching

Developed at Stanford University in the 1960s, microteaching is a behavioral approach for pre-service and in-service training that has substantial effects. It employs the explanation and modeling of selected teaching techniques; televised practice with small groups of students; discussion, correctives, and reinforcement while watching playback; and recycling through subsequent practice and playback sessions with new groups of students.

In-Service Education

In-service training for teachers also proves to have substantial effects. Somewhat like the case of in-service training of physicians, the biggest effects are on the teacher's knowledge, but effects on classroom behavior and student achievement are also notable.

For in-service training, authoritative planning and execution seem to work best; informal coaching by itself seems ineffective. Allowing the instructor to be responsible for the design and teaching of the sessions works better than relying on presentations by teachers and group discussions. The best techniques are observation and classroom practices, video/audio feedback, and practice. The most effective training combines lectures, modeling, practice, and coaching. The size of the training group, ranging from one to more than 60, makes no detectable difference.

Some apparent effects may be attributable to the selectivity of the program rather than to its superior efficacy. For example, federal-, state-, and university-sponsored programs appear more effective than locally initiated programs. Competitive selection of participants and the granting of college credit apparently work better as incentives than extra pay, renewal of certification, or no incentives. Independent study seems to have larger effects than workshops, courses, minicourses, and institutes.

CONCLUSION

Psychological research provides first-order estimates of the effects of instructional means on educational ends under various conditions. But some instructional practices may be costly—not in terms of dollars but in terms of new or complicated arrangements that may be difficult for some teachers and districts to adopt. Thus, estimates of effects are only one basis for decision making. We need to consider the productivity or value of effects in relation to total costs, including the time and energies of educators and students.

Knowledge from the field of psychology alone is not sufficient to prescribe practices, since different means bring about different ends. Educators must decide whether the learning effort is to be directed by teachers, by students, or by the curriculum. They must choose among a range of facts and concepts, breadth and depth, short- and long-term ends, academic knowledge and knowledge that has direct application in the real world, equal opportunity and equal results. They must decide which aspect of Plato's triumvirate of thinking, feeling, and acting will take precedence. Once these choices are made, educators can turn to the researchers' estimates of effects as one basis for determining the most productive practices.

ENDNOTES

1. Herbert J. Walberg, Diane Schiller, and Geneva D. Haertel, "The Quiet Revolution in Educational Research," *Phi Delta Kappan,* November 1979, pp. 179–183; Herbert J. Walberg, "Improving the Productivity of America's Schools," *Educational Leadership,* vol. 41, 1984, pp. 19–27; and Barry J. Fraser, Herbert J. Walberg, Wayne W. Welch, and John A. Hattie, "Syntheses of Educational Productivity Research," *International Journal of Educational Research,* vol. 11, 1987, pp. 73–145.

2. Neal Miller and John Dollard, *Social Learning and Imitation* (New Haven, CT: Yale University Press, 1941); and John Dollard and Neal Miller, *Personality and Psychotherapy* (New York: McGraw-Hill, 1950).

3. Eric A. Hanushek, "Throwing Money at Schools," *Journal of Policy Analysis and Management,* vol. 1, 1981, pp. 19–41; and Herbert J. Walberg and William F. Fowler, "Expenditure and Size Efficiencies of Public School Districts," *Educational Researcher,* vol. 16, 1987, pp. 515–526.

4. Benjamin S. Bloom, *Human Characteristics and School Learning* (New York: McGraw-Hill, 1976); and John B. Carroll, "A Model of School Learning," *Teachers College Record,* vol. 64, 1963, pp. 723–733.

5. The effects are expressed as differences between experimental and control groups in units of standard deviations. For further details and references, see my chapter in Merlin C. Wittrock, ed., *Handbook of Research on Teaching* (New York: Macmillan, 1986).

6. Margo A. Mastropieri and Thomas E. Scruggs, *Effective Instruction for Special Education* (Boston: Little, Brown, 1987).

7. John Hoetker and William P. Ahlbrand, "The Persistence of the Recitation," *American Educational Research Journal,* vol. 6, 1969, pp. 145–167.

8. For a full account of most views, see Penelope L. Peterson and Herbert J. Walberg, eds., *Research on Teaching* (Berkeley, CA: McCutchan, 1979); and Wittrock, op. cit.

9. Lev Vygotsky, *Mind in Society* (Cambridge, MA: Harvard University Press, 1978).

10. Anne Marie Palincsar and Anne Brown, "Reciprocal Teaching of Comprehension-Fostering and Comprehension-Monitoring Activities," *Cognition and Instruction,* vol. 1, 1984, pp. 117–176; David Pearson, "Reading Comprehension Instruction: Six Necessary Steps," *Reading Teacher,* vol. 38, 1985, pp. 724–738; and Paul R. Pintrich et al., "Instructional Psychology," *Annual Review of Psychology,* vol. 37, 1986, pp. 611–651.

11. Rose M. Giaconia and Larry V. Hedges, "Identifying Features on Effective Open Education," *Review of Educational Research,* vol. 52, 1982, pp. 579–602.

12. James A. Kulik and Chen-Lin Kulik, "Mastery Testing and Student Learning," *Journal of Educational Technology Systems,* vol. 15, 1986, pp. 325–345; Lorin W. Anderson and Robert B. Burns, "Values, Evidence, and Mastery Learning," *Review of Educational Research,* vol. 57, 1988, pp. 215–223; Thomas R. Guskey and S. L. Gates, "Synthesis of Research on the Effects of Mastery Learning in Elementary and Secondary Classrooms," *Educational Leadership,* May 1986, pp. 73–80; and Robert E. Slavin, "Mastery Learning Reconsidered," *Review of Educational Research,* vol. 57, 1988, pp. 175–213.

13. Herbert J. Walberg, "What Can We Learn from Japanese Education?," *The World and I,* March 1988, pp. 661–665.

14. Joel R. Levin, Gary J. Anglin, and Russell N. Carney, "On Empirically Validating Functions of Pictures in Prose," in D. M. Willows and H. A. Houghton, eds., *The Psychology of Illustration* (New York: Springer-Verlag, 1987).

15. Daniel Druckman and John A. Swets, eds., *Enhancing Human Performance* (Washington, DC: National Academy Press, 1988).

DISCUSSION QUESTIONS

1. How can teachers use or improve cues, engagement, correctives, and reinforcement to facilitate student achievement?

2. How do explicit teaching and comprehension teaching differ in terms of methods and elements?

3. Consider the advantages and disadvantages of open education. Is open education appropriate for all educational settings and students? Why? Why not?

4. How can knowledge from the field of psychology be used to guide curriculum development?

5. In what ways have programs and techniques developed for special populations influenced elementary and secondary curriculum development?

10 Honoring Diverse Styles of Beginning Teachers

EDWARD F. PAJAK
ELAINE STOTKO
FRANK MASCI

FOCUSING QUESTIONS

1. How would you describe a teacher's style of teaching?
2. How does teacher style differ from teacher characteristics? Teacher behavior? Teacher effectiveness?
3. How is a teacher's style influenced by his or her educational philosophy?
4. How would you describe a teacher's cycle of learning?
5. How does a teacher's professional learning differ from problem solving? Critical thinking? Transfer of learning?
6. What kind of supervisor would you prefer to have observing and mentoring your teaching?

Schools today face the responsibility of guaranteeing high-quality instruction for every student, while simultaneously having to recruit and retain unprecedented numbers of new and second-career teachers. This dual challenge is achievable, we believe, only by supporting teachers in ways that are compatible with how they most naturally learn and teach. In other words, those educators who provide support to new teachers should strive to work with them in the same way that teachers are expected to work with students—by recognizing and celebrating a diversity of styles and responding to differences in ways that enhance learning for everyone.

The standards movement in education has set for itself the admirable goal of high expectations for all students. Because students differ in their styles of learning, experienced teachers recognize the importance of providing alternative paths for achieving these agreed-upon outcomes. Similarly, the time has come for us to realize that new teachers do not all learn or teach the same way. Talk to several new teachers about why they are teachers, what teaching means to them, how they know when they are successful, and what gives them the most satisfaction, and you'll discover that some teachers place great emphasis on imparting knowledge to students, while others stress the importance of helping students discover knowledge for themselves. Some teachers believe in getting actively involved in their students' lives, while others prefer to maintain a more distanced professional relationship. Some teachers dedicate themselves to social change and justice for all students, while others concentrate their efforts on individual students who show promise of becoming leaders of their generation.

These different perspectives of teaching reflect various experiences or styles of teaching—inventing, knowing, caring, and inspiring—that highlight differences in how individuals perceive and process information (Pajak, 2003). When *inventing* teachers talk about teaching, for example, they tend to emphasize the importance of "having students solve problems" and of "seeing students apply their learning to real situations." *Knowing* teachers are more likely to focus on "helping kids learn content" and to believe they are successful when they "see students mastering the subject matter." *Caring* teachers often say that "providing opportunities for student growth" is most important, and they define success in terms of "building a classroom community." Finally, *inspiring* teachers tend to view teaching as "an opportunity to shape the future" and derive satisfaction from "seeing students make independent decisions."

These four ways of experiencing teaching are clearly evident in the literature on education. The *inventing* perspective is expressed, for example, in the scholarship of Jean Piaget and Hilda Taba; advocacy for the *knowing* viewpoint may be found in the writings of Benjamin Bloom and Mortimer Adler; the importance of the *caring* attitude is explained to us by Nel Noddings and Parker Palmer; and the *inspiring* stance is articulated in the work of Paulo Freire and Maxine Greene. The four styles can also be seen in depictions of teachers in popular culture.

Jaime Escalante, in the movie *Stand and Deliver*, is an example of an *inventing* teacher. Marva Collins, in the made-for-TV movie *The Marva Collins Story*, represents a *knowing* teacher. Roberta Guaspari, in the film *Music of the Heart*, depicts a *caring* teacher, and LouAnne Johnson, in *Dangerous Minds*, an *inspiring* teacher.

A TEACHER-PROOF TEACHER?

Why do different teacher styles matter? Forty or more years ago, during the Cold War and post-Sputnik era, some experts in education tried to develop what has been termed the "teacher-proof curriculum," in the belief that if instruction and curriculum were controlled to a sufficient degree, teachers would be forced into teaching only what was prescribed by the experts. Today, we fear, the inflexible enforcement of standards for teaching is moving us toward a "teacher-proof teacher," one who is standardized to the point of being unable to think independently or to act on personal convictions. Yet, we know from the study of teaching styles that real teachers are more complex, as the following vignettes demonstrate.

Inventing

Students in Ken Garry's eleventh-grade world history class have come to expect the unexpected. Still, on one memorable day at the beginning of the Russian history unit, even they were surprised to see a somewhat disheveled, unshaven Mr. Garry enter the room. They were certainly not prepared for what happened next. He took out a razor and began to shave. Then he posed a series of questions, beginning with "What did my shaving have to do with an event in Russian history?" A very lively discussion ensued around the fact that Peter the Great, in one of his efforts to westernize the country, ordered his nobles, the Boyars, to shave off their flowing beards. The students were likely not only to remember this event but, as a result of the discussion, to place it within the larger context of the modernization of Russia.

Knowing

To an observer entering Pam Gilbert's twelfth-grade English classroom, it is immediately apparent that each student has a clear idea of her expectations. Daily objectives are posted; each student is given a detailed agenda of what is to be covered during the lesson; and posters that describe rules, submission requirements for papers, and assignment deadlines are prominent throughout the room. Ms. Gilbert's lesson plans reveal that instruction is largely teacher-directed and focused on the learning of factual information and key concepts. Group work is also part of her instructional strategy; she typically assigns students to groups, giving each student a specific responsibility within the group. The classroom climate is one of efficiency and purpose.

Caring

Gloria Silverman loves children, and her eighth-grade mathematics students, if pressed, would admit to affection for her as well. They would cite her keen interest in their lives, her close contact with their parents (they might even give grudging appreciation for this), and her willingness to "go the extra mile" to help them understand the sometimes bewildering intricacies of the rudiments of algebra. Surprisingly large numbers of students attend her daily lunchtime help sessions and are grateful for her tenacious insistence on learning the subject matter, always couched in an almost parental concern for their well-being.

Inspiring

Second graders, at the very beginning of their educational experience, certainly represent a wealth of untapped possibility. They are impressionable and usually very eager to please. No one realizes this more and capitalizes on it better than their teacher, Joanna Chakitis. To describe her classroom environment as a wonderland is an understatement. The walls are covered with colorful and stimulating instructional materials, stations for work on individualized assignments, and job charts for student helpers. Even the ceiling contains examples of student work. The students in Ms. Chakitis's class are the beneficiaries of exceptionally creative and innovative teaching practices that are carefully designed to promote their growth and development.

SUPPORTING NEW TEACHERS

Beginning teachers often find themselves facing expectations and advice from university supervisors, mentor teachers, peer coaches, principals, and district office supervisors. How should support systems for new teachers that are provided by universities and schools respond to these diverse teaching styles? Our fundamental principle is simple, yet powerful. Those who provide support to new teachers—mentors, peer coaches, university supervisors, and principals—should make a deliberate effort to honor and legitimate perspectives and practices that differ from their own preferred styles of perceiving and judging reality. The starting point for helping new teachers succeed, in other words, should be the development of the teacher's preferred style. Once that style has been successfully developed, of course, the teacher should be encouraged to expand his or her repertoire of strategies and perspectives.

Teaching is much more than simply a job. For a great many people, teaching is a way of living their lives. Teaching is closely connected, in other words, to how teachers view themselves as people. Indeed, what teachers do in their classrooms is tightly wrapped up with, and difficult to separate from, their very identities. Support systems and mentoring practices that conflict with the teacher's identity and core values are, at the very least, useless and, at the worst, destructive.

Although any one of the experiences of teaching—*inventing, knowing, caring, inspiring*—can be a useful guide to practice, it is only a starting point. All of these paths must be traced if a teacher is to become truly effective. Supervisors (i.e., mentors, coaches, principals) are expected to ensure that new teachers know their subject matter and can teach, but in reality the support that new teachers need is much more complicated. An effective mentor is able to support the new teacher's personal and emotional needs and to help the teacher become an inquiring professional and reflective practitioner.

Each student that a teacher meets in the classroom requires different things at different times—explanations and reliable ways of thinking, high standards and understanding, nurturing care and emotional support, inspiration and values—and a teacher ought to be able to provide them all. Similarly, those who support beginning teachers should be able to offer differentiated support as well. Unfortunately, classroom observations and evaluations in most school systems rely on instruments or standards that favor only the organized and business-like demeanor of the knowing teacher. The innovation, creativity, and democratic goals of caring, inventing, and inspiring teachers are usually de-emphasized or even implicitly discouraged.

Adult learning theorist David Kolb (1984) identified four types of learners that roughly correspond to the teaching styles described here. Most people develop preferences for a particular style of learning, he believes, as a result of events in their lives, personality differences, environmental circumstances, and education. No one style is necessarily better or worse than another, he insists. The important thing is to recognize

that differences among learners do exist. His model portrays people as dynamic learners and problem solvers who constantly respond to their environments by engaging in new experiences, reflecting on these experiences from various perspectives, creating understandings and generalizations, and applying these understandings to their lives and to their work (Sims & Sims, 1995). Bernice McCarthy (1982, 1990) has long advocated linking Kolb's work to our understanding of teaching and learning.

Integrating the wisdom of three great educators—John Dewey, Jean Piaget, and Kurt Lewin—Kolb (1984) proposes a recurring cycle of learning that includes four phases. Teacher development can be understood as a recurring cycle of growth that begins with (a) concrete experience, followed by (b) empathic reflection, (c) construction of meaning, and (d) active experimentation. As teachers progress through the learning cycle, they complement their initial teaching style with functions that have lain dormant. Integrating the styles allows them to recognize and enact a wider range of choices and decisions when facing new situations. These phases of learning are best pursued with the support of a mentor, a clinical coach, or a team of colleagues. The descriptions of the four phases of learning, which appear below, are followed by an example of a clinical coach, Ms. Jeanette Greene, engaged in the process of observing and conferring with Gloria Silverman, the caring teacher described previously.

The Phases

1. The *concrete experience* phase of learning requires the clinical coach to actively engage the teacher in problem solving. Concrete data concerning teacher and student behavior and their relationship to curriculum, standards, objectives, methods, materials, or classroom artifacts are considered. A key question for

the teacher during this phase is "How well am I really doing?"

2. During the *empathic reflection* phase of learning, the coach displays and models empathy. Multiple perspectives are considered for the purpose of gaining insight into the subjective experience of students who inhabit the teacher's classroom. A question for the teacher to answer during this phase is "What is going on here for everyone involved, both for myself and for the students?"

3. In the *construction of meaning* phase of learning, the clinical coach encourages the teacher to raise theoretical and ethical issues, form generalizations, and propose hypotheses concerning cause-and-effect relationships. The central question for the teacher during this phase is "What does all this mean?"

4. Finally, during the *active experimentation* phase of learning, the coach steps back and empowers the teacher to take action. What has been learned is applied to practical problems in the classroom, accompanied by the collection of new data. The question for the teacher that guides this phase of the cycle is "How can I do things better?" (Pajak, 2003).

The key to applying these phases of learning is to help teachers enter the cycle at the phase that comes most naturally to them. When working with a caring teacher, for example, the mentor or coach should pay special attention to developing trust and a positive climate that will contribute to collaboration and mutual learning. Beginning a conversation that asks a caring teacher to empathically reflect on the experience of his or her students in the classroom will both be non-threatening and serve to engage the teacher in the learning cycle.

The Example

Jeanette Greene, as clinical coach, has done her homework. The day prior to her observation of Gloria Silverman, who exhibits a caring style of teaching, she scheduled a brief meeting for them to discuss the plan for the lesson. Having this conversation in advance demonstrates to Gloria that Jeanette respects her as a person and initiates the learning cycle by getting Gloria to focus on her teaching. The meeting also provides an opportunity for Jeanette to learn about the strategies that Gloria intends to use and how they relate to the purposes of the lesson.

The next day, Jeanette observes Gloria, recording a descriptive narrative of what is said and done by both the teacher and students, including some notes describing the feeling-tone within the classroom. Following the observation, Jeanette conducts an analysis of the data, looking for connections between observed events and student learning that will reinforce good practices, as well as patterns that relate to the interpersonal climate in the classroom. Later in the day, Jeanette meets with Gloria for the post-observation conference. For purposes of this example, we will assume that Gloria's lesson was generally positive, but there were several issues that Jeanette felt needed attention.

The first part of the conference, which corresponds to the *concrete experience* phase of learning, would be concerned chiefly with the data—in this case, a detailed discussion of the lesson that was observed. Jeanette would show Gloria the descriptive narrative she recorded along with specific events and patterns that relate to student learning and interpersonal behavior.

As Jeanette shifts to the *empathic reflection* phase, she needs to remember that caring teachers can be very sensitive and have their feelings easily hurt. While offering generous praise for positive aspects of the lesson, Jeanette should also tactfully introduce the areas of concern and even offer some concrete suggestions for Gloria to try. Because the major question of this phase is "What is going on here for everyone involved, both the teacher and the students?"

Jeanette can tap into Gloria's intense concern for her students and ask how her actions directly affect them as she encourages Gloria to expand her teaching repertoire.

Jeanette can begin the *construction of meaning* phase of learning by restating the major issues and by inviting Gloria to propose some strategies for modifying her instruction that are consistent with her personal values and beliefs about teaching and learning. Either Jeanette or Gloria might also propose concepts or theoretical perspectives that place their conversation within a broader framework. Again, by keeping the focus on the enhanced learning of Gloria's students, Jeanette honors Gloria's caring style, while facilitating her movement through the adult learning cycle.

The *active experimentation* phase of learning necessitates Gloria's implementing the recommendations collaboratively developed in the post-observation conference. Gloria's major motivation to carry out the recommendations should be in response to the questions "How can I do things better?" and "How can I become a better teacher?" Jeanette will work with Gloria to determine the focus of a subsequent observation to be conducted after Gloria has had time to try out some of the strategies identified. She will then establish with Gloria an appropriate time for the subsequent observation and follow-up conference to discuss Gloria's degree of success in implementing these innovations.

The intention is to gently nudge teachers out of their comfort zones and change their behavior by exposing them to alternative learning environments during each of the four phases (Rainey & Kolb, 1995). When Jeanette works with an inspiring teacher such as Joanna Chakitis, *construction of meaning* would be the starting point for discussion. In this case, Jeanette could begin with a conversation about personal values and beliefs about teaching and its purposes, and then encourage Joanna to move along to *active experimentation* by posing hypotheses about specific relationships between her behavior and student outcomes (How can I do things better?), with an eye toward the *concrete experience* phase (How well am I really doing?), which then would lead to *empathic* reflection.

When embedded in the reality of classroom experience, alternative learning environments structured around the four phases can allow teachers to take greater responsibility for their own professional growth and gradually develop a full range of teaching styles. Teams of teachers might be organized in a school according to their style preferences, perhaps by grade level or subject area, where they read and share instructional materials to more finely hone their natural abilities. Individual teachers could rotate through different teams as they gain fluency with different styles, or entire teams could explore different learning environments together over a period of time. The purpose of such teams is not to "track" teachers, but to create within a school "a cooperative human community that cherishes and utilizes individual uniqueness" (Kolb, 1984, p. 62). An awareness and appreciation of different styles can be helpful, for example, for improving communication, resolving conflicts amicably, selecting team members, and identifying mediators and as a framework for professional development.

MATCHING MENTORS AND TEACHERS

Honoring different teaching styles is not a technique to be used from time to time, but instead an entirely new way of thinking about support. At best, we typically offer teachers a "take it or leave it" form of support, because we have a natural tendency to want teachers to teach their classes the way we would if we were the teacher. But if a beginning teacher is forced to adopt a style of thinking and teaching by someone who is unsympathetic or inflexible, the beginning teacher is likely to become frustrated and discouraged and may never attain his or her full potential.

In an ideal world, every beginning teacher would be matched with a supervisor who shared his or her style, at least initially, to enhance communication and minimize frustration. Another workable strategy, however, may be to select clinical coaches who are knowledgeable about and sensitive to different teaching styles and who are comfortable allowing new teachers to teach to their strengths, while still understanding when and how to help the new teacher move out of his or her comfort zone and into an exploration of other styles.

Rather than advocating a particular way of behaving or thinking, this new form of support facilitates learning by modeling alternative behaviors and patterns of thinking. At each phase of the learning cycle, the supervisor or mentor becomes a clinical coach who is (a) a colleague who models and supports conscious awareness of the personal experience of teaching, (b) an empathic listener and sounding board who facilitates an understanding of the effect that teaching has on students, (c) a knowledgeable resource who helps interpret subjective and objective information to arrive at moral and conceptual meaning, and (d) a coach who empowers teachers toward action planning and hypothesis testing.

Attending to teacher differences requires flexibility and an environment that includes mutual respect, safety, shared responsibility for learning, and an emphasis on personal growth. Such change requires the clinical coach to meet teachers where they are and then build on their strengths, rather than relying on a remedial mentality. At a minimum, clinical coaches should:

- Reflect on their own beliefs about learning, teaching, and support.
- Assess and reflect on the needs of the new teacher as learner.

- Be sensitive to preferences for perceiving and processing information, on the part of both the teacher and the coach.
- Develop and use a variety of communication strategies.
- Develop and use a range of supervisory approaches.
- Clarify the roles of supervisor and teacher.
- Begin building an inclusive community of learners that welcomes diverse learning styles and preferences.

It is true that schools are not structured for individualized supervision, but then neither are classrooms designed for individualized instruction. Honoring diverse teaching styles is worth the extra effort, we believe, because it gives teachers greater choice and voice, which contributes to the coherence of their individual goals for professional development, is consistent with other reforms and classroom activities with which teachers are already involved, and can help build a schoolwide learning community that respects differences.

REFERENCES

Kolb, D. A. (1984). *Experiential learning.* Englewood Cliffs, NJ: Prentice Hall.

McCarthy, B. (1982). Improving staff development through CBAM and 4MAT. *Educational Leadership, 40* (1): 20–25.

McCarthy, B. (1990). Using the 4MAT system to bring learning styles to schools. *Educational Leadership, 48* (2): 31–37.

Pajak, E. (2003). *Honoring diverse teaching styles: A guide for supervisors.* Alexandria, VA: Association for Supervision and Curriculum Development.

Rainey, M. A., & Kolb, D. A. (1995). Using experiential learning theory and learning styles in diversity education. In R. R. Sims & S. J. Sims (Eds.), *The importance of learning styles.* Westport, CT: Greenwood Press.

Sims, R. R., & Sims, S. J. (1995). *The importance of learning styles.* Westport, CT: Greenwood Press.

DISCUSSION QUESTIONS

1. Which best describes your own teaching style: knowing, caring, inventing, or inspiring? Why?

2. Do you agree with the authors' assessment that certain education policies are attempting to move us toward a "teacher-proof teacher"?

3. What advantages and drawbacks exist in having a variety of teaching styles represented in a school?

4. Which of the four styles of teaching identified in this chapter is most popular today? Which is most often disregarded or overlooked?

5. When you were a beginning teacher, would a system of support that honored your preferred teaching style have been helpful to you?

11 Keeping Good Teachers: Why It Matters, What Leaders Can Do

Linda Darling-Hammond

FOCUSING QUESTIONS

1. How can a comfortable learning/teaching environment be created?
2. Why is teacher attrition such a large problem?
3. How can qualified teachers be encouraged to continue teaching?
4. What types of programs may be instituted to help fight teacher attrition?
5. What are some of the reasons teachers leave the profession? Change schools?

How teachers are paid was a part of it, but overwhelmingly the things that would destroy the morale of teachers who wanted to leave were the working conditions . . . working in poor facilities, having to pay for supplies, and so on.
> —A Los Angeles teacher talking about a high-turnover school

The first-grade classroom in which I found myself five years ago had some two dozen ancient and tattered books, an incomplete curriculum, and a collection of outdated content stand-ards. But I later came to thrive in my profession because of the preparation I received in my credential program: the practice I received developing appropriate curriculum; exposure to a wide range of learning theories; training in working with non-English-speaking students and children labeled "at risk."

It is the big things, though, that continue to sustain me as a professional and give me the courage to remain and grow: my understanding of the importance of asking questions about my own practice, the collegial relationships, and my belief in my responsibility to my students and to the institution of public education.
> —A California teacher from a strong urban teacher education program

What keeps some people in teaching while others give up? What can we do to increase the holding power of the teaching profession and to create a stable, expert teaching force in all kinds of districts? Some of the answers to these questions are predictable; others are surprising. The way schools hire and the way they use their resources can make a major difference.

Keeping good teachers should be one of the most important agenda items for any school leader. Substantial research evidence suggests that well-prepared, capable teachers have the largest impact on student learning (Darling-Hammond, 2000b; Wilson, Floden, & Ferrini-Mundy, 2001). Effective teachers constitute a valuable human resource for schools—one that needs to be treasured and supported.

THE CHALLENGE OF TEACHER ATTRITION

The No Child Left Behind Act's requirement that schools staff all classrooms with "highly qualified teachers" creates a major challenge, especially for schools in inner-city and poor rural areas. The problem does not lie in the numbers of teachers available; we produce many more qualified teachers than we hire. The hard part is *keeping* the teachers we prepare.

The uphill climb to staff our schools with qualified teachers becomes steeper when teachers leave in large numbers. Since the early 1990s, the annual number of exits from teaching has surpassed the number of entrants by an increasing amount (Figure 11.1), putting pressure on the nation's hiring systems. Less than 20 percent of this attrition is due to retirement (Henke, Chen, & Geis, 2000; Ingersoll, 2001).

Steep attrition in the first few years of teaching is a longstanding problem. About one-third of new teachers leave the profession within five years. Rates of attrition from individual schools and districts include these leavers, plus movers who go from one school or district to another. Taken together, leavers and movers particularly affect schools that serve poor and minority students. Teacher turnover is 50 percent higher in high-poverty than in low-poverty schools (Ingersoll, 2001), and new teachers in urban districts exit or transfer at higher rates than their suburban counterparts do (Hanushek, Kain, & Rivkin, 1999).

High-poverty schools suffer higher rates of attrition for many reasons. Salary plays a

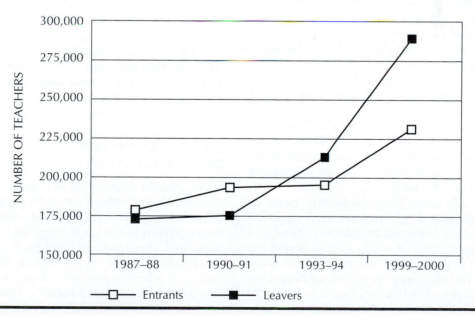

FIGURE 11.1   Trends in Teacher Entry and Attrition, 1987–2000
Source: Adapted from Ingersoll (2001).

part: Teachers in schools serving the largest concentrations of low-income students earn, at the top of the scale, one-third less than those in higher-income schools (National Center for Education Statistics [NCES], 1997). They also face fewer resources, poorer working conditions, and the stress of working with many students and families who have a wide range of needs. In addition, more teachers in these schools are underprepared and unsupported, factors that strongly influence attrition (Darling-Hammond, 2000a).

THE HEAVY COSTS OF ATTRITION

Early attrition from teaching bears enormous costs. A recent study in Texas, for example, estimated that the state's annual turnover rate of 15 percent, which includes a 40 percent turnover rate for public school teachers in their first three years, costs the state a "conservative" $329 million a year, or at least $8,000 per recruit who leaves in the first few years of teaching (Texas Center for Educational Research, 2000). High attrition means that schools must take funds urgently needed for school improvements and spend them instead in a manner that produces little long-term payoff for student learning.

Given the strong evidence that teacher effectiveness increases sharply after the first few years of teaching (Kain & Singleton, 1996), this kind of churning in the beginning teaching force reduces productivity in education overall. The education system never gets a long-term payoff from its investment in novices who leave.

In addition, large concentrations of underprepared teachers create a drain on schools' financial and human resources. In a startling number of urban schools across the United States, a large share of teachers are inexperienced, underqualified, or both. One recent estimate indicates that more than 20 percent of schools in California have more than 20 percent of their staffs teaching without credentials. These inexperienced teachers

are assigned almost exclusively to low-income schools serving students of color (Shields et al., 2001).

Such schools must continually pour money into recruitment efforts and professional support for these new teachers. Other teachers, including those who serve as mentors, are stretched thin and feel overburdened by the needs of their colleagues in addition to those of their students. Schools squander scarce resources trying to reteach the basics each year to teachers who come in with few tools and leave before they become skilled (Carroll, Reichardt, & Guarino, 2000). As a principal in one such school noted,

> Having that many new teachers on the staff at any given time meant that there was less of a knowledge base. . . . It meant there was less cohesion on the staff. It meant that every year, we had to recover ground in professional development that had already been covered and try to catch people up to where the school was heading. (cited in Darling-Hammond, 2002)

Most important, such attrition consigns a large share of students in high-turnover schools to a continual parade of ineffective teachers. Unless we develop policies to stem such attrition through better preparation, assignment, working conditions, and mentor support, we cannot meet the goal of ensuring that all students have qualified teachers.

FACTORS INFLUENCING TEACHER ATTRITION

In all schools, regardless of school wealth, student demographics, or staffing patterns, the most important resource for continuing improvement is the knowledge and skill of the school's best prepared and most committed teachers. Four major factors strongly influence whether and when teachers leave specific schools or the education profession entirely: salaries, working conditions, preparation, and mentoring support in the early years.

Salaries

Even though teachers are more altruistically motivated than are some other workers, teaching must compete with other occupations for talented college and university graduates each year. To attract its share of these graduates and to offer sufficient incentives for professional preparation, the teaching profession must be competitive in terms of wages and working conditions.

Unfortunately, teacher salaries are relatively low. Overall, teacher salaries are about 20 percent below the salaries of other professionals with comparable education and training. Data from the Bureau of Labor Statistics show that in 2001, the average teacher salary ($44,040) ranked below that of registered nurses ($48,240), accountants/auditors ($50,700), dental hygienists ($56,770), and computer programmers ($71,130) (National Commission on Teaching and America's Future [NCTAF], 2003).

Teachers are more likely to quit when they work in districts that offer lower wages and when their salaries are low relative to alternative wage opportunities, especially teachers in such high-demand fields as math and science (Brewer, 1996; Mont & Rees, 1996; Murnane & Olsen, 1990; Theobald & Gritz, 1996). Salary differences seem to matter more at the start of the teaching career (Gritz & Theobald, 1996; Hanushek et al., 1999), whereas experienced teachers appear to place more importance on working conditions (Loeb & Page, 2000).

Working Conditions

Surveys of teachers have long shown that working conditions play a major role in teachers' decisions to switch schools or leave the profession. Teachers' feelings about administrative support, resources for teaching, and teacher input into decision making are strongly related to their plans to stay in teaching and to their reasons for leaving (Darling-Hammond, 2000a; Ingersoll, 2001, 2002). High- and low-wealth schools differ greatly, on average, in the support that they give teachers. Teachers in more advantaged communities experience easier working conditions, including smaller class sizes and pupil loads and greater influence over school decisions (NCES, 1997).

The high attrition of teachers from schools serving lower-income or lower-achieving students appears to be substantially influenced by the poorer working conditions typically found in those schools. For example, a survey of California teachers (Harris, 2002) found that teachers in high-minority, low-income schools report significantly worse working conditions, including poorer facilities, less access to textbooks and supplies, fewer administrative supports, and larger class sizes. Further, teachers surveyed were significantly more likely to say that they planned to leave the school soon if the working conditions were poor.

An analysis of these California data found that serious turnover problems at the school level were influenced most by working conditions, ranging from large class sizes and poor facilities to multitrack, year-round schedules and low administrative support (Loeb, Darling-Hammond, & Luczak, 2003). Together with salaries, these factors far outweighed the demographic characteristics of students in predicting turnover at the school level. This finding suggests that working conditions should be one target for policies aimed at retaining qualified teachers in high-need schools.

Teacher Preparation

A growing body of evidence indicates that teachers who lack adequate initial preparation are more likely to leave the profession. A recent National Center for Education Statistics report found that 29 percent of new teachers who had not had any student teaching experience left within five years, compared with only 15 percent of those who had done student teaching as part of a teacher education program (Henke et al., 2000). The same study found that 49 percent of uncertified entrants left within five years, compared with only 14 percent of certified entrants. In California, the state standards board found that 40 percent of emergency-permit teachers left the profession within a year, and two-thirds never received a credential (Darling-Hammond, 2002).

In Massachusetts, nearly half of all recruits from the Massachusetts Institute for New Teachers program had left within three years (Fowler, 2002), and in Houston, Texas, the attrition rate averaged 80 percent after two years for Teach for America recruits (Raymond, Fletcher, & Luque, 2001).

Other research evidence suggests that the more training prospective teachers receive, the more likely they are to stay. For example, a longitudinal study of 11 programs found that those who graduate from five-year teacher education programs enter and stay in teaching at much higher rates than do four-year teacher education graduates from the same institutions (Andrew & Schwab, 1995). These longer, redesigned programs provide a major in a disciplinary field, as well as intensive pedagogical training and long-term student teaching. As Figure 11.2 shows, both four-year and five-year teacher education graduates enter and stay in teaching positions at higher rates than do teachers hired through alternative programs that give them only a few weeks of training (Darling-Hammond, 2000a).

Taking into account the costs to states, universities, and school districts for preparation,

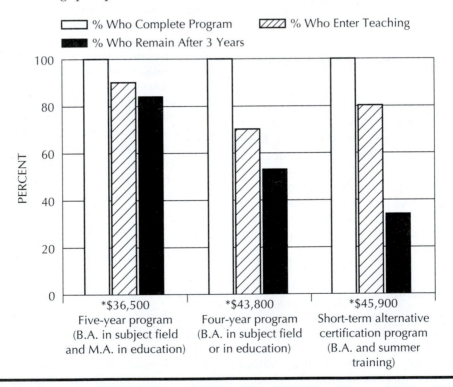

FIGURE 11.2   Average Retention Rates for Different Pathways into Teaching

*Estimated cost per third-year teacher.

Source: Darling-Hammond (2000a).

recruitment, induction, and replacement due to attrition, the actual cost of preparing a career teacher in the more intensive five-year programs is actually less than the cost of preparing a greater number of teachers in short-term programs of only a few weeks' duration. Graduates of extended five-year programs also report higher levels of satisfaction with their preparation and receive higher ratings from principals and colleagues.

In 2000, new teachers who had received training in specific aspects of teaching (for example, selection and use of instructional materials, child psychology, and learning theory), who experienced practice teaching, and who received feedback on their teaching left the profession at rates one-half as great as those who had no training in these areas (NCTAF, 2003). Similarly, first-year teachers who felt that they were well prepared for teaching were much more likely to plan to stay in teaching than those who felt poorly prepared. On such items as preparation in planning lessons, using a range of instructional methods, and assessing students, two-thirds of those reporting strong preparation intended to stay, compared with only one-third of those reporting weak preparation (see Figure 11.3). In these studies and others, graduates of teacher education programs

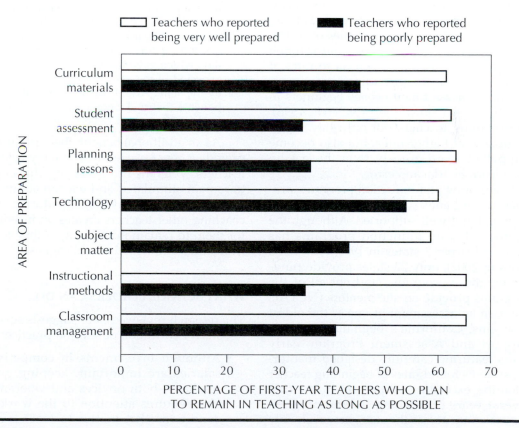

FIGURE 11.3   Effects of Preparedness on Beginning Teachers' Plans to Stay in Teaching
Source: Unpublished tabulations from Schools and Staffing Surveys, Teacher Questionnaire, 1999–2000.

felt significantly better prepared and more efficacious, and they planned to stay in teaching longer than did those entering through alternative routes or with no training (Darling-Hammond, Chung, & Frelow, 2002; NCTAF, 2003).

Mentoring Support

Schools can enhance the beneficial effects of strong initial preparation with strong induction and mentoring in the first years of teaching. A number of studies have found that well-designed mentoring programs raise retention rates for new teachers by improving their attitudes, feelings of efficacy, and instructional skills.

Such districts as Rochester, New York, and Cincinnati, Columbus, and Toledo, Ohio, have reduced attrition rates of beginning teachers by more than two-thirds (often from levels exceeding 30 percent to rates of under 5 percent) by providing expert mentors with release time to coach beginners in their first year on the job (NCTAF, 1996). These young teachers not only stay in the profession at higher rates, but also become competent more quickly than those who must learn by trial and error.

Mentoring and induction programs produce these benefits only if they are well designed and well supported. Although the number of state induction programs has increased (from 7 states in 1996–1997 to 33 states in 2002), only 22 states provide funding for these programs, and not all of the programs provide on-site mentors (NCTAF, 2003). In an assessment of one of the oldest programs, California's Beginning Teacher Support and Assessment Program, early pilots featuring carefully designed mentoring systems found rates of beginning teacher retention exceeding 90 percent in the first several years of teaching. As the program has scaled up across the state, however, only half of the districts have provided mentors

with time to coach novices in their classrooms (Shields et al., 2001).

Most effective are state induction programs that are tied to high-quality preparation. In Connecticut, for example, districts that hire beginning teachers must provide them with mentors who have received training in the state's teaching standards and its portfolio assessment system, which were introduced as part of reforms during the 1990s. These reforms also raised salaries and standards for teachers and created an assessment of teaching for professional licensure modeled after that of the National Board for Professional Teaching Standards. A beginning teacher noted of this connected system,

> One of the things that helped me a lot is that my cooperating teacher last year is a state assessor and she used to do live assessments. . . . She used to assess me using [state standards] for every lesson, every single day, which gave me a good idea of what is expected of me and how I will be assessed by the state. Also, I learned about the components that make good teaching. (Wilson, Darling-Hammond, & Berry, 2001)

As an additional benefit, these programs provide a new lease on life for many veteran teachers. Veterans need ongoing challenges to remain stimulated and excited about the profession. Many say that mentoring and coaching other teachers creates an incentive for them to remain in teaching as they learn from and share with their colleagues.

WHAT SCHOOL LEADERS CAN DO

The research reviewed here suggests several lessons for education policy and practice:

- Although investments in competitive salaries are important, keeping good teachers—both novices and veterans— also requires attention to the working conditions that matter to teachers. In addition to those often considered—class size, teaching load, and the availability of materials—key conditions include teacher participation in decision making, strong and supportive instructional leadership from principals, and collegial learning opportunities.

- Seeking out and hiring better-prepared teachers has many payoffs and savings in the long run in terms of both lower attrition and higher levels of competence.

- When the high costs of attrition are calculated, many of the strategic investments needed to keep good teachers—such as providing mentoring for beginners and creating ongoing learning and leadership challenges for veterans—actually pay for themselves to a large degree.

School systems can create a magnetic effect when they make it clear that they are committed to finding, keeping, and supporting good teachers. In urban centers, just as in suburban and rural areas, good teachers gravitate to schools where they know they will be appreciated and supported in their work. These teachers become a magnet for others who seek environments in which they can learn from their colleagues and create success for their students. Great school leaders create nurturing school environments in which accomplished teaching can flourish and grow.

REFERENCES

Andrew, M., & Schwab, R. L. (1995). Has reform in teacher education influenced teacher performance? An outcome assessment of graduates of eleven teacher education programs. *Action in Teacher Education, 17:* 43–53.

Brewer, D. J. (1996). Career paths and quit decisions: Evidence from teaching. *Journal of Labor Economics, 14*(2): 313–339.

Carroll, S., Reichardt, R., & Guarino, C. (2000). *The distribution of teachers among California's school districts and schools.* Santa Monica, CA: RAND.

Darling-Hammond, L. (2000a). *Solving the dilemmas of teacher supply, demand, and quality.* New York: National Commission on Teaching and America's Future.

Darling-Hammond, L. (2000b). Teacher quality and student achievement: A review of state policy evidence. *Educational Policy Analysis Archives, 8*(1) [Online journal]. Available: http://epaa.asu.edu/epaa/v8n1

Darling-Hammond, L. (2002). *Access to quality teaching: An analysis of inequality in California's public schools.* Stanford, CA: Stanford University.

Darling-Hammond, L., Chung, R., & Frelow, F. (2002). Variation in teacher preparation: How well do different pathways prepare teachers to teach? *Journal of Teacher Education, 53*(4): 286–302.

Fowler, C. (2002). Fast track . . . slow going? Education Policy Clearinghouse Research Brief, Vol. 2, Issue 1 [Online]. Available: http://www.edpolicy.org/publications/documents/updatev2i1.pdf

Gritz, R. M., & Theobald, N. D. (1996). The effects of school district spending priorities on length of stay in teaching. *Journal of Human Resources, 31*(3): 477–512.

Hanushek, E. A., Kain, J. F., & Rivkin, S. G. (1999). Do higher salaries buy better teachers? Working Paper No. 7082. Cambridge, MA: National Bureau of Economic Research.

Harris, P. (2002). *Survey of California teachers.* Rochester, NY: Peter Harris Research Group.

Henke, R., Chen, X., & Geis, S. (2000). *Progress through the teacher pipeline: 1992–1993 college graduates and elementary/secondary school teaching as of 1997.* Washington, DC: National Center for Education Statistics, U.S. Department of Education.

Ingersoll, R. M. (2001). Teacher turnover and teacher shortages: An organizational analysis. *American Educational Research Journal, 38*(3): 499–534.

Ingersoll, R. M. (2002). *Out-of-field teaching, educational inequality, and the organization of schools: An exploratory analysis.* Seattle, WA: Center for the Study of Teaching and Policy, University of Washington.

Kain, J. F., & Singleton, K. (1996, May/June). Equality of educational opportunity revisited. *New England Economic Review,* May issue, 87–111.

Loeb, S., Darling-Hammond, L., & Luczak, J. (2003). *Teacher turnover: The role of working conditions and salaries in recruiting and retaining teachers.* Stanford, CA: Stanford University School of Education.

Loeb, S., & Page, M. (2000). Examining the link between teacher wages and student outcomes. *Review of Economics and Statistics, 82*(3): 393–408.

Mont, D., & Rees, D. I. (1996). The influence of classroom characteristics on high school teacher turnover. *Economic Inquiry, 34:* 152–167.

Murnane, R. J., & Olsen, R. J. (1990). The effects of salaries and opportunity costs on length of stay in teaching: Evidence from North Carolina. *The Journal of Human Resources, 25*(1): 106–124.

National Center for Education Statistics (NCES). (1997). *America's teachers: Profile of a profession, 1993–1994.* Washington, DC: U.S. Department of Education.

National Commission on Teaching and America's Future (NCTAF). (1996). *What matters most: Teaching for America's future.* New York: Author.

National Commission on Teaching and America's Future (NCTAF). (2003). *No dream denied: A pledge to America's children.* New York: Author.

Raymond, M., Fletcher, S., & Luque, J. (2001). *Teach for America: An evaluation of teacher differences and student outcomes in Houston, Texas.* Stanford, CA: Center for Research on Educational Outcomes, The Hoover Institution, Stanford University.

Shields, P. M., Humphrey, D. C., Wechsler, M. E., Riel, L. M., Tiffany-Morales, J., Woodworth, K., Youg, V. M., & Price, T. (2001). *The status of the teaching profession, 2001.* Santa Cruz, CA: The Center for the Future of Teaching and Learning.

Texas Center for Educational Research. (2000). *The cost of teacher turnover.* Austin, TX: Texas State Board for Teacher Certification.

Theobald, N. D., & Gritz, R. M. (1996). The effects of school district spending priorities on the exit paths of beginning teachers leaving the district. *Economics of Education Review, 15*(1): 11–22.

Wilson, S., Darling-Hammond, L., & Berry, B. (2001). *A case of successful teaching policy: Connecticut's long-term efforts to improve teaching and learning.* Seattle, WA: Center for the Study of Teaching and Policy, University of Washington.

Wilson, S., Floden, R., & Ferrini-Mundy, J. (2001). *Teacher preparation research: Current knowledge, gaps, and recommendations.* Seattle, WA: University of Washington, Center for the Study of Teaching and Policy.

DISCUSSION QUESTIONS

1. What were the reasons that you became a teacher?
2. What are the reasons that you remain in the profession?
3. Have you ever seriously thought about leaving the classroom? Why or why not?
4. Which do you think would do most to improve teachers' effectiveness: higher salaries, better working conditions, better preparation, or better mentoring?
5. Which do you think would make the least difference?

Should teachers be held accountable for their teaching?

PRO	CON
1. Teaching should be guided by clear objectives and outcomes.	1. Many factors influence teaching and learning that have little to do with measurable objectives and outcomes.
2. Students have a right to receive a quality education, whereby professionals are held accountable for their behavior.	2. Educational accountability is a cooperative responsibility of students, teachers, parents, and taxpayers.
3. Accountability will encourage teachers to uphold high standards for instruction.	3. Teachers can provide instruction but they cannot force students to learn.
4. Feedback from accountability evaluation measures will provide teachers with information about their instructional strengths and weaknesses.	4. Mandating accountability will demoralize teachers and reduce their professional status.
5. Accountability will provide standards that are derived through consensual agreement and will offer objective assessment.	5. There will always be disagreement on who is accountable, for what, and to whom.

School District Proposes Evaluations by Students

Kamhi County School District in West Suburb had proposed to vote on implementing a change to their current teacher evaluation procedures. The proposed change would permit junior high students to participate in the evaluation process of their teachers, beginning in the spring. As a way of gathering feedback, all thirty principals were asked to complete an anonymous three-part survey. In Parts One and Two, the principals were asked to cite the advantages and disadvantages of this proposed change. In Part Three, they were asked to provide a plan that outlined how they would implement this approach in their building site if it were enacted.

While reading the survey responses, Marilyn Lauter, assistant superintendent for instruction, noticed two items, unsigned letters from both a student and a teacher, that caught her attention. The student argued that because students are consumers of teachers' services, they should have a right to have their voices heard. The teacher's letter expressed complete opposition to the proposed change, citing that students lacked the maturity to provide feedback. The teacher's letter also stated that such a change would advocate the philosophy and teaching styles of certain administrators, thereby limiting the teacher's voice. Furthermore, the letter stated that if the district voted to enact this change as policy, the teachers would probably strike. Lauter was feeling very uncomfortable with both letters, but also knew that more discussion was needed before any policy change should be taken to a vote.

Discuss the issues raised by the student and the teacher and consider the following questions:

1. Should junior high students be involved in the evaluation of their teachers? Why? Why not?
2. If you were the assistant superintendent for instruction, how would you handle this situation?
3. What other approaches might have been used to elicit feedback from the teachers, parents, and students concerning the proposed policy change to the teacher evaluation process?
4. In what ways might students' evaluations of teachers affect their instruction or your own instruction?
5. What evidence does research provide about the ability of junior high students to evaluate teachers?
6. How might teachers and parents in your school district react to this proposed policy change in teacher evaluation procedures?

PART THREE

Curriculum and Learning

What is the relationship between learning and curriculum? What role does active participation play in student achievement? To what extent are higher-order thinking, creativity, and moral education emphasized in curriculum delivery? How has standardized testing influenced student confidence? What is the role of character education in students' learning experiences?

In Chapter 12, Theodore R. Sizer and Nancy Faust Sizer argue that moral or character education is an intellectual endeavor that must allow students opportunities to act and think. Students should be encouraged to deal with important and relevant ideas, even when the outcome of their grappling with difficult situations is uncertain.

Next, in Chapter 13, Robert Sternberg and Todd Lubart discuss the factors that characterize creative thinking. The authors describe the type of instruction that fosters creative thinking. They suggest that students should be given more responsibility for selecting the type of problems that they investigate, rather than relying on teacher-constructed problems. In Chapter 14, Lawrence Kohlberg describes how moral education promotes the aims of education. He compares the cognitive-developmental approach with other approaches to moral education. Chester Finn then, in Chapter 15, presents several arguments against providing universal prekindergarten education in the United States. Adding a publicly financed program would be costly and unnecessary, he suggests, and the money that would have been spent on universal prekindergarten should instead be spent on innovation and experimentation to discover what must be done to make pre-K programs succeed.

In Chapter 16, Norman Eng explains how an increased demand for high-level cognitive skills and demographic changes in the United States will require an increased investment in academically high-potential students, particularly in the STEM fields. He calls for a differentiated approach to education policy that offers multiple pathways for student success as the fairest way to foster the abilities and interests of a demographically diverse student population while addressing the issue of American economic competitiveness. Finally, in Chapter 17,

Veronica Boix Mansilla and Howard Gardner call on teachers to teach the distinct ways of thinking that are represented in the various disciplines, rather than simply requiring students to simply memorized fact, formulas, and figures. Practical suggestions for stimulating student thinking in the classroom are offered.

12 Grappling

Theodore R. Sizer
Nancy Faust Sizer

FOCUSING QUESTIONS

1. Why should teachers be concerned with moral or character education?
2. How can teachers involve students more actively in their learning?
3. Why is it important for students to think deeply about what they learn?
4. What are the characteristics of a demanding curriculum?
5. What role should values play in student learning?

School is a frustration for Carl. He just can't see the good it does him. Even more, he can't see the good he does it. In social studies, the teacher tells him which U.S. presidents were the greatest. At least she also tells him exactly why. His parents say he should be grateful for that; they only got to memorize the list, never to hear the explanations, so it's more interesting to think about. Still, he'd like to have the chance to tell his teacher why he thinks a president who manages to avoid a war is as good as one who leads a nation in a war.

In math, he's told that there is one right answer and one way to get to that right answer. In English, he's told that the music lyrics he dotes on are inferior poetry. Even when he is asked to write, he's told how many paragraphs he should use to get his ideas across to "the reader." Which reader? Wouldn't it matter who he or she was?

And when his teacher takes his class to the computer room only to find a substitute there who doesn't know how to run the new machines, Carl is not allowed to read the computer manual so that he can help get the class started. He tries to argue that he's done this before at home and even at school and that he and his classmates need the time in the lab if they are to finish their projects. But he gets a little too near to rudeness, and the teacher, visibly upset, cuts him off. "I don't know what's happened to kids these days," she says to us as she turns the class back toward her classroom to wait out the period. "They're so irresponsible."

In fact, this last situation requires some deeper consideration. There is, of course, no guarantee that Carl could have figured out how to run the new machines and thus saved the time for his classmates and his teacher. It's hard to predict how much time his grappling would have taken or what its outcome would have been. The problem could have been "solved" on a superficial level, or it might have needed a lot more work. Carl's energy might have given out; he might even have damaged the equipment. Nor is there any excuse for the rudeness that those who know more than others about technology or any other subjects often display.

Still, Carl had been treated as if he were an empty vessel, as if his skills and his opinions were of no value to those around him. In the computer room, he was told that there was nothing that he or anyone else could do. Instead, they were all to go back to their classroom and act as if nothing had happened. The result was an intellectual and a moral vacuum.

Why does an intellectual vacuum so often lead to a moral one as well? Schools exist for children, but children are often seen as the school's clients, as its powerless people. They are told that they are in school not because of what they know but because of what they don't know. All over the world, powerless people lose the instinct to help, because they are so often rebuffed. Yet, even if he had ultimately been unsuccessful, struggling with the computer manual would have been a good use of Carl's mind. He would have been fulfilling the real purpose of schooling: to equip himself to be of use both to himself and to others. He would have used what he already knew to reach out and learn more about how computers work. And he would have put himself on the line in a good cause.

Putting oneself on the line may be valuable, but it invites the kind of criticism that is rarely applied to the young. Raising the young is exquisitely tricky business. A fiftyish father grumped to us about his daughter who was just graduating from high school. The young woman had announced to her parents that she was determined to become a writer. "A writer?" her dad snorted to us. "What would she write about? She doesn't know anything."

The young woman was full of passion. She liked to string words out, playing with them. She wrote exclusively about her own world, casting it as a revelation. She labored hard in English courses and had had several intense pieces published in the school's literary magazine. She had skimmed over her other courses, doing only the minimum. Nonetheless, she was an honors student. She surely would get a book award at graduation and deservedly so.

And yet her dad had a telling point. Behind his daughter's enthusiasms was glibness. Her skill was admirable, and her joy in the application of that skill was palpable. Her ability to describe her own thoughts and feelings was unusual. But the young woman did not even know that she knew relatively little, that there was important knowledge that required a broader context than her own life.

The father, caught in the practical demands of earning a living and tired of years of teenage hubris, is understandably cautious. But if he is smart, he will keep his concerns to himself. The energy, even the presumption, of the young writer should not be reined in just because so much of it is based on self-absorption and naïveté. Instead, in taking herself seriously and wanting to write for an ever-widening audience, she will be motivated to take an increased interest in the ways of the world. Time will tell.

In case after case, this is how we have seen growing up work. A student's hope and sense of agency often are dependent on her belief that there is something she can do that is valued by others. Not just other kids, but adults as well. And not empty "self-esteem building activities," but the outcome of her best efforts, in which she has real confidence. From that point on, talent intertwines constantly with content, as the student challenges herself to perform at higher levels for a broader audience.

And so it is with learning the habits of civil behavior. The skills are important: showing restraint; being willing to listen;

having empathy; feeling responsible for something and some people beyond oneself and one's personal coterie of friends; being nice; getting along in one's daily interactions.

But there must be more. Most interactions in life are complex; more than talent and good habits are needed to address them well. Few are mastered by merely applying a slogan such as "Just say no." Context is critical, if not crucial. The thoughts and resultant actions of, say, a Polish-German day laborer working near Auschwitz in 1944, a person who sees the full trains come and the empty trains go, might be appreciably different from the conclusions about the Holocaust reached by an outraged American teenager sitting in an unthreatened high school classroom 50 years later. It will help the teenager absorb the complexity of the situation if he can reflect as if from the shoes of the laborer, not necessarily to agree, but to empathize and to understand. In this Second World War moment there is powerful stuff: the particulars of a situation, in necessarily exquisite and painful detail. That stuff, if well and carefully considered, provides the perspective that is ultimately the heart of truly moral decisions. Educators call this "content."

The habits of civil behavior can do much to bring safety to a school's halls. But the meanings of civil behavior are much tougher to present. They transcend one's immediate environment. When fully and painstakingly constructed, they provide a distant mirror, the meaning of one's immediate condition viewed against a sweep of human and environmental experience, past and present.

One has to grapple with those meanings. If not, "behavior" is reduced to glib catchwords that provoke little more than periodic puffs of self-righteousness. A curriculum rich in content will teach young people that important matters of sensitive living have everything to do with hard, substantive, and often agonizingly painful thought. The students will write plays or stories or imagined memoirs that will help them get at the considerations inside that hypothetical day laborer's head.

Grappling is necessarily a balancing act. One tries to do what one has never done before and so learns more about what one wants to do. The reader's sense of his own power is built up by letting him try to understand the computer manual so the class can go forward. The writer's humility and appreciation of context are built up by asking her to take on another's complex identity before she tries to write about it. Each task is doable, but difficult; each requires that the student put him- or herself firmly on the line.

The first step in creating such a demanding curriculum is to believe that it can be done. Wise schoolpeople and parents should not underestimate the power that they can find in young minds, bodies, and hearts. Recently the newspapers reported that an 11-year-old took her younger cousin on a three-hour drive in the family car, crossing state lines, navigating effectively, looking for an uncle but settling for an aunt. Everyone who commented on the incident remarked on how naughty these children were, how neglectful the mother was who had left them and the keys in the car while she went to an exercise salon, how unobservant the gas station attendant was who sold them gas without noticing how young they were. No one wondered at the sheer competence lurking like a shadow underneath the youngsters' foolishness.

We're selling our children short when we believe that grappling is beyond them. In fact, most of them are engaging in dilemmas of intense seriousness while we're looking the other way. Most teenagers have watched one or another substance be abused, heard adults who are important to them treat each other harshly, and wondered why so many are poor in a rich country. Many have been mugged figuratively and some literally. The teenage mother or caregiver has been a fixture for centuries. Most modern wars have been fought (albeit neither started nor led) by teenage males. To treat adolescents as delicate flowers unable to act and think is a costly pretense, as patronizing as it is wasteful. Young people can do things, and they do do things now. Older folk should accept that fact and labor hard to provide the perspective that can affect, in a principled manner, the way that young people inform those actions that, willy-nilly, they will take.

Adolescents are no different from the rest of us. They resist mandates issued from on high, and most of them won't be forced into good habits. But they are willing to talk about moral choices, and they can decide that some courses of action are better than others. In fact, they are eager to formulate opinions on these matters, as long as they are trusted to take their time and examine their assumptions as carefully as they can. They can do this in school, by considering examples—some literary, some historical, some scientific—that are interesting and nuanced and in which a human must choose between possible actions. When they work it all through in a variety of assignments, they learn much about literature and history and about the human condition and the multiple ways in which it might develop. All of this considering is what helps the teenager deepen his or her understanding of values and thus construct a personal moral code. This last and most private step in the process is the most important one. Finally, the test of a good school is how its students behave when no one is looking, how they are in the mall as well as in the school's classrooms and corridors.

Most teachers are fond of the word "engagement," because it means that the students are really taking an interest in the work that the teacher has designed for them. Grappling, however, goes one step further. It presumes that the student has something to add to the story. Either hypothetically or actually, the student is asked to offer his or her input.

The input may be in the form of added information. High school students who are analyzing the racial and ethnic disagreements in their city may be asked to research immigration patterns, previous political relationships, or a number of other factors in order to get a clearer picture of what is in the minds of those who are involved in contemporary problems. The resultant information can be scrutinized carefully by their classmates, by their teacher, and by outside groups, both for the way it was gathered and for what it means. If it was gathered in the traditional ways of research, it can reinforce habits that are basically good ones: honesty, freedom from bias, the use of orderly procedures, and so forth. If it was gathered in unconventional ways, such as through chats with one's highly prejudiced uncle, those ways can be analyzed and even justified, at least on certain grounds. Once gathered, the research can be presented in graphs and photographs, essays and statistics, with much discussion of the way each format contributes to an overall understanding of the situation.

The students' input may also be in the form of opinion. Most high school students spend a lot of time considering such matters as pushing and shoving or even more violent activities and whether they are dangerous or are an inevitable part of life. They think about deterrence: when and how much a threatened punishment keeps them from doing something. They think about authority and about what its best and worst uses ought to be. They think about ethnicity and about how much it influences a person's overall approach to things. They question the religion that has been important to their family, the grandmother who believes that they ought to write thank-you notes, and the teacher who takes offense at sloppy work. They are at an unsettled time in their lives, while the many different thoughts they are having start to form themselves into opinions that they may keep all their lives.

We should be grateful for their confusion: It is part of life to think for oneself, and nature needs that little blip between generations. We can learn to live with and even harness (though that may be a "bad word" and suggest a "restrictive" concept) the energy of teenagers. The thoughts that are roiling around in the students' heads should be invited out and put to work. They should be applied to schoolwork, the better to develop and grow in the sunlight, the better to be made subject to others' questions.

Schoolwork is about violence and deterrence and authority and tradition and behavior. We should invite the students' input into the subject of whether the Civil War could have been avoided, of whether the southern states' desire to secede from the Union was legitimate self-determination or a dangerous threat to the very concept of democracy. School yard tensions and even family regroupings are not precisely analogous to the Civil War, of course. But the students' opinions will be refined and strengthened not by avoiding such analogies but by pressing to make them more accurate and appropriate. Insisting that the students tackle important and demonstrably relevant ideas, such as the meaning of justice, can be a tonic. It is one very important reason to be in school. And the students want more of it.

Text-based discussions are also amenable to grappling. For all sorts of reasons, many contemporary high school students read Harper Lee's *To Kill a Mockingbird*, a story of race, guilt, innocence, and courage set in the American South of the 1930s. The story shows the importance of evidence and argument. It portrays raw courage and the toughness of honesty. It is the sort of tale that usually provokes moral outrage and with that outrage the attention and engagement of high school students.

The litany of good questions that can arise is endless. To ponder them is to wrestle with specific and carefully described ideas that are freighted with values. Teachers can catch the heat that arises from the careful discussion of issues such as those raised by *To Kill a Mockingbird* and use it to deepen the talk, to broaden the questions, and to demand that the students use the text to support their arguments. Circling back over familiar ground, asking new sorts of questions about that ground, and looking for every scrap of data are necessary steps in building the habit of thoughtful grappling. A student who grapples is made aware of this complexity. And if there is an explicit assumption on the part of the school and its teachers that this sort of grappling is as worthy as it is complex, the student may get into the habit of the struggle.

When the students stick to a text such as *To Kill a Mockingbird* long enough to understand the abstractions in it, they are likely to apply that understanding to the next text they encounter. The exercise can thus lead a class into many places, with the depth of study growing as the interest deepens. Careful grappling is its own reward; it leads to further grappling.

Fiction is particularly useful in this kind of discussion because it gets the students outside themselves. It provides a new and unfamiliar setting to play out enduring issues and thus avoids the pressures of the immediate. The sense of suspense in the narrative draws in even those students who do not feel comfortable in moral discussions. History itself is stories, and the line between fiction and fact is a necessarily fuzzy one when it comes to the consideration of moral dilemmas. Questions about who writes history and why, about the role of ideas and of personality in communities, and about the varied and changing nature of government also are subject to debate. In science, there are many prominent moral questions in need of discussion, both on the basis of scientific evidence and on the basis of belief. One of the most important technological questions in our time is clearly "Just because we can do something, should we?" This is a particularly pressing question for adolescents. John F. Kennedy thought the answer was yes when it came to exploring space. The issues of developing and testing nuclear weapons, cloning animals and humans, and reaching children through the Internet, however, may lead to different answers.

One difference between grappling and other forms of learning is that, when the questions become the student's own, so do the answers. When simple curiosity about the birds visiting a winter feeder leads to questions about territory, sharing, cruelty, and the relationship between animals and humans, the process becomes a reality check. What is the evidence that some birds mate for life? That they return to the same feeder? How does this finding connect with other characteristics of birds? Is it real? Does it matter? If it matters, how am I affected? And finally and most important, How should I respond or behave? Should "last year's birds" have precedence over newcomers? Who am I to decide such things?

As adults, we must really be interested in what the students' "answers" are. If they are shallow, if they are biased, the teacher needs to help students develop them further but not necessarily replace them neatly with the teacher's own conclusions. The students may sense the teacher's personal views and be greatly influenced by them. However, they will also see that issues of weight are complex and that there are interpretations about which thoughtful, decent people can differ.

Few issues of value can be persuasively reduced to sharply painted absolutes. Even the dictum "Thou shalt not kill," for example, is a conflicted matter for those in the armed services or those in the part of the criminal justice system charged with carrying out legal executions. Depending on one's definition of when life begins, the issue of killing may arise in connection with abortion. There are few easy answers to central moral concerns. This is why young people must be given practice in grappling with them in as informed and principled a manner as possible.

In addition to providing additional information and offering informed opinion, a third kind of input that students can provide is their skills. Why should the local malls be the only agencies that know how to appreciate responsible teenagers? Besides the ability to do research, students have mathematical, artistic, writing, and speaking skills that can be valued in a complex world. Many high schools now have peer mediation programs, and students are learning much about identifying one another's needs and interests and finding common ground. These skills can be applied to a wider arena: at first in hypothetical role plays and under close supervision, but later with a somewhat more autonomous structure and in real situations, such as student-run businesses that raise money for the poor.

Unfortunately, the sort of grappling described here is all too rare in U.S. high schools. Few teachers have been offered the incentives or provided the support necessary to gain a deep grasp of their subjects. But a good deal of knowledge and authority on the teacher's part is usually required to teach in the interrogatory manner necessary to provoke the students to grapple. The larger the question, the more likely that the students will grow frustrated, at least at first. Only a confident coach can help his or her students move through that frustration to a greater clarity. It is much easier to give a lecture on the three causes of the French Revolution than to question the nature of revolution itself. The conventional metaphor for education is one of delivery, not of constructive, generative provocation. To teach grappling, teachers have to model it, which is difficult to do in a typical high school.

There are other factors as well. Given the sweeping nature of high school curricula—a bit of this and much of that, Cleopatra to Clinton, the history of China in two weeks, all branches of biology in a year—few schools are able to allow the time necessary for students to grapple. As long as the end result of high school is measured in "coverage" and as long as "coverage" is assessed by measuring the student's memory, there will be no time for students' own questions. Inquisitiveness, skepticism, and imagination are rarely priorities for state "curriculum frameworks" or, in all too many cases, for standardized tests. Indeed, the spiraling of ideas, the testing and retesting and testing again of hypotheses, the unpredictability of any one class, the messiness of this kind of inquiry will put the bravest and most effective teachers' students at a certain kind of short-term risk.

Another factor concerns deportment. High schools are such crowded places that certain norms seem only sensible. One is that people should listen to one another talk, which requires that only one person talk at a time. Most often, that person is the teacher, toward whom most students give the greatest respect. In many classrooms, the teacher has to shut a student up in order to open him up—that is, in order to give him the time to digest what is being said by the teacher or by other students.

In a classroom that puts a premium on developing ideas, everybody's hand would be up. No matter how pleased a teacher might be by this level of engagement, by the time it was any one student's turn to speak, any sense of coherence would be lost. Loosening up this structure by working in groups or by tolerating a certain amount of chaos would upset a lot of people. Some would be those students inside the classroom who need a degree of order and predictability to learn or who get intimidated by their classmates' ideas or even by their confidence. Other upset people might well be the folks who walk the school's halls. From such a distance, it is hard to tell the difference between excitement and cheekiness. Sometimes, it's the teacher whose initial convictions about the best kind of learning have been shaken or have put him on the line. He might be "grappling" with finding a new job by next spring.

And finally, many schools are afraid of the political ramifications of any sort of teaching that brings to the surface matters of value, matters that are often controversial and thus threatening. What if Susanna refuses to go to church on Sunday because she's offended by what she learned about abuses in the medieval church? What if Carlos can't sleep because he's upset about a predicted rise in the sun's temperature? What if Derek starts lecturing his parents about their smoking? If students take their education into their own hearts and begin to act according to their new discoveries, the dislocations in their own and their families' lives may well be difficult. The students will inevitably make some mistakes, and the school will be a convenient scapegoat.

Grappling with the tough issues is hard work. No matter how smart they sound, most students are new to the game of dealing with controversy. Recently, we observed a class that was learning about the Bill of Rights by discussing a case that involved downloading pornography, how much privacy a student should expect in school, who should decide what reasonable proof is, who has responsibility for the safety of students, and a host of other issues. One couldn't help but be struck not just by the students' commitment to the discussion but also by their skill at handling complex concepts, at looking at the background of the case, at imagining outcomes had the case been handled differently. One young man had an opinion on nearly every aspect; he was very well spoken and seemed confident and persuasive. Definitely a lawyer and a good one in the making, we thought. At the end of the class, though, he jumped up and, with a big smile, announced, "But what do we know? We're only children."

This young man wasn't undercutting the sophistication that he'd demonstrated so convincingly earlier. Indeed, he was adding to it by admitting that he had more that he needed to think about, more that he needed to learn. His perspective about his own place in life made it seem even more important to let him begin such discussions in school.

Few people in high schools believe that all young people are both capable of this level of work and ready to do it. Thus a self-fulfilling prophecy of lack of interest is at work. In matters such as the recent controversy over a national history curriculum, for example, adults with one perspective argued with adults with another perspective. The questions they argued over are important and enduring ones, such as how the experiences of Native Americans or African slaves or European immigrants should be presented. Much energy was being expended, and all these adults were honorable people trying to portray a complicated legacy in as fair and compelling a way as possible. They were mindful of the students they were teaching, in that they agreed that younger students should have a simpler and more complacent version of history than older ones. Teachers, too, try to design their lessons so carefully and to teach them so skillfully that there won't be any chance that they will misinform, or unnecessarily hurt, their students.

What these concerned adults leave out, however, is the dimension that each learner has to add to the material in order really to carry it in his or her head. There has to be a shred of interest present already on which the talented teacher can build. If the interest is based on a shared racial identity, a shared economic identity, or a shared psychological identity (such as seventh graders often feel with the rebellious American colonists struggling to get out from under a "mother country"), so be it. Building on these existing interests seems more important than presenting each unit in the recommended number of days.

When the external tests are administered, however, the honest grappling that the teacher has encouraged may end up harming her students. Other teachers may have prepared their students better for the tests by sticking to the prescribed curriculum, which "covered" immigration and railroad regulation in the same number of days. However, by emphasizing accuracy, by which they mean the ability to sort through semi-right clues to get to the all-right answer on a machine-graded test to the exclusion of all other aspects of the material, those teachers (and the principals and parents who are flogging them to get the test scores up) are neglecting an important part of the process.

The material that stays in a student's head only until the test will never make it into his or her outlook. When it is in a student's outlook—when he thinks, for example, of the losses and gains that immigration brought to those who engaged in it, or when she compares the immigration experience with a recent move that her family made—it gains moral importance.

When a student has gotten his juices up in some way, he will think about such material outside of school, argue about it at the dinner table, take a book about it out of the library, choose the topic for his next paper. Accuracy will start to matter, but only if it follows engagement, only if the student has put himself on the line. Only then will he care if he gets his dates right or if he finds himself changing his interpretation of something. He has started to grapple with a question of importance to him, and it may well emerge into a lifelong interest and a lifelong habit.

Few schools place a high value on questioning, even though it is the habit that is most likely to lead to consequential scholarship and responsible adulthood. Schools are such crowded places: crowded not only with restless bodies but with parents' dreams for their children. No wonder so much emphasis is put on order. But order discourages questioning. Surrounded by the disorderliness of too many children, most teachers find themselves waiting for 3 p.m., waiting for Friday, and waiting for vacation, all with a longing bordering on obsession, which makes them think in short-run rather than in long-run terms. In such a context, questions look messy and even rude. Besides, the students' own questions will take a lot more time to answer than the teachers' questions will, because the answers to most teachers' questions can be found on a page in the textbook. Better, most school systems seem to say, to present a watery diet of philosophical or psychological absolutes as a way to avoid conflict while appearing to attend to students' education in matters of value.

But more and more schoolpeople see things differently. They recognize that for humans the moral is embedded in the intellectual, that thinking hard by grappling in an informed and careful way is the most likely route to a principled and constructive life. The good person has both passion and restraint, respect for evidence and patience when evidence is not readily at hand.

These matters can be deeply embedded in the full academic curriculum. "Moral" or "character" education is neither a discrete curriculum added as an afterthought nor an unreflective activity, such as "community service," that has never been probed for its meaning. Truly moral education is an intellectual undertaking that must infuse the entire school. And it must be led by adults who know things, who themselves are regular grapplers with all the work and messiness and confusion that rich content entails.

DISCUSSION QUESTIONS

1. How do a teacher's concerns about moral or character education influence his or her instruction?
2. Why is grappling an important part of learning?
3. Is confusion a valuable or unavoidable step in the learning process?
4. What can adults do to provide a learning environment that challenges students to grapple?
5. Why is it important for moral education to infuse an entire school?

13 Creating Creative Minds

ROBERT J. STERNBERG
TODD I. LUBART

FOCUSING QUESTIONS

1. How are intelligence and creativity related?
2. What is the relationship between knowledge and creativity?
3. How are intellectual styles related to creativity?
4. What are the advantages and disadvantages of giving students the responsibility for selecting problems they would like to solve?
5. What distinguishes creative thinking and ordinary thinking?
6. How can the use of ill-structured problems help students think insightfully?
7. How do the norms of a school's environment influence the development of creativity?

Creativity is not simply inborn. On the contrary, schooling can create creative minds—though it often doesn't. To create creativity, we need to understand the resources on which it draws and to determine how we can help children develop these resources. In particular, we need to know how we can invest in our children's futures by helping them invest in their own creative endeavors.

We propose an "investment theory of creativity."[1] The basic notion underlying our theory is that, when making any kind of investment, including creative investment, people should "buy low and sell high." In other words, the greatest creative contributions can generally be made in areas or with ideas that at a given time are undervalued. Perhaps people in general have not yet realized the importance of certain ideas, and hence there is a potential for making significant advances. The more in favor an idea is, the less potential there is for it to appreciate in value, because the idea is already valued.

A theory of creativity needs to account for how people can generate or recognize undervalued ideas. It also needs to specify who will actually pursue these undervalued ideas rather than join the crowd and make contributions that, while of some value, are unlikely to turn around our existing ways of thinking. Such a theory will enable us and our children to invest in a creative future.[2] As is sometimes said, nothing is as practical as a good theory.

We hold that developing creativity in children—and in adults—involves teaching them to use six resources: intelligence, knowledge, intellectual style, personality, motivation, and environmental context. Consider each of these resources in turn.

INTELLIGENCE

Two main aspects of intelligence are relevant to creativity. These aspects, based on the triarchic theory of human intelligence, are the ability to define and redefine problems and the ability to think insightfully.[3]

Problem Definition and Redefinition

Major creative innovations often involve seeing an old problem in a new way. For example, Albert Einstein redefined the field of physics by proposing the theory of relativity; Jean Piaget redefined the field of cognitive development by conceiving of the child as a scientist; Pablo Picasso redefined the field of art through his cubist perspective on the world.

In order to *re*define a problem, a student has to have the option of defining a problem in the first place. Only rarely do schools give students this luxury. Tests typically pose the problems that students are to solve. And if a student's way of seeing a problem is different from that of the test constructor, the student is simply marked wrong. Similarly, teachers typically structure their classes so that they, not the students, set the problems to be solved. Of course, textbooks work the same way. Even when papers or projects are assigned, teachers often specify the topics. Some teachers, who view themselves as more flexible, allow students to define problems for themselves. These same teachers may then proceed to mark students down when students' definitions of problems do not correspond to their own.

In the "thinking-skills movement," we frequently hear of the need for schools to emphasize more heavily the teaching of problem-solving skills. Educators are then pleased when students do not merely memorize facts but rather use the facts to solve problems. Certainly, there is much to be said for a problem-solving approach to education. But we need to recognize that creative individuals are often most renowned not for solving problems, but for posing them. It is not so much that they have found the "right" answers (often there are none); rather, they have asked the right questions—they recognized significant and substantial problems and chose to address them. One only has to open almost any professional journal to find articles that are the fruit of good problem solving on bad—or at least fairly inconsequential—problems.

If we are to turn schooling around and emphasize creative definition and redefinition of problems, we need to give our students some of the control we teachers typically maintain. Students need to take more responsibility for the problems they choose to solve, and we need to take less. The students will make mistakes and attempt to solve inconsequential or even wrongly posed problems. But they learn from their mistakes, and if we do not give them the opportunity to make mistakes, they will have no mistakes to learn from. Instead of almost always giving children the problems, we more often need to let them find the problems that they are to solve. We need to help them develop their skills in defining and redefining problems, not just in solving them.

Insight Skills

Insight skills are involved when people perceive a high-quality solution to an ill-structured problem to which the solution is not obvious. Being truly creative involves "buying low"—that is, picking up on an idea that is out of favor. But just picking up on any idea that is out of favor is not sufficient. Insight is involved in spotting the *good* ideas. We have proposed a theory of insight whereby insights are of three kinds.[4]

The first kind of insight involves seeing things in a stream of inputs that most people would not see. In other words, in the midst of a stream of mostly irrelevant information, an individual is able to zero in on particularly relevant information for his or her purposes. For example, the insightful reader observes clues to an author's meaning that others may miss. An insightful writer is often one whose observations about human behavior, as revealed through writing, go beyond those of the rest of us.

The second kind of insight involves seeing how to combine disparate pieces of information whose connection is nonobvious and usually elusive. For example, proving mathematical theorems requires seeing how to fit together various axioms and theorems into a coherent proof. Interpreting data from a scientific experiment often involves making sense of seemingly disparate pieces of information.

The third kind of insight involves seeing the nonobvious relevance of old information to a new problem. Creative analogies and metaphors are representative of this kind of insight. For example, the student of history comes to see how understanding events of long ago can help us understand certain events in the present. A scientist might recall a problem from the past that was solved by using a certain methodology and apply this methodology to a current scientific problem.

Problems requiring insightful solution are almost always ill-structured; that is, there are no readily available paths to solution. Rather, much of the difficulty in solving the problem is figuring out what the steps toward solution might be. For example, when James Watson and Francis Crick sought to find the structure of DNA, the nature of the problem was clear. The way in which to solve it was not clear at all.

Problems presented in schools, however, are usually well structured; that is, there is a clear path—or several paths—to a prompt and expedient solution. In standardized tests, for example, there is always a path that guarantees a "correct" solution. The examinee's problem is, in large part, to find that guaranteed path. Similarly, textbook problems are often posed so that there can be an answer key for the teacher that gives the "correct" answers. Problems such as these are unlikely to require insightful thinking. One ends up trying to "psych out" the thought processes of the person who formulated the problem, rather than to generate one's own insightful thought processes.

While not exclusively limited to ill-structured problems, creative innovations tend to address such problems—not the well-structured ones that we typically use in school settings. If we want students to think insightfully, we need to give them opportunities to do so by increasing our use of ill-structured problems that allow insightful thinking. Project work is excellent in this regard, for it requires students not only to solve problems but also to structure the problems for themselves.

KNOWLEDGE

In order to make a creative contribution to a field of knowledge, one must, of course, have knowledge of that field. Without such knowledge, one risks rediscovering what is already known. Without knowledge of the field, it is also difficult for an individual to assess the problems in the field and to judge which are important. Indeed, during the past decade or so, an important emphasis in psychology has been on the importance of knowledge of expertise.

Schools can scarcely be faulted for making insufficient efforts to impart knowledge. Indeed, that seems to be their main function. Yet we have two reservations about the extent to which the knowledge they impart is likely to lead to creativity.

First, there is a difference between knowledge and usable knowledge. Knowledge can be learned in a way that renders it inert. Knowledge may be stored in the brain, but an individual may nonetheless be unable to use it. For example, almost every college undergraduate who majors in psychology takes a course in statistics as a part of that major. Yet very few undergraduates who have taken statistics are able to use what they have learned in the design and analysis of scientific experiments. (At the secondary level, many physics and chemistry students are unable to use basic algebra when they need to apply it.) Undergraduates in psychology do fine as long as they are given highly structured problems in which it is obvious which statistical technique applies. But they have trouble when they have to figure out which technique to apply and when to apply it. The context in which they acquired their knowledge is so different from the context in which they must use it that their knowledge is simply unavailable.

Our experience with knowledge learned in statistics courses is, we believe, the rule rather than the exception. Students do not generally learn knowledge in a way that renders it useful to them. To the contrary, they are likely to forget much of what they learn soon after they are tested on it. We have all had the experience of studying for an exam and then quickly forgetting what we studied. The information was learned in such a way as to make it useful in the context of a structured exam; once the exam is finished, so is that use of the knowledge.

Our second reservation about the knowledge that schools typically impart is that students are not taught in a way that makes clear to them why the information they are learning is important. Students do much better in learning if they believe that they can use what they learn. Foreign language provides a good example. People who need to use a foreign language learn it. Those who don't need it rarely retain much of it. Unless we show students why what they are learning should matter to them, we cannot expect them to retain what they are taught. Unfortunately, we often don't really know ourselves how students might use what we are teaching them. And if we don't know, how can we expect them to?

We also need to be concerned about the trade-off that can develop between knowledge and flexibility. We have suggested that increased expertise in terms of knowledge in a given domain often comes at the expense of flexibility in that domain.[5] We can become so automatic about the way we do certain things that we lose sight of the possibility of other ways. We can become entrenched and have trouble going beyond our very comfortable perspective on things. Because creativity requires one to view things flexibly, there is a danger that, with increasing knowledge, one will lose creativity by losing the ability to think flexibly about the domain in which one works. We need to recognize that sometimes students see things that we do not see—that they may have insights we have not had (and that initially we may not even recognize as insights). Teachers who have been doing the same thing year after year can become so self-satisfied and happy with the way they do things that they are closed to new ways of doing these things. They are unwilling to "buy low"—to try an idea that is different from those they have favored in the past.

On the one hand, we do not wish to underemphasize the importance of knowledge to creativity. On the other hand, we cannot overemphasize the importance of usable knowledge that does not undermine flexibility. Often we need to adopt the maintenance of flexibility as a goal to be achieved self-consciously. We might go to in-service training sessions, read new kinds of books, learn about a new domain of knowledge, seek to learn from our students, or whatever. If we want students to be creative, we have to model creativity for them, and we won't be able to do that if we seek to turn students' minds into safe-deposit boxes in which to store our assorted and often undigested bits of knowledge.

INTELLECTUAL STYLES

Intellectual styles are the ways in which people choose to use or exploit their intelligence as well as their knowledge. Thus intellectual styles concern not abilities, but how these abilities and the knowledge acquired through them are used in day-to-day interactions with the environment.

Elsewhere, one of the authors has presented details of a theory of intellectual styles based on a notion of "mental self-government."[6] Hence, we need not cover the theory in detail here. The basic idea is that people need to govern themselves mentally and that styles provide them with ways to do so. The ways in which people govern themselves are internal mirrors of the kinds of government we see in the external world.

Creative people are likely to be those with a legislative proclivity. A legislative individual is someone who enjoys formulating problems and creating new systems of rules and new ways of seeing things. Such a person is in contrast to an individual with an executive style: someone who likes implementing the systems, rules, and tasks of others. Both differ from an individual with a judicial style: someone who enjoys evaluating people, things, and rules. Thus the creative person not only has the ability to see things in new ways but likes to do so. The creative person is also likely to have a global—not just a local—perspective on problems. Seeing the forest despite all the trees is the mark of creative endeavor.

PERSONALITY

Creative people seem to share certain personality attributes. Although one can probably be creative in the short term without these attributes, long-term creativity requires

most of them. The attributes are tolerance of ambiguity, willingness to surmount obstacles and persevere, willingness to grow, willingness to take risks, and the courage of one's convictions.

Tolerance for Ambiguity

In most creative endeavors, there is a period of time during which an individual is groping—trying to figure out what the pieces of the puzzle are, how to put them together, how to relate them to what is already known. During this period, an individual is likely to feel some anxiety—possibly even alarm—because the pieces are not forming themselves into a creative solution to the problem being confronted. Creative individuals need to be able to tolerate such ambiguity and to wait for the pieces to fall into place.

In many schools, most of the assignments students are given are due the next day or within a very short period of time. In such circumstances students cannot develop a tolerance for ambiguity because they cannot spare the time to allow a situation to be ambiguous. If an assignment is due in a day or two, ambiguities need to be resolved quickly. A good way to help students develop a tolerance for ambiguity is to give them more long-term assignments and encourage them to start thinking about the assignments early on so that they can mull over whatever problems they face. Moreover, students need to realize that a period of ambiguity is the rule, not the exception, in creative work and that they should welcome this period as a chance to hatch their ideas, rather than dread it as a time when their ideas are not fully formed.

Willingness to Surmount Obstacles and Persevere

Almost every major creative thinker has surmounted obstacles at one time or another, and the willingness not to be derailed is a crucial element of success. Confronting obstacles is almost a certainty in creative endeavor because most such endeavors threaten some kind of established and entrenched interest. Unless one can learn to face adversity and conquer it, one is unlikely to make a creative contribution to one's field.

We need to learn to think of obstacles and the need to surmount them as part of the game, rather than as outside it. We should not think of obstacles as something only we have, but as something that everyone has. What makes creative people special is not that they have obstacles but how they face them.

Schools can be fairly good proving grounds for learning to surmount obstacles because we face so many of them while we are in school (whether as students or as teachers). But students sometimes leave school with the feeling that society is more likely to get in the way of creativity than to support it. Sometimes they are right, of course. And ultimately, they may have to fight for their ideas, as creative people have done before them. However, training to overcome resistance to new ideas shouldn't be the main contribution of the schools to students' creativity.

Willingness to Grow

When a person has a creative idea and is able to have others accept it, that person may be highly rewarded for the idea. It then becomes difficult to move on to still other ideas. The rewards for staying with the first idea are often great, and it feels comfortable to stick with that idea. At the same time, the person who has had a creative idea often acquires a deep-seated fear that his or her next idea won't be as good as the first one. Indeed, the phenomenon of "statistical" regression toward the mean would suggest that subsequent ideas actually will not be as good— that they will regress toward the mean. This is the same phenomenon that operates when

the "rookie of the year" in baseball doesn't play as well in his second year as in his first or when a restaurant that seemed outstanding when we first ate there isn't quite as good the second time. In short, there is a fair amount of pressure to stay with what one has and knows. But creativity exhibited over prolonged periods of time requires one to move beyond that first creative idea and even to see problems with what at one time may have seemed a superb idea. While schools often encourage the growth of a student's knowledge, such growth will by no means lead automatically to creativity, in part because schools do not encourage students to take risks with their newly acquired knowledge and abilities.

Willingness to Take Risks

A general principle of investment is that, on the average, greater return entails greater risk. For the most part, schools are environments that are not conducive to risk taking. On the contrary, students are as often as not punished for taking risks. Taking a course in a new area or in an area of weakness is likely to lead to a low grade, which in turn may dim a student's future prospects. Risking an unusual response on an exam or an idiosyncratic approach in a paper is a step likely to be taken only with great trepidation because of the fear that a low or failing grade on a specific assignment may ruin one's chances for a good grade in the course. Moreover, there is usually some safe response that is at least good enough to earn the grade for which one is aiming.

In addition, many teachers are not themselves risk-takers. Teaching is not a profession that is likely to attract the biggest risk-takers, and hence, many teachers may feel threatened by students who take large risks, especially if the teacher perceives those risks to be at his or her expense. Unfortunately, students' unwillingness to take risks derives from their socialization in the schools, which are environments that encourage conformity to societal norms. The result often is stereotyped thinking.

Courage of One's Convictions and Belief in Oneself

There are times in the lives of almost all creative people when they begin to doubt their ideas—and themselves. Their work may not be achieving the recognition it once achieved, or they may not have succeeded in getting recognition in the first place. At these times, it is difficult to maintain a belief in one's ideas or in oneself. It is natural for people to go through peaks and valleys in their creative output, and there are times when creative people worry that their most recent good idea will end up being their final good idea. At such times, one needs to draw upon deep-seated personal resources and to believe in oneself, even when others do not.

Schools do teach some students to believe in themselves: namely, those who consistently receive high grades. But the skills one needs to earn high grades are often quite different from those one needs to be creative. Thus those who go out and set their own course may receive little encouragement, whereas those who play the game and get good grades may develop a confidence in themselves that, though justified, is not necessarily related to their past or potential creative contributions. Those who most need to believe in themselves may be given every reason not to.

MOTIVATION

There is now good evidence to suggest that motivation plays an important part in creative endeavors. Two kinds of motivation are particularly important: intrinsic motivation and the motivation to excel. Both kinds of motivation lead to a focus on tasks rather than on the external rewards that performance of these tasks might generate.

Intrinsic Motivation

Teresa Amabile has conducted and reviewed a number of studies suggesting the importance of intrinsic motivation to creativity.[7] People are much more likely to respond creatively to a task that they enjoy doing for its own sake, rather than a task that they carry out exclusively or even primarily for such extrinsic motivators as grades. Indeed, research suggests that extrinsic rewards undermine intrinsic motivation.[8]

There is little doubt as to the way in which most schools motivate students today: namely, through grades. Grades are the ultimate criterion of one's success in school, and if one's grades are not good, love of one's work is unlikely to be viewed as much compensation. Therefore, many students chart a path in school that is just sufficient to get them an A. (If they put too much effort into a single course, they risk jeopardizing their performance in the other courses they are taking.) Students who once may have performed well for love of an intellectual challenge may come to perform well only to get their next A. Whatever intrinsic motivation children may have had at the start is likely to be drummed out of them by a system that rewards extrinsically, not intrinsically.

Motivation to Excel

Robert White identified as an important source of motivation a desire to achieve competence in one or more of a person's endeavors.[9] In order to be creative in a field, one generally will need to be motivated not only to be competent, but also to excel. The best "investors" are almost always those who put in the work necessary to realize their goals. Success does not just come to them—they work for it.

Schools vary in the extent to which they encourage students to excel. Some schools seem to want nothing more than for all their students to be at some average or "golden mean." Many schools, however, encourage excellence. Unfortunately, it is rare in our experience for the kind of excellence that is encouraged to be *creative* excellence. It may be excellence in grades, which generally does not require great creativity to attain; it may be excellence in sports or in extracurricular activities. There is nothing wrong with excellence of these kinds. Indeed, they are undoubtedly important in today's world. But seeking such excellences does not foster creativity—and may even interfere with it. When a student is simultaneously taking five or six courses, there is not much opportunity to spend the time or to expend the effort needed to be creative in any of them.

ENVIRONMENTAL CONTEXT

Creativity cannot be viewed outside an environmental context. What would be viewed as creative in one context might be viewed as trivial in another. The role of context is relevant to the creative enterprise in at least three different ways: in sparking creative ideas, in encouraging follow-up of these ideas, and in rewarding the ideas and their fruits.

Sparking Creative Ideas

Some environments provide the bases for lots of creative sparks, whereas other environments may provide the basis for none at all. Do schools provide environments for sparking creative ideas? Obviously, the answer to this question is necessarily subjective. Given the discussion above, we would have difficulty saying that they do. Schools provide environments that encourage learning about and dealing with existing concepts rather than inventing new ones. There is a lot of emphasis on memorization and some emphasis on analysis, but there is little emphasis on creative synthesis. Indeed, it is difficult for us to remember more than a handful of tests we ever took in school that encouraged creative thinking. On the contrary, the tests students typically take reward them for spitting back what they have learned—or, at best, analyzing it in a fairly noncreative way.

Encouraging Follow-up of Creative Ideas

Suppose a student has a genuinely creative idea and would like to pursue it within the school setting. Is there any vehicle for such follow-up? Occasionally, students will be allowed to pursue projects that encourage them to develop their creative thinking. But again, spending a great deal of time on such projects puts them at risk in their other courses and in their academic work. It is quite rare that any allowance is made whereby students can be excused from normal requirements in order to pursue a special interest of their own.

Evaluating and Rewarding Creative Ideas

Most teachers would adamantly maintain that, when grading papers, they reward creativity. But, if the experience of other teachers is similar to that of the teachers with whom we have worked, they don't find a great deal of creativity to reward. And we sometimes worry whether they would recognize creativity in student work were they to meet it. Please note that we do not except ourselves from this charge. We have failed more than once to see the value of a student's idea when we first encountered it, only to see that value later on—after the student had decided to pursue some other idea, partly at our urging. Teachers genuinely believe that they reward creativity. But the rewards are few and far between.

Look at any school report card, and assess the skills that the report card values. You will probably not find creativity anywhere on the list. One of us actually analyzed the report cards given to children in several elementary schools. A number of skills were assessed. However, not a single one of the report cards assessed creativity in any field whatsoever. The creative child might indeed be valued by the teacher, but it would not show up in the pattern of check marks on the report card.

TEACHING FOR CREATIVITY

How can we help develop students' creativity in the classroom? Consider an example. One of us had the opportunity to teach a class of 9- and 10-year-olds in a New York City school. The children ranged fairly widely in abilities and came from various socioeconomic backgrounds. The guest teacher was asked to demonstrate how to "teach for thinking" and decided to do so in the context of teaching about psychology. However, he wanted to impart not merely a set of decontextualized "facts" about the field, but rather the way psychologists think when they develop ideas for creative scientific theory and research.

He didn't tell the students what problem they were going to solve or even offer them suggestions. Rather, he asked each of them to share with the class some aspect of human behavior—their own, their parents', their friends'—that intrigued them and that they would like to understand better. In other words, the students were asked to *define problems* rather than have the teacher do it for them. At first, no one said anything. The children may never have been asked to formulate problems for themselves. But the teacher waited. And then he waited some more (so as not to teach them that, if only they said nothing, he would panic and start to answer his own questions).

Eventually, one student spoke up, and then another, and then another. The ice broken, the children couldn't wait to contribute. Rather than adopting the executive and largely passive style to which they were accustomed, they were adopting a *legislative style* whereby they enjoyed and actively participated in the opportunity to create new ideas. And create ideas they did. Why do parents make children dress up on special occasions? Why do parents sometimes have unreasonable expectations for their children? Why do some siblings fight a lot while others don't? How do we choose our friends?

Because these problems were the children's own problems and not the teacher's, the children were *intrinsically motivated* to seek answers. And they came up with some very perceptive answers indeed. We discussed their ideas and considered criteria for deciding which potential experiment to pursue as a group. The criteria, like the ideas, were the students' own, not the teacher's. And the students considered such factors as *taking risks* in doing experiments, *surmounting obstacles to doing an experiment,* and so on.

The children entered the class with almost no formal knowledge about psychology. But they left it with at least a rudimentary *procedural knowledge* of how psychologists formulate research. The teacher didn't give them the knowledge; they created it for themselves, in an environment that *sparked* and then *rewarded* creative ideas. To be sure, not all of the ideas were creative or even particularly good. But the students were encouraged to give it their best shot, and that's what they did.

The class didn't have time in one 75-minute period to complete the full design of an experiment. However, it did have time to demonstrate that even children can do the kind of creative work that we often reserve until graduate school. We can teach for creativity at any level, in any field. And if we want to improve our children and our nation, this is exactly what we need to do.

Does teaching for creativity actually work? We believe that it does. Moreover, the effectiveness of such teaching has been demonstrated.[10] After five weeks of insight training involving insight problems in language arts, mathematics, science, and social studies, students in grades 4 through 6 displayed significant and substantial improvements (from a pretest to a posttest) over an untrained control group on insight skills and general intelligence. In addition, the training transferred to insight problems of kinds not covered in the course, and a year later, the gains were maintained. These children had improved their creative skills with only a relatively small investment of instructional time.

Those who invest are taught that most obvious of strategies: buy low and sell high. Yet few people manage to do so. They don't know when a given security is really low or when it is really high. We believe that those who work in the schools do not have much better success in fostering creativity. We often don't recognize creativity when we see it. And although most of us believe that we encourage it, our analysis suggests that schools are probably as likely to work against the development of creativity as in its favor. The conventional wisdom is likely correct: Schools probably do at least as much to undermine creativity as to support it.

It is important to realize that our theory of creativity is a "confluence" theory: The elements of creativity work together interactively, not alone. The implication for schooling is that addressing just one—or even a few—of the resources we have discussed is not sufficient to induce creative thinking. For example, a school might teach "divergent thinking," encouraging students to see multiple solutions to problems. But children will not suddenly become creative in the absence of an environment that tolerates ambiguity, encourages risk taking, fosters task-focused motivation, and supports the other aspects of creativity that we have discussed.

It is also important to realize that obtaining transfer of training from one domain to another is at least as hard with creative thinking as with critical thinking. If you use trivial problems in your classroom (e.g., "What are unusual uses of a paper clip?"), you are likely to get transfer only to trivial problems outside the classroom. We are not enthusiastic about many so-called tests of creativity, nor about many training programs, because the

problems they use are trivial. We would encourage the use of serious problems in a variety of disciplines in order to maximize the transfer of training. Better to ask students to think of unusual ways to solve world problems—or school problems, for that matter—than to ask them to think of unusual ways to use a paper clip!

CONCLUSION

Perhaps the greatest block to the enhancement of creativity is a view of the "ideal student" that does not particularly feature creativity. Paul Torrance used an "Ideal Child Checklist," composed of characteristics that had been found empirically to differentiate highly creative people from less creative people.[11] A total of 264 teachers in the state of New York ranked the items in terms of desirability. The teachers' rankings showed only a moderate relation with the rankings of ten experts on creativity. The teachers supported more strongly than the experts such attributes as popularity, social skills, and acceptance of authority. The teachers disapproved of asking questions, being a good guesser, thinking independently, and risk taking. A replication of this study in Tennessee showed only a weak relation between the views of teachers and those of experts on creativity.[12] Clearly, to engender creativity, first we must value it!

Schools could change. They could let students define problems, rather than almost always doing it for them. They could put more emphasis on ill-structured rather than well-structured problems. They could encourage a legislative rather than (or in addition to) an executive style, by providing assignments that encourage students to see things in new ways. They could teach knowledge for use, rather than for exams; they could emphasize flexibility in using knowledge, rather than mere recall. They could encourage risk taking and other personality attributes associated with creativity, and they could put more emphasis on motivating children intrinsically rather than through grades. Finally, they could reward creativity in all its forms, rather than ignore or even punish it.

But for schools to do these things, it would take a rather fundamental re*valuation* of what schooling is about. We, at least, would like to see that process start now. Rather than put obstacles in their paths, let's do all that we can to *value* and encourage the creativity of students in our schools.

ENDNOTES

1. Robert J. Sternberg, "A Three-Facet Model of Creativity," in R. J. Sternberg, ed., *The Nature of Creativity* (New York: Cambridge University Press, 1988), pp. 125–47; and Robert J. Sternberg and Todd I. Lubart, "An Investment Theory of Creativity and Its Development," *Human Development*, vol. 34, 1991, pp. 1–31.

2. Herbert J. Walberg, "Creativity and Talent as Learning," in Sternberg, *The Nature of Creativity*, pp. 340–61.

3. Robert J. Sternberg, *Beyond IQ: A Triarchic Theory of Human Intelligence* (New York: Cambridge University Press, 1985); and Sternberg, *The Triarchic Mind: A New Theory of Human Intelligence* (New York: Viking, 1988).

4. Janet E. Davidson and Robert J. Sternberg, "The Role of Insight in Intellectual Giftedness," *Gifted Child Quarterly*, vol. 28, 1984, pp. 58–64; and Robert J. Sternberg and Janet E. Davidson, "The Mind of the Puzzler," *Psychology Today,* June 1982, pp. 37–44.

5. Robert J. Sternberg and Peter A. Frensch, "A Balance-Level Theory of Intelligent Thinking," *Zeitschrift für Pädagogische Psychologie,* vol. 3, 1989, pp. 79–96.

6. Robert J. Sternberg, "Mental Self-Government: A Theory of Intellectual Styles and Their Development," *Human Development*, vol. 31, 1988, pp. 197–224; and "Thinking Styles: Keys to Understanding Student Performance," *Phi Delta Kappan,* January 1990, pp. 366–71.

7. Teresa M. Amabile, *The Social Psychology of Creativity* (New York: Springer-Verlag, 1983).

8. Mark Lepper, David Greene, and Richard Nisbett, "Undermining Children's Intrinsic Interest with Extrinsic Rewards: A Test of the 'Overjustification' Hypothesis," *Journal of Personality and Social Psychology,* vol. 28, 1973, pp. 129–37.

9. Robert White, "Motivation Reconsidered: The Concept of Competence," *Psychological Review,* vol. 66, 1959, pp. 297–323.

10. Davidson and Sternberg, op. cit.

11. E. Paul Torrance, *Role of Evaluation in Creative Thinking* (Minneapolis: Bureau of Educational Research, University of Minnesota, 1964).

12. Bill Kaltsounis, "Middle Tennessee Teachers' Perceptions of Ideal Pupil," *Perceptual and Motor Skills,* vol. 44, 1977, pp. 803–806.

DISCUSSION QUESTIONS

1. How can curriculum workers plan instruction that encourages students to use legislative intellectual styles?
2. In what ways will the curriculum need to be structured to promote creative thinking?
3. What kinds of changes at the school level might be necessary to foster creative thinking?
4. What instructional approaches are most likely to promote creative thinking?
5. What personality attributes do creative people seem to share?

14 The Cognitive-Developmental Approach to Moral Education

LAWRENCE KOHLBERG

FOCUSING QUESTIONS

1. How does moral education promote the aims of education?
2. What are the levels of moral development?
3. How do moral judgment, content of moral judgment, and moral action differ?
4. How do conventional rules and principles influence moral choice?
5. How do indoctrination and values clarification differ as approaches to moral education?
6. What is the cognitive developmental approach to moral education?

In this chapter, I present an overview of the cognitive-developmental approach to moral education and its research foundations, compare it with other approaches, and report the experimental work my colleagues and I are doing to apply the approach.

MORAL STAGES

The cognitive-developmental approach was fully stated for the first time by John Dewey. The approach is called *cognitive* because it recognizes that moral education, like intellectual education, has its basis in stimulating the *active thinking* of the child about moral issues and decisions. It is called developmental because it sees the aims of moral education as movement through moral stages. According to Dewey:

> The aim of education is growth or *development*, both intellectual and moral. Ethical and psychological principles can aid the school in the *greatest of all the constructions—the building of a free and powerful character*. Only knowledge of the *order and connection of the stages in psychological development can insure this*. Education is the work of *supplying the conditions* which will enable the psychological functions to mature in the freest and fullest manner.[1]

Dewey postulated three levels of moral development: (1) the *premoral* or *preconventional* level "of behavior motivated by biological and social impulses with results for morals," (2) the *conventional* level of behavior "in which the individual accepts with little critical reflection the standards of his group," and (3) the *autonomous* level of behavior in which "conduct is guided by the individual thinking and judging for himself whether a purpose is good, and does not accept the standard of his group without reflection."[2]

Dewey's thinking about moral stages was theoretical. Building upon his prior studies of cognitive stages, Jean Piaget made the first effort to define stages of moral reasoning in children through actual interviews and through observations of children (in games with rules).[3] Using this interview material, Piaget defined the levels as follows: (1) the *premoral stage*, where there was no sense of obligation to rules; (2) the *heteronomous stage*, where the right was literal obedience to rules and an equation of obligation with submission to power and punishment (roughly ages four to eight); and (3) the *autonomous stage*, where the purpose and consequences of following rules are considered and obligation is based on reciprocity and exchange (roughly ages eight to twelve).[4]

In 1955, I started to redefine and validate (through longitudinal and cross-cultural study) the Dewey–Piaget levels and stages. The resulting stages are presented in Table 14.1.

We claim to have validated the stages defined in Table 14.1. The notion that stages can be *validated* by longitudinal study implies that stages have definite empirical characteristics.[5] The concept of stages (as used by Piaget and myself) implies the following characteristics:

1. Stages are "structured wholes," or organized systems of thought. Individuals are *consistent* in level of moral judgment.
2. Stages form an *invariant sequence*. Under all conditions except extreme trauma, movement is always forward, never backward. Individuals never skip stages; movement is always to the next stage up.
3. Stages are "hierarchical integrations." Thinking at a higher stage includes or comprehends within it lower-stage thinking. There is a tendency to function at or prefer the highest stage available.

Each of these characteristics has been demonstrated for moral stages. Stages are defined by responses to a set of verbal moral dilemmas classified according to an elaborate scoring scheme. Validating studies include the following:

1. A twenty-year study of fifty Chicago-area boys, middle- and working-class. Initially interviewed at ages ten to sixteen, they have been reinterviewed at three-year intervals thereafter.
2. A small, six-year longitudinal study of Turkish village and city boys of the same age.
3. A variety of other cross-sectional studies in Canada, Britain, Israel, Taiwan, Yucatan, Honduras, and India.

With regard to the structured whole or consistency criterion, we have found that more than 50 percent of an individual's thinking is always at one stage, with the remainder at the next adjacent stage (which he is leaving or which he is moving into).

With regard to invariant sequence, our longitudinal results have been presented in the *American Journal of Orthopsychiatry* (see endnote 12), and indicate that on every retest individuals either were at the same stage as three years earlier or had moved up. This was true in Turkey as well as in the United States.

With regard to the hierarchical integration criterion, it has been demonstrated that adolescents exposed to written statements at each of the six stages comprehend or correctly put in their own words all statements at or below their own stage but fail to comprehend any statements more than one stage above their own.[6] Some individuals comprehend the next stage above their own; some

TABLE 14.1   Definition of Moral Stages

I. Preconventional level

At this level, the child is responsive to cultural rules and labels of good and bad, right or wrong, but interprets these labels either in terms of the physical or the hedonistic consequences of action (punishment, reward, exchange of favors) or in terms of the physical power of those who enunciate the rules and labels. The level is divided into the following two stages:

Stage 1: *The punishment-and-obedience orientation.* The physical consequences of action determine its goodness or badness, regardless of the human meaning or value of these consequences. Avoidance of punishment and unquestioning deference to power are valued in their own right, not in terms of respect for an underlying moral order supported by punishment and authority (the latter being Stage 4).

Stage 2: *The instrumental-relativist orientation.* Right action consists of that which instrumentally satisfies one's own needs and occasionally the needs of others. Human relations are viewed in terms like those of the marketplace. Elements of fairness, of reciprocity, and of equal sharing are present, but they are always interpreted in a physical, pragmatic way. Reciprocity is a matter of "You scratch my back and I'll scratch yours," not of loyalty, gratitude, or justice.

II. Conventional level

At this level, maintaining the expectations of the individual's family, group, or nation is perceived as valuable in its own right, regardless of immediate and obvious consequences. The attitude is not only one of *conformity* to personal expectations and social order, but of loyalty to it, of actively *maintaining,* supporting, and justifying the order, and of identifying with the persons or group involved in it. At this level, there are the following two stages:

Stage 3: *The interpersonal concordance or "good boy-nice girl" orientation.* Good behavior is that which pleases or helps others and is approved by them. There is much conformity to stereotypical images of what is majority or "natural" behavior. Behavior is frequently judged by intention—"he means well" becomes important for the first time. One earns approval by being "nice."

Stage 4: *The "law and order" orientation.* There is orientation toward authority, fixed rules, and the maintenance of the social order. Right behavior consists of doing one's duty, showing respect for authority, and maintaining the given social order for its own sake.

III. Postconventional level

At this level, there is a clear effort to define moral values and principles that have validity and application apart from the authority of the groups or persons holding these principles and apart from the individual's own identification with these groups. This level also has two stages:

Stage 5: *The social-contract, legalistic orientation,* generally with utilitarian overtones. Right action tends to be defined in terms of general individual rights and standards, which have been critically examined and agreed upon by the whole society. There is a clear awareness of the relativism of personal values and opinions and a corresponding emphasis upon procedural rules for reaching consensus. Aside from what is constitutionally and democratically agreed upon, the right is a matter of personal "values" and "opinion." The result is an emphasis upon the "legal point of view," but with an emphasis upon the possibility of changing law in terms of rational considerations of social utility (rather than freezing it in terms of Stage 4 "law and order"). Outside the legal realm, free agreement and contract is the binding element of obligation. This is the "official" morality of the American government and Constitution.

Stage 6: *The universal-ethical-principle orientation.* Right is defined by the decision of conscience in accord with self-chosen *ethical principles* appealing to logical comprehensiveness, universality, and consistency. These principles are abstract and ethical (the Golden Rule, the categorical imperative); they are not concrete moral rules like the Ten Commandments. At heart, these are universal principles of *justice,* of the *reciprocity* and *equality* of human *rights,* and of respect for the dignity of human beings as *individual persons.*

do not. Adolescents prefer (or rank as best) the highest stage they can comprehend.

To understand moral stages it is important to clarify their relations to stages of logic or intelligence on the one hand and to moral behavior on the other. Maturity of moral judgment is not highly correlated with IQ or verbal intelligence (correlations are only in the 30s, accounting for 10 percent of the variance). Cognitive development, in the stage sense, however, is more important for moral development than such correlations suggest. Piaget has found that after the child learns to speak there are three major stages of reasoning: the intuitive, the concrete operational, and the formal operational. At around age seven, the child enters the stage of concrete logical thought: He can make logical inferences, classify, and handle quantitative relations about concrete things. In adolescence individuals usually enter the stage of formal operations. At this stage they can reason abstractly—i.e., consider all possibilities, form hypotheses, deduce implications from hypotheses, and test them against reality.[7]

Because moral reasoning clearly is reasoning, advanced moral reasoning depends upon advanced logical reasoning. A person's logical stage puts a certain ceiling on the moral stage he can attain. A person whose logical stage is only concrete operational is limited to the preconventional moral stages (Stages 1 and 2). A person whose logical stage is only partially formal operational is limited to the conventional moral stages (Stages 3 and 4). While logical development is necessary for moral development and sets limits to it, most individuals are higher in logical stage than they are in moral stage. As an example, over 50 percent of late adolescents and adults are capable of full formal reasoning, but only 10 percent of these adults (all formal operational) display principled (Stages 5 and 6) moral reasoning.

The moral stages are *structures of moral judgment* or *moral reasoning. Structures* of moral judgment must be distinguished from the *content* of moral judgment. As an example, we cite responses to a dilemma used in our various studies to identify moral stage. The dilemma raises the issue of stealing a drug to save a dying woman. The inventor of the drug is selling it for ten times what it costs him to make it. The woman's husband cannot raise the money, and the seller refuses to lower the price or wait for payment. What should the husband do?

The choice endorsed by a subject (steal, don't steal) is called the *content* of his moral judgment in the situation. His reasoning about the choice defines the structure of his moral judgment. This reasoning centers on the following ten universal moral values or issues of concern to persons in these moral dilemmas:

1. Punishment
2. Property
3. Roles and concerns of affection
4. Roles and concerns of authority
5. Law
6. Life
7. Liberty
8. Distributive justice
9. Truth
10. Sex

A moral choice involves choosing between two (or more) of these values as they *conflict* in concrete situations of choice.

The stage or structure of a person's moral judgment defines (1) *what* he finds valuable in each of these moral issues (life, law), i.e., how he defines the value, and (2) *why* he finds it valuable, i.e., the reasons he gives for valuing it. As an example, at Stage 1 life is valued in terms of the power or possessions of the person involved; at Stage 2, for its usefulness in satisfying the needs of the individual in question or others; at Stage 3, in terms of the individual's relations with others and their valuation of him; at Stage 4, in terms of social or religious law. Only at Stages 5 and 6 is each life seen as inherently worthwhile, aside from other considerations.

MORAL JUDGMENT VS. MORAL ACTION

Having clarified the nature of stages of moral *judgment,* we must consider the relation of moral judgment to moral *action.* If logical reasoning is a necessary but not sufficient condition for mature moral judgment, mature moral judgment is a necessary but not sufficient condition for mature moral action. One cannot follow moral principles if one does not understand (or believe in) moral principles. However, one can reason in terms of principles and not live up to these principles. As an example, Richard Krebs and I found that only 15 percent of students showing some principled thinking cheated as compared to 55 percent of conventional subjects and 70 percent of preconventional subjects.[8] Nevertheless, 15 percent of the principled subjects did cheat, suggesting that factors additional to moral judgment are necessary for principled moral reasoning to be translated into "moral action." Partly, these factors include the situation and its pressures. Partly, what happens depends upon the individual's motives and emotions. Partly, what the individual does depends upon a general sense of will, purpose, or "ego strength." As an example of the role of will or ego strength in moral behavior, we may cite the study by Krebs: Slightly more than half of his conventional subjects cheated. These subjects were also divided by a measure of attention/will. Only 26 percent of the "strong-willed" conventional subjects cheated; however, 74 percent of the "weak-willed" subjects cheated.

If maturity of moral reasoning is only one factor in moral behavior, why does the cognitive-developmental approach to moral education focus so heavily upon moral reasoning? For the following reasons:

1. Moral judgment, while only one factor in moral behavior, is the single most important or influential factor yet discovered in moral behavior.
2. While other factors influence moral behavior, moral judgment is the only distinctively *moral* factor in moral behavior. To illustrate, we noted that the Krebs study indicated that "strong-willed" conventional stage subjects resisted cheating more than "weak-willed" subjects. For those at a preconventional level of moral reasoning, however, "will" had an opposite effect. "Strong-willed" Stages 1 and 2 subjects cheated more, not less, than "weak-willed" subjects; i.e., they had the "courage of their (amoral) convictions" that it was worthwhile to cheat. "Will," then, is an important factor in moral behavior, but it is not distinctively moral; it becomes moral only when informed by mature moral judgment.
3. Moral judgment change is long-range or irreversible; a higher stage is never lost. Moral behavior as such is largely situational and reversible or "losable" in new situations.

AIMS OF MORAL AND CIVIC EDUCATION

Moral psychology describes what moral development is, as studied empirically. Moral education must also consider moral philosophy, which strives to tell us what moral development ideally *ought to be.* Psychology finds an invariant sequence of moral stages; moral philosophy must be invoked to answer whether a later stage is a better stage. The "stage" of senescence and death follows the "stage" of adulthood, but that does not mean that senescence and death are better. Our claim that the latest or principled stages of moral reasoning are morally better stages, then, must rest on considerations of moral philosophy.

The tradition of moral philosophy to which we appeal is the liberal or rational tradition, in particular the "formalistic" or "deontological" tradition running from Immanuel Kant to John Rawls.[9] Central to this tradition is the claim that an adequate morality is *principled*—i.e., that it makes judgments in terms of *universal* principles applicable to all mankind. *Principles* are to be distinguished from *rules*. Conventional morality is grounded on rules, primarily "thou shalt nots" such as are represented by the Ten Commandments, proscriptions of kinds of actions. Principles are, rather, universal guides to making a moral decision. An example is Kant's "categorical imperative," formulated in two ways. The first is the maxim of respect for human personality, "Act always toward the other as an end, not as a means." The second is the maxim of universalization, "Choose only as you would be willing to have everyone choose in your situation." Principles like that of Kant state the formal conditions of a moral choice or action. In the dilemma in which a woman is dying because a druggist refuses to release his drug for less than the stated price, the druggist is not acting morally, though he is not violating the ordinary moral rules (he is not actually stealing or murdering). But he is violating principles: He is treating the woman simply as a means to his ends of profit, and he is not choosing as he would wish anyone to choose (if the druggist were in the dying woman's place, he would not want a druggist to choose as he is choosing). Under most circumstances, choice in terms of conventional moral rules and choice in terms of principles coincide. Ordinarily, principles dictate not stealing (avoiding stealing is implied by acting in terms of a regard for others as ends and in terms of what one would want everyone to do). In a situation where stealing is the only means to save a life, however, principles contradict the ordinary rules and would dictate stealing. Unlike rules, which are supported by social authority, principles are freely chosen by the individual because of their intrinsic moral validity.[10]

The conception that a moral choice is a choice made in terms of moral principles is related to the claim of liberal moral philosophy that moral principles are ultimately principles of justice. In essence, moral conflicts are conflicts between the claims of persons, and principles for resolving these claims are principles of justice, "for giving each his due." Central to justice are the demands of *liberty, equality,* and *reciprocity.* At every moral stage, there is a concern for justice. The most damning statement a school child can make about a teacher is that "he's not fair." At each higher stage, however, the conception of justice is reorganized. At Stage 1, justice is punishing the bad in terms of "an eye for an eye and a tooth for a tooth." At Stage 2, it is exchanging favors and goods in an equal manner. At Stages 3 and 4, it is treating people as they desire in terms of the conventional rules. At Stage 5, it is recognized that all rules and laws flow from justice, from a social contract between the governors and the governed designed to protect the equal rights of all. At Stage 6, personally chosen moral principles are also principles of justice, the principles any member of a society would choose for that society if he did not know what his position was to be in the society and in which he might be the least advantaged.[11] Principles chosen from this point of view are, first, the maximum liberty compatible with the like liberty of others and, second, no inequalities of goods and respect which are not to the benefit of all, including the least advantaged.

As an example of stage progression in the orientation to justice, we may take judgments about capital punishment.[12] Capital punishment is only firmly rejected at the two principled stages, when the notion of justice as vengeance or retribution is abandoned. At the sixth stage, capital punishment is not condoned even if it may have some useful deterrent effect in promoting law and order. This is because it is not a punishment we would choose for a society if we assumed we had as much chance of being born into the position of a criminal or murderer as being born into the position of a law abider.

Why are decisions based on universal principles of justice better decisions? Because they are decisions on which all moral men could agree. When decisions are based on conventional moral rules, men will disagree, because they adhere to conflicting systems of rules dependent on culture and social position. Throughout history men have killed one another in the name of conflicting moral rules and values, most recently in Vietnam and the Middle East. Truly moral or just resolutions of conflicts require principles, which are, or can be, universalizable.

Alternative Approaches

We have given a philosophic rationale for stage advance as the aim of moral education. Given this rationale, the developmental approach to moral education can avoid the problems inherent in the other two major approaches to moral education. The first alternative approach is that of indoctrinative moral education, the preaching and imposition of the rules and values of the teacher and his culture on the child. In America, when this indoctrinative approach has been developed in a systematic manner, it has usually been termed "character education."

Moral values, in the character education approach, are preached or taught in terms of what may be called the "bag of virtues." In the classic studies of character by Hugh Hartshorne and Mark May, the virtues chosen were honesty, service, and self-control.[13] It is easy to get superficial consensus on such a bag of virtues—until one examines in detail the list of virtues involved and the details of their definition. Is the Hartshorne and May bag more adequate than the Boy Scout bag (a Scout should be honest, loyal, reverent, clean, brave, etc.)? When one turns to the details of defining each virtue, one finds equal uncertainty or difficulty in reaching consensus. Does honesty mean one should not steal to save a life? Does it mean that a student should not help another student with his homework?

Character education and other forms of indoctrinative moral education have aimed at teaching universal values (it is assumed that

honesty or service is a desirable trait for all men in all societies), but the detailed definitions used are relative; they are defined by the opinions of the teacher and the conventional culture and rest on the authority of the teacher for their justification. In this sense, character education is close to the unreflective valuings by teachers, which constitute the hidden curriculum of the school.[14] Because of the current unpopularity of indoctrinative approaches to moral education, a family of approaches called "values clarification" has become appealing to teachers. Values clarification takes the first step implied by a rational approach to moral education: the eliciting of the child's own judgment or opinion about issues or situations in which values conflict, rather than imposing the teacher's opinion on him. Values clarification, however, does not attempt to go further than eliciting awareness of values; it is assumed that becoming more self-aware about one's values is an end in itself. Fundamentally, the definition of the end of values education as self-awareness derives from a belief in ethical relativity held by many value-clarifiers. As stated by Peter Engel, "One must contrast value clarification and value inculcation. Value clarification implies the principle that in the consideration of values there is no single correct answer." Within these premises of "no correct answer," children are to discuss moral dilemmas in such a way as to reveal different values and discuss their value differences with each other. The teacher is to stress that "our values are different," not that one value is more adequate than others. If this program is systematically followed, students will themselves become relativists, believing there is no "right" moral answer. For instance, a student caught cheating might argue that he did nothing wrong, because his own hierarchy of values, which may be different from that of the teacher, made it right for him to cheat.

Like values clarification, the cognitive-developmental approach to moral education stresses open or Socratic peer discussion of value dilemmas. Such discussion, however, has an aim: stimulation of movement to the next stage of moral reasoning. Like values clarification, the developmental approach opposes indoctrination. Stimulation of movement to the next stage of reasoning is not indoctrinative, for the following reasons:

1. Change is in the way of reasoning rather than in the particular beliefs involved.
2. Students in a class are at different stages; the aim is to aid movement of each to the next stage, not convergence on a common pattern.
3. The teacher's own opinion is neither stressed nor invoked as authoritative. It enters in only as one of many opinions, hopefully one of those at a next higher stage.
4. The notion that some judgments are more adequate than others is communicated. Fundamentally, however, this means that the student is encouraged to articulate a position that seems most adequate to him and to judge the adequacy of the reasoning of others.

In addition to having more definite aims than values clarification, the moral development approach restricts value education to that which is moral or, more specifically, to justice. This is for two reasons. First, it is not clear that the whole realm of personal, political, and religious values is a realm that is nonrelative—i.e., in which there are universals and a direction of development. Second, it is not clear that the public school has a right or mandate to develop values in general. In our view, value education in the public schools should be restricted to that which the school has the right and mandate to develop: an awareness of justice, or of the rights of others in our Constitutional system.[15] While the Bill of Rights prohibits the teaching of religious beliefs, or of specific value systems, it does not prohibit the teaching of the awareness of rights and principles of justice fundamental to the Constitution itself.

When moral education is recognized as centered in justice and differentiated from value education or affective education, it becomes apparent that moral and civic education are much the same thing. This equation, taken for granted by the classic philosophers of education from Plato and Aristotle to Dewey, is basic to our claim that a concern for moral education is central to the educational objectives of social studies.

The term *civic education* is used to refer to social studies as more than the study of the facts and concepts of social science, history, and civics. It is education for the analytic understanding, value principles, and motivation necessary for a citizen in a democracy if democracy is to be an effective process. It is political education. Civic or political education means the stimulation of development of more advanced patterns of reasoning about political and social decisions and their implementation directly derivative of broader patterns of moral reasoning. Our studies show that reasoning and decision making about political decisions are directly derivative of broader patterns of moral reasoning and decision making. We have interviewed high school and college students about concrete political situations involving laws to govern open housing, civil disobedience for peace in Vietnam, free press rights to publish what might disturb national order, and distribution of income through taxation. We find that reasoning on these political decisions can be classified according to moral stage and that an individual's stage on political dilemmas is at the same level as on nonpolitical moral dilemmas (euthanasia, violating authority to maintain trust in a family, stealing a drug to save one's dying wife). Turning from reasoning to action, similar findings are obtained. In 1963 a study was made of those who sat in at the University of California, Berkeley, administration building and those who did not in the Free Speech Movement crisis. Of those at Stage 6, 80 percent sat in, believing that principles of free speech were being compromised, and that all efforts to compromise and negotiate with the administration had failed. In contrast, only 15 percent of the conventional (Stage 3 or Stage 4) subjects sat in. (Stage 5 subjects were in between.)[16]

From a psychological side, then, political development is part of moral development. The same is true from the philosophic side. In the *Republic,* Plato sees political education as part of a broader education for moral justice and finds a rationale for such education in terms of universal philosophic principles rather than the demands of a particular society. More recently, Dewey claims the same.

In historical perspective, the United States was the first nation whose government was publicly founded on postconventional principles of justice, rather than upon the authority central to conventional moral reasoning. At the time of our founding, postconventional or principled moral and political reasoning was the possession of the minority, as it still is. Today, as in the time of our founding, the majority of our adults are at the conventional level, particularly the "law and order" (fourth) moral stage. (Every few years the Gallup Poll circulates the Bill of Rights unidentified, and every year it is turned down.) The Founding Fathers intuitively understood this without benefit of our elaborate social science research; they constructed a document designing a government that would maintain principles of justice and the rights of man even though principled men were not the men in power. The machinery included checks and balances, the independent judiciary, and freedom of the press. Most recently, this machinery found its use at Watergate. The tragedy of Richard Nixon, as Harry Truman said long ago, was that he never understood the Constitution (a Stage 5 document), but the Constitution understood Richard Nixon.[17]

Watergate, then, is not some sign of moral decay of the nation, but rather of the fact that understanding and action in support of justice principles are still the possession of a minority of our society. Insofar as there is moral decay, it represents the weakening of conventional morality in the face of social and value conflict today. This can lead the less fortunate adolescent to fixation at the preconventional level, the more fortunate to movement to principles. We find a larger proportion of youths at the principled level today than was the case in their fathers' day, but also a larger proportion at the preconventional level.

Given this state, moral and civic education in the schools becomes a more urgent task. In the high school today, one often hears both preconventional adolescents and those beginning to move beyond convention sounding the same note of disaffection for the school. While our political institutions are in principle Stage 5 (i.e., vehicles for maintaining universal rights through the democratic process), our schools have traditionally been Stage 4 institutions of convention and authority. Today, more than ever, democratic schools systematically engaged in civic education are required.

Our approach to moral and civic education relates the study of law and government to the actual creation of a democratic school in which moral dilemmas are discussed and resolved in a manner that will stimulate moral development.

Planned Moral Education

For many years, moral development was held by psychologists to be primarily a result of family upbringing and family conditions. In particular, conditions of affection and authority in the home were believed to be critical, some balance of warmth and firmness being optimal for moral development. This view arises if morality is conceived as an internalization of the arbitrary rules of parents and culture, because such acceptance must be based on affection and respect for parents as authorities rather than on the rational nature of the rules involved.

Studies of family correlates of moral stage development do not support this internalization view of the conditions for moral development. Instead, they suggest that the conditions for moral development in homes and schools are similar and that the conditions are consistent with cognitive-developmental theory. In the cognitive-developmental view, morality is a natural product of a universal human tendency toward empathy or role taking, toward putting oneself in the shoes of other conscious beings. It is also a product of a universal human concern for justice, for reciprocity or equality in the relation of one person to another. As an example, when my son was four, he became a morally principled vegetarian and refused to eat meat, resisting all parental persuasion to increase his protein intake. His reason was "It's bad to kill animals." His moral commitment to vegetarianism was not taught or acquired from parental authority; it was the result of the universal tendency of the young self to project its consciousness and values into other living things, other selves. My son's vegetarianism also involved a sense of justice, revealed when I read him a book about Eskimos in which a real hunting expedition was described. His response was to say, "Daddy, there is one kind of meat I would eat—Eskimo meat. It's all right to eat Eskimos because they eat animals." This natural sense of justice or reciprocity was Stage 1— an eye for an eye, a tooth for a tooth. My son's sense of the value of life was also Stage 1 and involved no differentiation between human personality and physical life. His morality, though Stage 1, was, however, natural and internal. Moral development past Stage 1, then, is not an internalization but the reconstruction of role taking and conceptions of justice toward greater adequacy. These reconstructions occur in order to achieve a better match between the child's own moral structures and the structures of the social and moral situations he confronts. We divide these conditions of match into two kinds:

those dealing with moral discussions and communication and those dealing with the total moral environment or atmosphere in which the child lives.

In terms of moral discussion, the important conditions appear to be:

1. Exposure to the next higher stage of reasoning.
2. Exposure to situations posing problems and contradictions for the child's current moral structure, leading to dissatisfaction with his current level.
3. An atmosphere of interchange and dialogue combining the first two conditions, in which conflicting moral views are compared in an open manner.

Studies of families in India and America suggest that morally advanced children have parents at higher stages. Parents expose children to the next higher stage, raising moral issues and engaging in open dialogue or interchange about such issues.[18]

Drawing on this notion of the discussion conditions stimulating advance, Moshe Blatt conducted classroom discussions of conflict-laden hypothetical moral dilemmas with four classes of junior high and high school students for a semester.[19] In each of these classes, students were to be found at three stages. Because the children were not all responding at the same stage, the arguments they used with each other were at different levels. In the course of these discussions among the students, the teacher first supported and clarified those arguments that were one stage above the lowest stage among the children; for example, the teacher supported Stage 3 rather than Stage 2. When it seemed that these arguments were understood by the students, the teacher then challenged that stage, using new situations, and clarified the arguments one stage above the previous one: Stage 4 rather than Stage 3. At the end of the semester, all the students were retested; they showed significant upward change when compared to the controls, and they maintained the change one year later. In the experimental classrooms, from one-fourth to one-half of the students moved up a stage, while there was essentially no change during the course of the experiment in the control group.

Given the Blatt studies showing that moral discussion could raise moral stage, we undertook the next step: to see if teachers could conduct moral discussions in the course of teaching high school social studies with the same results. This step we took in cooperation with Edwin Fenton, who introduced moral dilemmas in his ninth- and eleventh-grade social studies texts. Twenty-four teachers in the Boston and Pittsburgh areas were given some instruction in conducting moral discussions around the dilemmas in the text. About half of the teachers stimulated significant developmental change in their classrooms—upward stage movement of one-quarter to one-half a stage. In control classes using the text but no moral dilemma discussions, the same teachers failed to stimulate any moral change in the students. Moral discussion, then, can be a usable and effective part of the curriculum at any grade level. Working with filmstrip dilemmas produced in cooperation with Guidance Association, second-grade teachers conducted moral discussions yielding a similar amount of moral stage movement.

Moral discussion and curriculum, however, constitute only one portion of the conditions stimulating moral growth. When we turn to analyzing the broader life environment, we turn to a consideration of the *moral atmosphere* of the home, the school, and the broader society. The first basic dimension of social atmosphere is the role-taking opportunities it provides, the extent to which it encourages the child to take the point of view of others. Role taking is related to the amount of social interaction and social communication in which the child engages, as well as to his sense of efficacy in influencing attitudes of others. The second dimension of social atmosphere, more strictly moral, is the level of justice of the environment or institution. The justice structure of an institution refers to the perceived rules or principles for distributing rewards, punishments, responsibilities, and privileges among institutional members. This structure may exist or be perceived at any of our moral stages. As an example, a study of a traditional prison revealed that inmates perceived it as Stage 1, regardless of their own level.[20] Obedience to arbitrary command by power figures and punishment for disobedience were seen as the governing justice norms of the prison. A behavior-modification prison using point rewards for conformity was perceived as a Stage 2 system of instrumental exchange. Inmates at Stage 3 or 4 perceived this institution as more fair than the traditional prison, but not as fair in their own terms.

These and other studies suggest that a higher level of institutional justice is a condition for individual development of a higher sense of justice. Working on these premises, Joseph Hickey, Peter Scharf, and I worked with guards and inmates in a women's prison to create a more just community.[21] A social contract was set up in which guards and inmates each had a vote of one and in which rules were made and conflicts resolved through discussions of fairness and a democratic vote in a community meeting. The program has stimulated moral stage advance in inmates.

Fenton, Ralph Mosher, and I received a grant from the Danforth Foundation (with additional support from the Kennedy Foundation) to make moral education a living matter in two high schools in the Boston area (Cambridge and Brookline) and two in Pittsburgh. The plan had two components. The first was training counselors and social studies and English teachers in conducting moral discussions and making moral discussion an integral part of the curriculum. The second was establishing a just community school within a public high school.

We have stated the theory of the just community high school, postulating that discussing real-life moral situations and actions as issues of fairness and as matters for democratic decision would stimulate advance in both moral reasoning and moral action. A participatory democracy provides more extensive opportunities for role taking and a higher level of perceived institutional justice than does any other social arrangement. Most alternative schools strive to establish a democratic governance, but none we have observed has achieved a vital or viable participatory democracy. Our theory suggested reasons why we might succeed where others failed. First, we felt that democracy had to be a central commitment of a school, rather than a humanitarian frill. Democracy as moral education provides that commitment. Second, democracy in alternative schools often fails because it bores the students. Students prefer to let teachers make decisions about staff, courses, and schedules, rather than to attend lengthy, complicated meetings. Our theory said that the issues a democracy should focus on are issues of morality and fairness. Real issues concerning drugs, stealing, disruptions, and grading are never boring if handled as issues of fairness. Third, our theory told us that if large democratic community meetings were preceded by small-group moral discussion, higher-stage thinking by students would win out in later decisions, avoiding the disasters of mob rule.[22]

We can report that the school based on our theory makes democracy work or function where other schools have failed.

Our Cambridge just community school within the public high school was started after a small summer planning session of volunteer teachers, students, and parents. At the time the school opened in the fall, only a commitment to democracy and a skeleton program of English and social studies had been decided on. The school started with six teachers from the regular school and sixty students, twenty from academic professional

homes and twenty from working-class homes. The other twenty were dropouts and troublemakers or petty delinquents in terms of previous record. The usual mistakes and usual chaos of a beginning alternative school ensued. Within a few weeks, however, a successful democratic community process had been established. Rules were made around pressing issues: disturbances, drugs, hooking. A student discipline committee or jury was formed. The resulting rules and enforcement have been relatively effective and reasonable. We do not see reasonable rules as ends in themselves, however, but as vehicles for moral discussion and an emerging sense of community. This sense of community and a resulting morale are perhaps the most immediate signs of success. This sense of community seems to lead to behavior change of a positive sort. An example is a fifteen-year-old student who started as one of the greatest combinations of humor, aggression, light-fingeredness, and hyperactivity I have ever known. From being the principal disturber of all community meetings, he has become an excellent community meeting participant and occasional chairman. He is still more ready to enforce rules for others than to observe them himself, yet his commitment to the school has led to a steady decrease in exotic behavior. In addition, he has become more involved in classes and projects and has begun to listen and ask questions in order to pursue a line of interest.

CONCLUSION

We attribute such behavior change not only to peer pressure and moral discussion but to the sense of community that has emerged from the democratic process in which angry conflicts are resolved through fairness and community decision. This sense of community is reflected in statements of the students to us that there are no cliques—that the blacks and the whites, the professors' sons and the project students, are friends. These statements are supported by observation. Such a sense of community is needed where students in a given classroom range in reading level from fifth grade to college.

There is very little new in anything we are doing. Dewey wanted democratic experimental schools for moral and intellectual development seventy years ago. Perhaps Dewey's time has come.

ENDNOTES

1. John Dewey, "What Psychology Can Do for the Teacher," in Reginald Archambault, ed., *John Dewey on Education: Selected Writings* (New York: Random House, 1964).
2. These levels correspond roughly to our three major levels: the preconventional, the conventional, and the principled. Similar levels were propounded by William McDougall, Leonard Hobhouse, and James Mark Baldwin.
3. Jean Piaget, *The Moral Judgment of the Child*, 2nd ed. (Glencoe, IL: Free Press, 1948).
4. Piaget's stages correspond to our first three stages: Stage 0 (premoral), Stage 1 (heteronomous), and Stage 2 (instrumental reciprocity).
5. Lawrence Kohlberg, "Moral Stages and Moralization: The Cognitive-Developmental Approach," in Thomas Lickona, ed., *Moral Development and Behavior* (New York: Holt, Rinehart and Winston, 1976).
6. James Rest, Elliott Turiel, and Lawrence Kohlberg, "Relations Between Level of Moral Judgment and Preference and Comprehension of the Moral Judgment of Others," *Journal of Personality*, vol. 37, 1969, pp. 225–52; and James Rest, "Comprehension, Preference, and Spontaneous Usage in Moral Judgment," in Lawrence Kohlberg, ed., *Recent Research in Moral Development* (New York: Holt, Rinehart and Winston, 1986).
7. Many adolescents and adults only partially attain the stage of formal operations. They do consider all the actual relations of one thing to another at the same time, but they do not consider all possibilities and form abstract hypotheses. A few do not advance this far, remaining "concrete operational."
8. Richard Krebs and Lawrence Kohlberg, "Moral Judgment and Ego Controls as Determinants of Resistance to Cheating," in Lawrence Kohlberg, ed., *Recent Research.*
9. John Rawls, *A Theory of Justice* (Cambridge, MA: Harvard University Press, 1971).
10. Not all freely chosen values or rules are principles, however. Hitler chose the "rule" "exterminate the enemies of the Aryan race," but such a rule is not a universalizable principle.
11. Rawls, *A Theory of Justice.*
12. Lawrence Kohlberg and Donald Elfenbein, "Development of Moral Reasoning and Attitudes Toward Capital Punishment," *American Journal of Orthopsychiatry*, Summer, 1975.
13. Hugh Hartshorne and Mark May, *Studies in the Nature of Character: Studies in Deceit*, vol. 1; *Studies in Service and Self-Control*, vol. 2; *Studies in Organization of Character*, vol. 3 (New York: Macmillan, 1928–30).
14. As an example of the "hidden curriculum," we may cite a second-grade classroom. My son came home from this classroom one day saying he did not want to be "one of the bad boys." Asked "Who are the bad boys?" he replied, "The ones who don't put their books back and get yelled at."
15. Restriction of deliberate value education to the moral may be clarified by our example of the second-grade teacher who made tidying up of books a matter of moral indoctrination. Tidiness is a value, but it is not a moral value. Cheating is a moral issue, intrinsically one of fairness. It involves issues of violation of trust and taking advantage. Failing to tidy the room may under certain conditions be an issue of fairness, when it puts an undue burden on others. If it is handled by the teacher as a matter of cooperation among the group in this sense, it is a legitimate focus of deliberate moral education. If it is not, it simply represents the arbitrary imposition of the teacher's values on the child.
16. The differential action of the principled subjects was determined by two things. First, they were more likely to judge it right to violate authority by sitting in. But second, they were also in general more consistent in engaging in political action according to their judgment. Ninety percent of all Stage 6 subjects thought it right to sit in, and all 90 percent lived up to this belief. Among the Stage 4 subjects, 45 percent thought it right to sit in, but only 33 percent lived up to this belief by acting.

17. No public or private word or deed of Nixon ever rose above Stage 4, the "law and order" stage. His last comments in the White House were of wonderment that the Republican Congress could turn on him after so many Stage 2 exchanges of favors in getting them elected.

18. Bindu Parilch, "A Cross-Cultural Study of Parent-Child Moral Judgment," unpublished doctoral dissertation, Harvard University, 1975.

19. Moshe Blatt and Lawrence Kohlberg, "Effects of Classroom Discussions upon Children's Level of Moral Judgment," in Lawrence Kohlberg, ed., *Recent Research.*

20. Lawrence Kohlberg, Peter Scharf, and Joseph Hickey, "The Justice Structure of the Prison: A Theory and an Intervention," *The Prison Journal,* Autumn-Winter, 1972.

21. Lawrence Kohlberg, Kelsey Kauffman, Peter Scharf, and Joseph Hickey, *The Just Community Approach to Corrections: A Manual, Part I* (Cambridge, MA: Education Research Foundation, 1973).

22. An example of the need for small-group discussion comes from an alternative school community meeting called because a pair of the students had stolen the school's video-recorder. The resulting majority decision was that the school should buy back the recorder from the culprits through a fence. The teachers could not accept this decision and returned to a more authoritative approach. I believe if the moral reasoning of students urging this solution had been confronted by students at a higher stage, a different decision would have emerged.

DISCUSSION QUESTIONS

1. Should moral and civic education be the responsibility of the schools? Why? Why not?

2. What type of curriculum design lends itself to promoting the aims of moral education?

3. How do the family and norms of school cultures influence children's moral development?

4. What is the role of the social atmosphere in moral education?

5. Should values be infused into the curriculum or explicitly taught? Why? Why not?

15 Targeted, Not Universal Pre-K

Chester E. Finn, Jr.

FOCUSING QUESTIONS

1. What role should pre-kindergarten serve for disadvantaged children?
2. What skills or competencies should we teach and assess at the pre-K level?
3. What are some reasons why certain children need intensive preschool interventions?
4. What are some advantages and disadvantages of universal preschool education?
5. Why might a targeted approach to pre-K reform make sense?

The universal-preschool-advocacy machine is running a bit low on gas. Its drivers are feeling neglected by the Obama Administration, semi-abandoned by their longtime funder at Pew, and thwarted by the perilous fiscal condition of nearly every state. This upsets them, of course, but it's no bad thing for the country, which needs to take a deep breath and ask whether universal is the right approach to preschool.

I've concluded that it's not. Not because preschool is in any way undesirable. To the contrary. My own granddaughters are getting plenty of it because preparing them to succeed in school is a top priority with their parents—and their grandparents. But for three important reasons, universal is the wrong policy to impose on the United States in 2013.

Reason #1: The overwhelming majority of three- and four-year-olds already have access to various forms of preschool. No, it's not always terrific, but their parents, many of them aided by a slew of federal and state programs, have found the means to pay for it. The United States benefits from an extensive, complex, and vibrant market in preschool and daycare, one with a host of providers and subsidy programs meeting many different child needs and family situations. To layer a new, publicly financed, universal program on top of all this would be a costly and unnecessary windfall for millions of households and be too clumsy and standardized to address the diversity of family preferences and challenges.

Reason #2: The children in greatest need of serious help in their early years are a relatively small population of kids for whom no universal program on anybody's horizon would be anywhere near sufficient. They are, for the most part, the severely impoverished progeny of young single mothers, many of them members of minorities and few of them with much education of their own. These youngsters (and their parents) require intensive interventions from the get-go, not a few hours a day when they're four years old. Yet, "universal" programs end up being tax-financed free rides for many millions of families and not nearly enough for the smaller population of kids who need major-league assistance.

Reason #3: The early childhood-education fraternity has not entirely accepted the concept of school readiness even though that is the main argument for any sort of publicly funded prekindergarten. (That many parents need childcare while they're at work mines a totally different policy vein.)

Much of the preschool world is queasy about setting academic expectations or mandating sophisticated curricula for its programs, much less aligning these with state (and, increasingly, multistate, even national) K–12 standards. It's queasier still about results-based accountability, whereby kids are assessed to determine whether they have the skills, knowledge, traits, and attitudes to succeed in kindergarten and beyond, and providers are judged according to their prowess at equipping their young charges with those attributes.

That's the seminal failure of Head Start, for example. Its four-decade-long refusal to view itself as a curriculum-based, school-readiness program is the primary (and wholly unsurprising) reason it's been so ineffective—as study after study has shown—in preparing its disadvantaged participants to prosper academically when they reach primary school.

WHAT DO YOU MEAN, "CURRICULUM"?

I'm not talking about heavy-duty academics for three- and four-year-olds. Nobody expects them to do algebra or read Dickens. This is about shapes, colors, and sounds, the difference between big and little, fast and slow, up and down. It's about learning the meanings of more words, following a story, responding to questions, being able to express a preference or recount an activity, etc. Such cognitive attainments—coupled with adequate motor skills, reasonable self-control, healthy attitudes, and acceptable social behavior—make an enormous difference in youngsters' school success and, according to some studies, in later life. They also can be assessed, though not usually with paper-and-pencil tests but with teacher-conducted "inventories" or clever game-like online instruments.

These are, of course, the very competencies that many low-income and minority children are not getting enough of at home. But such kids don't benefit much from preschool if the preschool program doesn't focus on these competencies—and agree to be evaluated on how well students acquire them. What's more, for severely disadvantaged kids to get the help they really need, such programs need to start very young, to be intense, and to involve parents.

On this front, the "universal" preschool crowd is either disingenuous or naïve. Their principal intellectual and moral argument—one for which I have considerable sympathy—is to give needy kids a boost. Serious pursuit of that objective calls for high-powered intervention programs that commence when the children are babies or toddlers.

Yet the programmatic and political strategy advanced by those same advocates is altogether different from their moral claim. They would furnish relatively skimpy preschool services to all 4 million of our nation's four-year-olds (and then, of course, to all 4 million three-year-olds), preferably under the aegis of public school systems.

Either this discordant plan is a front for public school expansionism—bent on annexing another grade or two to its current 13 and adding the staff (and dues-paying union members) that would accompany such growth; or it's a cynical calculation to appeal to the middle class in order for taxpayers to underwrite the routine childcare needs of working parents—and the heck with the poor kids who need more than that strategy will ever yield. The bona fide interests of disadvantaged children are being subordinated to the politics of getting something enacted.

ENTER BARACK OBAMA

Not long ago, the advocates—generously funded at the time by the Pew Charitable Trust and other national foundations—placed great hope in the new Obama administration. Twice during the campaign debates of 2008, candidate Obama termed early childhood education one of his top priorities, and soon after his election he pledged to that priority an additional $10 billion in annual federal funding. As a down payment, the American Recovery and Reinvestment Act that the new president pushed through Congress in early 2009 included $2.1 billion more for Head Start and $2 billion more for child care, plus additional funding for disabled preschoolers and some $54 billion in aid to strapped state and local education budgets.

But the Administration hasn't done a heck of a lot since then to lead a crusade for more preschool. Education Secretary Arne Duncan—an earnest backer of high-quality pre-K programs for kids who need them and the former overseer of a well-regarded program in Chicago—has given a couple of terrific speeches and testified in Congress on the Obama team's one major initiative in this sphere, the Early Learning Challenge Grants. This program would distribute about $1 billion per year on a competitive basis to states seeking to develop or expand high-quality early childhood programs. But as of this writing, that measure hasn't cleared Congress, and today nobody would term it a top Administration priority. Indeed, if you

search the White House web site, you find three times more hits for "childhood obesity" than for "early childhood education."

Along with less preschool action in Washington than advocates had hoped for, state capitals also are quieter these days. Governors' fiscal 2011 budgets held steady on preschool spending (at $5.3 billion), but barely one-third of these policy leaders even mentioned the topic in their 2010 state of the state addresses.

Will America's rush toward universal preschool resume when the fiscal picture brightens? I wouldn't be surprised. The political appeal is obvious: something for everyone, something that's said to be good for kids, something that might help your own child get ahead, something of value that others will pay for. And there's no shortage of advocates and experts asserting that America's future hinges on it.

WHO REALLY NEEDS IT?

Many youngsters arrive in kindergarten with learning deficits. For a large fraction of them, these deficits are mild and can be dealt with by competent teachers. For others, the shortfalls are already so severe that these hapless tykes are gravely unprepared to flourish in today's more "academic" kindergartens. This means that—barring a miracle—they won't be ready to flourish in first or second grade, either. They typically bring their deficits from disorganized homes in troubled neighborhoods, places where ill-prepared and overstretched adults offer their toddlers little true conversation, intellectual stimulation, and cognitive growth.

Research makes clear that children's acquisition of literacy skills in primary school correlates strongly with a half dozen "precursor" skills that they normally pick up between birth and age five, skills such as knowing the letters of the alphabet and their sounds and being able to write those letters—and one's own name. Middle-class kids with attentive, educated parents, grandparents, and other adults in their lives tend to acquire these (and many other) skills in the course of conventional child rearing.

But what about youngsters whose lives lack a sufficient number of such adults? The evidence indicates that they constitute about 10 percent, maybe 15 to 20 percent, of all children. There is evidence—much debated—to indicate that ultra-intensive pre-K programs can remedy such deficits and produce lasting gains of other kinds. But the programs commonly cited—notably Michigan's Perry Preschool and North Carolina's Abecedarian Project—turn out to be truly exceptional. They were very small, richly financed, uncommonly sophisticated, multifaceted interventions in the lives of extremely disadvantaged youngsters and their families, and they took place decades ago.

Some studies have found that programs of this kind had positive effects that endured for decades, such as reducing the rate of adult incarceration. That's surely good news, if somewhat remote from school readiness. But the long-term effects also turn out to be uneven and mostly small. The University of Maryland's Douglas Besharov notes, for example, that the gains of the Abecedarian Project "became ambiguous as time went on" and "did not lead to many improved outcomes in adulthood . . . with, for example, no statistically significant differences in high school graduation rates, employment, or criminal activity."

Even if their long-term impact were stronger, it's almost impossible to picture the conditions and financing of these boutique programs being replicated on a large scale. And it's naïve to suppose that their intensive features will be found in universal programs.

As for more-typical pre-K programs, a number of studies find that they have a positive effect—for a while. However, the big issue with pre-K education isn't whether it does participants some good in the short run. It's whether those gains last through school.

Here, the evidence is mostly bleak. Most of the gains that can be found at the end of pre-school ebb over time, and the differences attributable to various kinds of programs tend to wash out. Effects that may appear significant at the conclusion of the pre-K program typically fade to the vanishing point by third grade. That fading doubtless has more to do with what happens to students in the K–12 system—and with the continuing malign influences in their outside lives—than with preschool programs themselves. But it also suggests that universalizing the preschool experience is no way to achieve lasting gap reduction.

COSTS AND BENEFITS

The policy dilemma is inescapable: How important is it to expand participation in services whose effects are unpredictable, uneven, and transitory? It's a fine thing to give kids an early boost, but how much of a priority can this be when the pre-K advantage slowly ebbs?

A truly universal program, one that actually served all four-year-olds, would cost not less than $11.6 billion a year at the low end of the budget and as much as $58 billion at the high-cost Perry Preschool end. Including three-year-olds would at least double those sums. If we assume universal participation and pick a mid-level cost—say, $9,000 per child, which is close to where Head Start is today and approximates average per-pupil spending on K–12 public education—the outlay for four-year-olds would be about $36 billion per annum.

What's more troubling is that, because 85 percent of four-year-olds already participate in some sort of pre-K program, as much as $30 billion of the new funds would replace money that is currently being spent by government programs, private charity, and parents, while as little as $6 billion would go to pre-K services for children who currently have none. And that's if they participate.

Because no pre-K program will be compulsory, at least some of the families that don't sign on today will not do so tomorrow, either because they're too disorganized or because they truly don't want—or need—it for their daughters and sons.

Could this large additional public expenditure be worth it? The most dramatic claims for "investing in young children" have been made by economist James Heckman, who argues that this is a fundamental national strategy for building human capital, enhancing workforce productivity, and reducing welfare outlays. He finds lasting benefits both to individuals and to society, and his analyses are widely cited by pre-K advocates and politicians. However, Heckman confines himself to disadvantaged children, and the evidence he cites comes from Perry-style "hothouse" programs. Although this may strengthen the case for targeted, high-intensity intervention programs for acutely disadvantaged preschoolers, it does little to advance the argument for universal pre-K.

In fact, Heckman favors targeted pre-K programs. Writing in the Wall Street Journal in 2006, he acknowledged that, because "children from advantaged environments received substantial early investment" from their families, "there is little basis for providing universal programs at zero cost." Doing the latter, he explained, would be inefficient, wasteful of public dollars, and probably not effective in helping poor kids.

WHAT TO DO?

Society plainly has an interest in upgrading its human talent, as well as in narrowing damaging achievement gaps and ensuring that everyone has a fighting chance to develop their intellect and skills to the max. Yet it's not obvious that society has a compelling interest in paying for pre-K education that does not demonstrably and durably accomplish one or more of those objectives.

If states took the $5.4 billion that they're currently spending on pre-K programs and concentrated it on the roughly 10 percent of four-year-olds who most need intensive preschooling, they'd have close to $50,000 per child to spend. That's enough to pay for more than two years of Perry Preschool or Abecedarian-style programming. Even stretched from birth to age five, it would work out to about $10,000 per child per year, and that's without even touching the federal childcare dollars, leveraging the Head Start appropriation, or tapping into other current public spending on needy kids.

A powerful case can also be made for well-crafted experimentation and innovation. Despite all the pilot projects, studies, and evaluations, not enough is known with confidence about the essential ingredients of effective pre-K education and how to make those effects last. More also needs to be learned about the key elements of program quality (concentrating, one hopes, on results rather than inputs) that can successfully be brought to scale. Nobody has yet devised the perfect pre-K program, and it's likely that different approaches will work better for different kids and circumstances. It is therefore folly for states not to try diverse designs and evaluate them all.

Head Start needs urgent attention, too. Despite its popularity, despite the billions being spent on it, and notwithstanding the decent job it does of targeting services on needy kids, today's Head Start, when viewed through the lens of kindergarten readiness, amounts to a wasted opportunity.

In a rational world, it would make vastly more sense—and cost the taxpayer far less money—to overhaul Head Start (and pre-Head Start, Early Head Start, etc.), using existing programs that are already targeted, perhaps focusing them even more tightly on the neediest kids, starting them younger, extending them longer, and insisting that they emphasize preliteracy, vocabulary, and other school-readiness skills as well as the "softer" attributes (attentiveness, self-confidence, motivation, etc.) that Heckman links to later-life success. Such programs would be delivered by standards-based, outcomes-focused, rigorously assessed providers who are willing to be judged on the kindergarten readiness of their graduates.

But preschool policy cannot be made in a vacuum. Why its gains dissipate and the gaps that it narrows widen later has much to do with unchanging home and neighborhood situations. But we must also acknowledge, despite all the K–12 education reform of recent decades, the crummy, ineffectual schools that most poor children still end up in, the absence of decent choices among schools, and the system's still-widespread weak expectations, limp curricula, slipshod accountability, and ill-prepared, ill-compensated, and often inexperienced teachers.

Sustaining whatever pre-K gains can be produced, especially for poor kids, is principally a challenge for K–12 policy and practice. But that does not mean entrusting pre-K education to public school systems that today can't even sustain their own gains. (If they did, twelfth-grade NAEP results would show upticks akin to those in fourth grade.) Adding more years to the current public education mandate would simply give ineffectual school systems more time to fumble around while entangling pre-K education more tightly in the web of school politics, federalism disputes, bureaucratic rigidities, and adult interest groups.

Preschool—done right, tightly targeted, and intensively delivered, with sound cognitive standards, quality criteria, and readiness assessments—is the proper work of early childhood educators and America's vast preschool and childcare industry. Capitalizing on, maintaining, even magnifying the results of such early education is the proper work of the primary-secondary system—in addition, that is, to all the other serious challenges that confront it.

Perhaps the current lull in preschool expansionism will create the opportunity to take a deep breath and figure out just what is most urgent in this realm and what must be done to make it succeed.

DISCUSSION QUESTIONS

1. Should preschools be responsible to make children ready for K–12 education? Why or why not?
2. Do you believe that universal pre-K education is an investment in human capital or an inefficient drain of public resources? Explain.
3. Should targeted preschool education include nonacademic social services like health care, breakfasts, etc.? Explain.
4. What might be some challenges that a targeted pre-K program might face?

16 Demographics and Education in the Twenty-First Century

NORMAN ENG

FOCUSING QUESTIONS

1. What role do cognitive skills play in the twenty-first century?
2. How can knowledge of changing demographic patterns help educators teach students more effectively?
3. What internal and external factors influence one's cognitive ability?
4. What are some benefits and drawbacks to implementing a differentiated schooling approach based on students' abilities and interests?
5. Why is career and technical education (CTE) an essential component of differentiated schooling?

The National Academy of Sciences' (2007) report, Rising Above the Gathering Storm, called for more scientific and technical innovation to maintain America's economic growth and vitality. Countless other reports have called for more science, technology, engineering and math (STEM) education, culminating in Obama's 2009 Educate to Innovate initiative. The thinking goes, the more STEM knowledge students gain, the more prepared they will be for the twenty-first-century knowledge-based economy. The problem is that STEM jobs account for merely 5 percent of all U.S. jobs, which suggests that prudent allocation of resources is a principal consideration: Do all students need STEM education, or should it be focused primarily on the mathematically and scientifically inclined? And if so, what are the implications for the majority who are not? In this connection, demographics may hold the key to developing a more pragmatic twenty-first-century solution to educational equality and excellence.

THE IMPORTANCE OF DEMOGRAPHICS

Demographics tell us what issues we are dealing with and what kind of society we are becoming. For instance, a higher population of immigrants suggests that we need to increase bilingual education. A shrinking middle class foretells growing inequality, as well as social, economic, and political polarity. A graying population means that healthcare will become an important job sector. Understanding demographics helps us to better address employment opportunities and problems by matching demand and supply.

In the case of STEM education, policymakers are faced with a dilemma. They can consider the "quantitative" approach, which seeks to expand the number of scientists and engineers by requiring compulsory STEM education for all students (i.e., providing some STEM for all); or, they can follow the "qualitative" approach, which strives to optimize STEM development for the mathematically and scientifically inclined student. If the current education priority is STEM competitiveness, then the latter approach is more feasible and efficient, according to The Information Technology and Innovation Foundation (2010). Yet this approach is potentially exclusionary, because only a fraction of students will be extensively developed. On the other hand, the enduring American commitment to equality necessitates that no group or individual be excluded from opportunity. So how can this disparity be resolved?

First, it must be acknowledged that the two apparently competing concepts of individual differences and individual equality are central to America's unique heritage. While citizens in other nations have fought for human rights, they tend to be focused on the collective good (e.g., class equality in the French Revolution, political and economic freedom in China's Tiananmen Square protests, and racial equality for black South African inhabitants under Apartheid rule). America's founding principles, on the other hand, reflect the emphasis on individual liberty. Its subsequent history—through the Civil War, the Populist and Labor movements, and the Civil Rights movement—continues to chronicle the struggle for the right to be simultaneously different and equal. In fact, it has been the perennial tension to resolve this paradoxical ideal that

has cultivated bold progress, an American hallmark no other nation has matched in the modern era.

Many industries in the United States seem to realize that the concepts of individual differences and individual equality are not mutually exclusive. Professionals in the entertainment, food, and apparel industries pragmatically differentiate their communication to consider the diverse wants and needs of specific demographics (such as ethnicity, gender, and age) while striving to be inclusive. Advertisers for an athletic apparel company, for instance, might develop separate marketing campaigns for a sneaker, one that targets young urban males and another that caters to long distance runners.

How physicians use demographic characteristics to diagnose patients is illuminating. Despite similar pathological patterns, human beings have widely different health profiles that are affected by genetics and environment. Because of this, physicians perform what is called a "differential diagnosis," a determination of what has led to the system failure in a particular place and time. Often, these diagnoses take into account certain patterns that govern group behavior and characteristics, such as smoking, family history, and even ethnic membership. Troubleshooting complex systems such as the human body is notoriously challenging, but can be facilitated if doctors are aware of certain realities—that Jews and Asians, for example, are predisposed to lactose intolerance, or that high blood pressure and diabetes are more common among Hispanics and blacks. In turn, patients receive an equally unbiased, differentiated, and appropriate plan of treatment.

Politicians similarly craft distinct messages that target by geography (swing states), religion (the Christian vote), age (the Social Security vote), political view (Tea Party), lobbies (meat industry), and of course ethnicity (the Hispanic vote) when running for public office. The central point is that most industries in this hyper-specialized age recognize that individuals and groups are more receptive when you respect their distinctiveness and focus on addressing their particular needs. It is perhaps the most democratic approach.

However, this differentiated model has curiously eluded the education industry. Though it adjusts services for certain minority or protected groups (e.g., special education students, bilingual students), education primarily follows a "one-size-fits-all" instructional approach, ignoring differences, abilities, and interests, particularly at the secondary level. Schools still compel all students to take academic courses that muddle the connection between school and life. Invariably, the academically disinclined students lose interest and drop out. There is some evidence, in fact, that augmenting math and science requirements can even lead to lower high school graduation rates (Symonds, Schwartz, & Ferguson, 2011).

If educators followed a heterogeneous approach to instruction, they would be more mindful of individual abilities and—more importantly—offer a supportive curriculum that provides a visible pathway to achievement. Cultivating the link between potentiality and success would increase students' receptivity and ensure that employers invest in the development of future workers. Amazingly, this intuitive solution runs completely counter to current reform initiatives. If educators wish to match student skills with the specialized demands of a knowledge economy, then they will need to first acknowledge the limitations of a standardized curriculum paradigm.

Two interrelated demographic segments in particular illuminate the importance of a differentiated model and have critical implications for the twenty-first-century knowledge-based economy: the cognitive class and Asian American immigrants. In light of emerging research, the analysis of both groups reveals the folly of a homogenized education model, particularly at the secondary level. The intention is to shed light on a more relevant education paradigm that would ensure the United States remains economically competitive.

THE COGNITIVE CLASS

The cognitive class, also known as the intellectual class (Rindermann & Thompson, 2011), the smart fraction (La Griffe du Lion, 2002; Rindermann, Sailer, & Thompson, 2009), the creative class (Florida, 2003), or the gifted and talented, is not a traditionally recognized demographic segment such as immigrants, Hispanics, or women. In education for the twenty-first-century knowledge economy, however, recognizing the intellectual group—which can be composed of individuals representing all national, racial, and ethnic groups—is critically important.

Research has shown that a person's mental ability has a significant and positive relationship with income and educational attainment (Heckman, Stixrud, & Urzua, 2006; Ng, Eby, Sorensen, & Feldman, 2005; Scullin, Peters, Williams, & Ceci, 2000). On an individual level, it functions to open the doors of opportunity and to solve problems by increasing insight, foresight, and rationality that result in proximal consequences like higher-quality work and better health (Rindermann, 2008; Rindermann & Thompson, 2011).

On an aggregate level, cognitive ability has an enormous impact on economic growth, according to an emerging group of economists and cognitive science researchers. Lynn and Vanhanen (2002) revealed three major insights in a seminal study that collected data from 81 countries: (1) national IQ correlated significantly with per capita Gross Domestic Product (GDP) ($r = .62$); (2) IQ was similarly correlated with economic growth ($r = .64$); and (3) nations' IQs differed widely, with East Asian countries like Japan (IQ = 105) and South Korea (106) scoring high, and sub-Saharan African countries like South Africa (72) and Ghana (71) scoring low.

Although Lynn and Vanhanen's data drew wide scrutiny for its methodological limitations and racial implications, numerous studies have since confirmed the overall IQ-productivity relationship (e.g., Jones & Schneider, 2010; Hunt & Wittman, 2008; Hanushek & Woessmann, 2009). Lynn and Vanhanen (2006) and Rindermann (2007) further reinforced the validity of national IQ by associating it with international tests such as the Trends in International Mathematics and Science Study (TIMSS), the Programme for International Student Assessment (PISA), and the Progress in International Reading Literacy Study (PIRLS), with an r ranging from .80 to .90. Apparently, mathematical, scientific, and verbal abilities are suitable proxies for IQ.

Rather than focus on the average cognitive ability of a nation, several contemporaries have centered on the academic elite known as the cognitive class. Studies suggest that the IQ and test scores of those within the top ten percentile had a decisive effect on GDP and STEM achievement compared with national IQ, even after controlling for external factors like education level and degree of economic freedom (Gelade, 2008; Rindermann & Thompson, 2011). STEM achievement was determined by four indicators: (1) the number of patents per million people; (2) Nobel Prizes in science related to population size; (3) the number of scientists and engineers per million; and (4) the rate of high-technology exports as a percentage of manufacturing exports.

What makes these results compelling is not merely the high correlation between elite cognitive ability and national wealth, but rather the direction of causality and predictive effects as revealed by regression analyses, path analyses, longitudinal analyses, and cross-lagged panel designs. Although there were reciprocal effects between the two, the effect of intelligence on wealth is significantly stronger; that is, cognitive ability leads to higher wealth more than wealth leads to increased intelligence. Causal relationships are undoubtedly difficult to determine, but these studies have certainly demonstrated a clear connection between the two.

In concrete terms, Rindermann and Thompson (2011) discovered that an increase of one IQ point per person in the intellectual class raises average per capita GDP by U.S. $468 compared with only $229 by those from the mean group. Assuming that 5 percent of the 55 million public school students are considered gifted and talented (G&T), then each additional increase in IQ points for the G&T students would add almost $1.3 billion to the GDP. From another perspective, Hanushek and Woessmann's (2009) calculations suggested that the top 5 percent of students who increased their international scores by ten percentage points would have over four times greater impact on a nation's annual economic growth compared with those at the basic literacy level (1.3 vs. 0.3 percentage point annual growth, respectively). Simply put, the higher the IQ, the greater the impact on the economy.

Taken together, these studies suggest that the current lack of investment in academically high-potential students, particularly in the STEM fields, will have negative consequences for the U.S. economy. The federal government's simultaneous focus on academic low-achievers and STEM coursework for all students in the upper grades is admirable, but naïve and narrow-minded in a globally technological world. More resources are needed to better assess the diverse abilities of all students, as well as identifying and developing academically high potential students.

THE 2012 PEW STUDY: THE RISE OF THE ASIAN-AMERICANS

Another demographic segment that can significantly impact America's knowledge economy are the highly skilled immigrants, many of whom come from Asia. Asian immigrants, in fact, are granted three-quarters of all H-1B visas, for instance, with China and India alone accounting for 64 percent. Even so, such findings tell only a fraction of an emerging trend. According to the Pew Research Center's (2012) newest study, *The Rise of Asian Americans*, Asian Americans (the bulk of whom trace their roots to six countries—China, India, Japan, Korea, the Philippines, and Vietnam) are standing out as a select group, leading all other racial groups in population growth, income, and education in the United States.

Representing 6.2 percent of the total U.S. population (as of 2011), the Asian population (including mixed race Asians) grew 46 percent over the past decade and surpassed Hispanics as the fastest growing immigrant group in 2010. Though the Hispanic immigration rate has slowed significantly since the middle of last decade, those from Asia have continued to gain—quintupling from 1980 (3.6 million) to 2011 (18.2 million). Asian immigrants accounted for 36 percent (430,000) of new

immigrants—between 2007 and 2010—compared with 31 percent who were Hispanic (370,000). Based on the most recent U.S. Census Bureau's (2008a; 2008b) population projections, growth (or percentage change) for both groups will outpace blacks and whites by 2050 (173 percent Asians and 189 percent Hispanics); see Table 16.1. By then, it is estimated that Asians will number over 43 million and make up almost 10 percent of the total U.S. population. The growth rate of whites and mixed-race whites will decline in comparison, going from 81 percent of the population in 2010 to about 77 percent in 2050. If mixed-race whites are excluded, they represented 64.7 percent in 2010 and will steadily decline over the next four decades to 46.3 percent. By 2050, whites in the United States will be the minority population.

The Asians' level of growth is compounded by certain economic advantages. For one, Asian immigrants have a much lower undocumented rate compared to Hispanics (approximately 15 percent vs. 45 percent, respectively). Also, Asian immigrants

TABLE 16.1   Projections and Percent Distribution of the U.S. Population by Race Alone or in Combination*: 2010 to 2050 (in millions)

Race	2010	2020	2030	2040	2050	% Change 2010–2050
Asian	17.6 5.7%	23.1 6.8%	29.2 7.8%	35.9 8.9%	43.1 9.8%	173%
Hispanic	49.7 16.0%	66.4 19.4%	85.9 13.0%	108.2 26.7%	132.8 30.3%	189%
Black	42.2 13.6%	47.7 14.0%	53.5 14.3%	59.5 14.7%	65.7 15.0%	110%
White	251.4 81.0%	272.8 79.9%	294.9 79.0%	316.7 78.1%	339.4 77.3%	95%
Total	310.2 100%**	341.4 100%**	373.5 100%**	405.7 100%**	439.0 100%**	—

Note: *In combination* means in combination with one or more other races. **The sum of the race groups adds to more than 100% (the total population) because individuals may report more than one race. Source: U.S. Census Bureau (2008a; 2008b).

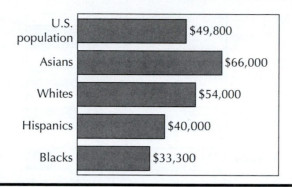

FIGURE 16.1   Median Household Income, 2010

Note: Asians include mixed-race Asian population, regardless of Hispanic origin. Whites and Blacks include only non-Hispanics. Hispanics are of any race. Household income is based on householders ages 18 and older; race and ethnicity are based on those of household head. Source: Pew Research Center analysis of 2010 American Community Survey, Integrated Public Use Microdata Sample (IPUMS) files, Pew Research Center (2012).

are notably more likely than other groups to be admitted with employment visas (27 percent received green cards based on employer sponsorship, compared with 8 percent of other immigrants). Most importantly, their median household income ($66,000) exceeds other groups, including whites ($54,000), even when adjusted for household size differences; see Figure 16.1. Their median household wealth, or sum of assets, also eclipses that of the median U.S. population ($83,500 vs. $68,529), although they still lag far behind whites ($112,000). Despite outperforming whites in income, Asians have a lower net worth as a result of immigration restrictions prior to 1965 that hindered long-term asset accumulation. If current trends continue, that gap should shrink significantly by 2050.

Such economic advantages are most likely because Asians are well educated overall; almost half have at least a bachelor's degree compared with 28 percent of the U.S. population. Among recent Asian immigrant adults, the percent is even higher: practically two-thirds who immigrated between 2007 and 2010 were enrolled in college or graduate school, or held a college degree (see Figure 16.2).

For now, overrepresentation is probably the most fitting description characterizing this ambitious demographic, especially within higher education. Asian Americans constitute 60 percent of all foreign students in U.S. educational institutions. Within STEM fields, both foreign- and native-born Asian students disproportionately held advanced U.S. degrees in 2010: A quarter of the 48,069 research doctorates granted at U.S. institutions; almost half of all engineering Ph.D. degrees, 38 percent of math and computer science doctorates; one-third of physical sciences doctorates; one-quarter of life science Ph.D. degrees; and almost one in five social sciences doctorates. Predictably, two-thirds of the Intel Science high school finalists in 2011 were of Asian heritage. Many finalists and winners of this talent search have subsequently won Nobel Prizes, MacArthur and Sloan research fellowships, or been elected to the National Academy of Sciences. They have been the key to keeping the United States competitive with China and India.

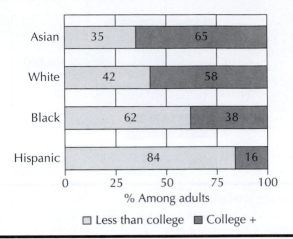

FIGURE 16.2 Education Characteristics of Recent Immigrants by Race and Ethnicity, 2010

Source: Pew Research Center analysis of 2010 American Community Survey, Integrated Public Use of Microdata Sample (IPUMS) files, Pew Research Center (2012).

Undergirding their economic and educational edge is a distinctive culture that strongly values marriage, parenthood, hard work, future orientation, and career success. The Pew survey reveals that Asians do in fact place the highest priorities on: (1) being a good parent (three-quarters of Asian-Americans vs. 50 percent of the general public); and (2) marriage (54 percent say that having a successful marriage is one of the most important things in life, compared with only 34 percent of all American adults); see Figure 16.3. As a result, they are more likely to be married (59 percent vs. 51 percent U.S. total), less likely to be an unmarried mother (16 percent vs. 41 percent), and their children are more likely than all American children to be raised in a household with two married parents (80 percent vs. 63 percent). Along with a larger than average household size, this stability coincides with middle class values and creates a strong network of support for children's growth and learning.

Hard work and success also rate highly among Asian Americans: 93 percent believed that "[Asian] Americans from my country of origin group are very hardworking," compared with only 57 percent who thought that Americans are very hardworking. Perhaps no other book captured the stereotype of strict parenting more than Yale law professor Amy Chua's (2011) *Battle Hymn of the Tiger Mother*, in which she unapologetically opined why "Chinese mothers are superior." In it, Chua extolled the virtues of authoritarian parenting where overriding children's preferences was crucial in getting them to practice harder and longer to become better at what they are doing. Asian parents are more demanding because they "assume strength, not fragility" in their child, unlike the archetypical American parent who constantly agonize over their child's psyche, according to Chua. Results from the Pew survey appear to support her parenting model, with six out of ten Asian Americans finding American parents put too little pressure on their children to succeed in school. Only 9 percent said the same about Asian-American parents. Interestingly, nearly four

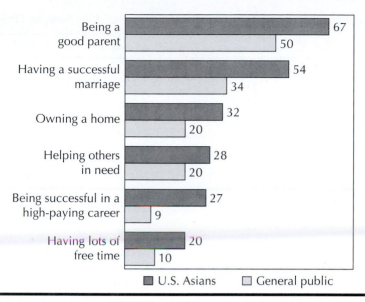

FIGURE 16.3   Life Goals and Priorities: Asian Americans vs. General Public
Source: Pew Research Center (2012): Asian-American Survey. Q19 a-g. General public results from January 2010 survey by the Pew Research Center. The question wording varied slightly from one survey to the other.

out of ten Asian Americans also agree that Asian parents put too much pressure on their children.

ASIANS' ACADEMIC PROFICIENCY

Educators and policymakers are well aware of Asian's overall academic proficiency at the school level. Out of all ethnic groups, Asians had the highest percentage of students who were proficient (a score of 3 or 4) on state tests in 2008: 83 percent of fourth and eighth graders were proficient in reading; whereas for math, 88 percent in fourth grade, 86 percent in eighth grade, and 81 percent in high school were deemed at least competent (Center on Education Policy, 2010); see Table 16.2. Only in high school reading did the same portion of whites score proficiently (78 percent). Asians similarly outperformed whites in 29 out of 34 states in math state tests at the advanced level, representing a median of 46 percent in the advanced category, compared with whites at 36 percent. As broadly acknowledged, a significant gap between Asian/Whites and African American/Hispanics exists across all levels, widening particularly in eighth grade and high school math. This plight has troubling implications for the twenty-first-century economy if America's education model rests on a one-size-fits-all approach.

In addition, Asian students are overrepresented among the gifted and talented (G&T). Asians make up only 5 percent of the total primary and secondary public school population but comprise 9.4 percent of the G&T population (Office for Civil Rights, 2006). Representation can be measured by comparing the percent of students in programs for G&T relative to their proportion in the overall student population, with 1.0 a perfect proportionate representation. Asian

TABLE 16.2 Median Percentages of Students' Scoring Proficiency on State Tests, by Ethnicity, 2008

Subject/Grade	Asian American	African American	Hispanic	White
Reading				
Grade 4	83	58	64	81
Grade 8	83	58	58	81
High school	78	53	56	78
Math				
Grade 4	88	56	67	82
Grade 8	86	46	55	77
High School	81	45	50	71

Source: Center on Education Policy (2010)

students are overrepresented compared to white students in G&T programs (see Figure 16.4), despite being outnumbered in total. It is possible that the percentage would be even higher if gifted and talented English language learners (i.e., limited in understanding English) also were included.

ASIANS' STEM CONTRIBUTIONS

High population growth, income, and education suggest significant potential, but do

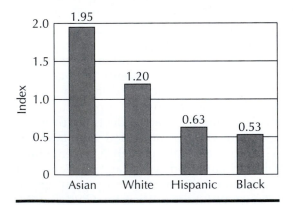

FIGURE 16.4 Gifted Representation Index
Note: 1.0 = perfect proportionate representation; > 1.0 = Overrepresentation; <1.0 = Underrepresentation.
Source: Office of the Civil Rights (2006).

not necessarily reveal impact. The Pew study showed that Asians earned a disproportionate number of degrees in science, technology, engineering, and math as well as of H-1B visas. But actual data of economic and intellectual contributions are needed to prove the value of demographic characteristics as the basis for a reimagined education model. Within the engineering and technology fields, for example, Asians—especially Chinese and Indians—are a driving force behind entrepreneurship and intellectual property that directly impact America's GDP.

In terms of immigrant-founded U.S. businesses, the four largest immigrant groups came from India, the United Kingdom, China, and Taiwan (Wadhwa, Saxenian, Rissing, & Gereffi, 2007). However, Asians comprised half of the top ten nations whose immigrants founded engineering and technology (E&T) companies in the United States. In particular, Indians were key founders of 26 percent of American E&T start-ups from 1995 to 2005. In fact, they dominated the entrepreneurial arena among immigrant-founded businesses—more than those from the next four nationalities combined (see Figure 16.5). Their growth, as illustrated in Silicon Valley, outpaced every other immigrant group over the past 20 years: Indian-led businesses in

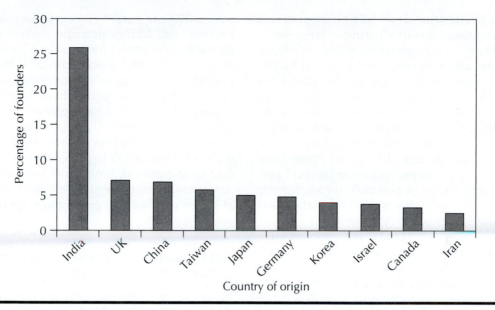

FIGURE 16.5   Birthplace of Engineering and Technology Immigrant Founders
Source: Wadhwa, Saxenian, Rissing, and Gereffi (2007).

Silicon Valley more than doubled (from 7 percent to 15.5 percent) between 1995 and 2005, whereas Chinese-led tech companies declined from 17 percent in 1998 (Saxenian, 1999) to 12.8 percent in 2005.

Aside from founding engineering and technology companies in the United States, Asians also played a significant role in other STEM fields. Whereas Figure 16.1 displayed the contributions of immigrants as a whole in each industry, Table 16.3 compares the influence between Asia and Europe (regions that contributed 10 percent or fewer in each industry, e.g., Middle East, Central/South America, and Australia were grouped together under "Others").

Workers from Asia represent the largest portion in four out of the five

TABLE 16.3   Industry Breakdown of Immigrant-Founded Companies, by Ethnic/Geographic Region

	Asia	Europe	Others*
Innovation/Manufacturing-Related Service	50%	19%	31%
Biosciences	32	37	31
Computers/Communications	63	20	17
Semiconductors	55	15	20
Software	48	24	28

*Others include nationalities whose companies comprised 10% or less: Middle East, Central/South America, Africa, Canada, and Australia.

Source: Wadhwa, Saxenian, Rissing, and Gereffi (2007)

immigrant-founded STEM industries (innovation/manufacturing-related service, computers/communications, semiconductors and software) in the United States. Those from India, in particular, stand out significantly, founding more companies in the innovation/manufacturing-related services sector (24 percent) than those from all of the European nations combined (19 percent). Indian immigrants also dwarf those from other Asian nations, including Japan (7 percent) and China (6 percent). As a reference point, the next highest non-Asian nation was the United Kingdom (6 percent).

The biosciences field was more evenly distributed. Indians, Germans, and Koreans each accounted for 10 percent of immigrant-founded start-ups in America, and British, French, and Israeli immigrants each contributed 6 percent. In total, those from Asia and Europe represented 32 percent and 37 percent, respectively.

Within both the computers/communications and the semiconductors industries, workers from China, Taiwan, and India were overrepresented. They accounted for over half of all immigrant start-ups in the former and 40 percent in the latter. Overall, the percentage of Asian immigrant-founders in the computer industry (63 percent) and semiconductors industry (55 percent) was more than triple that of Europeans (20 percent and 15 percent, respectively).

In the software industry, Indians alone dominated immigrants from all other nations, founding 34 percent of all new businesses in the United States. Their rate was almost four times that of the next highest group, the British (9 percent). Asians overall founded twice as many start-ups as those from Europe (48 percent vs. 24 percent).

Intellectual property, in the form of patents, is another concrete measure of STEM innovation. Data from the U.S. Patent & Trademark Office (USPTO), which measures domestic patenting activity, revealed a steadily increasing rate among Asian residents over a 30-year period (Foley & Kerr, 2012). Chinese and Indian patenting activity, for example, accounted for merely 5.3 percent from 1975 to 1982, but by the 2000 to 2004 period, their share increased three-fold to almost 17 percent. In contrast, patenting among ethnic whites has declined over the same 30-year period. Those of white Americans, who own the lion's share of patents in the United States, fell 16 percent (from 81 percent to 68 percent). Innovators from Europe saw patenting activity fall even more sharply at 25 percent (from 8.3 percent to 6.2 percent); see Figure 16.6.

THE CALL FOR EXCELLENCE BASED ON DIFFERENTIATED ABILITIES

Acknowledging the rise of Asian immigrants or the impact of the smart fraction is in no way meant to suggest any inherent abilities that other groups lack; in fact, many immigrants from Southeast Asian countries face much of the same poverty and low achievement as American minorities. However, with all the data on the economic contribution of Asian Americans and the intellectual class, it is nonetheless easy to dismiss these findings as elitist or even racist. In fact, it is merely acknowledging what parents, teachers, and others have long known to be true: that individuals have wide-ranging abilities, inclinations, and interests, and that various factors—fairly or unfairly—contribute to these gaps.

Heredity, for one, plays a significant part in determining one's cognitive abilities. Estimates in academic research vary widely, although social scientists generally assert that heredity accounts for between 45 percent (Jencks, 1972) and 80 percent (Jensen, 1969) of talent. Despite ongoing disagreements, they also agree that cognitive ability can be modified by external factors, and that they dynamically interact to determine realized differences in potential.

Both the micro-environment, which includes one's local milieu (e.g., family, home,

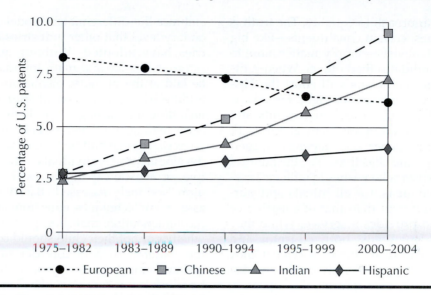

FIGURE 16.6   Growth in U.S. Patenting, by Ethnicity

Note: This table presents the share of patents in which inventors are of particular ethnicities, reside in the U.S. at the time of patent application, and work for a publicly listed corporation.

Source: Foley and Kerr (2012).

and school), and the macro-environment or broader forces (e.g., social class, education levels, and culture) have equally long-term influences. Within the macro forces, some have contended that accumulated advantages (or disadvantages) of geographical isolation and features (Nisbett, 2003; Ornstein, 2007) explain differences in human thought, behavior, and attitudes. Other researchers point to geo-political and economic realities such as voluntary migration (of Asians versus the involuntary migration of African slaves, for instance) and lack of opportunities in developing nations. The science of epigenetics, where gene expression of an offspring is influenced by parents' life experiences (e.g., the foods parents eat or the stresses they underwent when younger)—as opposed to parents' genetic code—has recently gained momentum as factors to explain mental, behavioral and physiological dispositions (Shulevitz, 2012).

Despite the reality of unequal abilities, progressive thinkers are reluctant to promulgate any kind of differentiated development in light of historical oppression and man's imperfect nature, so they invariably push for widespread teacher and school accountability in an effort to standardize outcomes. Inevitably, modern policies in the United States become captive to the unwavering push for equality at the expense of bona fide excellence, as demonstrated by compensatory funding, the focus on low-achieving and minority students, and the lowering of standards over the past decade in state tests and in higher education.

Marketers and politicians have it easier in some ways. They aren't explicitly held to the same equity imperatives and ideals that educators are to create equal opportunities and outcomes. Instead, those in other industries have a more grounded perspective about the existence of individual and group differences, and subsequently, a more pragmatic approach to equality. The truth is that, at times, certain constituents—like big donors or lobbyists—simply matter more to political candidates than others. When it fits their needs, politicians will court the Hispanic vote or the religious right. For advertisers, addressing the different wants and needs of suburban moms, baby boomers, or the millennial generation depends on their annual corporate objectives. Yet, the mindset of an advertiser who wishes to influence customer behavior is, for all intents and purposes, no different than that of a teacher or doctor who provides a service. While they have different goals, both educator and advertiser would be better served if they consider their target's individuality or distinctiveness. Context informs the approach; for educators, that means recognizing the circumstances and dispositions of their students and developing an appropriate plan. It also means embracing diversity of abilities and, often, unequal talents.

Ornstein (1977; 2002) asserted that inequality in the outcomes of schooling is a function of the natural inequality of talent among students (as well as a function of external forces). In fact, he argued that no more than 20 percent of educational outcomes are related to the combined influence of teachers and schools. Demographic patterns, as research on the cognitive elite and the rising Asian demographic has shown, illustrate the reality of these differences and sometimes magnify them. Accordingly, they should be scrupulously understood when formulating a more pragmatic egalitarianism. The solution is not to take on the Sisyphean task of equalizing abilities and outcomes of all students, as current reforms aim to do; rather, the solution lies in differentiating the curriculum by offering multiple pathways to success that take advantage of America's unique diversity.

First, despite educators' apprehension of importing business practices into education, a reframed education paradigm should embrace the differentiated model at the secondary level that other industries and countries have adopted. Without question, a rigorous literacy and math foundation must be laid at the primary, elementary, and the middle school levels for all students, given their differing starting points. However, at the early high school level—when abilities and interests emerge and become amplified—the development of individuals' athletic, cognitive, or artistic capabilities will need to be more seriously assessed. Based on formal assessment techniques, educators can provide recommendations that allow parents to decide whether or not their child should continue on the academic track or consider a career and nonacademic program, a process that families benefit from in countries like Germany, Finland, and Denmark.

As a result of the early assessment of academic potential and the implementation of an individualized plan, students will become engaged, fulfilled, and will significantly contribute to society. Profligate initiatives like the "STEM coursework for all" programs will be de-emphasized to more efficiently fund career and training initiatives (for a significant portion of students) and a more robust academic education (for those with potential in STEM, law, teaching, and other knowledge-based fields). Allocating resources to those with artistic, athletic, or interpersonal skills has long been accepted, so there is no reason why funds shouldn't also be distributed to the cognitively gifted and talented.

Concomitantly, schools must provide multiple pathways to graduation and success in the knowledge economy for the majority who will not go into STEM fields. Although Americans need to acknowledge that mathematical, verbal, and spatial skills are highly valued in a knowledge-based economy, this does not mean that that those with alternative abilities cannot contribute. As Murray (2008) asserted, the problem is the "misbegotten, pernicious, wrong-headed idea that not going to college means you're a failure" (p. 150). Is having a college education the only ticket to success? Going to or finishing college, in the traditional sense (i.e., the academic track), may not be an appropriate or desirable use of one's time and resources. Instead, policymakers should confront such cultural biases and expand niche secondary education services at the high school and community college levels to meet employer demand.

For example, a complex knowledge-based economy needs a diverse and large number of workers to implement the innovation strategies developed by scientists and engineers in a mutually enforcing way (Hanushek & Woessmann, 2009; Autor, Katz, & Kearney, 2006). These positions have been called "middle-skill" jobs—such as computer support, healthcare technicians, back office work in financial and healthcare companies, auto and airplane repair using computer diagnostic equipment—many of which require more than a high school degree but not necessarily a traditional four-year college degree. In fact, middle-skill jobs that require a post-secondary certificate/license or associate's degree are projected to be the fastest growing job sector, particularly in the healthcare, construction, and manufacturing industries (Council of Economic Advisors, 2009). Put simply, society also needs excellent technicians and skilled laborers.

High school students who pursue the vocational track or twenty-first-century career and technical education (CTE) programs like SkillsUSA, YearUp, and The Wisconsin Youth Apprenticeship Program will have the sought-after middle skills needed for jobs that pay better than those for high school graduates and pay comparably to or higher than those for many B.A. holders. It is worth noting that other developed European nations (e.g., Austria, Denmark, Finland, Germany, the Netherlands, Norway, and Switzerland) place far more emphasis on vocational education than Americans do:

between 40–70 percent of these European students opt for a "dual system approach" that combines classroom and workplace learning in high school, a pragmatic path that leads to real currency in the labor market (Symonds et al., 2011). The bottom line is that developing STEM skills, although important for a knowledge economy, should be but one part of America's twenty-first-century education paradigm, and that other career tracks have separate but complementary effects on economic growth as well. Given its diversity, the United States would also have an incomparable advantage in supplying hyper-specialized expertise over a wide range of industries—a benefit no other nation has.

Finally, these changes cannot be accomplished without robust support. Students with individualized pathway plans require highly qualified instruction and guidance. Understanding, recognizing, advising, and developing students' diverse abilities and talents are perennial teacher skills that take on considerably more importance in a differentiated paradigm; as such, building teacher capacity during the pre-service and in-service stage is of paramount importance. The role of career and guidance counselors will similarly be augmented, which will be particularly challenging with students who have no clear goals or exceptional talents. At the same time, a transparent process or system is needed to clearly delineate the major career pathways at the latter stages of middle school, so that students and their families can see the patterns of course-taking and other experiences that would best position them to gain access to that field (Symonds et al., 2011). Employers, parents, and schools subsequently will have a larger stake in developing each student's abilities.

CONCLUSION

The current school reform model, based on a standardized approach, is well intentioned and politically correct, but a hollow solution for unleashing diverse potential because it ignores real population differences. Although the United States should emphasize STEM education at the elementary and middle school levels, it can best remain committed to the ideal of equality and the value of the individual by recognizing students' heterogeneous capabilities—many of which will not lie in the STEM fields. More importantly, a reimagined model that offers multiple pathways for student success—whether through twenty-first-century CTE programs, intensive STEM education, or performing and visual arts career programs—is the fairest way to foster the abilities and interests of a demographically diverse student population while addressing the competitiveness issue. Individual equality and individual differences are uniquely American ideals worth fighting for, as long as they are honestly and pragmatically considered. The alternative, one in which equality and homogeneity are synonymous outcomes, would be utterly un-American.

In fact, former director of Common Cause John Gardner (1995) suggests that "Extreme egalitarianism . . . which ignores differences in native capacity and achievement, has not served democracy well. Carried far enough, it means . . . the end of striving for excellence which has produced mankind's greatest achievement." The implication is to develop individual capabilities in all domains that help make a successful transition from adolescence to adulthood, to "prepare more Americans for the new jobs that are being created in a world fueled by new technology. That's why investment in our people"—in more community colleges, Pell Grants and vocational-training classes—is "more important than ever," according to former president Bill Clinton at a recent convention speech (Friedman, 2012). Otherwise, we will be left with mismatched skills that result in what Uchitelle (2006) calls "disposable Americans," those caught in the cycle of unemployment and underemployment.

Diagnosing individual strengths, whether these are cognitive, artistic, or physical, is the ultimate realization of Gardner's excellence theme. It is the most ethical way to fulfill individual and collective potential. It is also the only way to allow for true human dignity.

REFERENCES

Autor, D., Katz, L., & Kearney, M. (2006). The polarization of the U.S. labor market. *American Economic Review, 96*(2): 189–194.

Center on Education Policy. (2010). *Policy implications of trends for Asian American students.* Washington, DC: Nancy Kober, Georgetown University.

Chua, A. (2011). *Battle Hymn of the Tiger Mother.* New York: Penguin Press.

Council of Economic Advisors. (2009). *Preparing the workers of today for the jobs of tomorrow.* Washington, DC. Retrieved from http://www.whitehouse.gov/assets/documents/Jobs_of_the_Future.pdf

Florida, R. (2003). *The rise of the creative class.* New York, NY: Basic Books.

Foley, C., & Kerr, W. (2012). Ethnic innovation and U.S. multinational firm activity (HBS Working Paper 12-006). Cambridge, MA: Harvard Business School. Retrieved from http://papers.ssrn.com/sol3/papers.cfm?abstract_id=1911295

Friedman, T. (2012). New rules. *The New York Times* (New York Ed.), SR13. Retrieved from http://www.nytimes.com/2012/09/09/opinion/sunday/friedman-new-rules.html?_r=1&emc=eta1

Gardner, J. (1995). *Excellence: Can we be equal and excellent too?* (Revised Ed.) New York, NY: W. W. Norton.

Gelade, G. (2008). IQ, cultural values, and the technological achievement of nations. *Intelligence, 36,* 711–718.

Hanushek, E., & Woessmann, L. (2009). Do better schools lead to more growth? Cognitive skills, economic outcomes, and causation (Discussion Paper No. 4575). Retrieved from Institute for the Study of Labor Web site: http://ftp.iza.org/dp4575.pdf

Heckman, J., Stixrud, J., & Urzua, S. (2006). The effects of cognitive and non-cognitive abilities on labor market outcomes and social behavior. *Journal of Labor Economics, 24,* 411–482.

Hunt, E., & Wittman, W. (2008). National intelligence and national prosperity. *Intelligence, 36,* 1–9.

Jencks, C. (1972). *Inequality: A reassessment of the effect of family and schooling in America.* New York, NY: Basic Books.

Jensen, A. (1969). How much can we boost IQ and scholastic achievement? *Harvard Educational Review, 39,* 1–123.

Jones, G., & Schneider, W. (2010). IQ in the production function: Evidence from immigrant earnings. *Economic Inquiry, 48*(3): 743–55.

La Griffe du Lion. (2002). The smart fraction theory of IQ and the wealth of nations. 4(1). Retrieved from http://lagriffedulion.f2s.com/sft.htm

Lynn, R., & Vanhanen, T. (2002). *IQ and wealth of nations.* Westport, CT: Praeger Publishers.

Lynn, R., & Vanhanen, T. (2006). *IQ and global inequality.* Augusta, GA: Washington Summit Publishers.

Murray, C. (2008). *Real education: Four simple truths for bringing America's schools back to reality.* New York, NY: Three Rivers Press.

National Academy of Sciences. (2007). *Rising above the gathering storm: Energizing and employing America for a brighter economic future.* Washington, DC: The National Academies Press. Retrieved from http://www.nap.edu

Ng, T. W. H., Eby, L. T., Sorensen, K. L., & Feldman, D. C. (2005). Predictors of objective and subjective career success: A meta-analysis. *Personnel Psychology, 58,* 367–408.

Nisbett, R. (2003). *The geography of thought: How Asians and westerners think differently…and why.* New York, NY: Free Press.

Office for Civil Rights. (2006). Civil rights data collection. Washington, DC: U.S. Department of Education. Retrieved from http://ocrdata.ed.gov/StateNationalEstimations/projections_2006

Ornstein, A. (1977). *An introduction to the foundations of education.* Chicago, IL: Rand McNally.

Ornstein, A. (2002). *Teaching and schooling in America: Pre- and post-September 11.* Boston, MA: Allyn & Bacon.

Ornstein, A. (2007). *Class counts: Education, inequality, and the shrinking middle class.* Lanham, MD: Rowman & Littlefield.

Pew Research Center. (2012). *The rise of Asian Americans.* Washington, DC: Paul Taylor (Ed.).

Rindermann, H. (2007). The g-factor of international cognitive ability comparisons: The homogeneity of results in PISA, TIMMSS, PIRLS and IQ-tests across nations. *European Journal of Personality, 21*(5): 667–706.

Rindermann, H. (2008). Relevance of education and intelligence at the national level for the economic welfare of people. *Intelligence, 36,* 127–142.

Rindermann, H., Sailer, M., & Thompson, J. (2009). The impact of smart fractions, cognitive ability of politicians and average competence of peoples on social development. *Talent Development & Excellence, 1*(1): 3–25.

Rindermann, H., & Thompson, J. (2011). Cognitive capitalism: The effect of cognitive ability on wealth, as mediated through scientific achievement and economic freedom. *Psychological Science, 22*(6): 754–763.

Saxenian, A. (1999). Silicon Valley's new immigrant entrepreneurs. San Francisco, CA: Public Policy Institute of California. Retrieved from http://www.ppic.org/content/pubs/report/R_699ASR.pdf

Scullin, M. H., Peters, E., Williams, W. W., & Ceci, S. J. (2000). The role of IQ and education in predicting later labor market outcomes. *Psychology, Public Policy, and Law, 6,* 63–89.

Shulevitz, J. (2012). Why fathers really matter. *The New York Times* (New York Ed.), SR1. Retrieved from http://www.nytimes.com/2012/09/09/opinion/sunday/why-fathers-really-matter.html?pagewanted=all

Symonds, W., Schwartz, R., & Ferguson, R. (2011). *Pathways to prosperity: Meeting the challenge of preparing young Americans for the 21st century.* Cambridge, MA: Pathways to Prosperity Project, Harvard Graduate School of Education.

The Innovation Technology and Innovation Foundation. (2010). *Refueling the U.S. innovation economy: Fresh approaches to science, technology, engineering and mathematics (STEM) education.* Washington, DC: Robert D. Atkinson and Merrilea Mayo.

Uchitelle, L. (2006). *The disposable American: Layoffs and their consequences.* New York, NY: Knopf.

U.S. Census Bureau (Population Division). (2008a). Table 4. Projections of the Population by Sex, Race, and Hispanic Origin for the United States: 2010 to 2050 (NP2008-T4). Retrieved from http://www.census.gov/population/www/projections/summarytables.html

U.S. Census Bureau (Population Division). (2008b). Table 6. Percent of the Projected Pop-ulation by Race and Hispanic Origin for the United States: 2010 to 2050 (NP2008-T6). Retrieved from http://www.census.gov/population/www/projections/summaryta-bles.html

Wadhwa, V., Saxenian, A., Rissing, B., & Gereffi, G. (2007). America's new immigrant entre-preneurs: Part I. Duke Science, Technology & Innovation Paper No. 23. Available at SSRN: http://ssrn.com/abstract=990152 or http://dx.doi.org/10.2139/ssrn.990152

DISCUSSION QUESTIONS

1. How do we strike the balance between addressing the nation's economic interests (or needs) and those of the individual?
2. Are the two ideals of excellence and equity compatible? Explain.
3. Is going to college a good decision for all students? Explain.
4. Compare the pros and cons of a standards-based education model with those of a differentiated schooling model. Which do you prefer and why?
5. Drawing on your perception of the current education system, do you think that the United States will move toward a differentiated approach? Explain.

17 Disciplining the Mind

Veronica Boix Mansilla
Howard Gardner

FOCUSING QUESTIONS

1. Compare learning subject matter and disciplinary thinking.
2. What are some limitations of subject matter learning?
3. Describe the four capacities the authors suggest as part of a quality precollegiate education.
4. How is learning history different from doing history?
5. How can teachers "nurture the disciplined mind" of their students?

The unit on industrialization was almost over. Phillip, a tenth-grade world history teacher, began to design the final test. In the past, he had included questions from his weekly quizzes as well as new questions about key events, people, and inventions. This approach had proven comfortable for both him and his students.

But this time he decided to raise the stakes. He wondered whether students' understanding of the process and meaning of industrialization had improved over the last six weeks. Could students explain why industrialization took place? Could they recognize how difficult it is for historians to build an empirically grounded portrait of an unfolding past or draw telling comparisons with today's communications revolution? These goals seemed far more important than the usual litany of names, dates, and locations. Yet Phillip worried that his students would see reflective questions of this kind in the final exam as foul play.

Phillip's dilemma permeates classrooms around the world and across the disciplines. It addresses issues of accountability, the nature of teacher-student interactions, and the rituals of schooling. Most striking, it reveals two colliding views of what it means to understand history, biology, mathematics, or the visual arts. From the conventional standpoint, students learn subject matter. In general, they and their teachers conceive of the educational task as committing to memory large numbers of facts, formulas, and figures. Fixed in textbooks, such facts are taken as uncontroversial, their mastery valued as a sign of cultural literacy.

In sharp contrast with teaching subject matter, an alternative perspective emphasizes teaching disciplines and disciplinary thinking. The goal of this approach is to instill in the young the disposition to interpret the world in the distinctive ways that characterize the thinking of experienced disciplinarians—historians, scientists, mathematicians, and artists. This view entrusts education institutions with the responsibility of disciplining the young mind (Gardner, 1999, 2006; Gardner & Boix Mansilla, 1994).

In our view, Phillip's transition from teaching subject matter to nurturing the disciplined mind is emblematic of a fundamental shift in the way in which educators, policymakers, and the general public conceive of curriculum, instruction, and assessment. Indeed, preparing students to understand the world in which they live today and to brace themselves for the future entails a necessary transformation.

TEACHING SUBJECT MATTER

Most students in most schools today study subject matter. In science, students memorize animal taxonomies, atomic weights, and the organs in the respiratory system. In mathematics, they learn algebraic equations and geometrical proofs by heart so they can plug in the appropriate numbers. In history, they are expected to remember key actors, events, and periods. In the arts, they classify works by artist and school.

Subject-matter learning involves mentally recording such propositions as, "The first Industrial Revolution took place in Britain at the end of the eighteenth century," "The chemical composition of water is H_2O," and "Picasso's Les Demoiselles d'Avignon is a cubist painting painted in 1907." From a subject-matter perspective, students come to see the subjects of history and science as the collection of dates, actors, facts, and formulas catalogued in textbooks and encountered in rooms 458 and 503, in second and third period.

THE POWER OF INGRAINED IDEAS

Clearly, there is much to admire in an individual who knows a great deal of information. Further, there is an appealing sense of efficiency in subject-matter teaching: Teachers can rapidly present large quantities of information to students and easily test this information. The apparent benefits pale, however, when we consider how the young human mind develops and how best to prepare that mind for the future.

In recent decades, cognitive psychologists have documented a phenomenon of vital importance for anyone interested in education. Although students have little trouble spewing forth information that they have committed to memory, they display great difficulty in applying knowledge and skills to new situations. Youngsters who have studied the solar system are unable to apply what they have learned to explain why it is warm in the summer in the northern hemisphere. When asked to explain how a particular species' trait or behavior has emerged, students studying biological evolution revert to pre-Darwinian "intentional" or teleological explanations. Students who are able to define cubism as a successful challenge to nineteenth-century aesthetic sensibilities naïvely equate a classical definition of "beautiful" with "good" when visiting a museum. Centuries of accumulated forms of expertise have simply bypassed these young minds despite a decade or more of formal education. Why is this so?

According to cognitive psychologists, early in life children develop powerful intuitive ideas about physical and biological entities, the operations of the human mind, and the properties of an effective narrative or graphic display. Some of these ideas are powerful precursors of sophisticated disciplinary understanding. For example, by age 5, children understand that narratives have beginnings, turning points, and endings and that the succession of events must "make sense" for the story to work, Historians, too, organize their accounts of the past in the form of narratives—intelligible accounts marked by turning points and preferred actors' perspectives.

Unfortunately, not all children's ideas are equally auspicious. Unlike historians, young students prefer simple explanations and clear distinctions between "good" and "mean" actors. They believe that events always result from intentional actions—especially the actions of leaders; they have difficulty understanding unintended consequences. Moreover, students often project contemporary knowledge and values onto the minds of actors in the past, making "presentism" one of the most difficult misconceptions to eradicate.

THE LIMITATIONS OF SUBJECT-MATTER LEARNING

Regrettably, subject-matter learning does not challenge such robust intuitive theories. Indeed, memorization does not even acknowledge the existence of these entrenched ways of making sense of the world. As a result, in subject-matter classrooms, students tend to momentarily retain the information presented, or they reorganize it in oversimplified linear plots. For example, students may record that the steam engine triggered the Industrial Revolution, then farmers rushed to the cities in search of work, then leading businessmen amassed enormous wealth and soon became abusive robber barons. In response, government and labor organized to regulate working conditions.

The plot demonstrates its fragility when students encounter apparent contradictions. Consider, for example, what happens when students learn that organized efforts to defend the rights of working people preceded the popularization of the steam engine. Students who have memorized a plotline—first industrialization, then unrest, then labor unions—cannot assimilate this information. More challenging still, the pre-disciplinary mind fails to appreciate that aspects of the Industrial Revolution are being recapitulated in the current digital upheavals around the globe.

Subject-matter learning may temporarily increase students' information base, but it leaves them unprepared to shed light on issues that are even slightly novel. A different kind of instruction is in order, one that seeks to discipline the mind.

THE DISCIPLINED MIND

For a historian, a statement such as "The first Industrial Revolution took place in Britain at the end of the eighteenth century" is not a fact to remember but rather a contestable claim that stems from deliberate ways to partition the past. It is constructed through close analysis of sources that capture the lives of Britons over centuries of progressive urbanization.

For students, learning to think historically entails understanding that historical accounts are sometimes conflicting and always provisional. Students learn that interpretations of the past are not simply a matter of opinion, nor must one account be "right" and the other "wrong" when differences occur. Rather, the disciplined mind weighs competing accounts through multiple considerations. For instance, a history of the nascent industrial working class will contrast with a history focusing on the captains of industry. Long-term accounts may capture slow population changes, whereas pointed accounts shed better light on the role of individuals and inventions. A disciplinary approach considers the types of sources consulted, such as letters, newsletters, and accounting and demographic records. It also assesses whether conflicting accounts could be integrated into a more comprehensive explanation.

All disciplines embody distinct ways of thinking about the world. Scientists hold theories about the natural world that guide their observations. They make hypotheses, design experiments to test them, revise their views in light of their findings, and make fresh observations. Artists, on the other hand, seek to shed novel light on the object of their attention, depict it with masterful technique, and stretch and provoke themselves and their audiences through deliberate ambiguities in their work.

Of course, it is unreasonable to expect all students to become expert scientists, historians, and artists. Nevertheless, quality precollegiate education should ensure that students become deeply acquainted with a discipline's fundamental perspectives on the world by developing four key capacities (Boix Mansilla & Gardner, 1999).

Capacity 1: Understanding the Purpose of Disciplinary Expertise

Disciplines inform the contexts in which students live. Supply-and-demand principles determine the products that line the shelves of supermarkets; biological interdependence shapes the life of animals and plants at the local park as well as in the rain forest.

Students of history grasp that the purpose of their discipline is to understand past human experience—not to make predictions but to meet the present and the future in informed ways. For example, understanding how novel forms of work accelerated the formation of class consciousness among eighteenth-century industrial workers prepares students to appreciate the experience of contemporary workers in China, India, or Malaysia. Although students learn to attend to important differences between past and present conditions—contemporary digital calling centers in India bear little resemblance to the early textile factories in Leeds, England—they also understand that rapid urbanization forces these workers, like their predecessors, to juggle economic opportunities with anxiety over challenges to family life and cultural tradition.

Capacity 2: Understanding an Essential Knowledge Base

An essential knowledge base embodies concepts and relations central to the discipline and applicable in multiple contexts. It also equips students with a conceptual blueprint for approaching comparable novel situations. For instance, in a unit on industrialization, students may examine the dynamic interaction between technology and society to decide whether they deem industrialization to be "progress" or "decline." Students can apply this blueprint to technological developments at different points in time, from the printing press, to the sewing machine, to today's Internet.

Capacity 3: Understanding Inquiry Methods

In contrast to naïve beliefs or mere information, disciplinary knowledge emerges from a careful process of inquiry and vetting claims. The disciplined mind considers forms of evidence, criteria for validation, and techniques that deliver trustworthy knowledge about the past, nature, society, or works of art.

In our own research, we have found that high school students trained in history recognize the demands of source interpretation, complex causal explanation, and the provisional nature of historical accounts (Boix Mansilla, 2005). However, becoming better historians does not make students better scientists, artists, or mathematicians—or vice versa. For example, when asked to adjudicate between competing accounts in science—a domain in which they have not been rigorously trained—the same students exhibit a subject-matter approach to inquiry. They view science as a domain in which one simply observes the world and writes down one's conclusions. Conversely, award-winning students in science tend to perceive history as all about dates and facts that one need only "find in sources" and "put together in a story." Cross-disciplinary transfer proves elusive.

Capacity 4: Understanding Forms of Communication

Disciplines communicate their expertise in preferred forms and genres. Historians see narratives as the best fit for their work, whereas scientists opt for data-heavy research reports. The disciplined mind understands these favored genres because it can place them in the broader context of their disciplinary origins. For example, the disciplined scientific mind understands that, unlike Darwin's *On the Origin of Species*, a biblical account of human creation cannot stand the test of empirical evidence, nor can it aspire to consideration as a scientific claim.

Students develop a disciplined mind when they learn to communicate with the symbol systems and genres of a discipline. In science, students learn how to write (and recognize) a well-crafted scientific report in which clear and testable hypotheses, methodology, results, and discussion are made public for readers to weigh. In history, knowledge about the past is embodied in vivid and well-footnoted narratives as well as in museum exhibits, monuments, and documentary films.

HOW TO NURTURE THE DISCIPLINED MIND

Teachers can help students develop disciplinary competencies in several ways (Gardner, 2006):

- Identify essential topics in the discipline. In our example about industrialization, some topics will address the knowledge base, such as the transformation of production systems and social organization during the Industrial Revolution. Some will address the methods of the discipline, such as understanding conflicting accounts of workers' experiences and worldviews during the early stages of the Industrial Revolution. Some will address the purposes of the discipline, such as understanding how changes in technology lead to changes in ways of thinking both then and now. Some topics will address the forms of communication in the discipline, such as understanding what makes a historical narrative masterful.

- Spend considerable time on these few topics, studying them deeply. By encouraging students to examine multiple perspectives on a topic and study them in depth, teachers help students become young experts in different topic areas.

- Approach the topic in a number of ways. Students may readily approach the social transformations associated with the Industrial Revolution by reading biographies and life stories. Other students may learn through careful analysis of demographic data or interpretation of artworks of the times. Still others may learn better when asked to debate a question like, "Did industrialization mean progress?". By providing a variety of entry points, teachers not only reach more students but also invite their students to think about important problems in multiple ways—a mental agility that characterizes the disciplined mind.

- Develop performances of understanding. Performances of understanding invite students to think with knowledge in multiple novel situations; they show whether students can actually make use of classroom material once they step outside the door. For example, in the unit on industrialization, teachers may present students with conflicting accounts of workers' experiences in the 1884 planned model industrial town of Pullman, Illinois—a case that students have not yet been coached to examine. In their analysis of the Pullman strike of 1894, some historians contend that Pullman's model community was a malicious design to exploit workers; other historians believe it was the result of naïve paternalism. Teachers might ask students to use what they have learned about historical inquiry to explain how expert historians could disagree. Students with a disciplinary mind in history would understand that they need to examine the conflicting accounts, check the sources used, take into consideration the date of the account, and clarify the historian's perspective. In doing so, students will develop a more informed understanding of historical accounts and will be able to apply their insights in other performances of understanding.

WHAT THE FUTURE REQUIRES

Today, the information revolution and the ubiquity of search engines have rendered having information much less valuable than knowing how to think with information in novel situations. To thrive in contemporary societies, young people must develop the capacity to think like experts. They must also be able to integrate disciplinary perspectives to understand new phenomena in such fields as medicine, bioethics, climate science, and economic development. In doing so, the disciplined mind resists oversimplification and prepares students to embrace the complexity of the modern world.

REFERENCES

Boix Mansilla, V. (2005). Between reproducing and organizing the past; Students' beliefs about the standards of acceptability of historical knowledge. In R. Ashby, P. Gordon, & P. Lee (Eds.), *International Review of History Education: Vol. 4* (pp. 98–115). Oxford, UK: Routledge.

Boix Mansilla, V., & Gardner, H. (1999). What are the qualities of understanding? In S. Wiske (Ed.), *Teaching for understanding: A practical framework* (pp. 161–196). San Francisco, CA: Jossey-Bass.

Gardner, H. (1999). *The disciplined mind: What all students should understand.* New York, NY: Simon and Schuster.

Gardner, H. (2006). *Five minds for the future.* Boston, MA: Harvard Business School Press.

Gardner, H., & Boix Mansilla, V. (1994). Teaching for understanding in the disciplines and beyond. *Teachers College Record, 96*(2): 198–218.

DISCUSSION QUESTIONS

1. Should teachers focus on teaching subject matter or disciplinary thinking? Explain.
2. How would a subject matter learning approach differ from teaching disciplinary thinking?
3. Is it possible to integrate both subject matter teaching and disciplinary thinking into a curriculum? Explain.
4. Should students learn the "basics" before engaging in disciplinary thinking? Explain.
   a. Or is it possible to learn disciplinary thinking without having a firm understanding of "the basics"? Explain.
5. Is it better to use the subject matter or disciplinary thinking approach to teach students twenty-first-century skills? Explain.
6. In this age of accountability and high-stakes testing, which educational approach is better? Which is more aligned with the high-stakes testing? Explain.

Should special education students be grouped (mainstreamed) into regular education classes?

PRO	CON
1. Schools should be organized so that all students achieve their maximum potential.	**1.** Serving the special education population diminishes resources for students who are most likely to benefit from public schooling.
2. Schools should implement a curriculum that is student-centered and responsive to the students' learning needs.	**2.** Schools should not have to provide an alternative curriculum designed for a small group of special needs students within a regular classroom setting.
3. Students need to work side by side with peers who have different learning needs.	**3.** Legislating to require teachers to fulfill the roles of parent, home, and counselor for special education students is unrealistic and unproductive.
4. Teachers must develop a broad-based repertoire of instructional strategies so that they can teach students with different needs and abilities in the same classroom.	**4.** Students who cannot conform to classroom structure and attend to learning tasks will not benefit from regular education instruction.
5. Mainstreaming can improve the social acceptance of special education students.	**5.** Most educators have not been adequately prepared to work with special education students.

CASE STUDY 3

Language and Standardized Testing

East High School in the big city has a large ethnic minority/immigrant population. Most of the immigrant students are placed in English as a Second Language (ESL) classes because of their initial English skill level. At East High School, ESL classes move at a slower pace than mainstream classes, and reading selections are often remedial to give students ample time to adapt to their new surroundings.

The ESL language teacher, Fred Davis, drills the students hard, and many become miraculously fluent in a short period of time. To pass out of the ESL classes into the mainstream classes, students must receive 85 percent or higher on the administered English test for ESL students. Many students in ESL find this practice unfair. They claim that their English skill levels surpass those of many of the mainstream students and that they are being unfairly held back in all of their schoolwork because of unfair scoring expectations on one English test. Only students in the mainstream classes are able to take advanced coursework, and ESL students believe that East High is hurting their ultimate potential.

Further, ESL students wishing to continue on to colleges and universities are afraid that they will not be prepared for future tests; that their scores will be adversely affected by their remedial coursework in high school. They also fear that the institutions of higher education will penalize them during the admission process because they were unable to advance into "normal" classes.

1. Is it fair for schools to use standardized testing as the sole measure of ability for determining advancement? Why? Why not? What are other methods that can be used?
2. Should subject tests be administered in a language of the student's choosing?
3. Is it good practice to separate non-English or limited-English immigrant students in all areas of coursework? Should they be integrated into mainstream courses even if their English language ability is limited?
4. How might a teacher handle a class differently if it were integrated with students of different cultural backgrounds? Different academic abilities? Is this beneficial? Why? Why not?
5. How does a cultural knowledge background affect a student's understanding?

PART FOUR

Curriculum and Instruction

How do curriculum and instruction influence each other? Which instructional strategies are most effective for learners? Why are students' learning experiences still based on highly structured curricula? How can we really know if a school is doing well? What role should standards play in education? In what ways are electronic and information technologies affecting instruction?

In Chapter 18, Yong Zhao uncovers the inconsistency between academic performance and entrepreneurial capabilities across different nations. He raises serious questions about the indicators of quality and purpose of education in the age of globalization. Next, in Chapter 19, Carol Ann Tomlinson and Edwin Lou Javius focus on the elusive goal of ensuring quality instruction for students regardless of race or income level. They describe seven principles of "teaching up" by which teachers can develop the skill—and will—to proliferate classrooms in which equal access to excellence is a reality for all learners.

In Chapter 20, Arthur L. Costa describes a "thought-filled curriculum" in which teachers instruct their students to think critically. Five themes emerge in which students learn how to think and eventually think "big" in order to build a "thought-filled world." In Chapter 21, Geneva Gay highlights a variety of multicultural issues that increasingly influence schools today. She offers a number of ideas that demonstrate the relevance of multiculturalism for professional practice, curriculum development, and closing the achievement gap.

In 22, David Perkins argues for inclusion of what he calls "knowledge arts" in the curriculum. The ability to communicate strategically and effectively, to think critically and creatively, and to apply knowledge to real-world problems can help to enliven teaching and learning. Finally, in Chapter 23, Grant Wiggins makes a case for abolishing the high school diploma, which he contends is less relevant in an increasingly unpredictable and pluralistic world. Tracing the historical sources of our rigid curriculum and criticizing the one-size-fits-all limitations of today's educational reforms, Wiggins recommends a more forward-looking, student-centered, and flexible approach to schooling that is better suited to an era where the curriculum is determined by the future, not the past.

18 Flunking Innovation and Creativity

Yong Zhao

FOCUSING QUESTIONS

1. What are the advantages and disadvantages of China and Singapore's education systems?
2. To what extent do China's educational practices hamper entrepreneurial qualities?
3. How do you explain China's recent economic growth and low patenting rates?
4. Explain the difference between academic skills and entrepreneurial qualities.
5. What is the relationship between national academic scores and entrepreneurial indicators?

East Asia's highly touted test scores in math, science, and reading are masking important failures in developing innovators and entrepreneurs. "We have a wake-up call now about America's kids," announced a worried Diane Sawyer on "ABC World News" in December 2010. Three weeks earlier, Sawyer had taken viewers to China to show them what she called "the ambition and energy of 1.3 billion people" competing for the American dream. "Today, the new international reading, math, and science scores were released, and Chinese students left American teens in the dust in all three categories," Sawyer said.

"In fact, these numbers are stunning for the entire world. Shanghai stunner, you could call it," said ABC reporter David Muir who accompanied Sawyer to China and further explained the significance of the scores. He pointed out that U.S. Secretary Arne Duncan labeled the scores a wake-up call for America and President Obama tagged the occasion "a modern day Sputnik moment to catch up." The rest of the $3^{1}/_{2}$-minute news clip featured stunning graphics showing how American students trailed Shanghai and several Asian countries, plus footage of President John F. Kennedy talking about the Soviet's Sputnik, the first man-made satellite to orbit the earth, launched in 1957 (Sawyer, 2010).

Sawyer was referring to the most recent results of the Programme for International Student Assessment (PISA), an international assessment of 15-year-olds in mathematics, reading, and science. In the most recent round, 65 nations participated in the study, with China's Shanghai ranking No. 1 in all three categories and the United States coming out average or below average (OECD, 2010). The results received extensive media coverage in the United States, all emitting a sense of shock, urgency, and anxiety. For example, Shanghai's students posted an average reading score of 556, compared to 500 for U.S. students, and they achieved the highest scores in math, 600, which was 113 points higher than the average for U.S. students (Associated Press, 2010). Considering the size of the gap between American students and Shanghai students, this sense of urgency and anxiety seems warranted.

WHY DIDN'T CHINA CELEBRATE?

Shanghai's stunning performance shocked other countries, too. For example, a recent report by Australia's Grattan Institute highlighted the extraordinary education achievement in Shanghai where "the average 15-year-old mathematics student is performing at a level two to three years, on average, above his or her counterpart in Australia, the United States, the U.K., and EU21 countries" (Jensen, 2012, p. 7). Although China has been thought of as a country with excellent education for a while now, Shanghai's PISA scores officially sealed its position as a world leader. It has become an education giant, one of the best-performing education systems, and a target of envy and learning. Surpassing Shanghai has become a goal for many countries, suggests the title of Marc Tucker's recent book, *Surpassing Shanghai: An Agenda for American Education Built on the World's Leading Systems* (Harvard Education Press, 2011).

But China did not have a big party celebrating this apparently outstanding achievement, which is unusual for a country eager to affirm its rise on the global stage with massive media coverage of any achievement in international competition, such as the number of Olympic medals. In fact, there was very little national coverage of the PISA results by the state-run mainstream media. And whenever the PISA story is mentioned, it is often accompanied with cautionary notes about why this news is not worth celebrating.

STEVE JOBS, AMONG OTHERS, IS ONE OF THE WHYS

"China needs (Steve) Jobs," China's Premier Wen Jiabao told business leaders in Jiangshu during his tour of one of China's most developed provinces in December 2011. "We must have products like Apple's that can dominate the world's markets" (Zhang, 2011). Wen's comments reflect China's burning desire for innovative and entrepreneurial talents to transform its labor-intensive economy to one built on innovation and creativity.

Despite its astounding economic growth for more than two decades, China's economy remains labor-intensive rather than knowledge-intensive. According to a report of the Chinese National Statistics Bureau, only about 2,000 Chinese companies owned the patent for the core technology used in the products they produced in 2005; that number represents less than 0.003 percent of all Chinese companies in that year (Zhao & Wu, 2005). Merely 473 innovations from China were recognized by the world's leading patent offices outside China in 2008 versus 14,399 from the United States (Gupta & Wang, 2011). As a result, although products worth billions of dollars are made in China, they are not made by China. Furthermore, an economy built on cheap labor is very volatile in a world where many countries can offer cheap labor. Rising labor costs and the increasing value of its currency already have threatened China's status as the world's factory.

But China can't have a Steve Jobs unless it fundamentally reforms its education, according to one of the most influential Chinese-American technology gurus, who has dedicated himself to incubating young entrepreneurs in China. "The next Apple, the next Google will come, but probably not in China," said Kai-fu Lee, founder of Innovation Works, an investment company aimed at cultivating innovative entrepreneurship in China. Lee was former founding president of Google China and former vice president of Interactive Services of Microsoft after working at Apple as a research and development executive (Caijing, 2010).

"At least not in the next 50 years or 100 years, there will not be an Apple or Google in China," Lee said in a controversial prediction at the World Economic Forum's Summer Davos in Tianjin, China, in September 2010. Lee migrated from Taiwan to the United States at age 11 and received his undergraduate education at Columbia and earned a Ph.D. from Carnegie Mellon University. "If China wants this (to have an Apple or Google), it must rebuild its education system," Lee said.

THE SAME IN SINGAPORE

Why is such an "excellent education system" held responsible for China's failure to produce a Steve Jobs? Why would the Chinese want to blow it up if it is as outstanding as its PISA performance suggests it is? Apparently, there is a mismatch of understanding of educational excellence.

The mismatch goes beyond China. Around the same time that China's Wen Jiabao said his country needs Steve Jobs, the iconic entrepreneur and the company he cofounded incited a discussion about creativity and entrepreneurship in another Asian country that has been viewed by outsiders to have the best education. In 2011, Steve Wozniak, who founded Apple with Jobs, said during an interview that a company like Apple could not emerge in structured countries like Singapore:

"When you're very structured almost like a religion . . . Uniforms, uniforms, uniforms . . . everybody is the same. Look at structured societies like Singapore where bad behavior isn't tolerated. You are extremely punished. Where are the creative people? Where are the great artists? Where are the great musicians? Where are the great singers? Where are the great writers? Where are the athletes? All the creative elements seem to disappear" (BBC, 2011).

Wozniak's comments quickly got the attention of Singaporeans, who have been working hard at promoting creativity and entrepreneurship. Although some disagreed with Wozniak's assessment, the overall reaction was that he told the truth. Singaporean entrepreneur Willis Wee wrote, "I'm not sure how much Wozniak knows about Singapore and its system. But as a Singaporean, who grew up in this tiny island, I have to agree with his words" (Wee, 2011).

In a CNN article, Singaporean journalist Alexis Ong concurred. "At first glance, it made the small pseudo-patriot in me annoyed, but for the most part, the great and mighty Woz speaks the truth," she said, adding that the culprit is Singapore's education system. "Wozniak's comments are really a scathing indictment of the Singapore education system, its strictly regimented curriculum and by-rote study techniques that sustain the city's formal culture," said Ong. Everybody is educated in Singapore, she added. "But clearly the Singaporean education isn't the kind of education that gives rise to the people like Sergey Brin and Mark Zuckerberg . . . In Singapore, where children are streamed into different academic tracks and under pressure to get into a reputable school before the age of 12, the push to conform is enormous" (Ong, 2012).

But outsiders believe Singapore has an excellent education system. Outsiders have envied and admired Singapore for its consistently high performance on international tests. Since the early 1990s, Singapore has ranked in the top five in the Trends in International Mathematics and Science Study

(TIMSS). In the most recent PISA, Singapore took second place in math, fourth place in sciences, and fifth in reading. Here again is a case of contradiction—an education giant that has trouble producing the creative and entrepreneurial talents it needs.

ACHIEVEMENT GAP VS. ENTREPRENEURSHIP GAP

This contradiction exists in other high-performing countries as well. Korea and Japan have consistently produced outstanding scores in international tests. In the most recent PISA administered in 2009, Korea ranked fourth in math, sixth in sciences, and second in reading, while Japan was ninth in math, fifth in sciences, and eighth in reading. Nonetheless, these countries have not traditionally shown a level of creativity and innovation-driven entrepreneurship that matched their test scores. According to the 2010 Global Entrepreneurship Monitor (GEM) report (Kelley, Bosma, & Amorós, 2010), Korea and Japan were at the bottom of the list of 22 innovation-oriented developed nations, taking 19th and 21st place respectively in terms of "nascent entrepreneurship rate," which is defined as the percentage of people actively engaged in early-stage entrepreneurial activities. (China and Singapore weren't included in the GEM study.)

That GEM report also said Korea ranked seventh and Japan 21st in the percentage of individuals who started and are still managing a business. An even more telling figure is that less than half of all the early entrepreneurship activities in Korea and Japan were driven by opportunity and improvement, while the rest were driven by necessity. In this category, Korea ranked 16th and Japan 18th.

The contradictory relationship between test scores and entrepreneurship activities is further affirmed by a comparison of PISA performance along with the entrepreneurship activities of nations. PISA scores in reading, math, and sciences are negatively correlated with entrepreneurship indicators in almost every category at statistically significant levels. In other words, countries with higher PISA scores have lower entrepreneurship activities. Specifically, countries with better performance on PISA tend to have fewer people who plan to start businesses and fewer people who have started new businesses.

The inverse relationship between PISA scores—often perceived as the measure of a nation's education quality and its students' academic abilities—and entrepreneurship activities seems to affirm the contradiction exemplified by Singapore and China. This means that the commonly used measures of educational quality have negative or no relationships with entrepreneurship.

The level of entrepreneurial activities in a nation is affected by many factors, but one of the most important factors is the percentage of individuals with entrepreneurial qualities because these are the individuals who undertake entrepreneurship activities. And one of the most significant elements of entrepreneurial qualities is perceived entrepreneurial capabilities—that is, an individual's confidence in his or her ability to succeed in entrepreneurship. Research suggests high-performing countries in international tests show a low level of perceived entrepreneurial capabilities (Zhao, 2012). For example, high-scoring countries on the PISA and TIMSS such as Singapore, Japan, Korea, and Taiwan scored much lower than Australia, the United Kingdom, and the United States in the category of perceived entrepreneurship capabilities of the GEM survey in 2011 (Bosma, Wennekers, & Amorós, 2012). Figure 18.1 shows the ranking of 23 countries and regions that participated in both the 2009 PISA math and 2011 GEM entrepreneurial capabilities. All 23 countries and regions are considered developed economies and thus are categorized as "innovation-driven economies" by the GEM study.

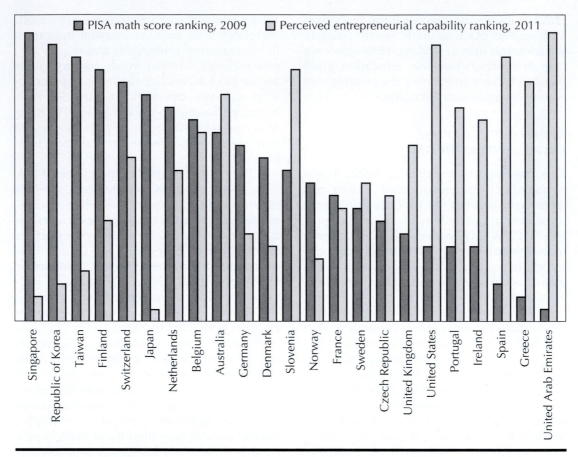

FIGURE 18.1 Ranking by PISA math scores vs. GEM Survey of Perceived Entrepreneurial Capability
Data Source: Bosma, Wennekers, and Amaros, 2012; OECD, 2010.

As Figure 18.1 shows, countries that scored higher in the 2009 PISA had lower scores in perceived entrepreneurial capabilities. Japan, Singapore, Korea, and Taiwan, among the top six on the PISA math score league table, are the lowest in terms of entrepreneurial capabilities, while the lowest ranked countries in PISA such as the United Arab Emirates, the United States, and Spain have the highest entrepreneurial capabilities. This inverse relationship is confirmed by a correlational analysis, which shows signifi-

cant negative correlation between PISA scores and entrepreneurial capabilities across countries (Zhao, 2012).

INTERPRETING THE GAPS

From China's and Singapore's blame of their supposedly excellent education for their inability to produce creative and entrepreneurial talents like Steve Jobs to the overall negative relationship between PISA scores and entrepreneurial capabilities, it seems reasonable to question the value and consequently the significance of educational excellence measured by international assessments such as the PISA. Entrepreneurship is directly related to economic prosperity and success. Thus, there should be little doubt that entrepreneurial capabilities may be a more worthwhile indicator than test scores. Even if we assume no causal relationship between the PISA and entrepreneurial activities and capabilities, the gap in PISA test scores may not warrant the level of anxiety and concern expressed by policy makers, the media, and the public.

But there is another possibility that should worry us: If the Chinese and Singaporeans are correct to blame their education for their shortage of creative and entrepreneurial talents, then the relationship between PISA scores and entrepreneurial capabilities and activities indeed could be causal. That would mean that pursuing academic achievement may come at the cost of entrepreneurial qualities. In other words, the educational practices and societal factors that help students achieve academically may hamper entrepreneurial qualities and reduce creativity. Standardized, narrow, and uniform educational experiences, high-stakes standardized testing, a push for conformity, and intolerance of exceptional talents are among the factors identified in China's and Singapore's education systems for destroying the nations' creativity and entrepreneurial spirits.

IMPLICATIONS

The world needs more creators, innovators, makers, and entrepreneurs. Numerous international organizations have produced reports about the importance of entrepreneurship and issued calls for countries to develop entrepreneurship (Schoof, 2006; World Economic Forum, 2011) because "innovation and entrepreneurship provide a way forward for solving the global challenges of the twenty-first century, building sustainable development, creating jobs, generating renewed economic growth, and advancing human welfare" (World Economic Forum, 2009, p. 7). In the United States, the Obama administration launched a $2 billion entrepreneurship initiative in 2011, which includes a significant piece for youth entrepreneurship education because, as President Obama said, "entrepreneurs are the engine of job creation in America, generating millions of good jobs" (2009). There is also an increasing call for adding entrepreneurship education to all school curriculum (Aspen Youth Entrepreneurship Strategy Group, 2008).

But, unfortunately, America is becoming more like Asia. American reformers have been steadily transforming schools into education environments hostile to creative and entrepreneurial talents. In an effort to close the achievement gap in test scores through measures such as No Child Left Behind, the United States has added a strong Asian flavor to its schools characterized by centralized standardized curriculum and high-stakes standardized testing. It is continuing down the same path with more rigor and force with the Common Core standards initiative and Race to the Top. Already, America has seen a significant narrowing of curricula (McMurrer, 2008) and a drastic shift toward teaching to the test (Nichols & Berliner, 2007). Coincidentally, America also saw a significant decline in creativity in the last few decades, as Newsweek reported in 2010 (Bronson & Merryman, 2010).

If America wants to continue its tradition of innovation and entrepreneurship, if President Obama is serious about out-innovating others and encouraging entrepreneurship, we must stop policies and practices that can harm creativity and entrepreneurship. This means attempts to narrow a child's educational experiences, to deprive children of opportunities to explore their interests and passions, or to label children incompetent or at risk just because they don't perform well on standardized tests. This also means any attempt to standardize and homogenize school experiences by forcing all teachers to teach the same thing at the same time for all children through test-based accountability measures for teachers and school leaders. Essentially, stop NCLB, stop the Common Core, and stop Race to the Top!

Of course, the most desirable situation is not just stopping efforts that can do harm, but developing an education that enhances human curiosity and creativity, encourages risk taking, and cultivates the entrepreneurial spirit in the context of globalization. Such an education requires a significant shift in our mindset about education from employment-oriented to entrepreneurship-oriented. An entrepreneurship-oriented education affords children autonomy, voice, and choice in what they learn, engages children in creating and making works that matter, and provides the learning in a global context.

REFERENCES

Aspen Youth Entrepreneurship Strategy Group. (2008). *Youth entrepreneurship education in America: A policy maker's action guide.* Washington, DC: Aspen Institute.

Associated Press. (2010, December 7). In ranking, U.S. students trail global leaders. *USA Today.*

BBC. (2011, Jan. 20). Steve Wozniak: "Think for yourself." http://www.bbc.co.uk

Bosma, N., Wennekers, S., & Amorós, J. (2012). Global entrepreneurship monitor: 2011 extended report: Entrepreneurs and entrepreneurial employees across the globe. London, England: Global Entrepreneurship Research Association.

Bronson, P., & Merryman, A. (2010, July 10). The creativity crisis. *Newsweek.*

Caijing. (2010). Kai-fu Lee: The next Apple will not be invented in China (translated). http://www.caijing.com.cn

Gupta, A., & Wang, H. (2011, July 28). Chinese innovation is a paper tiger. *The Wall Street Journal.*

Jensen, B. (2012). *Catching up: Learning from the best school systems in East Asia.* Melbourne, Australia: Grattan Institute.

Kelley, D., Bosma, N., & Amorós, J. (2010). Global *entrepreneurship monitor.* London, England: Global Entrepreneurship Research Association.

McMurrer, J. (2008). *Instructional time in elementary schools: A closer look at changes for specific subjects.* Washington, DC: Center on Education Policy.

Nichols, S., & Berliner. D. (2007). *Collateral damage: How high-stakes testing corrupts America's schools.* Cambridge, MA: Harvard Education Press.

Obama, B. (2009, March 10). President Obama's remarks to the Hispanic Chamber of Commerce. *The New York Times.*

OECD. (2010). *PISA 2009 results.* Paris, France: Author.

Ong, A. (2012, January 10). Singapore needs to encourage "bad behavior." CNN. http://www.cnngo.com

Sawyer, D. (2010, December 7). China beats U.S. in reading, math, and science. ABC News. http://abcnews.go.com

Schoof, U. (2006). *Stimulating youth entrepreneurship: Barriers and incentives to enterprise start-ups by young people.* Geneva, Switzerland: International Labor Organization.

Wee, W. (2011, December 15). Apple co-founder Steve Wozniak questions Singapore's creativity. Tech in Asia. http://www.techinasia.com/wozniak-questions-singapore-creativity

World Economic Forum. (2009). *Educating the next wave of entrepreneurs: Unlocking entrepreneurial capabilities to meet the global challenges of the 21st century.* Geneva, Switzerland: Author.

World Economic Forum. (2011). *Unlocking entrepreneur capabilities to meet the global challenges of the 21st century: Final report on the entrepreneurship education work stream.* Geneva, Switzerland: Author.

Zhang, S. (2011, December 21). Wen Jiabao: Zhongguo yao you qiaobusi (Wen Jiabao: China needs jobs). *China Daily.*

Zhao, X., & Wu, Q. (2005, December 20). End-of-year report: China to strengthen protection of intellectual properties and encourage domestic innovation. http://news.xinhuanet.com/politics/2005-12/20/content_3948433.htm

Zhao Y. (2012). *World class learners: Educating creative and entrepreneurial students*. Thousand Oaks, CA: Corwin Press.

DISCUSSION QUESTIONS

1. How can we stimulate students' entrepreneurial qualities and capabilities?
2. What portion of a school curriculum should be devoted to creative thinking?
3. Is an emphasis on standards and testing compatible with creativity?
4. Is the current accountability movement in the United States beneficial for both students and society?
5. What is the proper balance between having content knowledge and being able to apply it creatively?
6. What criteria would you use to define educational excellence?

19

Teach Up for Excellence

CAROL ANN TOMLINSON
EDWIN LOU JAVIUS

FOCUSING QUESTIONS

1. How is "separateness" in schools a problem?

2. Describe the seven core principles behind "teaching up."

3. What is the difference between a "growth" mindset and a "fixed" mindset?

4. What are some ways to cultivate a growth mindset?

5. How does understanding one's learning profile help teachers plan instruction?

6. What are the advantages of creating flexible classroom routines?

7. How does underestimating students hurt their learning?

Within the lifetime of a significant segment of the population, schools in the United States operated under the banner of "separate but equal" opportunity. In time, and at considerable cost, we came to grips with the reality that separate is seldom equal. But half a century later, and with integration a given, many of our students still have separate and drastically unequal learning experiences (Darling-Hammond, 2010).

Many of our schools are overwhelmingly attended by low-income and racially and linguistically diverse students, whereas nearby schools are largely attended by students from more affluent and privileged backgrounds (Kozol, 2005). Another kind of separateness exists within schools. It's frequently the case that students attend classes that correlate highly with learners' race and socioeconomic status, with less privileged students in lower learning groups or tracks and more privileged students in more advanced ones (Darling-Hammond, 2010).

The logic behind separating students by what educators perceive to be their ability is that it enables teachers to provide students with the kind of instruction they need. Teachers can remediate students who perform at a lower level of proficiency and accelerate those who perform at a higher level. All too often, however, students in lower-level classrooms receive a level of education that ensures they will remain at the tail end of the learning spectrum. High-end students may (or may not) experience rich and challenging learning opportunities, and students in the middle too often encounter uninspired learning experiences that may not be crippling but are seldom energizing. No group comes to know, understand, and value the others. Schools in which this arrangement is the norm often display an "us versus them" attitude that either defines the school environment or dwells just below the surface of daily exchanges.

DIFFICULT TO DEFEND

Research finds that sorting, this twenty-first-century version of school segregation, correlates strongly with student race and economic status and predicts and contributes to student outcomes, with students in higher-level classes typically experiencing better teachers, curriculum, and achievement levels than peers in lower-level classes (Carbonaro & Gamoran, 2003). Further, when lower-performing students experience curriculum and instruction focused on meaning and understanding, they increase their skills at least as much as their higher-achieving peers do (Educational Research Service, 1992).

These findings are even more problematic when combined with our current understanding that the human brain is incredibly malleable and that individuals can nearly always outperform our expectations for them. The sorting mechanisms often used in school are not only poor predictors of success in life, but also poor measures of what a young person can accomplish, given the right context (Dweck, 2007). Virtually all students would benefit from the kind of curriculum and instruction we have often reserved for advanced learners—that is, curriculum and instruction designed to engage students, with a focus on meaning making, problem solving, logical thinking, and transfer of learning (National Research Council, 1999).

In addition, the demographic reality is that low-income students of color and English language learners will soon become the majority of students in our schools (Center for Public Education, 2007; Gray & Fleischman, 2004). Given that low-level classes are largely made up of students from these groups and that students in such classes fare poorly in terms of academic achievement, the societal cost of continuing to support sorting students is likely to be high (Darling-Hammond, 2006).

Finally, Americans tend to be justly proud of the democratic ideals that represent this nation. We nourish those ideals when we invest in systems that enable each individual to achieve his or her best (Gardner, 1961). In contrast, we undercut those ideals when the systems we create contribute to a widening gap between those who have privilege and those who do not (Fullan, 2001).

Too few students—including those who excel academically—regularly have education experiences that stimulate and stretch them. Teaching up is one key approach that teachers can use to regularly make such experiences available to all students, regardless of their backgrounds and starting points.

SEVEN PRINCIPLES OF TEACHING UP

To create classrooms that give students equal access to excellence, educators at all levels need to focus on seven interrelated principles.

1. *Accept that human differences are not only normal but also desirable.* Each person has something of value to contribute to the group, and the group is diminished without that contribution. Teachers who teach up create a community of learners in which everyone works together to benefit both individuals and the group. These teachers know that the power of learning is magnified when the classroom functions effectively as a microcosm of a world in which we want to live. They craft culturally and economically inclusive classrooms that take into account the power of race, culture, and economic status in how students construct meaning; and they support students in making meaning in multiple ways (Gay, 2000).

2. *Develop a growth mind-set.* Providing equity of access to excellence through teaching up has its roots in a teacher's mindset about the capacity of each learner to succeed (Dweck, 2007). It requires doggedly challenging the preconception that high ability dwells largely in more privileged students. The greatest barrier to learning is often not what the student knows, but what the teacher expects of the student (Good, 1987).

A teacher with a growth mindset creates learning experiences that reinforce the principle that effort rather than background is the greatest determinant of success, a notion that can dramatically help students who experience institutional and instructional racism. A growth mindset also creates classrooms that persistently demonstrate to students and teachers alike that when a student works hard and intelligently, the result is consistent growth that enables people to accomplish their goals.

Teachers who teach up provide students with clear learning targets, guidelines, and feedback as well as a safe learning environment that supports them as they take their next steps in growth, no matter what their current level of performance is. Through words, actions, and caring, the teacher conveys to students "I know you have the capacity to do what's required for success; therefore, I expect much of you. Because I expect much, I'll support your success in every way I can. I'm here to be your partner in achievement."

3. *Work to understand students' cultures, interests, needs, and perspectives.* People are shaped by their backgrounds, and respecting students means respecting their backgrounds—including their race and culture. Teaching any student well means striving to understand how that student approaches learning and creating an environment that is respectful of and responsive to what each student brings to the classroom.

Many of us know the Golden Rule: Treat others as you would want to be treated. In classrooms that work for a wide spectrum of people, the Platinum Rule works better: Treat others as they want to be treated. This principle relates not only to teacher and student interactions, but also to teacher choices about curriculum and instruction.

For teachers who teach up, understanding students' learning profiles is the driving force behind instructional planning and delivery. A learning profile refers to how individuals learn most efficiently and effectively. How we learn is shaped by a variety of factors, including culture, gender, environmental preferences, and personal strengths or weaknesses. Teachers can talk with their students about preferred approaches to learning, offer varied routes to accomplishing required goals, and observe which options students select and how those options support learning (or don't). Teachers who teach up select instructional strategies and approaches in response to what they know of their students' interests and learning preferences, rather than beginning with a strategy and hoping it works. Teaching up is not about hope. It's about purposeful instructional planning that aims at ensuring high-level success for each student.

4. *Create a base of rigorous learning opportunities.* Teachers who teach up help students form a conceptual understanding of the disciplines, connect what they learn to their own lives, address significant problems using essential knowledge and skills, collaborate with peers, examine varied perspectives, and create authentic products for meaningful audiences. These teachers develop classrooms that are literacy-rich and that incorporate a wide range of resources that attend to student interests and support student learning.

Teachers who teach up also ensure that students develop the skills of independence, self-direction, collaboration, and production that are necessary for success. They commend excellence as a way of life and demonstrate to learners the satisfaction that comes from accepting a challenge and investing one's best effort in achieving it. They know that when tasks help students make sense of important ideas, are highly relevant to students' life experiences, and are designed at a moderate level of challenge, students are willing to do the hard work that is the hallmark of excellence. These teachers scaffold each student as he or she takes the next step toward excellence.

For example, a high school teacher began a study of *Romeo and Juliet* by having students think of instances in books, movies, TV shows, or their own lives when people's perceptions of others made it difficult to have certain friends, be in love with a particular person, or feel supported in their marriage. In this culturally diverse class, every student offered examples. They were fascinated with how often this theme played out across cultures, and they eagerly talked about what the examples had in common. As the teacher continued to guide them in relating the play to their own examples, the students remained highly engaged with a classic that might otherwise have seemed remote to them. When students make cultural and linguistic connections with content, they display more sophisticated thinking about essential learning goals (Gibbons, 2002).

5. Understand that students come to the classroom with varied points of entry into a curriculum and move through it at different rates. For intellectual risk-taking to occur, classrooms need to feel safe to students from a full range of cultural, racial, and economic backgrounds. Teachers who teach up understand that some students may feel racially and culturally isolated in their classes. Therefore, they find multiple ways for students to display their insights for the group. These teachers understand that every student needs "peacock" moments of success so classmates accept them as intellectual contributors.

For instance, a teacher might observe a student in a small-group setting who is questioning his peers about the solution to a math problem they are pursuing because it does not seem correct to him. A teacher who overhears the exchange might simply say to the group, "It seems important to me that Anthony raised the question he posed to you. His thinking brought to your attention the need to think further about your solution. The ability to ask a challenging question at the right time is a good talent to have." Elizabeth Cohen (1994) calls that attribution of status.

Teaching up means monitoring student growth so that when students fall behind, misunderstand, or move beyond expectations, teachers are primed to take appropriate instructional action. They guide all students in working with the "melody line" of the curriculum—the essential knowledge, understanding, and skills—while ensuring ample opportunity for individuals and small groups to work with "accompaniments"— that is, scaffolding for students who need additional work with prerequisites and extending depth for students who need to move ahead. For example, some students might need additional work with academic vocabulary, the cornerstone skills of literacy and numeracy, or self-awareness and self-direction. Other students will explore and apply understandings at more expert levels.

Teaching up also calls on teachers to use formative assessment data to guide instructional planning, scaffold the learning of struggling students, and extend learning for advanced students. In other words, teaching up requires both high expectations and high personalization.

For instance, in a middle school science study of simple machines, the teacher made certain to preteach key vocabulary to students who found academic vocabulary challenging. Students then examined and analyzed several Rube Goldberg contraptions, watched and discussed a video, and read designated sections from a text. This multimodal approach ensured that everyone had a solid baseline of experience with concepts they would then explore.

Following a formative assessment on the topic, students worked on one of two tasks. Students who needed additional reinforcement of how simple machines worked went on a guided tour of the school and speculated which simple machines were involved in mechanisms they came across in their tour, such as an elevator. Later, they used print and Web sources to confirm or revise their projections. Students who had already demonstrated solid mastery of the topic worked in teams to identify a problem at school or in their lives that three or more simple machines working together could solve; they also used Web and text sources to confirm or revise their projections.

6. *Create flexible classroom routines and procedures that attend to learner needs.* Teachers who teach up realize that only classrooms that operate flexibly enough to make room for a range of student needs can effectively address the differences that are inevitable in any group of learners. They see that such flexibility is also a prerequisite for complex student thinking and student application of content (Darling-Hammond, Bransford, LePage, & Hammerness, 2007). Teachers who teach up carefully select times when the class works as a whole, when students work independently, and when students work in groups. They teach their students when and how to help one another as well as how to guide their own work effectively. This kind of flexibility is commonly found in kindergarten classrooms—a strong indication that it's within reach of all grade levels.

An elementary math teacher in one such classroom regularly used formative assessment to chart students' progress. On the basis of what she learned, she built into her instructional plans opportunities for small-group instruction in which she could teach in new ways concepts that some students found difficult, extend the thinking of students who had mastered the concepts, and help students connect what they were learning to various interest areas. Occasionally, she modified the daily schedule so she could work with a portion of the class more intensively. In those instances, some students might work on writing assignments or with longer-term projects in the morning while the teacher met with a given group on a math topic and guided their work. In the afternoon, students would reverse assignments so that she could work with the morning's writers on math. She found that working with the small groups at key times in the learning cycle significantly increased the achievement of virtually all the students in the class.

In the same vein, a team of high school teachers took turns hosting a study room after school on Monday through Thursday. They expected students who hadn't completed their homework to attend. They also invited students who were having difficulty with course requirements and encouraged all students to come if they wanted additional support. Many students did. The sessions, which were less formal than class, also promoted sound relationships between the teachers and their students and among the students themselves.

7. *Be an analytical practitioner.* Teachers who teach up consistently reflect on classroom procedures, practices, and pedagogies for evidence that they are working for each student—and modify them when they're not. They are the students of their students. They are vigilant about noticing when students "do right," and they provide positive descriptive feedback so students can successfully recall or replicate the skill, knowledge, or behaviors in question. They empower students to teach them, as teachers, what makes students most successful. They share with students their aspirations for student success. They talk with students about what is and isn't working in the classroom, and they enlist students' partnership in crafting a classroom that maximizes the growth of each individual and of the group as a whole.

Consider a group of primary teachers who conducted individual assessments of kindergartners' understanding of symmetrical and asymmetrical figures and then discussed what they observed. They realized that vocabulary played a large role in the success of students who mastered the concept. As a result, they were better positioned to support the growth of students who were initially less successful by adding vocabulary practice to math instruction.

Or, consider a middle school teacher who talked often with his students about his confidence that they were engineers of their own success. To reinforce that point, he carefully observed students during whole-class, small-group, and independent work. He would make comments privately to students as he moved among them or as he stood at the door when they entered or left the room: "Josh, you provided leadership today when your group got off task. I wanted you to know it made a difference." "Ariela, you stuck with the work today when it was tough. Good job!" "Logan, are you still on track to bring in a draft of your paper tomorrow so you'll have a chance to polish it before it's due next week?"

A CHALLENGE WORTH TAKING

In her provocative book, *Wounded by School*, Kirsten Olson (2009) concludes that perhaps the deepest wounds schools inflict on students are wounds of underestimation. We underestimate students when they come to us with skills and experiences that differ from the ones we expected and we conclude they're incapable of complex work. We underestimate students when they fall short of expectations because they don't understand the school game and we determine that they lack motivation. We underestimate them when we allow them to shrink silently into the background of the action in the classroom. We underestimate them, too, when we assume they're doing well in school because they earn high grades, and we praise them for reaching a performance level that required no risk or struggle.

Classrooms that teach up function from the premise that student potential is like an iceberg—most of it is obscured from view—and that high trust, high expectations, and a high-support environment will reveal in time what's hidden.

Martin Luther King Jr. (1965) reminded us that human beings are:

> "caught in an inescapable network of mutuality, tied in a single garment of destiny. Whatever affects one directly affects all indirectly. I can never be what I ought to be until you are what you ought to be, and you can never be what you ought to be until I am what I ought to be. This is the interrelated structure of reality."

That truth has never been more evident than it is today. Schools have the still-untapped possibility of helping all kinds of learners become what they ought to be by developing the skill—and will—to proliferate classrooms in which equal access to excellence is a reality for all learners.

REFERENCES

Carbonaro, W., & Gamoran, A. (2003). The production of achievement inequality in high school English. *American Educational Research Journal, 39*(4): 801–827.

Center for Public Education. (2007). *The United States of education: The changing demographics of the United States and their schools.* Alexandria, VA: Author.

Cohen, E. (1994). *Designing groupwork: Strategies for the heterogeneous classroom.* New York, NY: Teachers College Press.

Darling-Hammond, L. (2006). Interview with Linda Darling-Hammond. PBS Nightly Business Report. Retrieved from http://www.pbs.org/nbr/site/features/special/WIP_hammond1

Darling-Hammond, L. (2010). *The flat world and education: How America's commitment to equity will determine our future.* New York, NY: Teachers College Press.

Darling-Hammond, L., Bransford, J., LePage, P., & Hammerness, K. (2007). *Preparing teachers for a changing world: What teachers should learn and be able to do.* San Francisco, CA: Jossey-Bass.

Dweck, C. (2007). *Mindset: The new psychology of success.* New York: Ballantine.

Educational Research Service. (1992). Academic challenge for the children of poverty: The summary report (ERS Item #171). Arlington, VA: Author.

Fullan, M. (2001). *The new meaning of educational change* (3rd ed.). New York, NY: Teachers College Press.

Gay, G. (2000). *Culturally responsive teaching: Theory, research and practice.* New York, NY: Teachers College Press.

Gardner, J. (1961). *Excellence: Can we be equal and excellent too?* New York: Harper and Row.

Gibbons, P. (2002). *Scaffolding language and scaffolding learning: Teaching second language learners in mainstream classrooms.* Portsmouth, NH: Heinemann.

Good, T. L. (1987). Two decades of research on teacher expectations: Findings and future directions. *Journal of Teacher Education, 38*(4): 32–47.

Gray, T., & Fleischman (2004/2005). Successful strategies for English language learners. *Educational Leadership, 62*(4): 84–85.

King, M. L., Jr. (1965). Commencement address for Oberlin College, Oberlin, Ohio.

Kozol, J. (2005). *The shame of the nation: The restoration of apartheid schooling in America.* New York, NY: Crown.

National Research Council. (1999). *How people learn: Brain, mind, school, and experience.* Washington, DC: National Academies Press.

Olson, K. (2009) *Wounded by school.* New York, NY: Teachers College Press.

DISCUSSION QUESTIONS

1. Are there certain instances where "separateness" works? Explain.
2. Why might mixed-ability classrooms benefit all students?
3. How much do nature and environment shape our mindset toward learning?
4. Can "teaching up" work for the "gifted and talented" population?
5. What are some other ways that a teacher might "teach up"?

20 The Thought-Filled Curriculum

Arthur L. Costa

FOCUSING QUESTIONS

1. How can a thought-filled curriculum promote student learning?
2. How can teachers teach their students to think?
3. How do Costa's five themes encourage thoughtful learning?
4. What tools are necessary to think "skillfully"?
5. What does it mean to think "skillfully"?

Everyone thinks. Keeping five themes in mind will ensure that every learner thinks skillfully. How do you know that your students need to learn how to think?

When I have posed this question to teachers of all grade levels in countries around the world, teachers have given surprisingly similar and consistent descriptions of their students' thinking:

- They just blurt out answers. They should think before they respond.
- They depend on me for their answers. I wish they would think for themselves.
- They give up so easily on difficult tasks. I'd like them to hang in there.
- They can't seem to work in groups. They must learn to cooperate and work together.
- They don't apply their knowledge. I want them to use what they know in other situations.
- They are afraid to take risks. I'd like them to be more creative, more adventure-some.

Such comments reflect teachers' awareness that to function in school, at work, and in life, students must persist when faced with adversity, solve cognitively complex problems, draw on vast reservoirs of knowledge, and work collaboratively. To strengthen these skills, instruction must become more reflective, complex, and relevant (Commission on the Whole Child, 2007). Curriculums must become more thought-filled in the sense of enlarging students' capacities to think deeply and creatively.

FIVE THEMES TO SHAPE CURRICULUM

I propose that educators make five themes part of any thought-filled curriculum. These themes provide lenses through which we can shape, organize, and evaluate curriculums.

1. Learning to Think

> Iron rusts from disuse; stagnant water loses its purity and in cold weather becomes frozen; even so does inaction sap the vigor of the mind.
>
> — Leonardo da Vinci

Humans are born with the capacity and inclination to think. Nobody has to "teach us how to think" just as no one teaches us how to move or walk. Moving with precision and style, however, takes much time and coaching. The distinction between awkwardness and grace is obvious to even an undisciplined observer. A superb ballerina, tai chi master, or gymnast needs years of practice, concentration, reflection, and guidance to perform intricate maneuvers on command with seemingly effortless agility.

Like strenuous movement, skillful thinking is hard work. And as with athletics, students need practice, reflection, and coaching to think well. With proper instruction, human thought processes can become more broadly applied, more spontaneously generated, more precisely focused, more complex, and more insightfully divergent.

Unlike athletics, however, thinking is usually idiosyncratic and covert. Awkwardness and agility are not as easily distinguished in thinking as they are in athletics. Definitions of thought processes, strategies for their development, and assessment of the stamina required for increased mastery, therefore, are elusive, as the following classroom interaction illustrates.

After showing a class of eighth graders how the Earth's population is likely to double in the next 50 years, a teacher asks students what could be done to solve the problem of population explosion.

STUDENT: I don't know.

TEACHER: Well, think about it. We may not have enough food and space. It's a problem we will need to solve.

STUDENT: We could send some people somewhere where they won't need food and space.

TEACHER: Where?

STUDENT: Uh, into space.

TEACHER: Why there?

STUDENT: They won't need to eat our food or live here anymore. (Swartz, Costa, Kallick, Beyer, & Reagan, 2007, p. 9)

Is this student thinking? Yes. Is this student thinking critically, skillfully, and creatively? It seems not.

Teachers who value thinking and habits of mind would ensure that students confront a problem like population expansion with a questioning attitude, arm themselves with attendant data, explore alternatives to the status quo, and predict the consequences of each of those alternatives. A contrasting teaching approach here might bring out strenuous thinking by taking time as a class to gather more information and understand why the problem exists. A teacher might pose such questions as, "Where in the world has this problem been encountered and resolved in the past?" "What alternative solutions might be generated?" or, "By what humane and just criteria might the consequences of each of those solutions be evaluated?".

Although thinking is innate and spontaneous, skillful thinking must be cultivated. One way to enhance such thinking is to get students intrigued by relevant, generative, conceptual knowledge. Cognition and content are inseparable. One cannot think about "nothing," and deep conceptual understanding requires such cognitive skills as comparing, analyzing, applying, translating, and evaluating (Wiggins & McTighe, 1998). Further, the deeper knowledge a learner has, the more analytical, experimental, and creative are that learner's thought processes (Willingham, 2007).

We can catalyze learning to think by making thinking skills explicit. We should use cognitive terminology and label and identify cognitive processes, saying, for example, "So as you're analyzing this problem ..." (Costa & Marzano, 2001). Teachers should also employ thinking maps and visual tools (Hyerle, 2004) and model problem solving, decision making, and investigating (Swartz et al., 2007).

It is not enough, however, for students to learn thinking and problem-solving skills in teacher-constructed classroom situations. They must also develop the inclination to use productive habits of mind, including persisting, managing impulsivity, thinking flexibly, striving for accuracy, and remaining open to continuous learning—on their own (Costa & Kallick, 2001).

2. Thinking to Learn

Learning is an engagement of the mind that changes the mind.

—Martin Heidegger

Meaning making is not a spectator sport. Knowledge is a constructive process; to really understand something, each learner must create a model or metaphor derived from that learner's personal world. Humans don't get ideas; they make ideas.

Content learning, therefore, should not be viewed as the only aim of instruction. Rather, teachers should select relevant, generative, wondrous content to serve as a vehicle for the joyride of learning. We can equip that vehicle by

- Posing challenging, content-embedded questions and problems that tax the imagination and stimulate inquiry.
- Inviting students to assess their own learning.
- Urging students to question their own and others' assumptions.

- Valuing students' viewpoints by maintaining a safe, nonjudgmental classroom atmosphere.

For example, to challenge students to dig deeper into historical perspectives, a teacher might have fifth graders compare and contrast two versions of the story of Pocahontas and John Smith by reading the fictionalized account *The Double Life of Pocahontas* (Fritz, 1987) and watching the Disney movie *Pocahontas*. Students could work in groups to take notes about the characters, setting, plot, and events depicted in the movie and to extract details from the text.

The teacher might direct student groups to draw conclusions about the accuracy of historical events after they identify significant patterns in the similarities and differences of the two sources (Reagan, in press). As each group shares its conclusions, the teacher should reinforce the skill of valuing others' viewpoints by reminding all students to paraphrase, clarify, or question what their peers in other groups report, so that they can better understand each group's conclusions rather than judging them. Following the discussion, students might reflect in their journals about skills to keep in mind when striving for accuracy and searching for truth; the value of listening to and empathizing with a speaker; how well they think they listened and empathized in this activity; and situations in school, home, and life that require them to strive for accuracy and listen with understanding and empathy.

3. Thinking Together

Friendship is one mind in two bodies.

—Mencius

Meaning making is not just an individual operation. Learning is a reciprocal process; the individual influences the group's thinking, and the group influences the individual's thinking (Marzano, Pickering, & Pollock, 2001; Vygotsky, 1978). Instructional techniques that encourage group activities help students construct both their own and shared knowledge.

When learners fail to see the interconnections and coherence of divergent views, collaborative thinking falters. If each student fixates on his or her own certainties, each perceives the solution to a problem solely from his or her own viewpoint. Such an egocentric view hinders serious reflection and honest inquiry.

Another purpose of a thought-filled curriculum, therefore, is to build an "ecology of thought"—a network of shared memories and awareness that links community members together (Isaacs, 1999). Collegial interaction is a crucial factor in the intellectual ecology of the school and classroom. Collaboratively individuals can elicit thinking that surpasses individual effort, but such collaboration is difficult because it means temporarily suspending what I, individually, think. It means relaxing our grip on certainties and opening our minds to new perspectives, abiding by and supporting group decisions that are arrived at through deep, respectful listening and dialogue. Learners must come to understand that as they transcend the self and become part of the whole, they will not lose their individuality, only their egocentricity.

Learning to listen with understanding and empathy may be one of the least-taught skills in school, yet it is one of the most powerful skills of intelligent problem solvers (Steil & Bommelje, 2007). Thought-filled curriculums should include instruction in and practice of

- Focusing mental energy on understanding others.
- Summarizing and paraphrasing others' thoughts.
- Empathizing.
- Monitoring clarity in communication.
- Setting aside judgments, solutions, and autobiographical responses.

4. Thinking About Our Own Thinking

> I thank the Lord for the brain he put in my head. Occasionally, I love to just stand to one side and watch how it works.
>
> —Richard Bolles

A broader intent of a thought-filled curriculum is the development of heightened consciousness of our own thinking among both teachers and students. The human species is known as *Homo sapiens sapiens*, which means "a being that knows its knowing." What distinguishes humans is our capacity for metacognition—the ability to stand back and examine our own thoughts while we engage in them. Although the human brain is capable of generating this reflective consciousness, generally we are not very aware of how we are thinking. Not everyone uses his or her capacity for metacognition equally (Csikszentmihalyi, 1993).

Learning to think begins with recognizing how we are thinking—by listening to ourselves and our own reactions and realizing how our thoughts may encapsulate us. Much of the kind of thinking people practice happens simply by virtue of their embedded habits, not because they closely examine their assumptions, their limited history, or their mental models.

Metacognition involves the whole of us: our emotions, bodily sensations, ideas, beliefs, values, character qualities, and the inferences we generate from interactions with others. When confronted with perplexing, ambiguous situations, skillful thinkers engage in an internal mental dialogue that helps them decide on intelligent actions. We can get students into the habit of such mindful probing by using self-reflective questions like these:

- How can I draw on my past successes to solve this new problem? What do I already know about the problem, and what resources do I have available or need to generate?

- How can I approach this problem flexibly? How might I look at the situation from a fresh perspective? Am I remaining open to new possibilities?
- How can I make this problem clearer, more precise, and more detailed? Do I need to check out my data sources? How might I break this problem down into its component parts and develop a strategy for approaching each step?
- What do I know or not know? What might I be missing, and what questions do I need to ask?
- What strategies are in my mind now? What values, beliefs, and intentions are influencing my approach? What emotions might be blocking or enhancing my progress?
- How is this problem affecting others? How might we solve it together, and what can I learn from others that would help me become a better problem solver?

Teachers can spur metacognition by directing students to verbalize plans and strategies for solving challenging problems—and by urging students to share their thinking as they monitor their progress, evaluate their strategies, and generate alternative strategies.

5. Thinking Big

> I learned to make my mind large, as the universe is large, so that there is room for paradoxes.
>
> —Maxine Hong Kingston

Building a thought-filled curriculum serves the larger agenda of building a more thought-filled world—an interdependent learning community where people continually search for ways to care for one another, learn together, and grow toward greater intelligence. We must deepen student thinking to hasten the arrival of a world community that

- Generates more thoughtful, peaceful approaches to solving problems, rather than resorting to violence to resolve differences.
- Values the diversity of other cultures, races, religions, language systems, time perspectives, and political and economic views.
- Shows greater consciousness of how humans affect Earth's limited resources and how we must live in harmony with our delicate environment.
- Engages in clear and respectful dialogue to resolve misunderstandings.

While designing each lesson, thought-filled teachers focus on this larger vision by asking themselves, Are these learnings essential? How do they contribute to building more thoughtful classrooms, schools, and communities, and a more thoughtful world? Teachers encourage students to "think big" when they lead them to inquire into such moral, ethical, and philosophical questions as, "What makes human beings human? What is beauty? What is justice? How can we learn to unite and not divide?".

These five themes constitute unfinished tasks for teachers and curriculum designers in building a more thought-filled curriculum. As noted computer scientist Alan Kay (1990) stated, "The best way to predict the future is to invent it." If we want a future that is vastly more thoughtful, cooperative, compassionate, and loving, then we have to create it. The future is in our schools and classrooms today.

REFERENCES

Commission on the Whole Child. (2007). *The learning compact redefined: A call to action.* Alexandria, VA: ASCD.

Costa, A., & Kallick, B. (2001). *Discovering and exploring habits of mind.* Alexandria, VA: ASCD.

Costa, A., & Marzano, R. (2001). Teaching the language of thinking. In A. Costa (Ed.),

Developing minds: A resource book for teaching thinking (pp. 379–383). Alexandria, VA: ASCD.

Csikszentmihalyi, M. (1993). *Flow: The psychology of optimal experience.* New York, NY: Harper and Row.

Fritz, J. (1987). *The double life of Pocahontas.* New York, NY: Puffin Books.

Hyerle, D. (Ed.). (2004). *Student successes with thinking maps.* Thousand Oaks, CA: Corwin Press.

Isaacs, W. (1999). *Dialogue and the art of thinking together.* New York, NY: Currency.

Kay, A. (1990, March). The best way to predict the future is to invent it. Keynote presentation at the annual conference of the Association for Supervision and Curriculum Development, San Francisco, CA.

Marzano, R., Pickering, D., & Pollock, J. (2001). *Classroom instruction that works.* Alexandria, VA: ASCD.

Reagan, R. (in press). Cognitive composition: Thinking based writing. In A. Costa & B. Kallick (Eds.), *Habits of mind: Voices from the field.* Alexandria, VA: ASCD.

Steil, L. K., & Bommelje, R. (2007). *Listening leaders: The ten golden rules to listen, lead and succeed.* Edina, MN: Beaver Pond Press.

Swartz, R., Costa, A., Kailick, B., Beyer, B., & Reagan, R. (2007). *Thinking based learning.* Norwood, MA: Christopher Gordon.

Vygotsky, L. S. (1978). *Mind in society: The development of higher psychological processes.* Cambridge, MA: Harvard University Press.

Wiggins, G., & McTighe, J. (1998). *Understanding by design.* Alexandria, VA: ASCD.

Willingham, D. (2007, Summer). Critical thinking: Why is it so hard to teach? *American Educator,* 9–16.

DISCUSSION QUESTIONS

1. How can you incorporate the five themes into your own teaching?

2. Do you agree with the author regarding the importance of teaching thinking explicitly? How would this most effectively be translated into classroom practice?

3. How interrelated are the five themes? Are they hierarchical or complementary? Can they be taught concurrently or must they be taught sequentially?

4. How can a thought-filled curriculum be integrated into an existing standards-based curriculum model?

5. How can we ensure that teachers are equipped with the requisite skills and pedagogy to explicitly teach thinking to their students?

21 The Importance of Multicultural Education

GENEVA GAY

FOCUSING QUESTIONS

1. How has multiculturalism changed in the United States?
2. How does lack of ethnic, racial, and cultural community harm schools? How does this extend into society?
3. How can multicultural education extend beyond the arts/humanities? Why is this important?
4. What are some steps to incorporating multicultural content into a curriculum?
5. How does cross-referencing subjects aid multicultural learning?
6. How do reality/representation and relevance shape a multicultural curriculum? How do they shape student learning?

Multiculturalism in U.S. schools and society is taking on new dimensions of complexity and practicality as demographics, social conditions, and political circumstances change. Domestic diversity and unprecedented immigration have created a vibrant mixture of cultural, ethnic, linguistic, and experiential plurality.

Effectively managing such diversity in U.S. society and schools is at once a very old and a very new challenge. Benjamin Barber (1992) eloquently makes the point that

> America has always been a tale of peoples trying to be a People, a tale of diversity and plurality in search of unity. Cleavages among [diverse groups] . . . have irked and divided Americans from the start, making unity a civic imperative as well as an elusive challenge. (p. 41)

Accomplishing this end is becoming increasingly important as the twenty-first century unfolds. People coming from Asia, the Middle East, Latin America, Eastern Europe, and Africa differ greatly from earlier generations of immigrants who came primarily from western and northern Europe. These unfamiliar groups, cultures, traditions, and languages can produce anxieties, hostilities, prejudices, and racist behaviors among those who do not understand the newcomers or who perceive them as threats to their safety and security. These issues have profound implications for developing, at all levels of education, instructional programs and practices that respond positively and constructively to diversity.

A hundred years ago, W. E. B. Du Bois (1994) proposed that the problem of the twentieth century was conflict and controversy among racial groups, particularly between African and European Americans. He concluded,

> Between these two worlds [black and white], despite much physical contact and daily intermingling, there is almost no community of intellectual life or point of transference where the thoughts and feelings of one race can come into direct contact and sympathy with the thoughts and feelings of the other. (p. 110)

Although much has changed since Du Bois's declarations, too much has not changed nearly enough. Of course, the color line has become more complex and diverse, and legal barriers against racial intermingling have been dismantled. People from different ethnic, racial, and cultural groups live in close physical proximity. But coexistence does not mean that people create genuine communities in which they know, relate to, and care deeply about one another. The lack of a genuine community of diversity is particularly evident in school curriculums that still do not regularly and systematically include important information and deep study about a wide range of diverse ethnic groups. As disparities in educational opportunities and outcomes among ethnic groups have continued to grow, the resulting achievement gap has reached crisis proportions.

Multicultural education is integral to improving the academic success of students of color and preparing all youths for democratic citizenship in a pluralistic society. Students need to understand how multicultural issues shape the social, political, economic, and cultural fabric of the United States as well as how such issues fundamentally influence their personal lives.

CONCEPTIONS OF MULTICULTURAL EDUCATION

Even though some theorists (Banks & Banks, 2002) have argued that multicultural education is a necessary ingredient of quality education, in actual practice educators most often perceive it either as an addendum prompted by some crisis or as a luxury. Multicultural education has not yet become a central part of the curriculum regularly offered to all students; instead, educators have relegated it primarily to social studies, language arts, and the fine arts and have generally targeted instruction for students of color.

These attitudes distort multicultural education and make it susceptible to sporadic and superficial implementation, if any. Textbooks provide a compelling illustration of such an attitude: The little multicultural content that they offer is often presented in sidebars and special-events sections (Loewen, 1995).

Another obstacle to implementing multicultural education lies with teachers themselves. Many are unconvinced of its worth or its value in developing academic skills and building a unified national community. Even those teachers who are more accepting of multicultural education are nevertheless skeptical about the feasibility of its implementation. "I would do it if I could," they say, "but I don't know how." "Preparing students to meet standards takes up all my time," others point out. "School curriculums are already overburdened. What do I take out to make room for multicultural education?"

A fallacy underlies these conceptions and the instructional behaviors that they generate: the perception of multicultural education as separate content that educators must append to existing curriculums as separate lessons, units, or courses. Quite the contrary is true. Multicultural education is more than content; it includes policy, learning climate, instructional delivery, leadership, and evaluation (see Banks, 1994;

Bennett, 2003; Grant & Gomez, 2000). In its comprehensive form, it must be an integral part of everything that happens in the education enterprise, whether it is assessing the academic competencies of students or teaching math, reading, writing, science, social studies, or computer science. Making explicit connections between multicultural education and subject- and skill-based curriculum and instruction is imperative.

It is not pragmatic for K–12 educators to think of multicultural education as a discrete entity, separated from the commonly accepted components of teaching and learning. These conceptions may be fine for higher education, where specialization is the rule. But in K–12 schools, where the education process focuses on teaching eclectic bodies of knowledge and skills, teachers need to use multicultural education to promote such highly valued outcomes as human development, education equality, academic excellence, and democratic citizenship (see Banks & Banks, 2001; Nieto, 2000).

To translate these theoretical conceptions into practice, educators must systematically weave multicultural education into the central core of curriculum, instruction, school leadership, policy making, counseling, classroom climate, and performance assessment. Teachers should use multicultural content, perspectives, and experiences to teach reading, math, science, and social studies.

For example, teachers could demonstrate mathematical concepts, such as less than/greater than, percentages, ratios, and probabilities, using ethnic demographics. Younger children could consider the ethnic and racial distributions in their own classrooms, discussing which group's representation is greater than, less than, or equal to another's. Older students could collect statistics about ethnic distributions on a larger scale and use them to make more sophisticated calculations, such as converting numbers to percentages and displaying ethnic demographics on graphs.

Students need to apply such major academic skills as data analysis, problem solving, comprehension, inquiry, and effective communication as they study multicultural issues and events. For instance, students should not simply memorize facts about major events involving ethnic groups, such as civil rights movements, social justice efforts, and cultural accomplishments. Instead, educators should teach students how to think critically and analytically about these events, propose alternative solutions to social problems, and demonstrate understanding through such forms of communication as poetry, personal correspondence, debate, editorials, and photo essays.

Irvine and Armento (2001) provide specific examples for incorporating multicultural education into planning language arts, math, science, and social studies lessons for elementary and middle school students and connecting these lessons to general curriculum standards. One set of lessons demonstrates how to use Navajo rugs to explain the geometric concepts of perimeter and area and to teach students how to calculate the areas of squares, rectangles, triangles, and parallelograms.

These suggestions indicate that teachers need to use systematic decision-making approaches to accomplish multicultural curriculum integration. In practice, this means developing intentional and orderly processes for including multicultural content. The decision-making process might involve the following steps:

- Creating learning goals and objectives that incorporate multicultural aspects, such as "Developing students' ability to write persuasively about social justice concerns."
- Using a frequency matrix to ensure that the teacher includes a wide variety of ethnic groups in a wide variety of ways in curriculum materials and instructional activities.

- Introducing different ethnic groups and their contributions on a rotating basis.
- Including several examples from different ethnic experiences to explain subject matter concepts, facts, and skills.
- Showing how multicultural content, goals, and activities intersect with subject-specific curricular standards.

Virtually all aspects of multicultural education are interdisciplinary. As such, they cannot be adequately understood through a single discipline. For example, teaching students about the causes, expressions, and consequences of racism and how to combat racism requires the application of information and techniques from such disciplines as history, economics, sociology, psychology, mathematics, literature, science, art, politics, music, and health care. Theoretical scholarship already affirms this interdisciplinary need; now, teachers need to model good curricular and instructional practice in elementary and secondary classrooms. Putting this principle into practice will elevate multicultural education from impulse, disciplinary isolation, and simplistic and haphazard guesswork to a level of significance, complexity, and connectedness across disciplines.

MULTICULTURALISM AND CURRICULUM DEVELOPMENT

How can teachers establish linkages between multicultural education and the disciplines and subject matter content taught in schools? One approach is to filter multicultural education through two categories of curriculum development: reality/representation and relevance.

Reality/Representation

A persistent concern of curriculum development in all subjects is helping students understand the realities of the social condition and how they came to be, as well as adequately representing those realities.

Historically, curriculum designers have been more exclusive than inclusive of the wide range of ethnic and cultural diversity that exists within society. In their haste to promote harmony and avoid controversy and conflict, they gloss over social problems and the realities of ethnic and racial identities, romanticize racial relations, and ignore the challenges of poverty and urban living in favor of middle-class and suburban experiences. The reality is distorted and the representations incomplete (Loewen, 1995).

An inescapable reality is that diverse ethnic, racial, and cultural groups and individuals have made contributions to every area of human endeavor and to all aspects of U.S. history, life, and culture. When students study food resources in the United States, for example, they often learn about production and distribution by large-scale agribusiness and processing corporations. The curriculum virtually ignores the contributions of the many ethnically diverse people involved in planting and harvesting vegetables and fruits (with the Mexican and Mexican American farm labor unionization movement a possible exception). School curriculums that incorporate comprehensive multicultural education do not perpetuate these exclusions. Instead, they teach students the reality—how large corporations and the food industry are directly connected to the migrant workers who harvest vegetables and pick fruits. If we are going to tell the true story of the United States, multicultural education must be a central feature in its telling.

School curriculums need to reverse these trends by also including equitable representations of diversity. For example, the study of American literature, art, and music should include the contributions of males and females from different ethnic groups in all genres and in different expressive styles. Thus, the study of jazz would examine various forms and techniques produced not just by African Americans but also by Asian, European, and Latino Americans.

Moreover, educators should represent ethnically diverse individuals and groups in all strata of human accomplishment instead of typecasting particular groups as dependent and helpless victims who make limited contributions of significance. Even under the most oppressive conditions, diverse groups in the United States have been creative, activist, and productive on broad scales. The way in which Japanese Americans handled their internment during World War II provides an excellent example. Although schools must not overlook or minimize the atrocities this group endured, students should also learn how interned Japanese Americans led dignified lives under the most undignified circumstances, elevating their humanity above their circumstances. The curriculum should include both issues.

Relevance

Many ethnically diverse students do not find schooling exciting or inviting; they often feel unwelcome, insignificant, and alienated. Too much of what is taught has no immediate value to these students. It does not reflect who they are. Yet most educators will agree that learning is more interesting and easier to accomplish when it has personal meaning for students.

Students from different ethnic groups are more likely to be interested and engaged in learning situations that occur in familiar and friendly frameworks than in those occurring in strange and hostile ones. A key factor in establishing educational relevance for these students is cultural similarity and responsiveness (see Bruner, 1996; Hollins, 1996; Wlodkowski & Ginsberg, 1995). For example, immigrant Vietnamese, Jamaican, and Mexican students who were members of majority populations in their home countries initially may have difficulty understanding what it means to be members of minority groups in the United States. Students who come from education environments that encourage active participatory learning will not be intellectually stimulated by passive instruction that involves lecturing and completing worksheets. Many students of color are bombarded with irrelevant learning experiences, which dampen their academic interest, engagement, and achievement. Multicultural education mediates these situations by teaching content about the cultures and contributions of many ethnic groups and by using a variety of teaching techniques that are culturally responsive to different ethnic learning styles.

Using a variety of strategies may seem a tall order in a classroom that includes students from many different ethnic groups. Research indicates, however, that several ethnic groups share some learning style attributes (Shade, 1989). Teachers need to understand the distinguishing characteristics of different learning styles and use the instructional techniques best suited to each style. In this scenario, teachers would provide alternative teaching techniques for clusters of students instead of for individual students. In any given lesson, the teacher might offer three or four ways for students to learn, helping to equalize learning advantages and disadvantages among the different ethnic groups in the classroom.

Scholars are producing powerful descriptions of culturally relevant teaching for multiethnic students and its effects on achievement. Lipka and Mohatt (1998) describe how a group of teachers, working closely with Native Alaskan (Yup'ik) elders, made school structure, climate, curriculum, and instruction more reflective of and meaningful to students from the community. For ten years, the teachers translated, adapted, and embedded Yup'ik cultural knowledge in math, literacy, and science curriculums. The elders served as resources and quality-control monitors of traditional knowledge, and they provided the inspiration and moral strength for the teachers to persist in their efforts to center the schooling of Yup'ik students around the students' own cultural orientations. In math, for instance, the teachers now habitually make connections among the Yup'ik numeration system, body measurements, simple and complex computations, geometry, pattern designs, and tessellations.

Similar attributes apply to the work of such scholars as Moses and Cobb (2001), Lee (1993), and Boykin and Bailey (2000), who are studying the effects of culturally relevant curriculum and instruction on the school performance of African American students. Moses and his colleagues are making higher-order math knowledge accessible to African American middle school students by teaching this material through the students' own cultural orientations and experiences. To teach algebra, they emphasize the experiences and familiar environments of urban and rural low-income students, many of whom are at high risk for academic failure. A key feature of their approach is making students conscious of how algebraic principles and formulas operate in their daily lives and getting students to understand how to explain these connections in nonalgebraic language before converting this knowledge into the technical notations and calculations of algebra. Students previously considered by some teachers as incapable of learning algebra are performing at high levels—better, in fact, than many of their advantaged peers.

Evidence increasingly indicates that multicultural education makes schooling more relevant and effective for Latino American, Native American, Asian American, and Native Hawaiian students as well (see McCarty, 2002; Moll, Amanti, Neff, & Gonzalez, 1992; Park, Goodwin, & Lee, 2001; Tharp & Gallimore, 1988). Students perform more successfully at all levels when there is greater congruence between their cultural backgrounds and such school experiences as task interest, effort, academic achievement, and feelings of personal efficacy or social accountability.

As the challenge to better educate underachieving students intensifies and diversity among student populations expands, the need for multicultural education grows exponentially. Multicultural education may be the solution to problems that currently appear unsolvable: closing the achievement gap; genuinely not leaving any children behind academically; revitalizing faith and trust in the promises of democracy, equality, and justice; building education systems that reflect the diverse cultural, ethnic, racial, and social contributions that forge society; and providing better opportunities for all students.

Multicultural education is crucial. Classroom teachers and educators must answer its clarion call to provide students from all ethnic groups with the education they deserve.

REFERENCES

Banks, J. A. (1994). *Multiethnic education: Theory and practice* (3rd ed.). Boston, MA: Allyn and Bacon.

Banks, J. A., & Banks, C. A. M. (Eds.). (2001). *Multicultural education: Issues and perspectives* (4th ed.). Boston, MA: Allyn and Bacon.

Banks, J. A., & Banks, C. A. M. (Eds.). (2002). *Handbook of research on multicultural education* (2nd ed.). San Francisco, CA: Jossey-Bass.

Barber, B. R. (1992). *An aristocracy of everyone: The politics of education and the future of America.* New York, NY: Oxford University Press.

Bennett, C. I. (2003). *Comprehensive multicultural education: Theory and practice.* Boston, MA: Allyn and Bacon.

Boykin, A. W., & Bailey, C. T. (2000). The role of cultural factors in school relevant cognitive functioning: Synthesis of findings on cultural context, cultural orientations, and individual differences. (ERIC Document Reproduction Service No. ED 441 880).

Bruner, J. (1996). *The culture of education.* Cambridge, MA: Harvard University Press.

Du Bois, W. E. B. (1994). *The souls of black folk.* New York, NY: Gramercy Books.

Grant, C. A., & Gomez, M. L. (Eds.). (2000). *Making school multicultural: Campus and classroom*

(2nd ed.). Upper Saddle River, NJ: Merrill/Prentice-Hall.

Hollins, E. R. (1996). *Culture in school learning: Revealing the deep meaning.* Mahwah, NJ: Erlbaum.

Irvine, J. J., & Armento, B. J. (Eds.). (2001). *Culturally responsive teaching: Lesson planning for elementary and middle grades.* New York, NY: McGraw-Hill.

Lee, C. (1993). Signifying as a scaffold to literary interpretation: The pedagogical implications of a form of African American discourse (NCTE Research Report No. 26). Urbana, IL: National Council of Teachers of English.

Lipka, J., & Mohatt, G. V. (1998). *Transforming the culture of schools: Yup'ik Eskimo examples.* Mahwah, NJ: Erlbaum.

Loewen, J. W. (1995). *Lies my teacher told me: Everything your American history textbook got wrong.* New York, NY: New Press.

McCarty, T. L. (2002). *A place to be Navajo: Rough rock and the struggle for self-determination in indigenous schooling.* Mahwah, NJ: Erlbaum.

Moll, L. C., Amanti, C., Neff, D., & Gonzalez, N. (1992). Funds of knowledge for teaching: Using a qualitative approach to connect homes and classrooms. *Theory into Practice, 31*(1): 132–141.

Moses, R. P., & Cobb, C. E., Jr. (2001). *Radical equations: Math literacy and civil rights.* Boston, MA: Beacon Press.

Nieto, S. (2000). *Affirming diversity: The sociopolitical context of multicultural education* (3rd ed.). New York, NY: Longman.

Park, C. C., Goodwin, A. L., & Lee, S. J. (Eds.). (2001). *Research on the education of Asian and Pacific Americans.* Greenwich, CT: Information Age Publishers.

Shade, B. J. (Ed.). (1989). *Culture, style, and the educative process.* Springfield, IL: Charles C. Thomas.

Tharp, R. G., & Gallimore, R. (1988). *Rousing minds to life: Teaching, learning, and schooling in social context.* Cambridge, UK: Cambridge University Press.

Wlodkowski, R. J., & Ginsberg, M. B. (1995). *Diversity and motivation: Culturally responsive teaching.* San Francisco, CA: Jossey-Bass.

DISCUSSION QUESTIONS

1. What issues related to multiculturalism have emerged in your school in recent years?
2. Do you agree with the author's claim that many teachers remain unconvinced that multicultural education has value?
3. What would be needed to bring theoretical concepts of multiculturalism into practice? Would this be of benefit to students? How?
4. How should considerations of multiculturalism influence the process of curriculum development?
5. Would a greater emphasis on multiculturalism help close the achievement gap? Why or why not?

CHAPTER

22 Knowledge Alive

DAVID PERKINS

FOCUSING QUESTIONS

1. How are knowledge arts used in society? How does this translate to schools?

2. How do schools fail to transmit the knowledge arts between subjects?

3. What are the ways by which a teacher can make knowledge visible? How does this relate to student understanding?

4. How can a teacher provide a culture of learning?

Perhaps the broadest and most basic question for educators—before matters of method, testing, or grading—is "What should we teach?" And perhaps the most basic answer is "knowledge." Knowledge in the broad sense—facts, ideas, and skills—provides the mainstay of the school curriculum from kindergarten through college.

But then there's the question of what you do with knowledge. Education has always been more generous about exposing learners to large volumes of knowledge than about teaching them the diverse skills involved in handling knowledge well—the knowledge arts.

The knowledge arts include communicating strategically, insightfully, and effectively; thinking critically and creatively; and putting school knowledge to work in what educators sometimes humbly call the "real world." The knowledge arts bundle together deep reading, compelling writing, strong problem solving and decision making, and the strategic and spirited self-management of learning itself, within and across the disciplines.

We need to put the knowledge arts on the table—to celebrate them for the depth and power they provide and for the ways they make knowledge meaningful. And we need to worry about their neglect.

THE KNOWLEDGE ARTS IN SOCIETY

To get a picture of how the knowledge arts work in schools, let's start with the bigger picture of how they work in society. We can tell the broad story of knowledge in four chapters, starting with creating it and moving on to communicating it, organizing it, and acting on it.

People create knowledge in various ways. Scientists examine the sky or the sea or quarks or viruses; historians puzzle over ancient documents and artifacts; pollsters survey public opinion; engineers design and test prototypes; newspaper reporters investigate political dogfights; police officers comb for evidence about crimes. Then we communicate that knowledge in various ways: through writing and reading; mathematical equations, maps, and diagrams; news broadcasts; electronic mailing lists; and works of art. We organize knowledge in various ways for ready access (notes, concept maps, Web sites) or for particular purposes, judgments, plans, and decisions (the court's verdict, the advertising campaign, the blueprints for a new building). And eventually, we act on all this knowledge: We carry out the judgment, erect the building, or launch the mission.

Of course, the story of knowledge in the form of these four chapters is far too linear. Creating, communicating, organizing, and acting on knowledge mix with one another in complex and generative ways. However, the four chapters provide a rough and ready overview.

THE KNOWLEDGE ARTS IN SCHOOL: A REPORT CARD

Keeping the four chapters in mind, how well does schooling develop the knowledge arts of learners? The report card for business-as-usual schooling would look like this:

> Creating knowledge: D
> Communicating knowledge: B
> Organizing knowledge: C
> Acting on knowledge: D

The first D reflects the fact that in typical schools, investigative, inquiry-oriented activities in which learners create knowledge are sparse. Of course, such activities occur here and there—for instance, in some kinds of science learning—but even then they often entail simply going through the motions of a laboratory experiment rather than genuinely wrestling with ideas.

Acting on knowledge also earns a D. We rarely ask students to do much with their learning outside school—except homework, of course. As a result, knowledge tends to become passive or inert. In both academic and practical contexts, learners fail to connect what they have learned to new situations or to act effectively on that knowledge (Bransford, Franks, Vye, & Sherwood, 1989). Students may memorize key information about biology for the science test but never ponder what that knowledge says about personal health care or public health issues.

Problems of transfer of learning have long plagued education (Bransford & Schwartz, 1999; Detterman & Sternberg, 1992; Perkins & Salomon, 1988). Typical schooling does not even encourage students to carry their knowledge from one classroom to another. Science instructors often complain that the math from math class somehow evaporates in the science room. History instructors grumble that some cognitive Bermuda Triangle in the corridor between the English and history classrooms has sucked away students' knowledge of writing.

Conventional education probably does best at communicating knowledge, so why does it rate only a B in this area? On the receptive side of communication, although learners spend a great deal of time loading up on knowledge, schools do not typically teach them to do so strategically. Many young readers can decode competently but have never learned to ask themselves what they are reading for, to monitor their reading as they go, to assess themselves afterward, and to fill in what they missed. The productive side of communication includes not only writing but also artistic expression, presentations, multimedia work, and so on. These areas, except for the mechanics of writing, typically receive little time or guidance.

Further, some schools direct dogged attention to skill and content learning in a narrow sense, with the unsettling consequence that skills become ritualized into mere recipes to follow (Perkins, 1992). For instance, students who know how to add, subtract, multiply, and divide can become quite confused about how to apply these operations to story problems, and they often fall back on limited keyword strategies, such as "all together means add." Students learn what they are supposed to say in class without really understanding it. Science educator Marcia Linn amusingly noted what one student made of a Newtonian principle of motion: "Objects in motion remain in motion in the classroom, but come to rest on the playground" (2002).

Organizing knowledge also receives little attention in typical schools—thus, the grade of C. In most school settings, strategic guidance in this skill appears only during review sessions or around such products as essays. Yet learning logs, concept mapping, debates, group presentations, and many other activities can dramatically expand students' skills in organizing knowledge.

At this point, dedicated educators will object: "My kids are deeply engaged in inquiry-oriented science learning!" "My students keep learning journals and review their learning every week!" "We stage a debate after every unit!" "Teams of youngsters are out there in the community investigating local history!" Good. These undertakings certainly cultivate the knowledge arts and deserve kudos when and where they occur. But we need to ask, "How often is this kind of teaching and learning happening, and how well?" Between the oases of glory stretch deserts of neglect.

BRINGING KNOWLEDGE TO LIFE

What does it look like to enliven teaching and learning through the knowledge arts? The following examples come from the work of my colleagues at Project Zero of the Harvard Graduate School of Education (www.pz.harvard.edu).

Making Thinking Visible

One way to advance the knowledge arts is to use thinking routines (Ritchhart, 2002) to make students' thinking visible, thus increasing their awareness of what goes into creating, communicating, organizing, and acting on knowledge.

For instance, Shari Tishman (2002) explored a simple way to make certain kinds of thinking visible by asking two key questions: "What's going on here?" and "What do you see that makes you say so?" She adapted this approach from a procedure for thoughtfully examining works of visual art (Housen, Yenawine, & Arenas, 1991), but learners can apply these questions to many different objects—for example, a short poem or a satellite photograph of a hurricane. Or a history instructor might show a historical artifact, like a crossbow, accompanied by the slightly tweaked questions "How does this work?" and "What do you see that makes you think so?"

Tina Grotzer and I have developed inquiry-oriented activities that engage students in communicating about the complex causal models that can often make science concepts difficult to understand—models that involve such invisible features as electrons, causal loops, and simultaneous cause and effect (Grotzer, 2003; Perkins & Grotzer, 2000). For instance, fourth graders studying electrical circuits compare different ideas about what the current does. Does it start at the battery and fill the circuit, as when a hot-water radiator system is turned on for the first time, and then continue to cycle? Or does the current of electrons move all at once, like a bicycle chain? Young learners lean toward the first idea, but the second is more scientifically accurate. The following discussion shows how the teacher can help students make visible their thinking about the scientific explanation of electrical flow (Grotzer, 2000):

> TEACHER: Let's compare how cause and effect works in these two different

kinds of cyclic models. In the cyclic sequential model [as in the radiator system analogy], what makes the electrons move?

STUDENT 1: They want to get out of the battery because of all the electrons so they go onto the wire.

TEACHER: And then what happens?

STUDENT 2: They go along the wire till they get to the bulb and that makes the bulb light up.

TEACHER: Why do the electrons move in the cyclic simultaneous model [as in the bicycle chain analogy]?

STUDENT 1: The electrons push the one in front but at the same time they are pushed by the one behind them. So everything moves at the same time.

TEACHER: Yes, each electron repels the next one but is repelled by the one behind it. It's both a cause and an effect at the same time. The whole thing turns like the chain on a bicycle. What causes the bulb to light?

STUDENT 3: When the electrons start to flow.

Grotzer's research shows that conversations like this one, along with simple experiments and activities, can make causal thinking visible and lead to higher levels of understanding.

Teaching for Understanding

Understanding is one of the most cherished goals of education. Teaching for understanding can bring knowledge to life by requiring students to manipulate knowledge in various ways. For instance, understanding a historical event means going beyond the facts to explain it, explore the remote causes, discuss the incident as different people might see it from their own perspectives, and skeptically critique what various sources say.

A number of years ago, several colleagues and I developed the Teaching for Understanding framework, which centers on the idea of performances of understanding (Blythe & Associates, 1998; Gardner, 1999; Perkins & Blythe, 1994). Here are two examples of classrooms using this framework, drawn from Wiske (1998).

Joan Soble employed the Teaching for Understanding framework to organize and deliver an introductory writing course for at-risk ninth graders—students whom she described as "perpetually overwhelmed." The students engaged in a wide range of understanding performances, including work with collages as preparation for writing; keeping and critically reviewing portfolios; and setting and pursuing goals individually, using a form that listed writing skills they wanted to improve, from sentence structure to revision practices to aspects of self-management. Thus, these students worked directly on the knowledge art of writing, learning how to practice it with more skill, confidence, and flair. Soble's approach also helped students with another knowledge art: the thoughtful management of their own learning.

Lois Hetland's seventh-grade class examined fundamental questions about Colonial America throughout the year. Some questions concerned the land: How does land shape human culture? How do people think about the land? How do people change the land? Another line of questioning concerned historical truth: How do we find out the truth about things that happened long ago or far away? How do we see through bias in sources? These throughlines, as Hetland called them, provided abiding points of reference for the learners. Discussing the same throughlines in connection with topic after topic helped students to develop not only a deeper understanding of Colonial America but also important knowledge arts: the ins and outs of historical inquiry and the management of their own learning through sustained questioning.

Such practices engage students in various mixes of the four broad activities identified earlier—creating, communicating, organizing, and acting on knowledge—in ways linked to the disciplines. Moreover, research has revealed something quite striking: Students who participate in Teaching for Understanding classrooms display shifts in their attitudes toward understanding. Compared with other students, they think of understanding in a more dynamic and exploratory way, rather than as a collection of facts and skills (Wiske, 1998). This stance toward understanding amounts to a knowledge art that equips students for deeper learning.

Creating a Culture of Learning

The knowledge arts—like any art—are more than skills: They involve passion, energy, and commitment (Tishman, Perkins, & Jay, 1995). Teachers promote the knowledge arts when they strive to establish a classroom culture of inquiry and excitement.

Ritchhart (2002) describes an algebra teacher who began the first day of school by displaying a mathematical puzzle problem from the newspaper, noting that a student had brought it in, saying that he loved little problems, and encouraging students to provide other puzzle problems throughout the year. Then he wrote on the chalkboard an elaborate arithmetic computation drawn from an episode in *The Phantom Tollbooth,* asking students to work out the answer and commenting that he had better figure it out himself. Inevitably, students came up with a variety of answers. The teacher gave his own answer but warned that he didn't think it was correct. He challenged students to find the right answer.

Through these actions and others like them—informal, welcoming, and inquiring—this teacher signaled that the coming school year would bring knowledge alive.

THE SECOND CURRICULUM

One natural reaction to these examples—and others from ingenious teachers across the world—is that they simply illustrate good teaching methods. They show ways of teaching content that enhance student engagement and make knowledge more meaningful.

True enough, but the knowledge arts are more than just tools for teachers to teach with; they encompass ideas, skills, and attitudes for learners to learn—a second curriculum. Thinking of the knowledge arts in this way creates new responsibilities for educators. As teachers teach science, history, or literature, they should be able to specify what skills of inquiry, strategies of communication, methods of organization, and ranges of application they are striving to develop in students; how they are spending time doing so; and how they are exciting students' interest and providing serious guidance. Without such an account, the second curriculum does not exist in any substantive sense.

The bad news: All this amounts to one more agenda in an era in which educators must prepare students for high-stakes tests that often emphasize *having* knowledge far more than *doing* something with it. The good news: The second curriculum is not just an add-on to the first. Instead, it's a meld, a fusion, an infiltration designed to bring knowledge to life and keep it alive. Taking the second curriculum seriously will not only equip students with knowledge-handling skills they need but also deepen and broaden their mastery of the first curriculum.

Behind the second curriculum is a simple idea: Education is not just about acquiring knowledge, but also about learning how to do significant things with what you know. It's not about dead knowledge, but about bringing knowledge to life. To educate for today and tomorrow, every school and every classroom should teach the knowledge arts seriously and well.

REFERENCES

Blythe, T., & Associates. (1998). *The teaching for understanding guide.* San Francisco, CA: Jossey-Bass.

Bransford, J. D., Franks, J. J., Vye, N. J., & Sherwood, R. D. (1989). New approaches to instruction: Because wisdom can't be told. In S. Vosniadou & A. Ortony (Eds.), *Similarity and analogical reasoning* (pp. 470–497). New York, NY: Cambridge University Press.

Bransford, J. D., & Schwartz, D. L. (1999). Rethinking transfer: A simple proposal with interesting implications. In A. Iran-Nejad & P. D. Pearson (Eds.), *Review of research in education* (Vol. 24, pp. 61–101). Washington, DC: American Educational Research Association.

Detterman, D., & Sternberg, R. (Eds.). (1992). *Transfer on trial.* Norwood, NJ: Ablex.

Gardner, H. (1999). *The disciplined mind.* New York, NY: Simon and Schuster.

Grotzer, T. A. (2000, April). *How conceptual leaps in understanding the nature of causality can limit learning: An example from electrical circuits.* Paper presented at the annual conference of the American Educational Research Association, New Orleans, LA.

Grotzer, T. A. (2003). Learning to understand the forms of causality implicit in scientific explanations. *Studies in Science Education, 39,* 1–74.

Housen, A., Yenawine, P., & Arenas, A. (1991). *Visual thinking curriculum.* (Unpublished but used for research purposes). New York, NY: Museum of Modern Art.

Linn, M. (2002, May). *The role of customization of innovative science curricula: Implications for design, practice, and professional development.* Symposium at the annual meeting of the National Association for Research in Science Teaching, New Orleans, LA.

Perkins, D. N. (1992). *Smart schools: From training memories to educating minds.* New York, NY: Free Press.

Perkins, D. N., & Blythe, T. (1994). Putting understanding up front. *Educational Leadership, 51*(5): 4–7.

Perkins, D. N., & Grotzer, T. A. (2000, April). *Models and moves: Focusing on dimensions of causal complexity to achieve deeper scientific understanding.* Paper presented at the annual conference of the American Educational Research Association, New Orleans, LA.

Perkins, D. N., & Salomon, G. (1988). Teaching for transfer. *Educational Leadership, 46*(1): 22–32.

Ritchhart, R. (2002). *Intellectual character: What it is, why it matters, and how to get it.* San Francisco, CA: Jossey-Bass.

Tishman, S. (2002). Artful reasoning. In T. Grotzer, L. Howick, S. Tishman, & D. Wise (Eds.), *Art works for schools.* Lincoln, MA: DeCordova Museum and Sculpture Park.

Tishman, S., Perkins, D. N., & Jay, E. (1995). *The thinking classroom.* Boston, MA: Allyn and Bacon.

Wiske, M. S. (Ed.). (1998). *Teaching for understanding: Linking research with practice.* San Francisco, CA: Jossey-Bass.

DISCUSSION QUESTIONS

1. What types of learning does the author include in the category "knowledge arts"?
2. Why does the author give schools low grades in the teaching of knowledge arts?
3. What suggestions are offered for enlivening teaching and learning?
4. Do the suggestions offered make you think differently about what goes on in your own classroom or school?
5. Which of the suggested changes would be easiest to make and which would be most difficult?

23 What Students Need to Learn: A Diploma Worth Having

GRANT WIGGINS

FOCUSING QUESTIONS

1. What is the major weakness of current high schools? Explain.
2. Describe the cardinal principles of secondary education.
3. What was Herbert Spencer's major critique of college-prep education?
4. Explain how does the standards movement might harm high school students.
5. What is quantitative literacy? Why is it important?

I have a proposal to make: It's time we abolished the high school diploma as we know it. In a modern, unpredictable, and pluralistic world, it makes no sense to demand that every 18-year-old pass the same collection of traditional courses to graduate.

Instead, we should do away with most course requirements, make all courses rigorous, and simply report what students have accomplished from year to year. Students should prepare for adult life by studying subjects that suit their talents, passions, and aspirations as well as needs. They should leave when they are judged to be ready for whatever next challenge they take on—whether it be college, trade school, the military, or playing in a band. Let's therefore abolish the diploma, if by diploma we mean that all students must graduate as though they were heading for the same twentieth-century future.

This plan would enable us to finally deal with the key weakness of high school, summarized in that term virtually all students and adults use to describe it: *bor-ing*. High school is boring in part because diploma requirements crowd out personalized and engaged learning. It is also boring because our graduation requirements have been produced the way our worst laws are; they are crude compromises, based on inadequate debate. Because of arbitrary policies that define preparation in terms of content instead of useful abilities, schools focus on "coverage," not meaningful learning.

A HISTORICAL PERSPECTIVE

Our belief in lockstep adherence to rigid curriculum requirements appears especially myopic and misguided if we look through the lens of the fundamental question, How well does the high school curriculum prepare all students for their adult lives? The Commission on the Reorganization of Secondary Education thought that asking this question was not only sensible but sorely needed—in 1918! Its report, Cardinal Principles of Secondary Education, yielded a sound set of criteria by which to rationally judge the high school curriculum. The commission underscored that these criteria must flow from the mission of schooling:

> Education in a democracy, both within and without the school, should develop in each individual the knowledge, interests, ideals, habits, and powers whereby he will find his place and use that place to shape both himself and society toward ever nobler ends. (p. 9)

The Cardinal Principles were a deliberate counterbalance to the policies that had arisen from the work of the Committee of Ten in 1892. That group had famously argued that a college-prep education, including multiple years of Latin and Greek, was appropriate for all students—even though fewer than 10 percent of high school students went to college. Chaired by the president of Harvard, the Committee of Ten was organized into subject-area groups and staffed by professors and teachers of those subjects. (Our current system, with its attention to a narrow collection of "traditional" academic subjects, still embodies the worst consequences of the work of this group.)

The Cardinal Principles, in contrast, were intentionally external to the traditional subjects and were based on an understanding of the broad mission of schooling as enabling individuals to better themselves and society. They proposed the following "main objectives of education": (1) health; (2) command of fundamental processes (reading, writing, arithmetical computations, and the elements of oral and written expression); (3) worthy home membership; (4) vocation; (5) citizenship; (6) worthy use of leisure; and (7) ethical character.

It's a bit startling to see health first in the list, ahead of "readin', writin', and 'rithmetic," isn't it? But that shock is also a helpful reminder of how much schools have lost their way. What could be more important in moving into adulthood than learning how to lead a healthy life, in the broadest sense?

This idea actually has much older roots. Herbert Spencer arguably wrote the first modern critique of out-of-touch college-prep education in his famous essay, "What Knowledge Is of Most Worth?" Spencer (1861) asserts that school exists to help us answer the essential question of how to live. Under this vision of education, health as an area of study rises to the top. Spencer writes that as vigorous health and its accompanying high spirits are larger elements of happiness than any other things whatever, then teaching how to maintain them is a teaching that yields in moment to no other whatever (p. 13). Spencer anticipates the protests with rapier wit:

> Strange that the assertion should need making! Stranger still that it should need defending! Yet are there not a few by whom such a proposition will be received with something approaching to derision. Men who would blush if caught saying Iphigénia instead of Iphigenía . . . show not the slightest shame in confessing that they do not know where the Eustachian tubes are, what are the actions of the spinal cord, what is the normal rate of pulsation, or how the lungs are inflated . . . . So overwhelming is the influence of established routine! So terribly in our education does the ornamental over-ride the useful! (p. 14)

But Spencer saves his greatest scorn for the failure to make child-rearing a core subject:

> If by some strange chance not a vestige of us descended to the remote future save a pile of our school-books or some college examination papers, we may imagine how puzzled an antiquary of the period would be on finding in them no sign that the learners were ever likely to be parents. "This must have been the curriculum for their celibates," we may fancy him concluding. (p. 20)

Spencer wisely notes that every subject will, of course, make a plea for its importance. Therefore, a curriculum can only be fairly justified using criteria about the purpose of schooling that are outside all "content."

In other words, we need to decide to include or exclude, emphasize or deemphasize any subject based on criteria related to school mission—a mission centered on improving the behavior and lives of students. Otherwise, our curricular decisions are arbitrary and school is aimless. Indeed, when we fail to seriously question the inclusion of algebra or the exclusion of ethics from graduation requirements, we can only fall back on custom: "We've always done it this way." But if that were the only real argument, we would still be requiring Greek of all graduates, as the Committee of Ten recommended.

THE UNWITTING HARM OF THE STANDARDS MOVEMENT

Our current situation is no better than when the Committee of Ten did its work. Think about it: We are on the verge of requiring every student in the United States to learn two years of algebra that they will likely never use, but no one is required to learn wellness or parenting.

The current standards movement, for all its good intentions, is perilously narrowing our definition of education, to the great harm of not only students but also entire fields of study: the arts, the technical arts and trades, and the social sciences. Gone are excellent vocational programs—as powerfully described by Matthew Crawford in *Shop Class as Soul Craft* (Penguin, 2010), arguably the best book on education in the last five years (Henderson, 2011, p. 92). Threatened are visual arts, theater, music, and dance programs despite their obvious value. Indeed, there are more musicians in this country than mathematicians, but you would never know it from the work of standards committees.

NOT WHICH STANDARDS, BUT WHOSE STANDARDS

At a meeting many years ago, I heard Ted Sizer respond to a proponent of national standards, "It's not which standards, it's whose standards!" In other words, don't make this sound so objective. It's a political determination, made by whoever has a seat at the table.

And who sits at the table? Representatives of all the traditional academic subjects. When have standards committees included working artists, journalists, Web designers, or doctors who could critique the usefulness or uselessness of traditional content standards? When have professors of bioethics, anthropology, or law been invited to critique content standards? Rather, the people who care most about their little corner of the traditional content world dictate that it is required.

True story: When I did a workshop as part of a standards-writing project in a large eastern state, I mentioned the problem of arcane elements in the history standards, in particular a mention of an obscure Chinese dynasty. A gentleman cried out, "But that was my dissertation topic, and it is important for students to know!" Worse: The speaker was the social studies coordinator for the state and had made sure to put this topic in the previous version of the standards.

Having worked with three different states on their standards writing and revision process, I can say with confidence that the way we organize standards-based work at the state and national levels dooms it from the start. The committees reflect typical people with typical backgrounds in education, charged to tinker with, but not radically overhaul, typical schooling; no criteria for choices are ever put forward to weed the document of pet topics. In short, these committees merely rearrange the furniture of the traditional core content areas; they replicate the past that they feel comfortable with rather than face the future that is on its annoying but inexorable way.

A CASE IN POINT: MATHEMATICS

For proof of the lack of forward thinking, look at the Common Core math standards. The recommended high school mathematics is unchanged from when I was a kid in prep school 45 years ago: four years of conventional topics in algebra, geometry, trigonometry, and calculus. The only improvement is greater emphasis on modeling and statistics. But the laying out of the standards in isolated lists of content (as opposed to summarizing the kinds of performance standards student work must meet) undercuts the likelihood of vital reform to make mathematics more engaging and useful to the majority of students.

Consider this dreary summary of a high school strand from the Common Core:

Trigonometric Functions

- Extend the domain of trigonometric functions using the unit circle.
- Model periodic phenomena with trigonometric functions.
- Prove and apply trigonometric identities.

This is a standard? With what justification? It almost goes without saying (but in the current myopia, it needs to be said): Few people need to know this.

Today, algebra is the new Greek that "all educated persons" supposedly need. This is clear from the work of the American Diploma Project (2004), launched a few years ago by Achieve, a group created by governors and corporate leaders. Achieve deserves credit for taking the idea of "backward design" of high school requirements from college and workplace readiness seriously, buttressed by research and analysis. But we should be cautious about accepting its narrow view of the high school curriculum, especially its claim that advanced algebra should be a universal requirement (Achieve, 2008). The data

Achieve cites to justify this claim include the following:

- Completing advanced math courses in high school has a greater influence on whether students will graduate from college than any other factor—including family background. Students who take math beyond Algebra II double their chances of earning a bachelor's degree.
- Through 2016, professional occupations are expected to add more new jobs—at least 5 million—than any other sector; within that category, computer and mathematical occupations will grow the fastest.
- Simply taking advanced math has a direct impact on future earnings, apart from any other factors. Students who take advanced math have higher incomes 10 years after graduating—regardless of family background, grades, and college degrees.

But hold on: All that this really says is that people who take advanced math courses are more likely to do well in college and be prepared for jobs that involve advanced math. But that doesn't mean that broad success in life depends on those courses. I have no doubt, for example, that most students who study Greek or astrophysics also end up in satisfying careers. Algebra is not the cause of adult success any more than Greek is. It is most likely the reverse: Those who take advanced courses are smart, motivated students who will succeed in any career they choose. As a recent study pointed out, only about 5 percent of the population actually need algebra II in their work (Handel, 2007).

Much the same criticism was made by the Partnership for 21st Century Skills (2010), whose critique of the draft Common Core math standards asserted that the standards should include more emphasis on practical mathematical application (for example, analyzing financial data); include statistics and probability in the elementary grades and emphasize these areas more in the secondary grades; and focus less on factual content mastery in favor of better integrating higher-order thinking skills throughout the curriculum.

Lerman and Packer (2010) remind us that employers tend to call for something far more general and useful than advanced algebra skills:

> Every study of employer needs made over the past 20 years . . . has come up with the same answers. Successful workers communicate effectively, orally and in writing, and have social and behavioral skills that make them responsible and good at teamwork. They are creative and techno-savvy, have a good command of fractions and basic statistics, and can apply relatively simple math to real-world problems such as those concerning financial or health literacy. Employers never mention polynomial factoring. (p. 31)

For a more enlightened approach to mathematics instruction, there is a fine body of work developed over the past 15 years under the heading of Quantitative Literacy (or Quantitative Reasoning). The Quantitative Literacy Manifesto (National Council on Education and the Disciplines, 2001) shares the concern of organizations like Achieve that most U.S. students leave high school without the math skills they need to succeed in either college or employment. But this report proposes a different solution—one better suited to the goal of universal education in a modern society:

> Common responses to this well-known problem are either to demand more years of high school mathematics or more rigorous standards for graduation. Yet even individuals who have studied trigonometry and calculus often remain largely ignorant of common abuses of data and all too often find themselves unable to comprehend (much less to articulate) the nuances of quantitative inferences. As it turns out, it is not calculus but numeracy that is the key to understanding our data-drenched society. (p. 2)

The Quantitative Literacy Manifesto calls for developing in students a predisposition to look at the world through mathematical eyes, to see the benefits (and risks) of thinking quantitatively about commonplace issues, and to approach complex problems with confidence in the value of careful reasoning (p. 22).

Alas, the Quantitative Literacy movement simply has less political clout than Achieve does. Again we see: It's not which standards, but whose standards.

REVISITING HIGH SCHOOL REQUIREMENTS

Mindful of the mission of schooling to prepare students to prosper in and contribute to a pluralistic and ever-changing democracy, I humbly offer my own update of Spencer's proposal and the work of the Cardinal Principles group. I think that if we consider future usefulness in a changing world as the key criterion, the following subjects represent more plausible candidates for key high school courses in the twenty-first century than those on the Achieve list:

- Philosophy, including critical thinking and ethics
- Psychology, with special emphasis on mental health, child development, and family relations
- Economics and business, with an emphasis on market forces, entrepreneurship, saving, borrowing and investing, and business start-ups
- Woodworking or its equivalent; you should have to make something to graduate
- Mathematics, focusing primarily on probability and statistics and math modeling
- Language arts, with a major focus on oral proficiency (as well as the reading and writing of nonfiction)
- Multimedia, including game and Web design

- Science: human biology, anatomy, physiology (health-related content), and earth science (ecology)
- Civics, with an emphasis on civic action and how a bill really becomes law; lobbying
- Modern U.S. and world history, taught backward chronologically from the most pressing current issues

Instead of designing backward from the traditions of college admission or the technical demands of currently "hot" jobs, this list designs backward from the vital human capacities needed for a successful adulthood regardless of school or job. How odd, for example, that our current requirements do not include oral proficiency when all graduates will need this ability in their personal, civic, social, and professional lives. How unfortunate for us personally, professionally, and socially that all high school and college students are not required to study ethics.

The financial meltdown of recent years underscores a related point: Understanding our economic system is far more important than learning textbook chemistry. In science, how sad that physics is viewed as more important than psychology and human development, as parents struggle to raise children wisely and families work hard to understand one another. (The principle of inertia from physics may explain it!)

Do not misunderstand my complaints as somehow too utilitarian or opposed to the liberal arts and higher math. I was educated in the classic tradition at St. John's College. I learned physics and calculus through Newton's *Principia* and geometry through Euclid and Lobachevski—in a college program with no electives—all based on the Great Books. I had arguably the best undergraduate education in the United States, if the aim is intellectual power. But would I mandate that all colleges look like St. John's? Absolutely not, any more than I would mandate that all schools adopt my proposed course list as

graduation requirements. On the contrary, my advocacy for injecting philosophy, economics, and human development into the terribly narrow conventional curriculum is a call to bring a richer array of options to students.

Everyone agrees that high school needs to be more rigorous. No one wants to perpetuate inequity of opportunity. But can't there be greater student choice that opens up rather than closes off opportunities? Can't vocational courses and courses in the arts be as demanding as upper-level courses in math or chemistry?

Setting standards in the way we do—mandating requirements for all by looking at our own generation's academic experience rather than forward to the developmental needs of all students—impedes progress rather than advancing it. Then, we add insult to injury: a one-size-fits-all diploma. In sum, it seems to me that we still do not have a clue about how to make education modern: forward-looking, client-centered, and flexible; adapted to an era where the future, not the past, determines the curriculum.

WHAT DO OUR STUDENTS NEED FROM SCHOOL?

I am not arguing for throwing out the Common Core Standards. At least they will impose reason on the current absurd patchwork of state standards and finally make it possible for authors, software designers, test makers, and textbook publishers to provide the most resources at the least expense. But let's not treat these standards as anything more than a timid rearrangement of previous state standards, promulgated by people familiar only with traditional courses and requirements.

Instead, let us face the future by pausing to consider anew the wisdom of Herbert Spencer and the authors of the Cardinal Principles. Let us begin a serious national conversation (all of us, not just the policy wonks, selected employers, and college admissions officers) about the questions, "What is the point of high school? What do our society and our students need from school, regardless of hidebound tradition or current policy fads?"

Then we might finally have a diploma worth giving and receiving in the modern age.

REFERENCES

Achieve. (2008). *Math works: All students need advanced math.* Washington, DC: Author. Retrieved from http://www.achieve.org/files/Achieve-MathWorks-FactSheet-All%20StudentsNeedAdvancedMath.pdf

American Diploma Project. (2004). *Ready or not: Creating a high school diploma that counts.* Washington, DC: Achieve.

Commission on the Reorganization of Secondary Education. (1918). *Cardinal principles of secondary education: A report of the Commission on the Reorganization of Secondary Education, appointed by the National Education Association.* Washington, DC: U.S. Department of the Interior.

Handel, M. J. (2007, May 23). *A new survey of workplace skills, technology, and management practices (STAMP): Background and descriptive statistics.* Boston, MA: Department of Sociology, Northeastern University.

Henderson, J. (2011). Book review. *Educational Leadership*, March, 92–93.

Lerman, R. I., & Packer, A. (2010, April 21). Will we ever learn? What's wrong with the common-standards project. *Education Week, 29*(29): 30–31.

National Council on Education and the Disciplines. (2001). *Mathematics and democracy: The case for quantitative literacy.* Princeton, NJ: Author. Retrieved from Mathematical Association of America at http://www.maa.org/ql/mathanddemocracy.html

Partnership for 21st Century Skills. (2010). *P21 comments on Common Core state standards initiative—mathematics.* Retrieved from http://www.p21.org/documents/P21_CCSSI_Comments_MATH_%20040210.pdf

Spencer, H. (1861). What knowledge is of most worth? In H. Spencer, *Essays on education and kindred subjects* (pp. 1–44). London: Author.

DISCUSSION QUESTIONS

1. Do you believe taking rigorous courses increases adult success or that smarter students take harder courses? Explain.
2. What should the goal of high school be? Explain.
3. What types of people would you include in a standards committee? Why?
4. What rationale would you use to decide the worth of a particular subject in a high school curriculum?
5. How would you answer the author's question: What is the point of high school?

Should academic content standards be used in place of curriculum guides?

PRO	CON
1. Content standards ensure high expectations for every student in every classroom.	1. Raising expectations will hurt students who are already not achieving by making a difficult challenge impossible.
2. Standards make public what all students should know and be able to do.	2. Curriculum guides and textbooks are public documents that already exist and serve the same purpose.
3. Standards ensure that important content is not overlooked and that students are exposed to new content at each grade.	3. Teachers need flexibility when covering content to meet the needs of diverse groups of students who may be at different stages in their development.
4. Standards focus teaching, student work, and assessment on the knowledge and skills that are most important for success in life.	4. Students need to learn how to be responsible for their own learning, because no one really knows what knowledge and skills will be most important in the future.
5. Standards can reduce the wide variability in the quality of curriculum, instruction, and assessment that exists from one classroom to another.	5. Teachers deserve to be treated as professionals who employ academic freedom to help students to construct knowledge that is personally meaningful.
6. Rubrics and scoring guides that describe the specific criteria that must be met at each level of achievement help to communicate what students should know to both students and parents.	6. Standards are really nothing but a smokescreen for one-shot, high-stakes tests.

CASE STUDY 4

An Advocate for Longer School Days

Jack Pierce, curriculum coordinator of Ipsid Elementary District, handed a written proposal to the superintendent, Dick Bosio, which suggested that the district lengthen the school day by forty minutes beginning in the fall. Pierce cited research to support his claim that academic learning time is the most important variable associated with student learning for most types of learners. He also reported research that showed significant relationships between increased academic time and gains in student achievement. While explaining his rationale for increasing the length of the school day, Pierce said he felt confident that overall the district would demonstrate an increase in students' Iowa Test of Basic Skills scores. He suggested that this change would probably satisfy the public that Ipsid was promoting excellence in education. Pierce emphasized that, because time spent on relevant academic tasks is measurable, the district would be able to show that better test scores were the result of the increased academic instruction. Furthermore, he said that increased instructional time was advisable according to the research on teaching that emphasized student outcomes.

The Ipsid superintendent listened closely to Pierce's proposal. He had some concerns, but decided that Pierce had analyzed almost all the critical factors. Noting some of the considerations that might need to be addressed, Bosio thought to himself that because engaged time was equivalent to time devoted to actual work, asking teachers to stay a little longer each day would not be an issue. Bosio turned to Pierce and said, "I think this is a good idea. Go ahead and implement this change."

1. Assume you are Bosio and discuss how you would implement an extension of your school's instructional day by forty minutes.
2. Do you think that student achievement is directly correlated with academic engaged time? Why? Why not?
3. Based on your experience, what factors other than time on task influence student outcomes?
4. In what ways does the use of different instructional models influence student outcomes?
5. What alternatives might be considered to promote student outcomes, instead of lengthening the school day?
6. What is the relationship among content, quality of teaching, academic engaged time, and student outcomes?
7. How do subject matter content and social atmosphere of the classroom affect academic engaged time?

PART FIVE

Curriculum and Supervision

How do developments and curriculum influence each other? What are the issues changing our views of supervision and leadership? How would new conceptions of supervision influence practice and professional programs of preparation?

In Chapter 24, Thomas Sergiovanni describes how conceptions of school leadership practice would be reconceived if the politics of division were replaced with the politics of virtue. He explores how the role of the principal as steward differs from perceptions of transformational leadership. He also claims that students as well as teachers will be able to embrace the concept of civic virtue. In Chapter 25, Harry Wong, Ted Britton, and Tom Ganser point out that induction of new teachers in the United States is either entirely lacking or not well structured, typically involving support from a single mentor. The authors describe more systematic approaches to induction that other countries have adopted.

In Chapter 26, Edward Pajak describes how various models of clinical supervision are linked to the concept of psychological style. He explains why and how clinical supervisors can better communicate by applying approaches that coincide with teachers' psychological types. Pajak also suggests that supervisors should strive to work with teachers in ways that are consistent with how teachers are expected to work with students by celebrating diversity and responding to that diversity in ways that enhance learning for all. Next, in Chapter 27, Richard Ingersoll traces trends that show a recent surge in the number of new teachers employed in schools. He provides empirically based ideas for improving the induction experiences of these novices as a kind of education reform that will ensure their satisfaction, retention, commitment, and success.

In Chapter 28, W. James Popham discusses the importance of identifying the instructional sensitivity of assessments. He defines instructional sensitivity as how closely students' performance on an assessment reflects what they learned. Popham contends that instructional sensitivity is important when assessments are used in accountability and describes how the instructional sensitivity of an assessment can be evaluated. Finally, in Chapter 29, Daniel Duke describes the importance of identifying previously well performing schools that have begun to "slip." Duke identifies issues, including budget cuts, state and federal mandates, increase in at-risk students, and loss of staff, which can affect school performance. Likewise, he cites factors such as increases in class size and ineffective professional development that can lead to school decline.

CHAPTER

24

The Politics of Virtue: A New Framework for School Leadership

Thomas J. Sergiovanni

FOCUSING QUESTIONS

1. What is the politics of virtue?
2. In what ways are the politics of virtue and the democratic legacy related?
3. How would practice emanating from a pluralistic conception of politics influence school leadership?
4. What are the basic principles of formal organization theories?
5. If the politics of division were replaced with the politics of virtue, how would conceptions of leadership need to be redefined?
6. In what ways does the role of the principal as steward differ from current conceptions of school leadership?
7. What are the similarities and differences between conceptions of stewardship and transformational leadership?

Margaret Mead once remarked, "Never doubt that a small group of thoughtful, committed citizens can change the world; indeed, it's the only thing that ever has." Her thought suggests that perhaps there is something to the 1,000 points of light theory of change. Is it possible to rally enough small groups of thoughtful and committed citizens to create the kind of schools we want? I think so, if we are willing to change the way politics is thought about in schools.

Rarely does a day go by without the media telling us still another story about divisions, hostilities, factions, and other symptoms of disconnectedness in schools. Teachers disagreeing over methods; parents bickering with teachers over discipline problems; board members squabbling over curriculum issues; administrators complaining about encroachments on their prerogatives; everyone disagreeing on sex education; and students, feeling pretty much left out of it all, making it difficult for everyone in the school by tediously trading their compliance and goodwill for things that they want. This mixture of issues and this mixture of stakeholders, all competing for advantage, resembles a game of bartering where self-interest is the motivator and individual actors engage in the hard play of the politics of division. The purpose of this game is to win more for yourself than you have to give back in return. Allison (1969) summarizes the game of *politics of division* as follows:

> Actions emerge neither as the calculated choice of a unified group nor as a formal summary of a leader's preferences. Rather the context of shared power but separate judgment concerning important choices determines that politics is the mechanism of choice. Note the environment in which the game is played: inordinate uncertainty about what must be done, the necessity that something be done and crucial consequences of whatever is done. These features force responsible men to become active players. The *pace of the game*—hundreds of issues, numerous games, and multiple channels—compels players to fight to "get others' attention," to make them "see the facts," to assure that they "take the time to think seriously about the broader issue." The *structure of the game*—power shared by individuals with separate responsibilities—validates each player's feeling that "others don't see my problem," and "others must be persuaded to look at the issue from a less parochial perspective." The *rules of the game*—he who hesitates loses his chance to play at that point, and he who is uncertain about his recommendation is overpowered by others who are sure—pressure players to come down on the side of a 51–49 issue and play. The *rewards of the game*—effectiveness, i.e., impact on outcomes, as the immediate measure of performance—encourage hard play. (p. 710)

The politics of division is a consequence of applying formal organization theories of governance, management, and leadership to schools. At root, these theories assume that human nature is motivated by self-interest and that leadership requires the bartering of need fulfillment for compliance. Would things be different if we applied community theories instead? Communities, too, "play the game" of politics. But it is a different game. It is a game of politics more like that envisioned by James Madison, Alexander Hamilton, John Jay, Thomas Jefferson, and other American founders and enshrined in such sacred documents as the Declaration of Independence, the Constitution of the United States, and the amendments to that Constitution that represent a bill of rights and a bill of responsibilities for all Americans. It is a game called the *politics of virtue*—a politics motivated by shared commitment to the common good and guided by protections that ensure the rights and responsibilities of individuals.

CIVIC VIRTUE

Is it possible to replace the politics of division with a politics of virtue? I think so, if we are willing to replace the values that have been borrowed from the world of formal organizations with traditional democratic values that encourage a commitment to civic virtue. This would entail development and use of different theories of human nature and leadership. For example, the rational choice theories of human nature we now use will need to be replaced with a normative and moral theory of human nature. And the executive images of leadership that we now rely on will need to be replaced with collegial images aimed at problem solving and ministering.

Creating a politics of virtue requires that we renew commitments to the democratic legacy that gave birth to our country. This is the legacy that can provide the foundation for leadership in schools. The American founders had in mind the creation of a covenantal polity within which "The body is one but has many members. There can be unity with diversity. . . . The great challenge was to create a political body that brought people together and created a 'we' but still enabled people to separate themselves and recognize and respect one another's individualities. This remains the great challenge for all modern democracies" (Elshtain, 1994, p. 9). The cultivation of commitment to civic virtue is a key part of this challenge.

During the debate over passing the Constitution of 1787, America was faced with a choice between two conceptions of politics: *republican* and *pluralist*. In republican politics, civic virtue was considered to be the cornerstone principle—the prerequisite for the newly proposed government to work. Civic virtue was embodied in the willingness of citizens to subordinate their own private interests to the general good (e.g., see Sunstein, 1993) and was therefore the basis for creating a politics of virtue. This politics of virtue emphasized self-rule by the people, but not the imposition of their private preferences on the new government. Instead, preferences were to be developed and shaped by the people themselves for the benefit of the common good.

Haefele (1993) believes that it is easier to provide examples of how civic virtue is expressed than to try to define it with precision. In his words:

> It is fashionable nowadays for both the left and the right to decry the loss of civic virtue; the left on such issues as industry rape of the environment and the right because of the loss of patriotism. Both sides are undoubtedly right, as civic virtue belongs to no single party or creed. It is simply a quality of caring about public purposes and public destinations. Sometimes the public purpose is chosen over private purposes. A young Israeli economist investigating a Kibbutz came across the following case. The Kibbutz had money to spend. The alternatives were a TV antenna and TV sets for everyone or a community meeting hall. The economist found that everyone preferred the TV option but that, when they voted, they unanimously chose the meeting hall. Call it enlightened self-interest, a community preference or something else, it is civic virtue in action. (p. 211)

When the republican conception of politics is applied to schools, both the unique shared values that define individual schools as communities and our common democratic principles and conceptions of goodness that provide the basis for defining civic virtue are important.

The pluralist conception of politics differs from the republican. Without the unifying power of civic virtue, factions are strengthened and the politics of division reigns. In the ideal, the challenge of this politics is to play people and events in a way that the self-interests of individuals and factions are mediated in some orderly manner. "Under the pluralist conception, people come to the political process with preselected interests that they seek to promote through political conflict and compromise" (Sunstein, 1993, p. 176). Deliberate governmental processes of conflict resolution and compromise, of checks and balances, are needed in the pluralist view because preferences are not shaped by the people themselves as they strive to control self-interests that happen to dominate at the time.

Civic virtue was important to both Federalists, who supported the proposed Constitution, and Anti-Federalists, who opposed the Constitution, though it was the centerpiece of Anti-Federalist thinking. The Anti-Federalists favored decentralization in the form of democracy tempered by a commitment to the common good. The Federalists, by contrast, acknowledged the importance of civic virtue, but felt the pull of pluralistic politics was too strong for the embodiment of virtue to be left to chance. They proposed a representative rather than a direct form of government that would be guided by the principles of a formal constitution that specified a series of governmental checks and balances to control factionalism and self-interest.

The positions of both the Federalists and the Anti-Federalists have roles to play in the governance of schools. In small communities, for example, the politics of virtue expressed within a direct democracy that is guided by *citizen* devotion to the public good seems to make the most sense. Small schools and small schools within schools would be examples of such communities. They would be governed by autonomous school councils that are responsible for both educational policy and site-based management—both ends and means. This approach to governance represents a significant departure from present policies that allow principals, parents, and teachers in local schools to decide how they will do things, but not what they will do. The decisions that local school councils make would be guided by shared values and beliefs that parents, teachers, and students develop together. Schools, in this image, would not function as markets where self-interests reign or bureaucracies where entrenched rule systems reign, but as morally based direct democracies within which parents, teachers, and students, guided by civic virtue, make the best decisions possible for learning.

At the school district level, by contrast, the position of the Federalists might make the most sense. A representative form of government spearheaded by elected school boards, guided by an explicit constitution that contains the protections and freedoms needed to enable individual school communities to function both responsibly and autonomously, would be the model. School communities would have to abide by certain school district regulations regarding safety, due process, equity, fiscal procedures, and a few basic academic standards. But, beyond these, schools would be free to decide for themselves not only their management processes, but their policy structures as well. They would be responsible for deciding their own educational purposes, educational programs, scheduling and ways of operating, and means to demonstrate to the school district and to the public that they are functioning responsibly. Accountability in such a system would be both responsive to each school's purposes and, in light of those purposes, to tough standards of proof.

How can schools be held accountable for different standards? First, we will need to create standards for standards. Then we will

be able to assess whether the standards that individual schools set for themselves are good ones. Once standards are accepted, each school is then assessed on its own terms. Here is how such a strategy would work: Schools make promises to the people; the promises must be good ones; school boards and states hold schools accountable for keeping their promises.

THE RATIONAL CHOICE QUESTION

Formal organization theories of human nature can be traced back to a few principles that are at the center of classical economic theory. Prime among them is the *utility function,* which is believed to explain all consumer behavior. The reasoning behind this belief is as follows. Humans are by their nature selfish. They are driven by a desire to maximize their self-interests and thus continually calculate the costs and benefits of their actions. They choose courses of action that either make them winners (they get a desired payoff) or keep them from losing (they avoid penalties). So dominant is this view and so pervasive is the concept of utility function that emotions such as love, loyalty, obligation, sense of duty, belief in goodness, commitment to a cause, and a desire to help make things better are thought to count very little in determining the courses of actions that humans choose. This view of human nature comprises a model of economics called *rational choice theory.*

Rational choice theory, expressed simply as "What gets rewarded gets done," undergirds much of the thinking in schools about how to motivate teachers to perform, how to introduce school improvement initiatives in schools, how to motivate people to accept change, and how to motivate students to learn and to behave. By emphasizing self-interest, rational choice theory discourages the development of civic virtue.

Two additional motivational rules need to be recognized if we are to have a more complete picture of human nature: "What is *rewarding* gets done," and "What people value and believe in gets done." Both rules compel people to perform, improve, change, and meet their commitments from within, even if doing so requires that self-interest be sacrificed. Both rules address the intrinsic and moral nature of human nature. Both rules are essential to the cultivation of civic virtue.

IS CIVIC VIRTUE FOR STUDENTS, TOO?

Some readers might concede that perhaps we should move away from a rational choice view of motivation. Perhaps we should acknowledge the capacity of parents and teachers to respond less in terms of their self-interest and more in terms of what they believe is right and good. But what about students? Can they too respond to the call of virtue?

Children and young adults in schools have different needs and different dispositions. They function developmentally at different levels of moral reasoning than do adults. But the evidence is clear that students from kindergarten to grade 12 have the capacity to understand what civic virtue is and to respond to it in ways that are consistent with their own levels of maturation.

Reissman (1993) and several other teachers in New York City's District 25, for example, have been working with elementary school children (even first and second graders) on developing "bills of responsibilities." The bills are designed to teach the meaning of civic virtue and to introduce students to sources of authority that are more morally based than the usual behavioristic ways to get students to do things. Key is the emphasis on reciprocal responsibilities—a critical ingredient in community building. Communities of mind, for example, evolve from commitments to standards that apply to everyone in the school, not just to students. Thus, if students must be respectful, so must

parents, teachers, principals, and everyone else who is a member of the school community or who visits the school.

Events at the Harmony School in Bloomington, Indiana, illustrate civic virtue in action (Panasonic Foundation, 1994). A well-known sculptor had removed his limestone rhinoceros from its place in front of an art gallery in Bloomington to keep it from being vandalized. The kindergarten through twelfth grade students at the Harmony School launched a campaign to return the rhino to Bloomington. They raised $6,000 and purchased the rhino, which now stands in front of the school for the entire community to enjoy.

One year Harmony High School students decided that, instead of the traditional field trip to Chicago, they would go to Quincy, Illinois, where the Mississippi floods had devastated the city. One of the students explained, "They have plenty of food, and plenty of relief supplies, but they don't have anybody to help get life in order." Harmony students helped by clearing mud, garbage, and debris from the streets and by planting flowers and shrubs. Many similar stories, I know, are coming to your mind as you read about and think about the events at Harmony.

Harmony High School is private, and Bloomington, Indiana, is hardly downtown Kansas City, Miami, or San Antonio. But students everywhere are pretty much the same. They have the capacity to care. They want to be called to be good, and they know the difference between right and wrong. The fact is that students, too, under the right conditions, not only will be responsive to the calls of civic virtue, but they need to be responsive if they are to develop into the kinds of adults that we want them to be.

NEW LEADERSHIP IMAGES

Replacing the politics of division with a politics of virtue requires a redefined leadership. Civic virtue is encouraged when leadership aims to develop a web of moral obligations that administrators, teachers, parents, and even students must accept. One part of this obligation is to share in the responsibility for exercising leadership. Another part of this obligation is to share in the responsibility for ensuring that leadership, whatever its source, is successful. In this redefinition, teachers continue to be responsible for providing leadership in classrooms. But students, too, have a moral obligation to help make things work. They, too, provide leadership where they can and try as best they can to make the teacher's leadership effective. Similarly, administrators, parents, and teachers would accept responsibility together for the provision and the success of leadership.

Key to leadership in a democracy is the concept of social contract. Heifetz (1994) notes, "In part, democracy requires that average citizens become aware that they are indeed the principals, and that those upon whom they confer power are the agents. They have also to bear the risks, the costs, and the fruits of shared responsibility and civic participation" (p. 61).

It is through morally held role responsibilities that we can understand school administration as a profession in its more traditional sense. School administration is bound not just to standards of technical competence, but to standards of public obligation as well (Bellah et al., 1985, p. 290). The primacy of public obligation leads us to the roots of school leadership—stewardship defined as a commitment to administer to the needs of the school by serving its purposes, by serving those who struggle to embody these purposes, and by acting as a guardian to protect the institutional integrity of the school.

Principals function as stewards by providing for the overseeing and caring of their schools. As stewards, they are not so much managers or executives but administrators. According to Webster's dictionary,

to "manage" means to handle, to control, to make submissive, to direct an organization. "Superintend," in turn, means attending to, giving attention to, having oversight over what is intended. It means, in other words, supervision. As supervisor, the principal acts *in loco parentis* in relationship to students, ensuring that all is well for them. And as supervisor the principal acts as steward, guarding and protecting the school's purposes and structures.

Supervision in communities implies accountability, but not in the tough, inspectoral sense suggested by factory images of inspection and control. Instead, it implies an accountability embedded in tough and tender caring. Principals care enough about the school, the values and purposes that undergird it, the students who are being served, the parents whom they represent, and the teachers upon whom they depend that they will do whatever they can to protect school values and purposes, on the one hand, and to enable their accomplishment on the other.

In a recent interview, Deborah Meier, then co-director of the celebrated Central Park East Secondary School in New York City, was asked, "What is the role of the principal in an effective school?" (Scherer, 1995). Her response shows how the various ministerial roles of the principal are brought together by supervision understood as an expression of stewardship:

> Someone has to keep an eye on the whole and alert everyone when parts need close- or long-range attention. A principal's job is to put forth to the staff an agenda. The staff may or may not agree, but they have an opportunity to discuss it. I'll say, "Listen, I've been around class after class, and I notice this, don't notice this, we made a commitment to be accountable for one another, but I didn't see anybody visiting anybody else's class. . . ." Paul [Schwartz, Meier's co-director] and I also read all the teachers' assessments of students. Once we noticed that the 9th and the 10th grade math teachers often said the kids didn't seem to have an aptitude for math. We

asked the math staff, "How can these kids do nicely in 7th and 8th grade, and then seem inept in 9th and 10th? Are we fooling ourselves in 7th and 8th, or are we fooling ourselves in 9th and 10th? Because they are the same kids." (p. 7)

Meier and Schwartz both practiced leadership that is idea based. The source of authority that they appealed to is the values that are central to the school and the commitments that everyone has made to them. And because of this, their supervisory responsibilities do not compromise democratic principles, dampen teacher empowerment, or get in the way of community building. Both directors were committed to creating a staff-run school with high standards—one where staff must know each other, be familiar with each other's work, and know how the school operates. As Meier (1992) explained,

> Decisions are made as close to each teacher's own classroom setting as possible, although all decisions are ultimately the responsibility of the whole staff. The decisions are not merely on minor matters—length of classes or the number of field trips. The teachers collectively decide on content, pedagogy, and assessment as well. They teach what they think matters . . . governance is simple. There are virtually no permanent standing committees. Finally, we work together to develop assessment systems for our students, their families, ourselves, and the broader public. Systems that represent our values and beliefs in as direct a manner as possible. (p. 607)

This process of shared decision making is not institutionalized into a formal system, but is embedded in the daily interactions of everyone working together.

In stewardship the legitimacy of leadership comes in part from the virtuous responsibilities associated with the principal's role and in part from the principal's obligation to function as the head follower of the school's moral compact. In exercising these responsibilities and obligations, it is not enough to make the right moves for just any purpose or just any vision. The noted historian and leadership theorist James MacGregor Burns (1978) pointed out that purposes and visions should be socially useful, should serve the common good, should meet the needs of followers, and should elevate followers to a higher moral level. He calls this kind of leadership *transformational.*

Many business writers and their imitators in educational administration have secularized this original definition of transformational leadership to make it more suitable to the values of formal organizations. They "conceive of transformation, not in Burns's sense of elevating the moral functioning of a polity, but in the sense of inspiration, intellectual stimulation, and personal considerations . . . , or altering the basic normative principles that guide an institution . . ." (Heifetz, 1994, pp. 228–229; see also Bass, 1985, and Hargrove, 1989). This revisionist concept of transformational leadership might be all right for managers and CEOs in business organizations. But when it comes to the kind of leadership that they want for their children's schools, few businesspersons are likely to prefer the corporate definition over Burns's original definition.

When principals practice leadership as stewardship, they commit themselves to building, serving, caring for, and protecting the school and its purposes. They commit themselves to helping others to face problems and to make progress in getting problems solved. Leadership as stewardship asks a great deal of leaders and followers alike. It calls both to higher levels of commitment. It calls both to higher levels of goodness. It calls both to higher levels of effort. And it calls both to higher levels of accountability. Leadership as stewardship is the *sine qua non* for cultivating civic virtue. Civic virtue can help to transform individual stakeholders into members of a community who share common commitments and who feel a moral obligation to help each other embody those commitments.

ENDNOTE

This chapter is drawn from *Leadership for the School-house: How Is It Different? Why Is It Important?* San Francisco: Jossey-Bass. 1996

REFERENCES

Allison, G. T. (1969). Conceptual models and the Cuban missile crisis. *American Political Science Review, 63*(3): 689–718.

Bass, B. M. (1985). *Leadership and performance beyond expectations.* New York, NY: Free Press.

Bellah, R. N., and others. (1985). *Habits of the heart: Individualism and commitment in American life.* New York, NY: HarperCollins.

Burns, J. M. (1978). *Leadership.* New York, NY: HarperCollins.

Elshtain, J. B. (1994). Democracy and the politics of difference. *Responsive Community, 4*(2): 9–20.

Haefele, E. T. (1993). What constitutes the American republic? In S. L. Elkin and K. E. Soltan (eds.), *A new constitutionalism.* Chicago, IL: University of Chicago Press (pp. 207–233).

Hargrove, E. C. (1989). Two conceptions of institutional leadership. In B. D. Jones (ed.), *Leadership and politics: New perspectives in political science.* Lawrence, KS: University of Kansas Press.

Heifetz, R. (1994). *Leadership without easy answers.* Cambridge, MA: Harvard University Press.

Meier, D. (1992). Reinventing teaching. *Teacher's College Record, 93*(4): 594–609.

Panasonic Foundation. (1994). *Panasonic partnership program.* A newsletter of the Panasonic Foundation, 4(1).

Reissman, R. (1993). A bill of responsibilities. *Educational Leadership, 51*(4): 86–87.

Scherer, M. (1995). On schools where students want to be: A conversation with Deborah Meier. *Educational Leadership, 52*(1): 4–8.

Sunstein, C. R. (1993). The enduring legacy of republicanism. In S. L. Elkin and K. E. Soltan (eds.), *A new constitutionalism.* Chicago, IL: University of Chicago Press (pp. 174–207).

DISCUSSION QUESTIONS

1. What is the relationship between the politics of division and the application of formal organization theories of governance, management, and leadership in schools?
2. What are the implications of applying the politics of virtue to the practice of school leadership?
3. What are the disadvantages of applying rational choice theory to change initiatives and student motivation?
4. What evidence is there to support the belief that students of all ages have the capacity to understand and support civic virtue?
5. Why are the concepts of social contract and obligation key to the practice of leadership in a democracy?
6. In your opinion, is the notion of school leadership based on the politics of virtue a (a) practical, (b) feasible, or (c) desirable idea? Why? Why not?

25   What the World Can Teach Us about New Teacher Induction

Harry K. Wong
Ted Britton
Tom Ganser

FOCUSING QUESTIONS

1. What are some new teacher induction techniques?

2. How does extended teacher assistance training shape a new teacher's experience? What are the benefits?

3. How does teacher induction aid in teacher retention?

4. How can teacher induction aid seasoned teachers (those that have been teaching over five years)? The administration? The community?

5. What are some ways to combat isolation/alienation in U.S. schools? What are ways in which teachers, administration, and community can do this?

An effective teacher is perhaps the most important factor in producing consistently high levels of student achievement.[1] Thus, the profession must see to it that teachers are continually learning throughout their careers, and that process begins with those newest to the profession. A new teacher induction program can acculturate newcomers to the idea that professional learning must be a lifelong pursuit.

A book edited by Ted Britton, Lynn Paine, David Pimm, and Senta Raizen provides a more detailed look at how five countries—Switzerland, Japan, France, New Zealand, and China (Shanghai)—acculturate their new teachers, specifically their science and mathematics teachers, and shape their entry into the profession.[2] In this chapter, we share a brief summary of the findings reported in that volume.

The five countries studied provide well-funded support that reaches all beginning teachers, incorporates multiple sources of assistance, typically lasts at least two years, and goes beyond the imparting of mere survival skills. For example, in Switzerland, new teachers are involved in practice groups, in which they network to learn effective problem solving. In Shanghai, new teachers join lesson-preparation and teaching-research groups. New teachers in New Zealand take part in a 25-year-old Advice and Guidance program that extends for two years. Lesson study groups are the mode in

Japan, while in France, new teachers work for an extended time with groups of peers who share experiences, practices, tools, and professional language.

Before we go into more detail about these programs, a basic definition of induction is in order. *Induction* is a highly organized and comprehensive form of staff development, involving many people and components, that typically continues as a sustained process for the first two to five years of a teacher's career. Mentoring is often a component of the induction process.

The exponential growth in the number of induction programs in the United States attests to the value that staff developers and other school leaders ascribe to them. Educational leaders have eagerly adapted their approaches to induction to reflect the many changes in the teaching profession.[3] But induction programs are a global phenomenon, and here we offer to U.S. leaders a summary of the best practices of the international programs reported by Britton and his colleagues.

SWITZERLAND

In the Swiss system, teachers are assumed to be lifelong learners. From the start, beginning teachers are viewed as professionals, and induction focuses on the development of the person as well as on the development of the professional.

Induction begins during student teaching as teams of three students network with one another. It continues for beginning teachers in practice groups of about half a dozen teachers and is carried forward in mutual classroom observations between beginning teachers and experienced teachers. Thus induction moves seamlessly from a teacher's preservice days to novice teaching to continuing professional learning.

The Swiss philosophy explicitly rejects a deficit model of induction, which assumes that new teachers lack training and competence

and thus need mentors. Instead, several cantons provide a carefully crafted array of induction experiences for new teachers, including the following:

- *Practice groups.* These are a form of structured, facilitated networking that supports beginning teachers from different schools as they learn to be effective solvers of practical problems.
- *Standortbestimmung.* Practice groups generally conclude with a group Standortbestimmung—a form of self-evaluation of the first year of teaching that reflects the Swiss concern with developing the whole person as well as the teacher.
- *Counseling.* Counseling is generally available for all teachers, but a greater number of beginning teachers take part. It can grow out of the practice groups and can involve one-on-one mentoring of classroom practice. In some cantons, counseling is mandatory for beginning teachers.
- *Courses.* Course offerings range from obligatory courses to voluntary courses available on a regular basis to impulse courses, which are put together on short notice to meet a short-term need.

These practices are supported with training for practice-group leaders, counselors, and mentors.

A professional team heads the whole set of induction activities and is in charge of the practice-group leaders. These leaders, all active teachers themselves, are the key to the quality of the practice groups and other components of induction, such as classroom visits and individual counseling. These individuals are relieved of some of their teaching duties to make time for their responsibilities as practice-group leaders. They also receive additional pay and are themselves supported by the central team. The group leaders are trained to carry out their responsibilities and take part in a wide range of professional development offerings to increase their competence as leaders.

CHINA (SHANGHAI)

The teaching culture in Shanghai features research groups and collective lesson planning. It is a culture in which all teachers learn to engage in joint work to support their teaching and their personal learning, as well as the learning of their pupils. The induction process is designed to help bring new teachers into this culture.

There is an impressive array of learning opportunities at both the school and the district levels; among them are the following:

- Welcoming ceremonies at the school
- District-level workshops and courses
- District-organized teaching competitions
- District-provided mentoring
- A district hot line for new teachers that connects them with subject specialists
- District awards for outstanding novice/ mentor work
- Half-day training sessions at colleges of education and in schools for most weeks for the first year of teaching
- Peer observation, both in and outside of school
- Public, or open, lessons, with debriefing and discussion of the lesson afterwards
- Report lessons, in which a new teacher is observed and given comments, criticisms, and suggestions
- Talk lessons, in which a teacher (new or experienced) talks through a lesson and provides justification for its design, but does not actually teach it
- Inquiry projects and action research carried out by new teachers, with support from those on the school or district teaching research section or induction staff
- District- or school-developed handbooks for new teachers and mentors
- End-of-year celebrations of teachers' work and collaboration

In keeping with the collective and collaborative focus of the teaching culture in Shanghai, a number of other critical components play a role in the induction process for new teachers.

Lesson-Preparation Groups

The heart of the professional learning culture is the lesson-preparation group. These groups engage new and veteran teachers in discussing and analyzing the lessons they are teaching.

Teaching-Research Groups

A beginning teacher is also a member of a teaching-research group, which provides a forum for the discussion of teaching techniques. Each teacher, new or experienced, must observe at least eight lessons a semester, and most teachers observe more. It is very common for teachers to enter others' classrooms and to engage in discussion about mutually observed teaching. These conversations help new teachers acquire the language and adopt the norms of public conversation about teaching, and that conversation becomes a natural part of the fabric of any teacher's professional life.

Teaching Competitions

Districts organize teaching competitions with the goal of motivating new teachers and encouraging the serious study of and preparation for teaching. The competitions also identify and honor outstanding accomplishment. Lessons are videotaped so that the district can compile an archive for future use. Teaching thus becomes community property, not owned privately by one teacher, but shared by all.

NEW ZEALAND

In New Zealand, the induction phase is called the Advice and Guidance (AG) program. The

AG program is seen as the initial phase of the lifelong professional development of teachers. Every beginning teacher is released from 20 percent of work time to participate in the program.

Teachers and school-level administrators are willing to invest in the effort to support beginning teachers partly because schools are required to provide an AG program. Provisionally registered teachers must document the AG support they received during their first two years when they apply for a permanent certificate. But many of those who provide support for new teachers view their assistance as a commitment to the teaching profession.

The National Ministry of Education also provides limited regional resources for professional development services to beginning teachers. Regional meetings, which attract teachers from different schools, provide for the free exchange of induction experiences among a wide variety of participants. Although there is a national handbook outlining the goals of the AG program, the extent, nature, and quality of the local programs vary widely.

At the local school, an administrator or a staff member is typically the coordinator of the AG program. The people involved most directly in supporting beginning teachers are typically the AG coordinator, department heads, "buddy teachers," and, to a lesser extent, all other school staff members. In schools that have more than one beginning teacher, the AG coordinator convenes all the beginning teachers every two weeks throughout most of the year. Observation of teaching is a key activity in school-level induction programs and comes in several varieties. As in Switzerland, facilitated peer support is an important induction strategy.

Ted Britton explains that one reason New Zealand was chosen as a subject for study was the contrast it offered to countries that place a great deal of the responsibility for assisting beginning teachers on a single mentor or on just a couple of people. (He was alluding to the United States.) Indeed, we were struck by the variety of the sources of support in New Zealand and by how the schools make use of a range of induction activities. Throughout the education system in New Zealand, there is a universal commitment to supporting beginning teachers.

JAPAN

Teaching in Japan is regarded as a high-status occupation, a dignified profession. New teachers have a reduced teaching load and are assigned guiding teachers. The guiding teacher is the key to success in the Japanese system.

In-School Teacher Education

In their first year, all new teachers typically teach two or more demonstration lessons, which are viewed by prefectural administrators, the guiding teacher, the school principal or assistant principal, and other teachers in the school. The demonstration, or "study teaching," lesson, a traditional Japanese method for improving teaching, is a formal public lesson, which is observed and then subjected to critique by colleagues.

James Stigler and James Hiebert view these lessons and their subsequent public analysis as the core activity of in-school teacher education.[4] To prepare for their public lessons, the new teachers write and rewrite their lesson plans, practice teaching the lesson with one of their classes, and modify the lesson with the help of a guiding teacher. They might even call teachers from neighboring schools, whom they know from their university or prefectural classes, and seek their help and advice.

In Japan, as in Shanghai, teaching is viewed as a public activity, open to scrutiny by many. The induction process welcomes beginners into that open practice and provides beginning teachers with many regular opportunities to observe their peers, their guiding teachers, and other teachers in their school, as well as those in other schools. No special arrangements need to be made, for schools and teaching are organized to allow for such open observations. Indeed, the method is universal, so that all teachers have experienced it, and all seem to see its wisdom and believe in its efficacy. The most critical factor is that it is the lesson that is criticized, not the teacher.

New teachers are also required to submit a culminating "action research" project based on a classroom lesson they would like to investigate. This project is usually about 30–40 pages in length and is handed in to the prefectural education office (though no formal feedback on it is provided). These projects are accumulated in the prefectural inservice offices and are available for other teachers to use.

Japanese teachers do not have their own, isolated offices. Rather, teams or even an entire staff occupy one large room with individual desks and the accompanying equipment and supplies. Thus a new teacher receives help from many teachers, because most veteran teachers believe it is their responsibility to help new teachers become successful.

Out-of-School Teacher Education

Most out-of-school activity occurs under the guidance of a city or prefectural inservice center. Such a center is usually housed in a rather large building, is well staffed with specialists in most disciplines, and is dedicated to the inservice development of local teachers.

Induction is only the first phase of a teacher's professional learning. All Japanese teachers must participate in sponsored inservice programs five, ten, and twenty years after their induction program has been completed.

FRANCE

To become a certified secondary teacher in France, one must successfully pass a highly competitive national recruitment examination, both oral and written. A new teacher is referred to as a *stagiaire*, which translates roughly as someone who is undertaking a stage of development or formation.

A pedagogical advisor, appointed by a regional pedagogical inspector, is provided for all secondary school stagiaires. When new teachers need advice, the advisors give it, but the teachers are encouraged to proceed on their own. Stagiaires observe one another's classes on numerous occasions.

All new teachers are required to attend off-campus sessions several days per week at the nearest Institut Universitaire de Formation des Mâitres (IUFM), an institution created in 1991 specifically to handle teacher education and development. The main goal of the IUFM is to increase both the intellectual status of teacher education and the professionalism of teachers.

At the IUFM, groups of stagiaires meet, and their work is directed by their *formateur*, an experienced teacher educator who teaches in the classroom part time and is employed part time by the IUFM. *Formation*, which translates roughly as development or shaping, is the process a new teacher undergoes to become a member of the teaching profession, and the formateur is the person who provides formative experiences. A typical day for a new teacher might include the following activities:

- Preparing several lessons, teaching the lessons, and marking the pupils' homework
- Tutoring a smaller group of pupils
- Observing the pedagogical advisor teach and discussing features of the lesson
- Observing, participating in, and discussing lessons taught by a teacher in a different school in the same town
- Working on aspects of teaching for a day and a half at the IUFM

A professional *memoir*, written under the guidance of a memoir tutor, is required of every new teacher. The memoir is a report on some detailed exploratory work relating to some aspect of teaching practice or to an academic issue. It can be done either individually or by a pair of stagiaires.

The compulsory learning opportunities for stagiaires are varied. In France, first-year teaching and learning about teaching take place in a number of settings, and a certain amount of flexibility is required, as stagiaires move between institutional settings. The French view working with different teachers as ideal for formation, because these experiences bring the stagiaires into contact with a considerable number of different people in varied roles: the formateurs; the pedagogical advisors; the school staff in different schools, including administrators and teachers of various subjects; the memoir tutor; different groups of pupils; parents; and possibly the regional pedagogical inspectors.

Stagiaires can come to think of the group with which they work at the IUFM as a "tribe," a group of same-subject teachers working together in their joint area of specialization. And the notion of tribe is an important one. Various things support the integrity of a tribe: shared experience, shared practices, shared tools, and shared language.

To an outsider, this process might look like induction that ends after the first year of teaching. But the French view it as simply part of teacher formation; it is the method by which the system takes in new members.

APPLICATION TO U.S. SCHOOLS

Although the approaches to the induction of new teachers in these five countries differ from one another, they do have three major similarities that can provide useful ideas for staff developers responsible for induction programs in the United States. First, the induction approaches are highly structured, comprehensive, rigorous, and seriously monitored. There are well-defined roles for staff developers, administrators, and instructors, mentors, or formateurs.

In contrast, the professional development programs in the United States are often sporadic, incoherent, and poorly aligned, and they lack adequate follow-up.[5] The amount of time devoted to professional development in a given area is most commonly about one day during the year for any given teacher.[6]

Second, the induction programs of the five countries focus on professional learning and on the growth and professionalism of teachers. They achieve these ends through an organized, sustained professional development system that employs a variety of methods. These countries all consider their induction programs to be one phase or a single part of a total lifelong professional learning process.

In contrast, in more than 30 states, the nearly universal U.S. practice seems remarkably narrow: mentoring predominates, and often there is little more.[7] In many schools, one-on-one mentoring is the dominant or even the sole strategy for supporting new teachers, and it often lacks real structure and relies on the willingness of the veteran teacher and the new teacher to seek each other out. Many mentors are assigned to respond to new teachers' need for day-to-day survival tips, and so they function primarily as a safety net for the new teachers.

Third, collaboration is a strength of each of these five induction programs. Collaborative group work is understood, fostered, and accepted as a part of the teaching culture in all five countries surveyed. Experiences, practices, tools, and language are shared among teachers. And it is the function of the induction phase to engender this sense of group identity in new teachers and to help experienced teachers begin treating them as colleagues.

In contrast, isolation is the common thread and complaint among new teachers in

U.S. schools. New teachers want more than a job. They want to experience success. They want to contribute to a group. They want to make a difference. Thus collegial interchange, not isolation, must become the norm for U.S. teachers.[8]

Indeed, the most successful U.S. induction programs go beyond mentoring.[9] They are structured, sustained, intensive professional development programs that allow new teachers to observe others, to be observed by others, and to be part of networks or study groups, in which all teachers share with one another and learn to respect one another's work. Michael Garet and his colleagues confirmed this finding when they showed that teachers learn more in teacher networks and study groups than with mentoring.[10]

In their examination of over 30 new teacher induction programs in the United States, Annette Breaux and Harry Wong also found the inevitable presence of a leader.[11] These leaders have created organized and comprehensive induction programs that stress collaboration and professional growth. Teacher induction programs that rely on networking and collaboration can be found in such places as the Flowing Wells Schools in Tucson, Arizona (the Institute for Teacher Renewal and Growth); the Lafourche Parish Schools in Lafourche, Louisiana (the Framework for Inducting, Retaining, and Supporting Teachers program); and the Dallas Public Schools in Dallas, Texas (New Teacher Initiatives: New Teacher Support and Development Programs and Services).

The district staff developer and the building principal are the keys to establishing the commitment to teacher improvement and student achievement. But the bottom line remains: Good teachers make the difference. Districts that provide structured, sustained induction, training, and support for their teachers achieve what every school district seeks to achieve—improved student learning through improved professional learning.

ENDNOTES

1. Eric A. Hanushek, John F. Kain, and Steven G. Rivkin, "Why Public Schools Lose Teachers," Working Paper 8599, National Bureau of Economic Research (Cambridge, Mass., 2001); and Aubrey Wang et al., *Preparing Teachers around the World* (Princeton, N.J.: Educational Testing Service, 2003), available at www.ets.org/research/pic.

2. Edward Britton et al., eds., *Comprehensive Teacher Induction: Systems for Early Career Learning* (Dordrecht, Netherlands: Kluwer Academic Publishers and WestEd, 2003), available at www.WestEd.org.

3. Tom Ganser, "The New Teacher Mentors: Four Trends That Are Changing the Look of Mentoring Programs for New Teachers," *American School Board Journal*, December 2002, pp. 25–27; and Tom Ganser, "Sharing a Cup of Coffee Is Only a Beginning," *Journal of Staff Development*, Fall 2002, pp. 28–32.

4. James Stigler and James Hiebert, *The Teaching Gap* (New York: Free Press, 1999).

5. Wang et al., *Preparing Teachers.*

6. Basmat Parsad, Laurie Lewis, and Elizabeth Farris, *Teacher Preparation and Professional Development, 2000* (Washington, DC: National Center for Education Statistics, 2001).

7. Edward Britton et al., "More Swimming, Less Sinking. Perspectives from Abroad on U.S. Teacher Induction," paper prepared for the National Commission on Mathematics and Science Teaching in the 21st Century, San Francisco, 2000.

8. Harry K. Wong, "Collaborating with Colleagues to Improve Student Learning," Eisenhower National Clearinghouse, ENC Focus, vol. 11, no. 6, 2003, available at www.enc.org/features/focus; and "Induction Programs That Keep Working," in Marge Scherer, ed., *Keeping Good Teachers* (Alexandria, VA.: Association for Supervision and Curriculum Development, 2003), chap. 5, available at www.newteacher.com—click on "Published Papers."

9. Annette L. Breaux and Harry K. Wong, *New Teacher Induction: How To Train, Support, and Retain New Teachers* (Mountain View, Calif.: Harry K. Wong Publications, 2003).

10. Michael Garet, "What Makes Professional Development Effective?" *American Educational Research*, Winter 2001, pp. 915–946.

11. Breaux and Wong, *New Teacher Induction.*

DISCUSSION QUESTIONS

1. What kind of professional support did you receive when you first became a teacher? Was this support adequate?
2. Is the support that beginning teachers receive today any better than the support that you received?
3. Which country's induction program described in this chapter sounds most appealing to you?
4. Which induction practices do you think are least likely to be adopted in the United States? Why?
5. What changes in induction practices would be of most benefit to teachers in the United States?

26 Clinical Supervision and Psychological Functions

EDWARD F. PAJAK

FOCUSING QUESTIONS

1. What is clinical supervision, and how has it evolved over time?
2. What are psychological functions?
3. How do psychological functions influence communication styles?
4. What are the implications of psychological functions for the practice of clinical supervision?
5. How can supervisor–teacher relationships be improved?

Clinical supervision of instruction has a fairly long history in the United States, stretching back more than three decades. The seminal work began with Morris Cogan (1973) and Robert Goldhammer (1969) at Harvard University in the 1960s and continued later at the University of Pittsburgh. Since its inception, scholars have commented and elaborated on the fundamental clinical cycle at great length and from a wide variety of perspectives. So many volumes and articles have been published about clinical supervision over the years, in fact, that fresh insights and refinements may seem improbable at this point. This article asserts, on the contrary, that the theory of psychological functions introduced by Carl Jung (1971) and popularized by others (Briggs & Myers, 1977; Keirsey, 1998) can bring some conceptual clarity to the field of clinical supervision and also serve as a guide to practitioners when communicating with teachers.

Because the number of authors who have written about clinical supervision during recent decades is so very large, a complete account of every perspective is well beyond the scope of this article. The most prominent approaches, however, have been classified according to certain shared qualities into four families (see Figure 26.1). These four families of clinical supervision emerged chronologically in approximately the order in which they are listed (Pajak, 2000). The *original clinical* models of Goldhammer (1969) and Cogan (1973), which appeared in the late 1960s and early 1970s, for example, were followed during the mid- to late-1970s by what may be described as the *humanistic– artistic* models of Blumberg (1974) and Eisner (1979). In turn, the *technical–didactic* models advocated by Acheson and Gall (1980) and Hunter (1984) gained ascendancy in the

Original clinical models	The models proposed by Goldhammer, Mosher and Purpet, and Cogan offer an eclectic blending of empirical, phenomenological, behavioral, and developmental perspectives. These models emphasize the importance of collegial relations between supervisors and teachers, cooperative discovery of meaning, and development of individually unique teaching styles.
Humanistic–artistic models	The perspectives of Blumberg and Eisner are based on existential and aesthetic principles. These models forsake step-by-step procedures and emphasize open interpersonal relations and personal intuition, artistry, and idiosyncrasy. Supervisors are encouraged to help teachers understand the expressive and artistic richness of teaching.
Technical–didactic models	The work of Acheson and Gall, Hunter, and Joyce and Showers draws on process–product and effective teaching research. These models emphasize techniques of observation and feedback that reinforce certain effective behaviors or predetermined models of teaching to which teachers attempt to conform.
Developmental–reflective models	The models of Glickman, Costa and Garmston, Schon, Zeichner and Liston, Garman, Smyth and Retallick, Bowers and Flinders, and Waite are sensitive to individual differences and the organizational, social, political, and cultural contexts of teaching. These models call for supervisors to encourage reflection among teachers, foster professional growth, discover context-specific principles of practice, and promote justice and equity.

FIGURE 26.1   Four Families of Clinical Supervision
Source: Pajak (2000).

early to mid-1980s and were followed by the *developmental–reflective* models. The latter category arose during the mid-1980s and continued proliferating through the 1990s; it includes models proposed by Glickman (1985), Costa and Garmston (1994), and Zeichner and Liston (1996), among others (Garman, 1986; Waite, 1995). These four families of clinical supervision and the models comprising them differ greatly in the purposes toward which they strive, their relative emphasis on objectivity versus subjectivity, the type of data collected and the procedures for recording it, the number and series of steps or stages involved, the degree of control exercised by the supervisor versus the teacher, and the nature and structure of pre- and post-observation conferences (Pajak, 2000).

What could possibly be the source of so many divergent perspectives on what is essentially a straightforward process involving a preobservation conference, a classroom observation, and a postobservation conference? How can such a multiplicity of models that differ among themselves in fundamental ways conceivably coexist and retain adherents among theorists and school practitioners? More practically, how can anyone sort through this profusion of advice and reasonably decide which version of clinical supervision may actually be appropriate for oneself or for any given situation? A number of supervision scholars have recently suggested that concepts derived from the psychology of Carl Jung may offer a promising perspective for answering these and other questions related to the supervision of instruction (Champagne & Hogan, 1995; Garmston, Lipton, & Kaiser, 1998; Hawthorne & Hoffman, 1998; Norris, 1991; Oja & Reiman, 1998; Shapiro & Blumberg, 1998).

JUNG'S PSYCHOLOGICAL FUNCTIONS

Among many other important discoveries related to conscious and unconscious mental processes, Jung (1971) proposed that people exhibit four psychological functions with respect to their perceptions. Two of these functions, intuition (N) and sensing (S), characterize the way that we gather data about and perceive reality, while another two functions, thinking (T) and feeling (F), refer to the ways that we appraise or judge the reality that is perceived. Although gathering data and making judgments about perceptions are obviously central issues for clinical supervision, Champagne and Hogan (1995) appear to be alone in having applied Jung's formulations to the field in a thorough and systematic way. (Their book includes a useful assessment instrument for determining psychological type and function and speculates about the effect that these mental processes have on both teaching and supervision.) The concept of psychological functions already productively informs other areas of study, including learning styles (Silver, Strong, & Perini, 1997), leadership (Fitzgerald & Kirby, 1997), and organizational dynamics (Hirsch & Kummerow, 1998), all of which have clear relevance for understanding classrooms and schools. It seems worthwhile, therefore, to further explore the implications of Jung's formulations for clinical supervision.

According to Jung (1971), people who draw primarily on *intuition* to collect data and perceive reality prefer exploring and discussing ideas and theories, untried possibilities, and what is new. They easily become bored with specifics, details, data, and facts that are unrelated to concepts. Intuitive people tend to think and communicate with spontaneous leaps of intuition and may omit or neglect details. In contrast, those who draw on the *sensing* function to gather data and perceive reality prefer focusing on what is real, concrete, and tangible in the here and now. They tend to be more concerned with facts and data than with theory and abstractions. Sensing people think and communicate carefully and accurately, referring to and emphasizing facts and details, but may miss seeing the *gestalt*, or big picture.

People who favor *thinking* over feeling when making judgments about the reality that they perceive prefer using evidence, analysis, and logic. They are more concerned with being rational than with empathy, emotions, and values. Thinking types communicate in an orderly and linear manner, emphasizing if–then and cause–effect linkages. On the other hand, those who prefer using *feeling* to guide their judgments do so on the basis of empathy, warmth, personal convictions, and a consistent value system that underlies all their decision processes. They are more interested in people, emotions, and harmony than in logic, analysis, or attaining impersonal goals. Feeling people communicate by expressing personal likes and dislikes, as well as feelings about what is good versus bad and right versus wrong.

Jung (1971) compared the four functions to the points on a compass and suggested that their interplay was just as indispensable as this navigational device for psychological orientation and discovery. Displaying the functions in a compasslike configuration (see Figure 26.2) highlights the manner in which the two psychological processes of getting information and making decisions interact, resulting in four possible function pairs: sensory–thinking (S–T), sensory–feeling (S–F), intuitive–thinking (N–T), and intuitive–feeling (N–F). These four combinations (bracketed by parentheses in the quadrants illustrated in Figure 26.2) have distinctive effects on how individuals relate to the

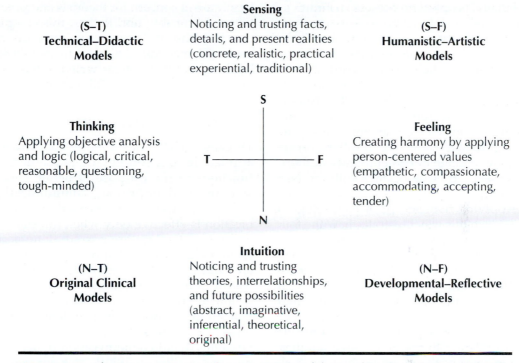

FIGURE 26.2 The Four Functions as Compass Points and the Resulting Combinations Related to Clinical Supervision Families

world. They also appear to correspond well with the four families of clinical supervision described earlier.

People characterized by an intuitive–thinking (N–T) function pair, for example, are concerned with competence and tend to concentrate on the future, ideas, and possibilities. They are guided by theoretical concepts and work by testing hypotheses. N–Ts are likely to consider the big picture and are distressed by what they view as incorrect or faulty principles. This worldview most closely parallels the original clinical models, particularly those of Goldhammer (1969) and Cogan (1973).

In comparison, those individuals who display a sensory–feeling (S–F) combination primarily want to be helpful to others. They focus attention on the present and facts, but are most concerned with people. S–Fs want

to provide support and are guided by a sense of service. They work by meeting people's needs and are troubled by conflict and disagreements. An S–F orientation, in turn, would seem to most closely resemble the humanistic–artistic family of models represented by Blumberg (1974) and Eisner (1979).

People possessing a sensory–thinking (S–T) orientation mainly strive to be efficient. They focus on the present and facts and attend closely to current reality. They prefer to follow established policies and procedures and believe that their work and the work of others is facilitated by having such processes and structures in place. S–Ts want to see results produced and are annoyed when work is done incorrectly. The technical–didactic models of Acheson and Gall (1980) and Hunter (1984) appear to match up well with this perspective.

Finally, people who possess an intuitive–feeling (N–F) combination seek to empower others and are strongly concerned with the future, people, and possibilities. Guided by ideals that they believe are worthy, N–Fs work by expressing and acting on their values. These individuals seek to promote growth and are troubled when values are absent or are viewed as incorrect. The developmental–reflective models, represented by a range of contemporary authors, would seem to be associated with the N–F viewpoint.

Applying the concept of psychological functions in this way illustrates how the four clinical supervision families are related and complement one another despite their obvious differences. Rather than solely expressing the *Zeitgeist* of the decade when it emerged or the worldview of particular authors, each family of models may be viewed as expressing a logic that is complete only in relation to the other three families. Chronologically, the intuitive–thinking qualities of the original clinical supervision models that emerged in the 1960s were mirrored by their psychological opposite, the sensory–feeling orientation of the humanistic–artistic models in the 1970s, following what could be conceived as a sort of Hegelian thesis–antithesis dialectic (Friedrich, 1954). The tension between them was then resolved by a synthesis of the two, which incorporated the sensing and thinking functions of each and resulted in the technical–didactic models that were prominent in the 1980s. This synthesis became a new thesis, in turn, giving rise to its own antithesis, the N–F-oriented developmental–reflective models of the 1990s. This final grouping, thus, rounded out the range of psychological possibilities.

Does this mean that the potential for developing entirely new approaches to clinical supervision has been exhausted? Probably. Could this *fin de siècle* explain the dearth of new clinical supervision models during the last five years or so? Perhaps. Should it

be a cause of concern for theorists and practitioners? Probably not. Rather, this completion of the pattern may provide an unprecedented foundation for further theory building and research, as well as a basis for more precise and successful practice.

THE COMMUNICATION WHEEL

Thompson (2000) has recently adapted and applied Jung's concept of psychological functions to the purpose of better understanding and improving communication within organizations. He notes that communication is effective only when information and understanding are passed along accurately from a sender to a receiver. Problems are likely to arise when individuals or groups encode or decode messages differently while trying to communicate with one another. Not all communication problems can be traced to differences in psychological type, he cautions, but communication preferences do serve as filters that influence our perceptions. These perceptions ultimately become the realities to which we all respond.

Of particular relevance and interest to theorists and practitioners of clinical supervision is Thompson's (2000) assertion that attending to psychological functions can enhance the quality of interaction between coaches (i.e., supervisors) and their clients within all types of organizations. He proposes that the functions (S, N, T, and F) can be thought of as four languages that people use when communicating. Thompson further hypothesizes the existence of eight communication dialects (T–N, N–T, S–T, T–S, S–F, F–S, N–F, and F–N), which are determined by whether an individual usually relies more heavily on his or her dominant or auxiliary function. Everyone can use both, but people tend to rely more heavily on their dominant function during times of stress. Drawing on this finer differentiation, the relationship among the various models of clinical supervision can be depicted in terms

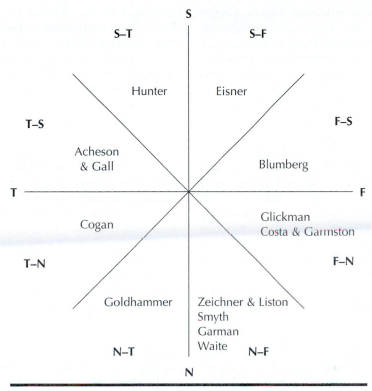

FIGURE 26.3   Models of Clinical Supervision as Communication Dialects

of these eight communication dialects, as in Figure 26.3.

Communication works best, Thompson (2000) suggests, when both parties speak the same primary language. If they differ, one or the other must adjust or else communication will break down. On the other hand, the better an individual can approximate the language and dialect of others, the more communication should improve. Understanding how psychological type affects communication can be useful for diagnosing causes of communication problems, both interpersonally and in groups. Possible solutions to existing problems can be identified and potential problems in supervisory situations may be avoided entirely by anticipating communication difficulties in advance. In any case, listening

for cues about the communication preferences of other people is obviously the key.

By aligning the models of clinical supervision with the function-based communication dialects, fine conceptual distinctions among the models that fall within the various families can be explained (see Figure 26.3). Despite many similarities between the perspectives of Goldhammer (1969) and Cogan (1973), for example, these models of clinical supervision differ substantially in their respective justifications for clinical supervision. Goldhammer (1969) begins his book by "generating images of what school can be like, particularly in the children's experience" (p. 1). He offers a scathing indictment of the meaninglessness of much that occurs in classrooms and recommends clinical supervision as a way of making instruction more consciously purposeful and responsive to students' needs. Cogan (1973) grounds his argument for clinical supervision, in contrast, along organizational and professional development lines. He advocates clinical supervision as a practical means for "disseminating and implementing new practices" more effectively and for professionalizing the teaching corps (p. 3). Cogan and Goldhammer also differ in the relative importance that each places on objective versus subjective issues. Both authors are concerned with observable behaviors and meanings and the relationship between them as expressed in the teacher's unique teaching style. Cogan (1973) urges supervisors to focus attention primarily on teacher behaviors, however, arguing that a change in style will naturally follow if behavior changes: "The proper domain of the clinical supervisor is the classroom behavior of the teacher. That is, the proper subject of supervision is the teacher's classroom behavior, not the teacher as a person" (p. 58). Goldhammer (1969), on the other hand, advocates consideration of how supervisory processes affect the teacher's "ideas and feelings about himself," beyond "substantive technical learning" (p. 133). Supervisors themselves are advised by Goldhammer (1969) to submit their own behavior to "reflexive examination" during the postconference analysis stage (p. 337), intriguingly anticipating the reflective practice associated with the adjacent N–F perspective (see Figure 26.3).

Such differences between the two seminal theorists may be due to the communication dialect that each expresses in his writings. Although both original models of clinical supervision are highly consistent with an intuitive–thinking function pair, Goldhammer's views lean closer to conceptual abstraction, while Cogan clearly places greater emphasis on issues of practical application. Goldhammer's model appears to reflect a communication preference for intuition over thinking (N–T), in other words, while Cogan's model demonstrates a stronger preference for thinking over

intuition (T–N). Although we will never know if such preferences were rooted in the personalities of these men, it is interesting to note that Goldhammer, who was Cogan's student, published his book on clinical supervision in 1969. Cogan had spoken and written articles about clinical supervision many years before, however, and he is said to have finished three or four drafts of his own book before deciding in 1973 that his ideas were finally ready for public scrutiny (personal communications with Robert H. Anderson and David W. Champagne). Even then, he referred to his work rather tentatively as a "rationale," apparently anticipating further refinement.

Moving to the technical–didactic family, the approaches to clinical supervision advocated both by Acheson and Gall and by Hunter plainly give voice to a sensory–thinking (S–T) combination (see Figure 26.3). Yet the former carry objective analysis to an extreme. Where Goldhammer had five stages and Cogan had eight phases, Acheson and Gall (1980) propose no less than *thirty-two* discrete behavioral techniques for classroom observation and conferencing, indicating an exceptionally heavy reliance on the thinking function. They contrast their *techniques* with competing texts, noting that other authors "have emphasized theory and research on clinical supervision. Our book is practical in intent. We emphasize the techniques of clinical supervision, the 'nuts and bolts' of how to work with teachers to help them improve their classroom teaching" (p. xiii).

In comparison, Hunter (1984) draws heavily on her personal experience to inform practice and is concerned with obtaining a complete and accurate record, through "script-taping" of everything that is said and done in the classroom by teachers and students. While every bit as linear and rational as Acheson and Gall's approach, Hunter's version requires the clinical supervisor to directly experience and record sensory input, unmediated and unimpeded by observation instruments or mechanical devices. A major advantage of script-taping, she notes, is that "the observer can quickly 'swing' focus from one part of the group to another (something not possible for a camera). This enables an observer to scan and record many parts of the room almost simultaneously" (pp. 185–186). Thus, although both models express an S–T preference, Acheson and Gall place greater emphasis on the thinking function (T–S), whereas Hunter emphasizes sensing (S–T) more heavily.

Blumberg's (1974) model of clinical supervision is highly sensing as well, but, coupled with a dominant feeling function, the primary focus is on people and the quality of their interpersonal relations. As typifies an F–S function pair, Blumberg's model of clinical supervision is built on the assumption that much of the difficulty that teachers and supervisors face in working together stems from behavioral conflicts that originate in the organizational context of schools. Blumberg (1974) advises supervisors to concentrate on issues of trust, affection, and influence that he believes create psychological barriers between teachers and supervisors. He suggests that three conditions must be in place for instructional supervision to be successful: "the teacher must want help, the supervisor must have the resources to provide the kind of help required or know where the resources may be found, and the interpersonal relationships between a teacher and supervisor must enable the two to give and receive in a mutually satisfactory way" (p. 18).

Along with Blumberg, Eisner (1979) eschews following a step-by-step formula, as would be expected of any S–F combination. But Eisner is considerably less concerned with improving interpersonal relations. By relying on personal sensitivities and experiences, Eisner proposes that an instructional supervisor can become the major instrument through which the classroom and its context are perceived and understood. He views

clinical supervisors ideally as "connoisseurs" who perceive what is important yet subtle in classroom behavior and who can eloquently describe its essential expressive value. This esthetic aspect of Eisner's (1979) model suggests an affinity with the N–F function pairing, but a closer reading of the process that he outlines indicates a very strong emphasis on visual, auditory, and kinaesthetic sensing accompanied by the subjective feeling function (S–F dialect). That is, a combination of heightened sensing and feeling are critical for informing an artistic appreciation of the teaching act:

> By artistic I mean using an approach to supervision that relies on the sensitivity, perceptivity, and knowledge of the supervisor as a way of appreciating the significant subtleties occurring in the classroom, and that exploits the expressive, poetic, and often metaphorical potential of language to convey to teachers or to others whose decisions affect what goes on in schools, what has been observed. (p. 59)

Finally, the developmental and reflective models, respectively, appear to represent the F–N and N–F communication dialects, as depicted in Figure 26.3. Costa and Garmston's (1994) and Glickman's (1985) versions of clinical supervision place a high premium on both feeling and intuition (F–N), with a focus on facilitating the cognitive growth and decision-making ability of teachers through empathetic understanding and flexible response to teachers' current levels of functioning. Both aim to influence the way that teachers mentally process information and strongly favor abstract over concrete thinking as a goal to pursue. They concentrate primarily on the matter of how supervisors can guide teachers toward conscious understanding and control of their actions in the individual classroom, as well as when working collectively, to attain desirable learning outcomes for students. For example, Glickman (1985) defines "the key to successful schools as instructional supervision that fosters teacher development by promoting greater abstraction, commitment and collective action" (p. 381). Similarly, Costa and Garmston (1994) explain that "cognitive coaching enhances the intellectual capacities of teachers, which in turn produces greater intellectual achievement in students" (p. 6). A major goal of cognitive coaching is "enhancing growth toward *holonomy*," which they define as "individuals acting *autonomously* while simultaneously acting *interdependently* with the group" (p. 3).

Advocates of reflective practice, such as Zeichner and Liston (1987), Garman (1986), Waite (1995), and Smyth (1985), also seek to influence cognitive processes, but their position more closely approximates the value-driven N–F orientation. Accordingly, these authors urge supervisors and teachers to question the hierarchical nature of interpersonal relationships in schools, to raise issues of gender, race, and culture to conscious levels, and to challenge the knowledge embodied in the books, curriculum, lessons, and examinations that are part of schooling. Teachers and supervisors are encouraged to consider those aspects of classrooms and schools (including their own professional identities) that disempower other educators and debilitate students. This potential transformation of schooling is to be fueled by collaborative inquiry and guided by the moral principles of justice and equity.

DISCUSSION AND IMPLICATIONS

Choosing the proper communication style when working with teachers has been a perennial concern in the clinical supervision literature. Although general consensus exists that the process of selecting a communication style should include consideration of the needs of teachers, experts conflict substantively in the specific advice that they offer on this point. Goldhammer (1969), writing from an intuitive–thinking point of view, for example, cautions supervisors to refrain from being overly direct when working with inexperienced teachers lest these teachers become dependent on the supervisor and fail to develop a personal teaching identity. He advises that experienced veterans can more easily tolerate a supervisor's forthrightness and assimilate into their teaching repertoire what seems appropriate to them, without feeling unduly pressured or intimidated. In contrast, Hunter (1984), writing from a sensing–thinking perspective, asserts that a direct communication style is exactly the tonic for inducting newcomers into the teaching profession, because novices are inexperienced and sorely need the expert advice that a supervisor can readily provide. Collaborative communication, she believes, should be reserved for teachers who possess the experience and expertise to engage in dialogue with the supervisor on a more equal footing.

Which of these rationales is correct? Each view seems sound and plausible until the other is considered, because both positions are consistent within their own internal logic. Yet each remains diametrically opposed to the other. Rather than quibble about the *right* way and the *wrong* way to treat teachers with varying levels of experience and expertise on the basis of general principles, an understanding of psychological functions and communication dialects allows us to accept *both*—and a range of other alternatives that may be appropriate under different sets of circumstances. Instead of stereotyping beginning teachers and experienced teachers as being all alike, a *functional* perspective on clinical supervision enables us to see that each situation is defined by the psychological processes of the individuals who happen to be involved in the teacher–supervisor relationship. While this insight greatly complicates things for both supervision theorists and practitioners, it also promises a refinement of our understanding and an improvement of our chances for success by moving us beyond the *direct* versus *indirect* communication controversy.

The application of psychological functions to clinical supervision sheds light on another contemporary issue, as well: shaping the content of communication with teachers on the basis of the hierarchical goals that a supervisor hopes to accomplish. Several authors, all writing from a developmental–reflective perspective, have independently recommended that a supervisor's practice should be guided by whether the object is to improve a teacher's technical competence, conceptual understanding, or sensitivity to issues of an ethical nature (e.g., Grimmett, 1989; Zeichner & Liston, 1996). In each instance, a preference for goals favoring moral sensitivity over technical competence is explicitly stated. A view of clinical supervision that considers psychological functions suggests that this hierarchical device is essentially arbitrary, except from the perspective of those who favor intuition and feeling as ways of perceiving and evaluating reality. A supervisor with a sensing–thinking preference, in contrast, is likely to consider an idealistic and well-intentioned teacher who lacks the skills needed to help students to learn as more problematic than a motivated and technically proficient teacher who expresses little concern for principles of social justice. A view informed by psychological functions suggests, as well, that in addition to technical (S–T), conceptual (N–T), and moral (N–F) considerations, a relational (S–F) dimension of growth is also possible, desirable, and seriously worth considering as an outcome of instruction and supervision. Without questioning the value of moral commitment or more abstract thinking, in other words, the legitimacy and importance of development along other lines for students, teachers, and supervisors become evident.

The major implication of psychological functions for practice, however, is that clinical supervisors ought to interact with teachers in the manner through which the teachers, themselves, learn best. Wiles (2001) reported preliminary findings that Florida teachers who were nominated by their superintendents as "the best" differ from other teachers on a learning styles inventory based on Jung's psychological functions and other measures. The teachers who were nominated as exemplary "tend to be more flexible, more experimental, and more student-centered than the regular population of teachers in Florida" (p. 7). Yet much of what supervisors do, say, and think when they interact with teachers, consciously or unconsciously, is typically determined by their own psychological preferences for perceiving and judging. Indeed, Goldhammer (1969) very clearly anticipated this very point. Until supervisors become conscious of their own preferences and more sensitive to those of teachers, they will inadvertently tend to favor, reward, and reinforce teachers who behave, speak, and think as they do, while misunderstanding and failing to communicate with teachers who differ from themselves.

The bases of a true collegial relationship include trust and a willingness to share and understand personal meanings, understandings, and frames of reference. Clinical supervision should provide support for teachers with an aim toward increasing professional responsibility and openness and the capacity for self-analysis and self-direction. By attending carefully to psychological functions, clinical supervisors can recognize and build on existing strengths. Instead of calling attention to deficits and shortcomings, supervisors can open alternative paths for teachers to reach their professional goals. Teachers can be helped to perfect their uniquely personal teaching styles and also round out their repertoires by developing styles that reflect other modes of thinking. Clinical supervisors should initially be willing to accept each teacher's unique style and enter into dialogue with the assumption that the teacher is professionally competent, even though the two of them may experience and respond to the world very differently. Indeed, tracking teachers according to the supervisor's subjective judgments of their ability is as indefensible as the placing of students into different curriculum tracks according to the teacher's perceptions of their academic aptitude.

Clinical supervisors, no less than teachers, should make a deliberate effort to honor and legitimate perspectives and strategies that are not harmonious with their own preferred tendencies for perceiving and judging reality. That is to say, clinical supervisors should strive to work with teachers in ways that are consistent with how teachers are expected to work with students—by celebrating diversity and responding to that diversity in ways that enhance learning for all.

REFERENCES

Acheson, K. A., & Gall, M. D. (1980). *Techniques in the clinical supervision of teachers.* White Plains, NY: Longman.

Blumberg, A. (1974). *Supervisors and teachers: A private cold war.* Berkeley, CA: McCutchan.

Briggs, K. A., & Myers, I. B. (1977). *Myers–Briggs type indicator.* Palo Alto, CA: Consulting Psychologists Press

Champagne, D. W., & Hogan, R. C. (1995). *Consultant supervision: Theory and skill development,* 3rd ed. Wheaton, IL: CH Publications.

Cogan, M. L. (1973). *Clinical supervision.* Boston, MA: Houghton Mifflin.

Costa, A. L., & Garmston, R. J. (1994). *Cognitive coaching: A foundation for renaissance schools.* Norwood, MA: Christopher–Gordon.

Eisner, E. W. (1979). *The educational imagination: On the design and evaluation of educational programs.* New York, NY: Macmillan.

Fitzgerald, C., & Kirby, L. (Eds.) (1997). *Developing leaders: Research and applications in psychological type and leadership development.* Palo Alto, CA: Davies–Black.

Friedrich, C. J. (1954). *The philosophy of Hegel.* New York, NY: Random House.

Garman, N. B. (1986). Reflection, the heart of clinical supervision: A modern rationale for practice. *Journal of Curriculum and Supervision, 2*(1): 1–24.

Garmston, R. J., Lipton, L. E., & Kaiser, K. (1998). The psychology of supervision. In Gerald R. Firth and Edward F. Pajak (Eds.), *Handbook of Research on School Supervision.* New York, NY: Simon & Schuster Macmillan (pp. 242–286).

Glickman, C. D. (1985). *Supervision of instruction: A developmental approach.* Boston, MA: Allyn and Bacon.

Goldhammer, R. (1969). *Clinical supervision: Special methods for the supervision of teachers.* New York, NY: Holt, Rinehart & Winston.

Grimmett, P. P. (1989) A commentary on Schon's view of reflection. *Journal of Curriculum and Supervision,* 5.

Hawthorne, R. D., & Hoffman, N. E. (1998). Supervision in non-teaching professions. In Gerald R. Firth and Edward F. Pajak (Eds.), *Handbook of research on school supervision.* New York, NY: Simon & Schuster Macmillan (pp. 555–580).

Hirsch, S. K., & Kummerow, J. M. (1998). *Introduction to type in organizations.* Palo Alto, CA: Consulting Psychologists Press.

Hunter, M. (1984). Knowing, teaching, and supervising. In. P. L. Holford (Ed.), *Using what we know about teaching.* Alexandria, VA: Association for Supervision and Curriculum Development.

Jung, C. G. (1971). *Psychological types.* A revision by R. F. C. Hull of the translation by H. G. Baynes. Princeton, NJ: Princeton University Press.

Keirsey, D. (1998). *Please understand me II: Temperament, character, intelligence.* Del Mar, CA: Prometheus Nemesis.

Norris, C. J. (1991). Supervising with style. *Theory Into Practice, 30* (Spring 1991), 129–133.

Oja, S. N., & Reiman, A. J. (1998). Supervision for teacher development across the career span. In Gerald R. Firth and Edward F. Pajak (Eds.), *Handbook of research on school supervision.* New York, NY: Simon & Schuster Macmillan (pp. 463–487).

Pajak, E. F. (2000). *Approaches to clinical supervision: Alternatives for improving instruction,* 2nd ed. Norwood, MA: Christopher–Gordon.

Shapiro, A. S., & Blumberg, A. (1998). Social dimensions of supervision. In Gerald R. Firth and Edward F. Pajak (Eds.), *Handbook of research on school supervision.* New York, NY: Simon & Schuster Macmillan (pp. 1055–1084).

Silver, H., Strong, R., & Perini, M. (1997). Integrating learning styles and multiple intelligences. *Educational Leadership, 55* (September), 22–27.

Smyth, J. W. (1985). Developing a critical practice of clinical supervision. *Journal of Curriculum Studies, 17* (January–March), 1–15.

Thompson, H. L. (2000). *Introduction to the communication wheel.* Watkinsville, GA: Wormhole Publishing.

Waite, D. (1995). *Rethinking instructional supervision: Notes on its language and culture.* Washington, DC: Falmer Press.

Wiles, J. (2001). Some of our best teachers. *Wingspan, 13* (March), 4–9.

Zeichner, K. M., & Liston, D. P. (1987). Teaching student teachers to reflect. *Harvard Educational Review, 57* (February), 23–48.

Zeichner, K. M., & Liston, D. P. (1996). *Reflective teaching: An introduction.* Mahwah, NJ: Erlbaum.

DISCUSSION QUESTIONS

1. How effective and how collegial have your experiences been with clinical supervision?
2. In your experience, do teachers tend to exhibit the various psychological types described?
3. How could a principal or peer coach apply the concept of psychological functions when working with a teacher?
4. Would understanding and use of psychological types make clinical supervision more collegial? Why or why not?
5. Would understanding and use of psychological types make clinical supervision more effective? Why or why not?

27 Beginning Teacher Induction: What the Data Tell Us

RICHARD INGERSOLL

FOCUSING QUESTIONS

1. Why is induction important for new teachers?
2. Why is induction reform so relevant now?
3. What are the "ballooning" trend and the "greening" of the teaching force?
4. What are the some negative consequences to high teacher turnover?
5. What typical induction activities do beginning teachers participate in?
6. What types of induction support matter?

Since the advent of public schools, education commentators and reformers have perennially called attention to the challenges encountered by newcomers to school teaching. Although elementary and secondary teaching involves intensive interaction with youngsters, the work of teachers is done largely in isolation from colleagues. This isolation can be especially difficult for newcomers, who, upon accepting a position in a school, are frequently left to succeed or fail on their own within the confines of their classrooms—often likened to a "lost at sea" or "sink or swim" experience. Other commentators go further, arguing that beginners tend to end up in the most challenging and difficult classroom and school assignments, akin to a "trial by fire." Indeed, some have assailed teaching as an occupation that "cannibalizes its young." These are the very kinds of issues and problems that effective employee entry, orientation, and support programs—widely known as induction—seek to address. Teaching, however, has traditionally not had the kind of induction programs for new entrants common to many skilled blue- and white-collar occupations and characteristic of many traditional professions.

This has changed in recent decades; induction for beginning teachers has become a major topic in education policy and reform. The theory behind such programs holds that teaching is complex work, that pre-employment teacher preparation is rarely sufficient to provide all the knowledge and skill necessary to successful teaching, and that a significant portion of this knowledge can be acquired only on the job. This view holds that schools must provide an environment where novices can learn how to teach, survive, and succeed as teachers. These programs aim to improve the performance and retention of new hires and to enhance the skills and prevent the loss of new teachers with the ultimate goal of improving student growth and learning.

While teacher induction has received much attention in the policy realm, until recently, empirical research on these reforms has been limited. It has been unclear how widespread induction programs are across the nation, what activities, supports, and components the induction experience usually includes, and, most importantly, whether receiving such support has any positive effect on teachers and students. All of this poses difficulties for those engaged in the very important and very practical matter of deciding which, if any, program or activity to offer in schools.

To answer these questions, I began a series of research projects several years ago with my colleagues Tom Smith and Michael Strong and a doctoral student, Lisa Merrill. In order to investigate the larger context surrounding teacher induction, we used the best national data available to explore demographic changes in the teaching force as a whole in recent decades. We analyzed how widespread beginning teacher induction programs are across the nation, whether their prevalence has increased over the past decade, and what types and amounts of induction beginning teachers actually get. In addition, we conducted our own statistical analysis of how participating in these induction programs affects the retention of beginning teachers. Finally, we reviewed the existing empirical studies that have evaluated the effects of induction on teachers and students.

What we learned is very revealing. Induction is a timely and growing reform, but, for those responsible for funding, designing, and implementing induction,

there is both good news and sobering news.

CHANGES IN THE TEACHING FORCE

For several decades, we've heard much about a "graying" trend in the teaching force. The conventional wisdom has been that the aging of the baby-boomer generation has led to massive teacher retirements, in turn, precipitating a teacher shortage crisis. Our data analyses show that the teaching force has indeed gotten steadily older in recent decades, and this has led to more teacher retirements. But, the data also suggest that the peak of retirements may have passed; we found that the numbers of teachers retiring slowed between 2005 and 2009. In contrast, we've identified three larger, but lesser-known, changes in the demographic character of the teaching force, all of which have strong implications for induction (Ingersoll & Merrill, 2010).

The first trend is what we call the "ballooning" of the teaching force. After two decades of flat growth, since the mid-1980s, the teaching force in the United States has dramatically increased in size. The U.S. Census Bureau indicates that K–12 teaching has long been one of the largest occupational groups, if not the largest, in the nation, and it is growing even larger. In the mid-1980s, student enrollments began to grow, and they have done so ever since; the teaching force has grown at the same time. The rates of these student and teacher increases have not matched those of the post-war, baby-boom years, with one large difference: The rate of increase for teachers has far outpaced the rate of increase for students. That is, the number of teachers is going up far faster than the number of students. For example, from the late 1980s to 2008, total K–12 student enrollment went up by 19 percent. During the same period, the teaching force increased at over 2.5 times that rate, by 48 percent.

This trend immediately raises two large questions: First, why? What are the reasons for and sources of the trend? What is driving this upsurge in teacher employment? And, second, what are the implications and consequences of the trend? In particular, how are school districts paying for this? We have begun to explore these questions elsewhere (Ingersoll & Merrill, 2010). Here, we will focus on the implications of this ballooning for induction.

The ballooning has meant an upsurge in hiring and has resulted in another equally dramatic trend that we have called a "greening" of the teaching force. In 1988, there were about 65,000 first-year teachers; by 2008, this number had grown to over 200,000 (see Figure 27-1). In 1988, the most common teacher was a veteran with 15 years of teaching experience. By 2008, the most common teacher was not a gray-haired veteran; he or she was a beginner in the first year of teaching. By that year, a quarter of the teaching force had five years or less of experience.

A third and final trend we discovered reveals a sobering side to this greening.

Teacher attrition—teachers leaving teaching—is especially high in the first years on the job. Several studies, including our own analyses (Ingersoll, 2003; Ingersoll & Perda, in press), have estimated that between 40 percent and 50 percent of new teachers leave within the first five years of entry into teaching. Moreover, we have found that the attrition rates of first-year teachers have increased by about one-third in the past two decades. So, not only are there far more beginners in the teaching force, but these beginners are less likely to stay in teaching. In short, both the number and instability of beginning teachers have been increasing in recent years.

All organizations and occupations, of course, experience some loss of new entrants—either voluntarily because newcomers decide to not remain or involuntarily because employers deem them unsuitable. Moreover, some degree of employee turnover, job, and career change is normal, inevitable, and beneficial. However, teaching has relatively high turnover compared to many other occupations and professions, such as lawyers,

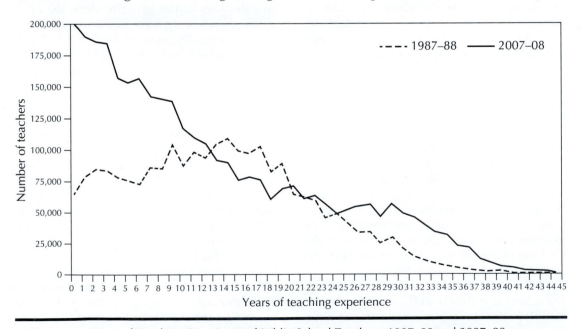

FIGURE 27.1 Years of Teaching Experience of Public School Teachers, 1987–88 and 2007–08

engineers, architects, professors, pharmacists, and nurses, and these departures are not cost free (Ingersoll & Perda, in press).

For instance, one negative consequence of the high turnover in teaching is its link to the teacher shortages that seem to annually plague many schools. In analyses of national data, we've found that neither the much-heralded mathematics and science teacher shortage (Ingersoll & Perda, 2010) nor the minority teacher shortage (Ingersoll & May, 2011) is primarily due to insufficient production of new teachers, as is widely believed. In contrast, the data indicate that these school staffing problems are to a significant extent the result of a "revolving door," where large numbers of teachers depart teaching long before retirement. Moreover, the data show that beginning teachers, in particular, report that one of the main factors behind their decision to depart is a lack of adequate support from school administrators (Ingersoll, 2003).

INDUCTION PROGRAMS PROLIFERATE

These demographic changes in the teaching force have large implications for induction. Our analyses show there has been a simulta-neous increase in beginners and decrease in veterans. Beginners are now the largest group within one of the largest occupations in the nation, and these beginners have steadily become more prone to quickly leave teaching. All of this suggests a strong increase in the need for support programs.

Not surprisingly, our data indicate that over the past couple of decades, the number of induction programs also has grown considerably. The percentage of beginning teachers who report that they participated in some kind of induction program in their first year of teaching has steadily increased in recent decades—from about 50 percent in 1990 to 91 percent by 2008 (see Figure 27-2). Moreover, these percentages don't tell the whole story. The large increase in the number of first-year teachers—the greening discussed above—has meant that, numerically, far more beginners are receiving support. In 1991, about 61,000 first-year teachers participated in an induction or mentoring program; by 2008, this had almost trebled, to about 179,000. As of the 2010–2011 school year, 27 states required some kind of induction program for new teachers (Goldrick et al., 2012).

However, while most beginning teachers now participate in some kind of formal

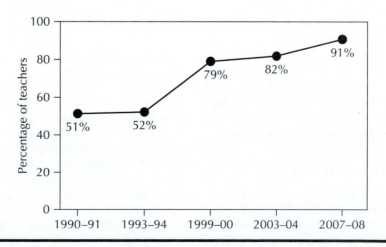

FIGURE 27.2   Trends in the Percent of Beginning Teachers Participating in Induction or Mentor Programs

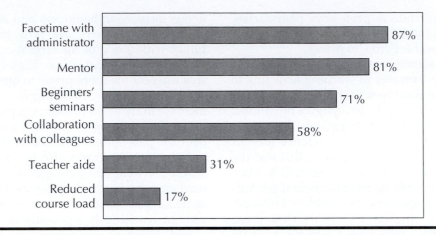

FIGURE 27.3   Percent of First-Year Teachers Who Received Various Induction Supports (2007–2008)

induction program, the kinds of support that schools provide to them vary (see Figure 27-3). The most recent data available—from the 2007–2008 school year—show that the most common induction activity that beginners participated in was having regular supportive communication with their principal, other administrators, or their department chair (87 percent). Slightly fewer beginning teachers, about 80 percent, said they received ongoing guidance and feedback from a mentor teacher. Just over half of beginning teachers said they had common collaboration and planning time with other teachers in the same subject area. Interestingly, almost one-third received extra classroom assistance, such as a teacher aide. On the other hand, fewer than 20 percent of beginning teachers reported receiving a reduced teaching load or schedule to ease their transition—a support that is probably more common for beginning professors in higher education.

DOES INDUCTION MATTER?

Of course, the key question is this: Does participating in induction matter? One subset of this question involves retention—does participation in induction slow the high attrition of beginners? To answer this question, we undertook a series of advanced statistical analyses to examine the effect of induction on the likelihood that beginning teachers stayed in or left their schools at the end of their first year on the job (Smith & Ingersoll, 2004; Ingersoll & Smith, 2004).

After controlling for the background characteristics of teachers and schools, we did find a link between beginning teachers' participation in induction programs and their retention. But we also found that the strength of the effect depended on the types and number of supports that beginning teachers received. Participation in some types of activities in the first year was more effective at reducing turnover than was participation in other types. The factors with the strongest effect were having a mentor teacher from one's subject area and having common planning or collaboration time with other teachers in one's subject area.

The data also revealed that the various types of induction supports, activities, or practices rarely existed alone; schools or districts usually provide beginning teachers with different "packages" or "bundles" of components or supports. Collectively, getting multiple induction components had a strong effect on whether beginning teachers stayed or left. Moreover, as the number of components in the packages increased, both the number of teachers receiving the package and the likelihood of their turnover decreased.

For example, the most common package consisted of just two basic components: working with a mentor and having regular supportive communication with one's principal, another administrator, or one's department chair. Beginners receiving just these two supports had better retention than those who received no induction at all, but the difference was small. In contrast, other beginners received a far more comprehensive package: the above two supports plus others, such as participation in a seminar for beginning teachers, common planning time with other teachers in the same subject, a reduced course load, and assistance from a classroom aide. Getting this comprehensive package had a very large effect; the likelihood that beginners who received this package would leave at the end of their first year was less than half that of those who participated in no induction activities. But only 5 percent of beginners received such a comprehensive package in 2007–2008. Our conclusion was that induction helps, but it depends on how much one gets. The more comprehensive the induction program, the better the retention.

Our study looked at just one outcome—retention—which raises several questions. Have there been other empirical studies done on the effects of induction? Have any studies looked at the effect on other outcomes, such as whether participating in induction improves beginning teachers' classroom instructional practices and, in turn, improves student learning and achievement?

To answer these questions, we recently undertook a thorough review of existing empirical studies that evaluated the effects of induction (Ingersoll & Strong, 2011). The objective of our review was to give researchers, policy makers, and educators a reliable and current assessment of what is known, and not known, about the effectiveness of teacher induction and mentoring programs. After an extensive search, we found 15 empirical studies that were solid enough to merit inclusion in our review. Each evaluated the effects of induction on an outcome, by comparing data from both participants and nonparticipants in particular induction components, activities, or programs.

When we began our review, we weren't sure what to expect. In educational research, as in many other fields, the existing base of research evaluating particular programs or reforms often yields contradictory findings and mixed conclusions. Whether the target of evaluation is a new curricular product, the value of teachers' credentials, the performance of charter schools, or whatever, typically some studies find negative effects, some find no effects, and some find positive effects. In the research on the effects of induction, we also found a few mixed and contradictory findings. But, interestingly, overall we found mostly consensus: Induction has a positive effect. Most of the studies that looked at the effect on teachers' job satisfaction, commitment, and retention found positive effects on beginning teachers who participated in some kind of induction. Likewise, most of the studies that we reviewed of teachers' classroom practices showed that beginning teachers who participated in some kind of induction performed better at various aspects of teaching, such as keeping students on task, developing workable lesson plans, using effective student questioning practices, adjusting classroom activities to meet students' interests, maintaining a positive classroom atmosphere, and demonstrating successful classroom management. Finally, for student achievement, most of the studies also showed that students of beginning teachers who participated in some kind of induction had higher scores, or gains, on academic achievement tests.

CONCLUSION

Induction is an education reform whose time has come. Over the past two decades, there has been a large increase in the number of states, districts, and schools offering support, guidance, and orientation programs. Importantly, the data also indicate that induction can help retain teachers and improve their instruction. The data also show that the kinds and amounts of support vary. And some research suggests that content, intensity, and duration are important: The effect depends on how much induction one gets and for how long.

Over the past couple of decades the number of beginning teachers has ballooned and so has the number of beginners eligible for induction in any given school. This is important because induction is not free—especially the more comprehensive programs. Thus far, we don't have much data and research on the relative costs and benefits of induction. Along with content and duration, induction programs also vary in their financial costs, and beyond the question of which kinds and amounts of assistance are most effective lies the question of which kinds and amounts of assistance are most cost-effective. Especially in periods of budget shortfalls, the "bang for the buck" of such programs is, of course, crucial information for policy makers faced with deciding which programs to fund. This is an area in which the research community could provide useful guidance to the policy community.

REFERENCES

Goldrick, L., Osta, D., Barlin, D., & Burn, J. (2012). *Review of state policies on teacher induction.* Santa Cruz, CA: New Teacher Center.

Ingersoll, R. (2003). *Is there really a teacher shortage?* Philadelphia, PA: University of Pennsylvania, Consortium for Policy Research in Education.

Ingersoll, R., & May, H. (2011). *Recruitment, retention, and the minority teacher shortage.* Philadelphia, PA: University of Pennsylvania, Consortium for Policy Research in Education.

Ingersoll, R., & Merrill, L. (2010). Who's teaching our children? *Educational Leadership, 67*(8), 14–20.

Ingersoll, R., & Perda, D. (2010). Is the supply of mathematics and science teachers sufficient? *American Educational Research Journal, 47*(3), 563–595.

Ingersoll, R., & Perda, D. (in press). *How high is teacher turnover and is it a problem?* Philadelphia, PA: University of Pennsylvania, Consortium for Policy Research in Education.

Ingersoll, R., & Smith, T. (2004). Do teacher induction and mentoring matter? *NASSP Bulletin, 88*(638), 28–40.

Ingersoll, R., & Strong, M. (2011). The impact of induction and mentoring for beginning teachers: A critical review of the research. *Review of Educational Research, 81*(2), 201–233.

Smith, T., & Ingersoll, R. (2004). What are the effects of induction and mentoring on beginning teacher turnover? *American Educational Research Journal, 41*(3), 681–714.

DISCUSSION QUESTIONS

1. How would you define a successful induction program? (or, What outcome defines a successful induction program?) Explain.
2. As a beginning teacher, what topics would you like addressed as part of the induction process?
3. Why do you think teaching has relatively high turnover compared with other professions?
4. How long do you think induction should last for new teachers? Explain.

28 Instructional Insensitivity of Tests: Accountability's Dire Drawback

W. James Popham

FOCUSING QUESTIONS

1. Describe what is meant by instructional sensitivity.
2. What role do judgmental evidence and empirical evidence play in determining instructional sensitivity of assessments?
3. Identify and describe the four dimensions used to evaluate an assessment.
4. Why is it important to evaluate the instructional insensitivity of an assessment?
5. Who should be involved in evaluating the instructional sensitivity of an assessment? Explain.

ABSTRACT

If we plan to use tests for purposes of accountability, we need to know that they measure traits that can be influenced by instruction. In this chapter, the author offers a model procedure for judging our tests.

Large-scale accountability tests have become increasingly important. They influence the deliberations of policy makers and affect the day-by-day behaviors of teachers in their classrooms. The premise underlying the use of these accountability tests is that students' test scores will indicate the quality of instruction those students have received. If students score well on accountability tests, we conclude that those students have been well taught. Conversely, if students score poorly on accountability tests, we believe that those students have been poorly taught.

Furthermore, advocates of these tests make two assumptions: (1) that teachers who realize they are going to be judged by their students' test scores will try to do a better instructional job, and (2) that higher-level authorities can take action to bolster the quality of instruction in schools or districts where test results indicate ineffective instruction is taking place. For either of these assumptions to make sense, the accountability tests being employed must actually be able to determine the effect of instruction on students' test scores. However, all but a few of the accountability tests now having such a profound impact on our nation's schools are instructionally insensitive. That is, they are patently unsuitable for use in any sensible educational accountability program.

INSTRUCTIONAL SENSITIVITY

A test's instructional sensitivity represents the degree to which students' performances on that test accurately reflect the quality of the instruction that was provided specifically to promote students' mastery of whatever is being assessed. In other words, an instructionally sensitive test would be capable of distinguishing between strong and weak instruction by allowing us to validly conclude that a set of students' high test scores are meaningfully, but not exclusively, attributable to effective instruction. Similarly, such a test would allow us to accurately infer that a set of students' low test scores are meaningfully, but not exclusively, attributable to ineffective instruction. In contrast, an instructionally insensitive test would not allow us to distinguish accurately between strong and weak instruction.

Students' performances on most of the accountability tests currently used are more heavily influenced by the students' socioeconomic status (SES) than by the quality of teachers' instructional efforts. That is, such instructionally insensitive accountability tests tend to measure the SES composition of a school's student body rather than the effectiveness with which the school's students have been taught.

Instructionally insensitive tests render untenable the assumptions underlying a test-based strategy for educational accountability. How can the prospect of annual accountability testing ever motivate educators to improve

their instruction once they've realized that better instruction will not lead to higher test scores? How can officials accurately intervene to improve instruction on the basis of low test scores if those low scores really aren't a consequence of ineffective instruction?

There is ample evidence that, instead of improving instructional quality, ill-conceived accountability programs can seriously diminish it. Teachers too often engage in a curricular reductionism and give scant, if any, instructional attention to content not assessed by accountability tests. Too often teachers impose excessive test-preparation drills on their students and thereby extinguish the genuine joy those students should experience as they learn. And too often, we hear of teachers or administrators disingenuously portraying students' test scores as improved when, in fact, no actual improvement has taken place.

Yet, while the distinction between instructionally sensitive and insensitive accountability tests may be readily understandable and the classroom consequences of using instructionally insensitive accountability tests are all too apparent, it accomplishes little when educators complain, even profusely, about policy makers' reliance on the wrong kinds of accountability tests. Educators who simply carp about accountability tests are usually seen as individuals eager to escape evaluation. Only when we can convincingly demonstrate that an accountability program is relying on instructionally insensitive tests will we be able to remedy the current absurdity. Clearly, we need a credible procedure to determine the instructional sensitivity of a given accountability test.

This article describes the main features of a practical procedure for ascertaining the instructional sensitivity of any test, whether it is already in use or is under development. Because the instructional sensitivity of an accountability system's tests is the dominant determinant of whether that system helps or harms students, this approach should be used widely. Although the chief ingredients of the approach are described here, devils hide in details, and thus, a more detailed description of the procedures is available from wpopham@ucla.edu or at www.ioxassessment.com.

GATHERING EVIDENCE

There are two main categories of evidence for determining the instructional sensitivity of an accountability test: judgmental evidence and empirical evidence. Judgmental evidence can be collected by using panels of trained judges to rate specified attributes of a test. Empirical evidence can be provided by students' actual test scores, but these test scores must be collected under specific conditions—for instance, by comparing differences between the test scores of "taught" and "untaught" students.

Regardless of whether the instructional sensitivity of a test is determined by reliance on judgmental evidence alone, empirical evidence alone, or a combination of both, instructional sensitivity should be conceived of as a continuum rather than a dichotomy. Rarely will one encounter an accountability test that is totally sensitive or insensitive to instruction. The task facing anyone who wishes to determine an accountability test's instructional sensitivity is to arrive at a defensible estimate of where that test falls on such a continuum.

For practical reasons, the chief evidence to be routinely gathered about a test should be judgmental, not empirical. If resources permit, empirical studies should be used to confirm the extent to which judgmental data are accurate. But in today's busy world of education, the collection of even judgmental evidence regarding instructional sensitivity would be an improvement. The assembly of confirmatory empirical evidence is desirable but not absolutely necessary when embarking on an appraisal of an accountability test's

instructional sensitivity. A number of key test-appraisal procedures currently rely only on judgment-based approaches; for instance, studies focused on content-related evidence of validity are based on judges' reviews of a test's items.

There is nothing sacrosanct about the kinds of judgmental evidence for appraising instructional sensitivity or how to go about assembling such evidence. One practical method is to create panels of 15 to 20 curriculum specialists and teachers who are knowledgeable about the content. If the results of an instructional sensitivity review are to be released to the public, it is sensible to include several noneducators as panelists for the sake of credibility.

After receiving ample orientation and training, panelists would use 10-point scales to rate the tests on four evaluative dimensions. For each evaluative dimension, panelists would be given a rubric that contains sufficient explanatory information and, as necessary, previously judged exemplars so that all panelists would use similar evaluative perspectives.

Panelists could use a variety of procedures for their tasks. But most likely their procedures would be similar to either the iterative models that have been commonly employed in setting standards for the past couple of decades or the judgmental methods used in recent years to ascertain the alignment between a state's accountability tests and the content standards those tests are ostensibly assessing. In both of those approaches, panelists typically make individual judgments and then share them with the entire panel. After that, an open discussion of panelists' judgments occurs, followed by another set of individual judgments. As many iterations of this procedure are carried out as are necessary for the group to reach a consensus. Another method uses the average of the panelists' final ratings as the overall judgment.

The four evaluative dimensions that should be used are (1) the number of curricular aims assessed, (2) the clarity of assessment targets, (3) the number of items per assessed curricular aim, and (4) the instructional sensitivity of items. As noted above, panelists would be given sufficient information to allow them to rate each dimension on a 10-point scale. Then the four separate ratings would be combined to arrive at an overall rating of a test's instructional sensitivity. Those who are designing an instructional sensitivity review need to determine whether to assign equal weight to each of the four dimensions or to assign different weights to each dimension.

NUMBER OF CURRICULAR AIMS ASSESSED

Experience makes it all too clear that teachers cannot realistically focus their instruction on large numbers of curricular aims. In many states, lengthy lists of officially approved curricular aims often oblige teachers to guess about what will be assessed on a given year's accountability tests. More often than not, there are far too many "official" curricular aims to be tested in the available testing time (or, in truth, to be taught in the available teaching time). After a few years of guessing incorrectly, many teachers simply abandon any reliance on the state's sanctioned curricular aims. If an accountability test is to be genuinely sensitive to the impact of instruction, all teachers should be pursuing the same curricular aims, not teacher-divined subsets of those aims.

Clearly, therefore, one evaluative dimension to be considered when determining an accountability test's instructional sensitivity should be the number of curricular aims assessed by the test. Note that there is no reference here to the worth of those curricular aims. Obviously, the worth of a set of curricular aims is extremely important, but the appraisal of that worth should be a separate, albeit indispensable, activity. A test's instructional sensitivity is not dependent on the grandeur of the curricular aims being measured.

To evaluate the number of curricular aims assessed, it is necessary to deal with those curricular aims at a grain size (that is, degree of breadth) that meshes with teachers' day-to-day or week-to-week instructional decisions. Evaluators must be wary of aims that are too large. If the grain size of a curricular aim is so large that it prevents a teacher from devising activities sensibly targeted toward that curricular aim, then the curricular aim's grain size is too broad. For example, some states have very general sets of "content standards," such as "measurement" or "algebra" in mathematics. This grain size is much too large for panelists to make sense of when using this evaluative dimension. Instead, a panelist's focus needs to be on the smaller curricular aims typically subsumed by more general standards. These smaller curricular aims are often labeled "benchmarks," "indicators," "objectives," or something similar.

The rubric for this evaluative dimension should be organized around a definition in which higher ratings would be given to a set of curricular aims whose numbers would be regarded by teachers as easily addressed in the instructional time available. In other words, if teachers have enough instructional time to teach students to achieve all of the curricular aims to be assessed, panelists would give the highest ratings. In contrast, lower ratings would be given to sets of curricular aims regarded as too numerous to teach in the available instructional time, because teachers would be uncertain about which of the aims would be assessed on a given year's accountability test.

CLARITY OF ASSESSMENT TARGETS

The second evaluative dimension revolves around the degree to which teachers understand what they are supposed to be teaching. If teachers have only a murky idea of what constitutes the knowledge or skills they are supposed to be teaching—as exemplified by what's measured on an accountability test— then those teachers will often end up teaching the wrong things. Thus an instructionally sensitive accountability test should be accompanied by descriptive information that describes not only the types of items eligible to be used on the test but, more important, the essence of the skills or knowledge the test will be measuring. If teachers have a clear understanding of what is to be measured, then their instructional efforts can be directed toward those skills and bodies of knowledge rather than toward specific test items. A test consisting of items that measure instructional targets that teachers understand is surely more apt to accurately measure the degree to which those targets have been hit.

The manner in which an accountability test describes what it's supposed to be measuring can, of course, vary considerably. Sometimes state officials supply no descriptive information beyond the curricular aims themselves. In other instances, a state's educational authorities provide explicit assessment descriptions intended to let the state's teachers know what is to be measured by the state's accountability tests. And, of course, there are many other ways of describing what is to be assessed by an accountability test. Thus, in carrying out a judgmental appraisal of an accountability test's descriptive clarity, the material under review should be whatever descriptive information is readily available to teachers. If this turns out to be only the state's official curricular aims, then that is the information to be used when panelists render their judgments about this second dimension of instructional sensitivity. If a state's tests have more detailed assessment descriptions, then this is the information to use. The descriptive information to be reviewed by panelists must be routinely accessible to teachers, not hidden in the often fugitive technical reports associated with an accountability test.

The rubric for this evaluative dimension should emphasize the teachers' likely understanding of the nature of the skills and knowledge to be assessed. Higher ratings would be supplied when panelists believe

teachers can readily comprehend what is to be assessed well enough to design appropriate instructional activities.

Ideally, before ratings on this evaluative dimension are collected, a separate data-gathering activity would be carried out in which a half-dozen or so teachers are first given copies of whatever materials are routinely available that describe the accountability test's assessment targets, are asked to read them carefully, and then are directed to put that descriptive information away. Next, in their own words and without reference to the previously read descriptive material, the teachers would be asked to write, independently, what they understood to be the essence of each skill or body of knowledge to be assessed. The degree to which such independently written descriptions are homogeneous would then be supplied to the panelists before they render a judgment. This information would supply panelists with an idea of just how much ambiguity appears to be present in the test's descriptive materials. Although not necessary, this optional activity would clearly strengthen the conclusions reached by the panel.

ITEMS PER ASSESSED CURRICULAR AIM

The third evaluative dimension on which an accountability test's instructional sensitivity can be judged deals with whether there are enough items on a test to allow teachers (as well as students and students' parents) to determine if each assessed curricular aim has been satisfactorily achieved. The rationale for this evaluative factor is straightforward. If teachers can't tell which parts of their instruction are working and which parts aren't, they'll be unable to improve ineffectual instructional segments for future students. Moreover, if there are too few items to determine a student's status with respect to, say, a specific skill in mathematics, then a student (or the student's parents) can't tell whether additional instruction appears to be needed on that skill. Similarly, if teachers are given meaningful information regarding their incoming students' skills and knowledge at the beginning of a school year, then more appropriately tailored instruction can be provided for those new students. Although not strictly related to a test's instructional sensitivity, the reporting of students' status on each curricular aim can transform an instructionally sensitive test into one that is also instructionally supportive.

The number of items necessary to arrive at a reasonably accurate estimate of a student's mastery of a particular assessed skill or body of knowledge depends, of course, on the curricular aim being measured. Broad curricular aims require more items than do narrower ones. Thus the number of items on a given test might vary for the different curricular aims to be measured. Panelists need to make their ratings on this evaluative dimension by reviewing the general pattern of a test's distribution of items per assessed curricular aim after taking into consideration the particular outcomes being assessed.

The rubric to appraise this evaluative dimension should take into account the number and representativeness of the sets of items being used. Panelists would first be asked to review any materials describing what the test is supposed to measure, then consider the degree to which a designated collection of items satisfactorily provides an estimate of a test-taker's achievement. High ratings would reflect both excellent content representativeness and sufficient numbers of items. In other words, to get a high rating on this evaluative dimension, there would need to be enough items to assess a given skill or body of knowledge, and those items would need to satisfactorily sample the key components of the skill or knowledge being measured. Low ratings would be based on too few items, insufficient representativeness of the items, or both.

ITEM SENSITIVITY

The fourth and final evaluative dimension is the degree to which the items on the test are judged to be sensitive to instructional impact. The panelists must either be able to render judgments themselves on a substantial number of actual items from the test or have access to item-by-item judgments rendered by others. In either scenario, the item reviewers must make judgments, one item at a time, about a sufficiently large number of actual items so that a defensible conclusion can be drawn about the instructional sensitivity of a test. Sometimes, because of test-security considerations, these judgments may be made in controlled situations by individuals other than the regular panelists. Ideally, the panelists would personally review a test's items one at a time.

There are three aspects of this evaluative dimension that, in concert, can allow panelists to arrive at a rating of a test's item sensitivity. First, three separate judgments need to be rendered about each item. These judgments might take the form of Yes, No, or Not Sure and would be made in response to three questions:

1. *SES influence.* Would a student's likelihood of responding correctly to this item be determined mostly by the socioeconomic status of the student's family?
2. *Inherited academic aptitudes.* Would a student's likelihood of responding correctly to this item be determined mostly by the student's innate verbal, quantitative, or spatial aptitudes?
3. *Responsiveness to instruction.* If a teacher has provided reasonably effective instruction related to what is measured by this item, is it likely that a substantial majority of the teacher's students will respond correctly to the item?

An instructionally sensitive item should receive a flock of No responses for the first two questions and a great many Yes responses for the third question. For each item, then, the reviewers' judgments indicating the degree to which the item is instructionally sensitive would be reported on all three of these questions. Then the panel would use the per-item data to arrive at a judgment on the test as a whole.

It should be noted that many current accountability tests, especially those constructed along traditional psychometric lines, contain numerous items closely linked to students' SES or to their inherited academic aptitudes. This occurs because the mission of traditional achievement tests is to permit comparisons among test-takers' scores. In order for those comparisons to work properly, however, there must be a reasonable degree of score spread in students' tests scores. That is, students' test results must be meaningfully different so that fine-grained contrasts between test-takers are possible. Because students' SES and inherited academic aptitudes are both widely dispersed variables, and ones that do not change rapidly, test items linked to either of these variables efficiently spread out students' test scores. Accordingly, builders of traditional achievement tests often end up putting a considerable number of such items into their tests, including those tests used for accountability purposes.

To the extent that accountability tests measure what students bring to school rather than what they are taught there, the tests will be less sensitive to instruction. It is true, of course, that SES and inherited academic aptitudes are themselves substantially interrelated. However, by asking panelists to recognize that either of those variables, if pervasively present in an accountability test, will contaminate the test's ability to gauge instructional quality, we have a reasonable chance to isolate the magnitude of such contaminants.

INSTRUCTIONAL SENSITIVITY REVIEWS

The vast majority of today's educational accountability tests are fundamentally insensitive to instructional quality. If these tests cannot indicate whether students' scores are affected by the quality of a teacher's instruction, then they prevent well-intentioned accountability programs from accomplishing what their architects had hoped. If educators find that the quality of their instructional efforts is being determined by students' scores on accountability tests that are inherently incapable of detecting effective instruction, they should take steps to review the tests' instructional sensitivity. The judgmental procedures set forth here provide the framework for a practical process for carrying out such a review.

If the review of an accountability test reveals it to be substantially sensitive to instruction, then it is likely that other test-influenced elements of the accountability program are acceptable. However, if a review indicates that an accountability program's tests are instructionally insensitive, then two courses of action seem warranted. First, there should be a serious attempt made to replace the instructionally insensitive tests with those that are sensitive to instruction. If that replacement effort fails, it is imperative to inform the public, and especially education policy makers, that the accountability tests being used are unable to detect successful instruction even if it is present. In that case it is particularly important to involve noneducators as review panelists so that the public does not see the instructional sensitivity review as the educators' attempt to escape accountability. Parents and members of the business community can be readily trained to function effectively as members of an instructional sensitivity panel.

An evaluation of the instructional sensitivity of the nation's accountability tests is long overdue. We must discover whether the key data-gathering tools of the accountability movement have been claiming to do something they simply cannot pull off.

DISCUSSION QUESTIONS

1. With the emphasis on high-stakes testing, how important is it to determine the instructional sensitivity of an assessment?
2. How important is it that teachers be involved in the evaluation of assessments? Explain.
3. If a test is determined to be instructionally insensitive, what should the course of action be?
4. Can the four dimensions of evaluation be modified to examine classroom-made tests and assessments? Explain how evaluation of teacher-made assessments might look.
5. Do you agree with the author about the importance of including noneducators in the evaluation process? Explain.

29 Diagnosing School Decline

Daniel L. Duke

FOCUSING QUESTIONS

1. What are some signs that a school is in decline?
2. What factors lead to school decline?
3. How can school decline be counteracted?
4. How is a school in decline different from a chronically low-performing school?
5. What is the purpose in identifying schools that are in decline?

When we run a fever, we suspect that something is wrong with our bodies—a virus perhaps or a bacterial infection. The elevated temperature is a symptom of a deeper problem, though left untreated it can become a cause for additional problems. Such is the case with scores on standardized tests. If test scores start to drop, that may be an indication of deeper problems. Left unaddressed, declining test scores can become the cause of other problems, both for individual students and for entire schools.

Researchers know a great deal about how to improve schools, but they have spent less time trying to understand what causes schools to decline in the first place.[1] One probable reason for the scarcity of research is the reluctance of declining schools to place themselves under the microscope. Here I argue that knowing the possible causes of school decline, especially an initial drop in performance, is critical for educators who want to intervene early. Failing to nip student achievement problems in the bud can set into motion a dangerous downward spiral in which every downturn triggers new problems and accelerates the school's rate of decline.[2]

Of course, some low-performing schools do not experience decline, because they have never performed well. My focus here is on schools that once were characterized by adequate or even good performance but have begun to slip. A number of these schools have participated over the past four years in the University of Virginia's School Turnaround Specialist Program (STSP). This unique outreach program combines the talents of experienced educators and faculty members from the Curry School of Education and the Darden Graduate School of Business Administration. The goal is to train principals to be school turnaround specialists and to support them in their efforts to reverse a downward trend in school performance.

As research director for the STSP, I have spent the past four years working with a team of researchers to understand the circumstances that confront these school turnaround specialists and to discover how they deal with them. This knowledge, combined with what we know from previous investigations of school decline, has led us to identify a number of potential indicators of school decline. By attending to these indicators when they first surface, educators are more likely to prevent a school from slipping into a self-perpetuating downward spiral.

The approach I take here may best be characterized as a challenge-and-response analysis. Schools face challenges from time to time. Among the challenges associated with school decline, I want to focus on four that are common: serious budget cuts, new state and federal mandates, the loss of key personnel, and an influx of at-risk students.[3] Strictly speaking, these challenges do not cause schools to decline, but decline is a consequence of failing to address these challenges effectively. In medicine, specialists in iatrogenic medicine study medical problems created or exacerbated by improper medical practice. Education needs an equivalent enterprise devoted to examining the academic problems created or exacerbated by inadequate educational practice.

Problems in addressing challenges can be found at the levels of the individual, the group, and the school. Individual teachers may fail to recognize when particular students need help, or they may prescribe a "treatment" that actually makes matters worse. Groups of educators may invest more energy in diverting blame for low performance than in correcting problems, thereby delaying much-needed reforms. School leaders may fail to recognize systemic issues that undermine a school's ability to raise achievement. In some cases, these failures are ones of omission. Nothing is done to address a challenge. In other cases, the problem is a failure of commission. Actions are taken, but they are inadequate or inappropriate.

Here I want to identify 11 early indicators of school decline that are associated with inadequate and inappropriate responses to the aforementioned quartet of challenges.[4] I should note that these challenges sometimes travel in packs. New mandates, for example, may cause some veteran educators to retire or seek other employment. An influx of at-risk students without an increase in funding may have the effect of reducing resources.

Undifferentiated assistance. One indicator of school decline is the absence of systematic efforts to identify the learning problems and knowledge deficits of struggling students who have not been placed on an IEP (individualized education program). Instead of providing assistance that targets each student's specific issues, the school assigns all students judged to be in academic difficulty to a common supplementary program or intervention. Help takes the form of repetition and extended practice. Some students, however, may require assistance that targets particular learning problems, such as problems with decoding, comprehension, sequencing, and information processing. Repetition and extended practice are of little benefit to these students.

Another problem with generic interventions is that students may be compelled to cover material that they already understand, as well as material that they do not understand. Valuable time is wasted, and the risk of students' becoming bored increases. Furthermore, if students receive assistance at the same time that their classmates are moving ahead in the curriculum, the initial problem is compounded because the struggling students fall further behind.

Inadequate monitoring of progress. One reason why assistance may be undifferentiated is the absence of efforts to systematically monitor student progress in learning required content. All states, in order to comply with their own accountability mandates as well as the federal No Child Left Behind (NCLB) Act, test students annually on state curriculum standards. Teachers are provided with pacing guides in many school systems to ensure that they cover all of the curriculum requirements for which their students are responsible. In an effort to cover this content, however, some teachers feel that they cannot take time to carefully assess student progress on a regular basis. As a consequence, students may go weeks or even months without grasping key concepts and skills. In certain subjects, such as mathematics, the results can be disastrous.

Schools that have successfully combated decline often discover efficient ways to monitor student progress and provide differentiated assistance. Training in classroom assessment and the use of periodic benchmark testing aligned to state curriculum standards enable teachers to spot student deficits and provide timely and targeted assistance. Waiting until students take end-of-year standardized tests to identify learning deficits is a sure prescription for performance problems.

Unadjusted daily schedule. Another reason that students may not receive timely and targeted assistance is the inflexibility of the daily school schedule. In order to address content-related problems and skill deficits, teachers need to work with students during times other than regular class periods. It is typically of little value for students to receive help while their classmates are moving forward with new material. Low-performing schools that have turned around often modify the daily schedule in ways that provide struggling students with extended learning time. Sometimes these schools offer double-block classes in core subjects like language arts and mathematics so that low-achieving students can receive an additional period of instruction during the regular school day. In other cases, the school day is lengthened on certain days to provide students who need help with supplementary instruction.

A modified schedule also makes it possible for teachers working as a team to meet during the regular school day. Meetings allow for collaborative planning, curriculum alignment, professional development, and discussions of students experiencing problems. Schedules that do not facilitate teacher collaboration increase the likelihood of communication and coordination problems, thereby contributing to school decline.

Alignment problems. In the wake of pressure for greater accountability, states have adopted curriculum standards and standardized tests based on these standards. Students stand the best chance of mastering the standards and performing well on the state tests when their teachers align class content with state standards and tests. A decline in student achievement may reflect the fact that teachers are neglecting required content.

One indicator of instructional neglect can be found in an analysis of student answers on standardized tests. Results on state tests often can be broken down by specific curriculum standards. When student errors are randomly distributed, the problem may be traceable to variations in how individual students prepared for the tests. When lots of students miss the same questions, however, the fault probably lies with alignment problems and teachers' failure to cover or adequately explain certain subject matter.

Alignment is not just a matter of individual teachers making adjustments in content to reflect curriculum standards. Teachers at the same grade level, as well as across grade levels, need to review their content to make certain that (1) students at the same grade level are exposed to the mandated curriculum and (2) students at one grade level learn the content necessary to succeed at the next grade level. When teachers do not meet on a regular basis to review their coverage of curriculum standards and analyze student progress, the prospects for school decline increase.

Ineffective staff development. Some form of staff development is available to teachers in practically every school, but the mere availability of such training is no guarantee of instructional effectiveness. Schools that begin to decline are frequently the recipients of one-shot inservice programs and staff development that is only tangentially related to core academic concerns. When teachers complain about irrelevant workshops and useless staff development, school leaders need to take heed.

The most worthwhile staff development opportunities are often associated with a sustained focus on a key aspect of the required curriculum, such as literacy. Teachers benefit from learning how to use a new textbook, refine classroom assessment skills, improve classroom management, and detect learning problems. Using the same consultant or trainer over an extended period can provide continuity and avoid the confusion and mixed messages that often attend sporadic staff development involving multiple providers.

Lost focus. One of the first signs of school decline may be the loss of a clear academic focus. Discussions with school personnel may reveal a lack of clarity regarding priorities. If everything seems to be a priority, the concentration of time and resources on critical elements of the school program is apt to be inadequate. Lack of focus makes it difficult to provide effective staff development and targeted assistance for struggling students.

While it may be "politically correct" in public schools to act as if all subject matter and all aspects of schooling were of equal importance, the hard, cold fact is that some subjects and teaching functions are more important than others when dealing with a drop in student achievement. When we studied declining schools that participated in our program at the University of Virginia, we discovered that every school had substantial numbers of students with reading problems. Improving instruction and assistance in reading needed to be a top priority in these

schools. Students' success in every other subject, including mathematics, depended on their ability to read and comprehend written material. To have chosen any focus other than reading and literacy would have made little sense.

Another focus in many low-performing schools must be student attendance. It is difficult for students to master essential content when they are not in school. The lack of a well-coordinated initiative to address student absenteeism can be another early indicator of school decline.

Lack of leadership. Leadership is synonymous with focus and direction.[5] Leaders are expected to see that priorities are identified and addressed. More than just a set of skills or traits, leadership is a perception, a perception that one or more individuals grasp what must be done in order to achieve the mission at hand.[6] The first individual to whom people look for leadership in schools is the principal. Key members of school faculties can also play important leadership roles.

Not surprisingly, declining schools frequently are characterized by a lack of leadership. An effective principal or veteran teacher may have retired or been reassigned. The replacement is not perceived to have the competence, commitment, or clarity of purpose of the one who departed. Teachers begin to feel adrift without a rudder. Where once there was a shared understanding of what needed to be done, now there is disagreement. Confusion displaces consensus.

The critical role of leadership in arresting school decline was driven home to me last year when my colleagues and I searched for examples of low-performing schools where teachers took the initiative and spontaneously organized themselves to turn their school around. We combed the literature on school turnarounds and even placed an advertisement in *Education Week*. We were unable to locate a single example. It would seem that there is no substitute for capable leaders when it comes to reversing a downward slide in performance.

Hasty hiring. One aspect of the school turnaround process where capable leaders make their impact felt is hiring. Many of our most successful turnaround specialists had to replace staff members during their first year or two. In some cases, individuals left of their own accord. In other instances, principals had to document deficiencies and initiate an employment termination process. When it came to new hires, however, our principals did not panic, nor did they settle for questionable replacements.

It is tempting for principals in declining schools to approach the hiring process fatalistically. They assume that highly qualified educators are unlikely to want to work in a troubled school. Consequently, they rush to judgment and select individuals about whom they have reservations. Declining schools need top-notch teachers if they are to combat falling test scores. Settling for "warm bodies" is likely to compound rather than resolve academic problems. Successful turnaround specialists find that retaining a long-term substitute and continuing to search for a qualified teacher is preferable to hiring someone who is unlikely to make a positive impact on student achievement.

Increased class size. Even highly qualified teachers may have difficulty when class sizes are allowed to increase to the point where it is difficult to maintain order and provide targeted assistance. Large classes are especially problematic when the classes involve critical academic subjects such as reading, language arts, and mathematics. Some states and school systems have mandated maximum class sizes for early elementary grades, clearly a step in the right direction. Few states and school systems, however, have taken similar action with regard to middle and high school courses that enroll large percentages of at-risk students.

A declining school is apt to lose some students as parents take advantage of the provisions in NCLB that permit transfers from a low-performing school. Quite often the students who are withdrawn from these schools are high-achieving students, not the struggling students who presumably would most benefit from a change. As a result, the proportion of low-achieving students may climb in a declining school. If this occurs, it is especially important for class sizes to remain as low as possible.

Overreliance on untrained helpers. No declining school wants to be caught without programs to help struggling students. Simply offering assistance programs, however, is no guarantee of success, especially when these programs rely heavily on volunteers, teacher aides, and other individuals who may lack the expertise to recognize learning problems and provide effective help.

Schools that have successfully turned around tend to place the responsibility for assisting struggling students into the hands of qualified teachers and specialists. Supplementary programs are evaluated regularly to determine whether they are making a difference in academic achievement. Ineffective programs are either improved or eliminated.

More rules and harsher punishments. Decreases in student achievement often are accompanied by increases in student behavior problems. Such problems rob struggling students of precious instructional time as teachers are compelled to devote more energy to maintaining order and dealing with discipline. Confronted with rising behavior problems, declining schools often rely on promulgating more rules and harsher punishments. This prescription can backfire. Teachers may find themselves devoting even more time to enforcing rules and monitoring punishments. Less time is available for instruction, assistance, and building relationships with students. Meanwhile, students chafe under greater restrictions and a more punitive climate. Some rules and punishments may be necessary, but they are no substitute for caring and concern.

FOREWARNED IS FOREARMED

The purpose of identifying characteristics of declining schools is to give educators some tangible indicators for which to be on the alert. Early intervention can prevent a precipitous slide. Many of the schools in the School Turnaround Specialist Program have experienced the benefits of early intervention. A major reason for their success is the fact that principals recognized the initial signs of decline. They also understood what needed to be done to address these concerns.

Of course, the 11 indicators I've identified here do not constitute an exhaustive list. There are no doubt a number of more subtle indicators of decline, including certain shared beliefs and aspects of school culture. For example, I suspect that teachers in declining schools are more likely to give up on struggling students and less likely to hold themselves to high standards of professional practice. These 11 indicators should be regarded as no more than a starting place for diagnosing school decline. Educators can refine and expand this list so that improvements can be made in the early detection and reversal of school decline.

ENDNOTES

1. Daniel L. Duke, "Understanding School Decline," unpublished manuscript, Partnership for Leaders in Education, Charlottesville, Virginia, 2007; and idem, "What We Know and Don't Know About Improving Low-Performing Schools," *Phi Delta Kappan*, June 2006, pp. 729–34.
2. Daniel L. Duke and Jon S. Cohen, "Do Public Schools Have a Future? A Case Study of Retrenchment and Its Implications," *The Urban Review*, vol. 15, 1983, pp. 89–105.
3. Duke, "Understanding School Decline."
4. The research from which the indicators of school decline are drawn includes the following: Daniel L. Duke, "Keys to Sustaining Successful School Turnarounds," *ERS Spectrum*, Fall 2006, pp. 21–35; idem, "Understanding School Decline"; Daniel L. Duke et al., *Liftoff: Launching the School Turnaround Process in 10 Virginia Schools* (Charlottesville, Va.: Partnership for Leaders in Education, 2005); and Daniel L. Duke et al., "How Comparable Are the Perceived Challenges Facing Principals of Low-Performing Schools?," *International Studies in Educational Administration*, vol. 35, no. 1, 2007, pp. 3–21.
5. Michael Fullan, *Leading in a Culture of Change* (San Francisco: Jossey-Bass, 2001).
6. Daniel L. Duke, "The Aesthetics of Leadership," *Educational Administration Quarterly*, Winter 1986, pp. 7–27.

DISCUSSION QUESTIONS

1. What role can teachers play in identifying and combating school decline?
2. Is it possible to turn around a school without the strong leadership of a principal? Explain.
3. The author identifies ineffective staff development as a factor contributing to school decline. What type of staff development do you find beneficial? How should it be delivered effectively?
4. According to Duke, behavior issues often accompany declines in school performance and this hampers effective instruction. How should behavior issues be addressed?
5. The author identifies a variety of factors in diagnosing school decline. Which factor do you believe is the most influential in leading to school decline? Explain.
6. Should the approaches to improve a declining school and a chronically low performing school be the same? Explain.

Should the person who helps teachers improve instruction also evaluate their performance?

PRO	CON
1. The threat of evaluation can stimulate reluctant teachers to improve.	1. Supervision requires an environment where new skills can be safely practiced without threat.
2. Evaluation is simply the final step in an extended period of formative supervisory feedback.	2. Supervision and evaluation, like formative and summative assessment, are entirely separate categories of thought and practice.
3. Trust and honesty are built by people working closely together over a long period of time.	3. The threat of evaluation irrevocably eliminates trust and makes open communication impossible.
4. The relationship between supervisor and teacher is very similar to the relationship between teacher and student.	4. Supervisors should always treat teachers as professional colleagues, not as subordinates who know less than they do.
5. The person who has been working with a teacher all year long is best qualified to make a judgment about whether the teacher's employment should continue.	5. The person who has been working with a teacher all year long in a helping relationship cannot be relied on to provide an objective judgment of performance.

CASE STUDY 5

A Principal Works for Inclusion

Imagine you are the principal at Northmore High School, in a small, rural town. Northmore's surrounding population is fairly homogenous, as is the student body. The school counselor has approached you concerning a number of students who are mildly handicapped or have special needs and who have recently become targets of unwelcoming comments in the hallways and schoolyard. The comments come from a specific group of students who participate on various athletic teams.

It is a basic concern of yours that all students feel welcome at the school and do not have to be subjected to behavior or remarks that make them uncomfortable.

1. Do you approach the teachers first and discuss how to deal with the issue in the classroom?

2. How should the teachers approach the subject in the classroom to establish a healthy relationship among all students?

3. What programs can you present in the school to make the environment more accepting: clubs, peer and outside discussion groups, films, classroom discussions, parent-teacher conferences, guest speakers, and so on?

4. Is it better to work with outside groups to provide a forum for discussion that puts the issue in a larger community or national context? To what extent should the issue be put in a larger sociological perspective, and to what extent should it be dealt with locally?

5. Should the coaches of the respective athletic teams be notified so that they can announce that they will suspend the athletes or limit playing time if there is another occurrence?

6. Is it better to inform parents in writing about their children's misbehavior and warn them that another incident could lead to suspension or worse?

7. To what extent, if at all, should the school district's attorney be consulted? Are the incidents a legal matter?

Curriculum and Policy

In Part Six, the relationship between policy and curriculum is considered. What are the implications of current demographic trends for curriculum? How are issues of diversity globalization, educational equity, and practice-based assessment influencing the curriculum? Do academic standards help or hinder the pursuit of equitable student learning outcomes? How are school reform and restructuring efforts affecting the curriculum, and what policy alternatives are available?

In Chapter 30, Allan Odden calls for strategically managing the human resource system in schools as a way of managing them toward supporting the strategic directions of the organization. Aligning management practices with a district's overall improvement strategy, instructional program, and goals for improving student achievement, he suggests, will help a school attract, develop, and retain talented people. In Chapter 31, Andy Hargreaves and Dennis Shirley examine the educational policies of Finland, England, Canada, and the grassroots movement in the United States. Through their examination they identify principles of improvement required for educational policy reform.

In Chapter 32, Carl Glickman argues that single models, structures, methods, and systems of education should be avoided. A diversity of approaches is preferable, he contends, as long as every school and district is held responsible for providing an education for all students that increases their choices for exercising their rights to life, liberty, and the pursuit of happiness. In Chapter 33, Linda Darling-Hammond and Laura McCloskey compare the curricula and assessment methods of the United States and other internationally competitive countries. In countries such as Finland, teachers play an active role in assessment development and local assessments are used to inform and influence the national standards. Other high-performing countries use portfolio-based assessments and school-based tasks rather than the standardized tests the United States uses under No Child Left Behind.

In Chapter 34, Larry Cuban describes how the public's goals for education have structured school time in this country. Additionally, Cuban identifies proposals put forth over the past quarter century to extend school time and factors that have prevented the success of extended school time reform. He also examines how the belief that college is for all has affected policymakers' attitudes towards school time. Finally, in Chapter 35, Allan Ornstein examines how the purposes of education have changed during the course of American history, especially in light of sometimes competing values like excellence and equality. Reviewing current economic, policy, and social trends that seem to signal growing inequality in American society, he challenges educators to ask whether and how schools can ensure excellence while equalizing differences.

30 Manage "Human Capital" Strategically

ALLAN ODDEN

FOCUSING QUESTIONS

1. Why do we need to strategically manage human capital in education?
2. Describe the two major ingredients to educate all children effectively.
3. Describe the steps needed to strategically managing human capital.
4. What are the benefits of organizing teacher work in collaborative teams?
5. Describe some of the core ideas behind the strategic management of human capital.

Education is a people-intensive proposition. By most estimates, 85 percent of school and district budgets are devoted to salaries and benefits, a figure that means that the manner in which leaders identify and develop their most important asset determines to a great degree the success of the enterprise. That figure also means that cutting school and district budgets significantly without reducing employees or their compensation is next to impossible.

In the awkward argot of policy and research, what was once known as "human resource management" has become "strategic management of human capital." That phrasing may sound a bit cumbersome, but it neatly captures the new thinking about the strategic role that managing educator talent plays in a district's success. When school and district leaders understand the potential for such strategic management, human resources will no longer be relegated to a back-bench position.

Strategically managing human capital in education is about restructuring the entire human resource system. That means that recruitment, selection, distribution, induction, professional development, performance management and evaluation, compensation, and career progression are all restructured to boost teacher and principal effectiveness in ways that dramatically improve instructional practice and student learning.

In order to accomplish current education goals to educate all children, and especially low-income and minority children, to world-class performance standards, schools need talented and well-prepared teachers and leaders. But the current system doesn't recruit, train, hire, induct, deploy, develop, retain, or strategically manage the top talent needed to accomplish these goals. These shortcomings are most acute in the largest urban districts and in many rural districts. The worst problems include the following:

- Lack of a comprehensive and strategic human resource management system;
- Historic inability to recruit the best and brightest into education;
- Difficulty staffing high-needs schools, too many of which have excess numbers of unqualified and ineffective teachers and principals;
- Chronic shortages of teachers in such subjects as math, science, and technology;
- High teacher turnover;
- Professional development systems that spend lots of money with little effect on teaching practice or student achievement; and
- Compensation systems that pay teachers for factors unrelated or weakly related to effective instruction or gains in student learning.

No system with these severe and systemic dysfunctions can hope to dramatically improve its performance.

Schools need two key ingredients. The first is talented people. All school systems need smart and capable people at all levels. However, poor urban and rural districts have been on the short end of the educator talent stick for decades. They suffer the most talent shortages and are most in need of strategic talent management. Thus one of their prime emphases should be creating strategies to recruit, place, develop, and retain top talent.

The second ingredient is strategic management of that talent. Just finding talented people and turning them loose is not sufficient. As businesses and other organizations have learned over the past decades, the highest performing organizations not only recruit and retain smart and capable individuals, they also manage them in ways that support the organization's strategic direction. This requires aligning all aspects of the human resource management system (much more than just the personnel or human resource office) around

multiple measures of teaching effectiveness. The goal is to redesign the entire human capital management system so that effective teacher talent is acquired, placed strategically and distributed equitably in schools and districts, developed to the district's vision of instructional effectiveness and student performance, and retained over time.

Strategic talent management has two outcomes that allow educators to measure progress: student performance and teaching performance. Though the country has significant expertise in how to test students, measuring teaching performance and effectiveness and using the measures as a management tool are only at the beginning stages. If one objective of strategically managing human capital in education is to produce better classroom instruction, then related objectives are to create and use valid ways to measure teaching effectiveness and to redesign human capital management systems to ensure that all teachers are providing the most effective instruction. Furthermore, the measured elements of instructional practice must be statistically linked to improvements in student performance to indicate what effective teachers must do to boost student achievement.

In 2008, a set of district and state leaders came together as the Strategic Management of Human Capital (SMHC) Task Force to discuss the shortcomings of human capital management in public education and to further a reform agenda. This task force developed a set of principles for the strategic management of human capital in public education as well as reform proposals to seriously address human capital in education (see www.smhc-cpre.org). These proposals were bolstered by the teacher and principal effectiveness initiatives of the Obama administration's Race to the Top program.

THE NEED FOR STRATEGIC MANAGEMENT

If they are to be strategic, human capital management practices must align with a district's education improvement strategy and its view of effective instructional practice as well as its goals for student achievement. But districts can't implement a powerful improvement strategy unless they have both the management and teaching talent to execute the complex actions such comprehensive strategies require. Conversely, administrators can't improve student academic achievement just with talented people, high expectations, and random acts of good practice. Administrators must systemically manage top talent around a well-designed education improvement strategy, including effective instructional practice, if they're to be effective.

This view of strategic management draws from emerging approaches to talent management in the private sector. Current thinking in that sector emphasizes the importance of (1) organizational strategy as a basis for a human capital management program design and (2) the strategic management of human capital in carrying out organizational strategies to improve performance. During the past 15 years, many organizations concluded that people, talent, and human capital need to be placed on strategic agendas. These organizations found that strategic human resource management strategies should be formally linked vertically to their organization's improvement programs and linked horizontally across all the specific HR elements. Many analyses have shown empirical links between these kinds of aligned human capital management practices and improved organizational performance.

Developing a strategic approach to managing human capital starts from understanding the need to dramatically improve organizational performance, specifically student achievement. Figure 30-1 depicts how the strategic management of human capital is linked vertically to the district's education improvement strategy.

The starting point for making the complex and politically charged human capital management changes is to understand that organizational performance—student achievement—needs to be increased by considerable levels. Once an understanding is reached that very substantial improvements in student performance are needed, districts need to figure out how to do it, that is, how to create their education improvement strategy. And central to an effective improvement strategy is an explicit and well-articulated vision of effective instructional practice. Furthermore, to make the human resource management system strategic, the instructional vision must drive the organization's human resource programs. For example, one study of the use of HR metrics, including special metrics developed on instructional practice, found that centralized professional development was more effective than site-based professional development and that consistency of effective instructional practice across classrooms within schools produced higher levels of student performance.

The next step is to identify the key staff who will carry out that strategy. The key district roles include the superintendent, chief academic officer, chief talent officer, the HR office, data and accountability, and the office of professional development. The key roles at the school level are the core content teachers, teacher leaders, and principals. These are key because instruction happens in classrooms and in schools. Teachers have multiple instructional leadership roles, such as grade-level leaders, coordinator of multi-grade teacher teams, school-wide instructional coaches, instructional facilitators, professional development leaders, curriculum team coordinators, mentors, and so on. Principal roles can include lead principal, assistant principal for curriculum and instruction, and others. Principals also are the lead managers of human capital at the site.

After the primary roles are identified, the next step is identifying the key competencies

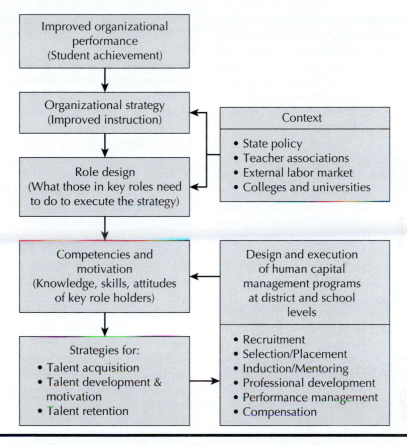

FIGURE 30.1   How Performance Goals Determine Strategic Human Capital Management Program Designs

for each key role. For example, each teacher clearly would need the core competency of instructional expertise. In addition, schools want teachers' expertise to increase over time. An explicit instructional vision can be important for delineating the range of necessary expertise, and a set of rubrics can indicate the level of performance of each individual teacher and how that aligns with the instructional vision. In addition to content-rich instructional expertise, each teacher leadership role would also have a set of required competencies specific to that role.

It should be clear that the description of teacher leadership roles overlaps the instruc-tional leadership roles of the principal or assistant principal, thus providing a potential career ladder for teachers and a leadership development pathway through which schools "grow" school and district leaders over time.

Once the key teacher and principal roles are identified—together with their requisite knowledge, skills and expertise, and competencies—the next step in strategically managing human capital is to identify strategies for acquiring, developing, and retaining talent with these competencies. These strategies will guide the development of the specific human resource management programs, including recruitment, selection, placement, induction, development, career progression, and compensation, as well as such key decisions as tenure and dismissal. Designing, implementing, and staying true to new approaches to teacher and principal human capital development requires a huge change in the normal operation of school systems.

Three examples help illuminate these changes. First, many urban districts are discovering that by partnering with the two national talent recruiting organizations—Teach for America and The New Teacher Project—they can recruit large numbers of the country's best and brightest into schools, particularly high-poverty schools, that have been starved for top talent. These new teachers have a substantial positive effect on student learning.

Second, the best way to organize teacher work is in collaborative teams working with formative student data to plan instruction and assessment strategies that are part of curriculum units. This way of organizing teachers' work is the most effective context for teacher development. New teachers immediately have access to curriculum units, lesson plans, and the thinking of senior teachers as they discuss current formative assessment data and its implications for changes in instruction, and ongoing development can focus on the needs and directions of collaborative teacher teams. However, few schools currently organize teachers this way, though more such teams are formed each year. It will take several years—and changes in how teachers view "plan time"—for this way of organizing teachers' work to dominate the education system.

A third example is the shift to develop multiple measures of teacher effectiveness and to use the results to promote, pay, dismiss, and grant tenure to teachers. Many critics have seen these elements of the education system as almost impossible to change, yet states and districts are taking them on, reinforced by both Race to the Top and foundation support.

A good example of foundation support is the empowering effective teachers strategies suggested by the Bill & Melinda Gates Foundation. There are plans to implement these strategies in the Gates Intensive Partnership Sites: Hillsborough, Florida; Memphis, Tennessee; Pittsburgh, Pennsylvania; and a charter school consortium in Los Angeles. These systems have agreed to develop multiple measures of teaching effectiveness—ranging from measures of instructional practice to tests of teacher pedagogical content knowledge to value-added measures of effect on student achievement—and to use them in teacher recruitment, the equitable distribution of effective teachers, redesigned teacher tenure, focused professional development, new forms of performance-based teacher compensation, and teacher dismissal. Washington, DC, is probably the leading urban school district implementing these powerful efforts to assess teaching effectiveness and using the results to strategically manage teacher talent—and the district's increases in student performance show that the strategies work. This represents "radical" and, as the Washington, DC, example shows, controversial change in the "personnel administration" and human resource management of schools as we know them.

SCHOOL LEADERS

The strategic management of human capital is a distributed responsibility, extending beyond the district human resource department and its formal programs of recruitment, evaluation, and compensation. The key leader of the district, of course, is the superintendent. This person must place a high value on organizational improvement and all that flows from it: commitment to a vision of how to improve instructional practice and an insistence that all elements of the human capital management system be aligned with that vision. Many organizations that are talent-centric also have a chief talent officer whose prime role is to orchestrate the system's effort to recruit, develop, motivate, compensate, and retain its effective talent.

But the "street-level" human capital managers in education are mostly school principals. School leaders are responsible for interviewing, selecting, evaluating, and providing feedback to teachers and teacher leaders and for overseeing these functions.

CONCLUSION

One underlying concept of strategic talent management is that for each key strategic job in the system—primarily those of teacher, teacher leader, and principal—strategic human capital management means structuring the HR system around the knowledge, skills, and desired effects those jobs require, and thus horizontally aligning each individual program element of the HR system. Herbert Heneman and Anthony Milanowski (2007) have developed a process and a tool that districts can use to determine the degree to which each of the human resource management program elements is currently aligned around the key competencies for teachers.

Strategic management of human capital includes the following core ideas:

1. The strategic needs for acquiring, developing, and retaining talent should flow from the education system's improvement strategy, which usually includes an explicit vision of effective instructional practice and identifies the key people needed to implement the improvement strategy.
2. The strategic management of human capital begins with aggressive and comprehensive strategies to recruit—from whatever talent channel—top teaching and leadership talent into schools and districts. This is especially true for poor urban and rural districts because their

challenges are the toughest in the country and deserve the best talent to address them successfully.
3. Teacher talent needs to be professionally managed to produce in classrooms and schools the content-rich, effective instructional practices that boost student learning to high levels.
4. To produce these effective instructional practices, improve them over time, and achieve the desired gains in student learning, the system needs to horizontally align all the key pieces of the HR system—recruitment, selection, staffing, induction/mentoring, professional development, performance management/evaluation, and compensation—to multiple measures of teaching effectiveness. Similarly, for other key staff, the HR pieces and related measures of effectiveness need to be designed around the knowledge, skills, and expertise that teacher leaders, principals, and other key district leaders need to successfully execute their roles in the improvement strategy.
5. In the process of designing and implementing both the improvement strategy and the human capital management program, the education system should produce a professional school culture that is characterized by high expectations for student achievement, a common vision of effective instruction, and accountability for student performance results.

If all of the elements of strategic human capital management work as intended, the district and each school should have sufficient quantities and quality of talent, and instructional practice should continuously improve, students should be able to attain ever higher levels of academic achievement, and districts should be able to significantly reduce the large achievement gaps linked to poverty and race that exist across America's schools.

REFERENCES

Heneman, H. G., III., & Milanowski, A. T. (2007). *Assessing human resource alignment: The foundation for building total teacher quality improvement.* Madison, WI: University of Wisconsin, Wisconsin Center for Education Research, Consortium for Policy Research in Education.

Odden, A. (2011). *Strategic management of human capital in education.* New York, NY: Routledge.

DISCUSSION QUESTIONS

1. How much input should talented teachers have about where they are being placed?
2. Why is managing educator talent critical to improving student learning?
3. What are some potential challenges for administrators and districts in managing teacher talent?
4. How important is it to have a "chief talent officer" as a key leader in a district? Explain.

Beyond Standardization: Powerful New Principles for Improvement

ANDY HARGREAVES
DENNIS SHIRLEY

FOCUSING QUESTIONS

1. Explain the integration between education and economic policy in Finland.

2. How has Ontario, Canada, reformed its highly standardized educational system?

3. Describe the successes and limitations of the networking program undertaken in England.

4. What types of grassroots programs are influencing education reform in the United States?

5. Describe the principles of improvement that emerge from examining the educational policies of Finland, Canada, and England in addition to the grassroots movement in the United States.

A new phase of reforms promises to move us past standards and accountability and into an era that allows greater creativity, flexibility, inclusiveness, and inspiration.

We are entering an age of post-standardization. Improvement in terms of tested achievement has reached a plateau. The curriculum is shrinking, classroom creativity is disappearing, and dropout rates are frozen. Top-down prescriptions without support and encouragement at the grassroots and local level are exhausted. If you find that you are in the midst of another grueling year of trying to meet Adequate Yearly Progress (AYP) targets, if you dread teaching the standardized literacy program that your district has adopted, and if your classroom coaches and mentors have turned into curriculum compliance officers, then "post-standardization" might sound like more academic argot coined by ivory-tower intellectuals. But hold on! Especially when we look beyond the American context, signs are emerging that the era of market competitiveness between schools in delivering standardized curriculum and teaching practices is on its last legs.

High-stakes and high-pressure standardization, where short-term gains in measurable results have been demanded at any price, have turned many U.S. schools not into learning-enriched environments, but into enervating "Enrons of educational change."[1]

When policy makers turn up the heat; define reading, writing, and math as core subjects to be tested; and threaten to close struggling schools that can't make AYP and to disperse their pupils, educators respond—and with a vengeance! They slash social studies at the same time the country is internationally isolated; they skimp on science when there is unprecedented global competition for technological breakthroughs; and they decimate the arts, foreign languages, and physical education with the prospect that America's next generation will be uncouth, uncultured, and unfit.

And what has the United States gained from its obsession with raising test scores? Although more time has been spent on language arts and math since 2001, this has come at the cost of reducing time for such subjects as science, history, and the arts.[2] NAEP reading scores for fourth and eighth graders have remained flat for more than a decade. Math scores show more encouraging signs of progress, especially for pupils in the bottom 10th percentile, so here we have the proverbial silver lining in the dark clouds.[3] But U.S. teachers have suffered mightily through the nation's new policies, and they resent it. Only 15 percent indicate on surveys that the No Child Left Behind Act is improving local education,[4] indicating a loss of faith in the government's ability to galvanize the very people who care the most about educating this nation's children.

Confronted by data on the limits of existing strategies and challenged by the economic need for increased innovation and creativity, a new shift in education reform is upon us. This is already evident in recent developments in Finland, Canada, England, and the United States. Besides and beyond standardization, each of the alternatives outlined here contains different theories of action, of how and what to change, and carries different consequences—though all, to some degree, wed proposals for future change with traces and legacies from the past.

FINNISHING SCHOOLS

In January 2007, with colleagues Gabor Halasz and Beatriz Pont, one of us undertook an investigative inquiry for the Organisation for Economic Co-operation and Development (OECD) into the relationship between leadership and school improvement in one of the world's highest performing education systems and economies: Finland.

At the core of Finland's success and sustainability is its capacity to reconcile, harmonize, and integrate elements that have divided other developed economies and societies—a prosperous, high-performing economy and a decent, socially just society. While the knowledge economy has weakened the welfare state in many other societies, a strong welfare state is a central part of the Finnish narrative that supports and sustains a successful economy.

The contrast with Anglo-Saxon countries, where material wealth has been gained at the expense of increasing social division and also at the cost of children's well-being, could not be more striking. The United Kingdom and United States rank dead last and next to last, respectively, on the UNICEF 2007 survey on children's well-being, while Finland ranks near the top.[5]

The Finnish education system is at the center of this successful integration that, in less than half a century, has transformed Finland from a rural backwater into a high-tech economic powerhouse.[6] Respondents interviewed by the OECD team indicated that Finns are driven by a common and articulately expressed social vision that connects a creative and prosperous future to the people's sense of themselves as having a creative history and a common social identity.

Technological creativity and competitiveness connect the Finns to their past in a unitary narrative of lifelong learning and societal development. This occurs within a strong welfare state that supports education and the economy. Schooling is free as a universal right from well-funded early childhood education through higher education—including free school meals and all necessary resources, equipment, and musical instruments. Science and technology are high priorities. Almost 3 percent of GDP is allocated to scientific and technological development, and a national committee that includes leading corporate executives and university presidents, and is chaired by the prime minister, steers and integrates economic and educational strategy.[7] Yet Finland also boasts the highest number of composers per capita in the world.[8]

This educational and economic integration occurs in a society that values children, education, and social welfare. Finland's high school graduates rank teaching as their most desired occupation. As a result, entry into teaching is demanding and highly competitive, with teaching applicants having only a 10 percent chance of acceptance.[9]

In Finland, the state steers but does not prescribe in detail the national curriculum. Trusted teams of highly qualified teachers write much of the curriculum at the local level, adjusting it to the students they know best. In schools characterized by an uncanny calmness, teachers exercise their sense of professional and social responsibility to care especially for children at the bottom, so as to lift them to the level of the rest. Individual assistants are available for children who struggle, special educational support is provided for those with more serious difficulties, and school teams including teachers, administrators, welfare workers, and the school nurse meet regularly to discuss and support children in danger of falling behind.

By law, Finnish principals must have been teachers themselves, and most continue to teach at least two hours per week. By remaining tethered to the daily details of teaching and interacting with children, principals enjoy credibility among their teachers and overcome the traditional divide between administrators and teachers.

How is it, school principals in Finland were asked, that they could still teach as well as lead in their high-performing education system on the leading edge of the global economy? "Because," one said, "unlike the Anglo-Saxon countries, we do not have to spend our time responding to long, long lists of government initiatives that come from the top."

Of course, there are dramatic differences between Finland and the United States. For example, Finland has only four million people and little ethnic diversity; the United States has more than 300 million people and extraordinary cultural and linguistic diversity. We cannot duplicate Finland, but we also should not dismiss it.

Finland contains essential lessons for societies that aspire, educationally and economically, to be successful and sustainable knowledge societies, societies that go beyond an age of low-skill standardization. Building a future by wedding it to the past; fostering strong connections between education and economic development without sacrificing culture and creativity; raising standards by lifting the many rather than pushing a privileged few; developing a highly qualified profession that brings about improvement through commitment, trust, cooperation, and responsibility; and sharing responsibility for all of our children's futures, not just those in our own schools or classes—these are just some of the signs about possible lessons to be learned from Finland's exceptional educational and economic achievements.

CAN-DO CANADA

If Finland seems too far away geographically, demographically, and politically to offer lessons for educational improvement to the United States, then let's move closer to home—into Canada. In the latter half of the 1990s and beyond, the Canadian province of Ontario was the epitome of standardization. Its conservative agenda of diminished resources and reductions in teachers' preparation time, high-stakes tests linked to graduation, and accelerating reform requirements exacted high costs on teaching and learning. Research one of us conducted in six secondary schools exposed the pernicious impact of its policies.[10] Teachers complained of "too many changes, too fast," "too much, too quickly," "just so much, so soon," to an extent that was overwhelming. Having to take shortcuts meant teachers did not always feel they could do their best work. "What a waste of my intelligence, creativity, and leadership potential!" one teacher concluded. Ontario's education system was about as far removed from the needs of a fast-paced new knowledge economy as a country could get.

This changed in 2003 when the Liberal Party replaced the Progressive Conservative government. Appointing a well-published education policy scholar in the education ministry's most senior position, and being formally advised by international change consultant Michael Fullan, the province wedded a continuing commitment to test-based educational accountability with initiatives that built capacity for improvement and provided professional support.[11]

A Literacy and Numeracy Secretariat has driven instructional improvement by using teams of consultants and coaches supported by quality materials and by avoiding the worst excesses of the overly prescriptive models that characterized literacy strategies in the United Kingdom and United States.[12] Though provincial targets are fixed, schools and districts also are encouraged to commit to and set their own goals.

Within this framework of high aspirations, building professional capacity is emphasized. The province has allocated $5 million to teacher unions to spend on professional development, successful practices are networked across schools, and underperforming schools are encouraged (not compelled) to seek assistance from government support teams and higher performing peers.

As with other alternatives, this reform strategy also has imperfections. For instance, the measurement-driven emphasis on literacy and math seems to be a politically expedient (if slightly modified) import from England more than an educationally necessary improvement strategy, given Ontario's already strikingly high performance in literacy on international tests.[13] But these limitations could be remedied by widening the reform focus, developing professionally shared rather than politically imposed targets, and testing sample populations rather than administering a complete census for accountability purposes.

Notwithstanding these limitations, Ontario's theory of action offers many lessons. Intelligent accountability, increased investment, heightened trust, and strengthened professional networking provide a noteworthy contrast to policies endorsed south of the border that cut funding, pit teachers and schools against one another, and reduce teacher professionalism to the hurried implementation of policy makers' ever-changing mandates.

ENGLAND'S EDGE

Across the Atlantic is one of America's closest policy partners, Britain. We recently evaluated a major project in England involving more than 300 secondary schools that had experienced a dip in measured performance over one or two years. These schools were networked with one another, provided with technical assistance in interpreting achievement results, given access to support from mentor schools, and offered a modest discretionary budget to spend in any way they chose, provided that it addressed the goals of improvement.[14] Participating schools also had a practitioner-generated menu of proven strategies for short-, medium-, and long-term improvement.

The initial results of the project were remarkable. More than two-thirds of these networked schools improved at double the rate of the national average over one or two years, and they entirely avoided the characteristic top-down mandates and prescriptions that typified English educational reforms before this point.

In this high-trust culture of schools helping schools and the strong supporting the weak, teachers and administrators praised the flexible budgeting that focused on improvement, applauded the network's conferences for their inspirational input and practical assistance, and greatly appreciated the availability (rather than forced imposition) of mentor schools and principals who shared practical strategies and advice.

Schools were especially successful in improving in the short term, stimulated by the menu of short-term strategies provided by experienced colleagues. Teachers and schools excitedly implemented and exchanged short-term change strategies, such as providing students with test-taking strategies, paying past students to mentor existing ones, feeding students with bananas and water before examinations, bringing in examiners and university teachers to share their grading criteria with students, collecting mobile phone numbers to contact students who did not show up on exam days, introducing motivational speakers for such vulnerable groups as working-class boys in old mill towns, providing Web-based support for home learning, and so on.

Such short-term strategies do not bring about deeper transformations of teaching and learning, but they do give instant lifts in measured attainment—and in ways that largely avoid the unethical manipulation of test-score improvement in regimes of standardization (e.g., selecting only higher-performing students, narrowing the curriculum, or teaching only to the test). Useful in their own right, these strategies have even greater value when they are confidence-building levers that assist more challenging long-term improvements.

But this approach also has limitations. Strategies are "so gimmicky and great," as one principal put it, that they do not challenge or encourage teachers to question and revise their existing approaches to teaching and learning. The rush to raise achievement injects teachers with an addictive "high" of short-term success. The result is a somewhat hyperactive culture of change that can be exhilarating but also draining and distracting.

The project's successful short-term strategies, therefore, seem to serve less like levers to longer-term transformation than like lids upon it. In part, this is because the project—successful as it is—remains embedded in a wider national policy culture of short-term funding and proposal cycles, pressure for quick turnarounds and instant results, proliferation of multiple initiatives, and language that emphasizes moving students into the right achievement cells. Educators talk about "targeting" the right groups, "pushing" students harder, "moving" them up, "raising aspirations," "holding people down," and "getting a grip" on where youngsters are.

Yet, despite this limitation, the success of high-trust networks, school-to-school collaboration, discretionary budgeting, and a combination of proven insider experience with powerful outside-in evidence, points to a potential for an even greater transformation still to be unleashed. This alternative theory of action holds great promise if it can be separated from the surrounding context of bureaucratic accountability and wedded instead to higher-level professional and peer-driven principles of accountability. The English example suggests that it is the "peer factor" more than the "fear factor" that offers our best hope for raising achievement further.

GROWING THE GRASSROOTS IN AMERICA

American educators who teach poor and working-class children can only look with envy at the broad social safety net enjoyed by children and youth in other western nations, where educators are not expected to achieve everything by themselves. Rather than learn from other nations about policies that increase economic performance and social cohesion, reduce income disparities, and expand educational access for all, American policy makers have endorsed the untested and ideologically driven strategy of more markets, more privatization, and more pupil testing as the path to academic achievement.

Yet policy makers are not the only shapers of public education. One of the more inspiring recent developments in the United States has been the emergence of community and youth organizing as drivers of change and creators of "civic capacity" in urban education.[15] For years, these local initiatives were bit players in school reform. Symbolic language about "parent involvement" rarely went beyond one-on-one deals between individual parents and the educators who served their children.[16] Larger efforts to organize parents indicated that they were usually divided among themselves, incapable of galvanizing anything beyond episodic protests, and sidestepped in the push for standardization and control. Moreover, this pattern of fragmented and fractious engagement has occurred within a new context of "diminished democracy," in which fewer Americans participate in the traditional forms of civic life and prefer large voluntary associations that represent their interests but do not bring them into deliberative processes in the public sphere.[17]

Yet perhaps the tide is starting to turn. A new wave of community and youth organizing, supported by such powerful funders as the Ford, Hazen, Mott, and Gates foundations, is helping to get us beyond the "deep reforms with shallow roots" that Michael Usdan and Larry Cuban decried as endemic patterns in American change efforts.[18] In New York City, the Community Collaborative to Improve District 9 Schools in the South Bronx developed a teacher support program with that city's public schools that reduced teacher attrition from 28 percent to 6.5 percent in targeted schools in a single year.[19] In Philadelphia, high school activists with Youth United for Change exposed the way by which one of the only three secondary schools in the city that achieved AYP did so: by having teachers coach students on test items and by posting answers to anticipated test questions on walls where tests were administered.[20] In Chicago, the Logan Square Neighborhood Association and other community groups have created a Grow Your Own teacher preparatory program linked with area universities to prepare poor and working-class parents to become certified teachers.[21]

In these and other cases, community and youth organizers have moved beyond 1960s-style protest politics to conduct research with university allies, create and lead charter schools, provide professional development for teachers, and educate parents in how to combine data analyses of pupil achievement with in-class observations of teaching and learning.

Earlier work by one of us has documented efforts by the Industrial Areas Foundation in Texas to turn around struggling urban schools in the 1990s—efforts that developed a network of roughly 150 Alliance Schools that linked schools with faith-based institutions and community organizations, although these promising efforts fell on hard times as new accountability systems led principals to view working with parents as a distraction from the quest for AYP.[22]

Yet Oakes and Rogers in Los Angeles have described how UCLA faculty provided crucial expertise to community and youth organizing groups that has ranged from high-level legal representation to the day-to-day politics of improving large urban high schools.[23]

We do not yet know whether these diverse efforts will be sustainable. But if government does not meet its obligations, then activist parents and communities must become the prime movers of educational change. The emerging educational activism of grassroots America indicates that powerful reform efforts need not all begin with governments or guiding coalitions that come from the top. Instead, with the support of foundations and other organizations, these reforms can unleash the immense commitment and capacity locked up in our children's homes and communities.

CONCLUSION

When we put together what we can learn from the Finns, the Canadians, and the Brits, as well as from the grassroots activism of ordinary Americans, we begin to see the evolution of powerful new principles of improvement. These are different from the principles of markets, standardization, and the quick but fleeting turnarounds that have dominated U.S. reform efforts for more than a decade—the same strategies now being abandoned by other nations. These new principles suggest that:

- A compelling, inclusive, and inspirational vision for economic, social, and educational development that offers people more individual choice is in the best American traditions of freedom and justice, appeals to public spiritedness, and includes financial responsibility for the development of others.
- Learning and achievement priorities should follow the vision, which means much more than narrowing numerical achievement gaps in tested basics. We must attend to the basics but also move far beyond them. Creativity and innovation for the knowledge economy, cosmopolitan identity and global engagement in an age of insecurity, environmental awareness if we are to avert a planetary catastrophe, physical fitness for all to turn back the epidemic of obesity, and cultivation of the arts and humanities

that enrich our spirit and develop our responsibility toward others—these are the learning priorities of a sustainable knowledge society. Americans need a more enriching and engaging curriculum for all, not to replace the basics, but to bolster and move us beyond them.

- This kind of powerful learning calls for high-quality teaching. But high-performing countries elsewhere do not create and keep quality teachers by using the market to manipulate the calculus of teachers' pay. Rather, good and smart people are called to teaching and kept in the profession by an inspiring and inclusive social vision to which the society subscribes and for which it accords high status.
- Trust, cooperation, and responsibility create the collegiality and shared, committed, professional learning that improve classroom effectiveness and raise standards with students. Shared targets rather than externally arbitrary AYP keeps pushing teachers to higher and higher levels of performance. Such strong professional learning communities depend on inspirational and more widely distributed leadership, rather than fleeting and heroic turnarounds that rely on single individuals. At a time of extraordinary demographic turnover in school and school leadership, the time is ripe for America to undertake significant investment in developing and renewing its next generation of leaders.
- Data can inform and enhance teacher decisions and interventions, but they should never "drive" instruction. Teaching entails gathering information from a variety of sources; and some valuable teacher traits have more in common with the skilled thespian who responds instantly to a demanding and vocal audience and with the doctor who combines evidence and intuition to diagnose a

patient than with the civil engineer who relies on scientific data to design roads, bridges, or tunnels. Evidence collected by teachers that enables schools to compare themselves to similar schools and that stresses how schools and teachers make a difference to the students they serve is a more fair and instructive guide to improvement than are the crude data that too often are used to rank and shame struggling schools.

- The evidence from almost everywhere else points to how much teachers and schools can learn from being networked with peers and how achievement gaps can be narrowed by systems that encourage and support strong schools to help their weaker counterparts. It would make immense sense for Americans to reallocate resources to peer learning and to systems of teachers helping teachers and schools helping schools.

- Governments are often pushed into politically popular though educationally ineffective strategies for change because they feel they must pander to parental nostalgia for schools as they remember them. Treating parents as customers and clients, as recipients of services, or as targets of external interventions only intensifies this sense of defensive nostalgia. But the activist element in American communities demonstrates what can be achieved when parents and communities are engaged and empowered to advocate for and help improve the quality of education for some of the nation's poorest children. Great value can be added to educational investment through parallel investment in parent and community development. Educators cannot be expected to do everything themselves.

A bigger and better vision; a bolder view of enriching and engaging learning; the inspiration, support, and professional discretion that will attract and retain the very best teachers; a national strategy that will develop and renew the leadership that can build and constantly improve strong professional learning communities; intelligent accountability that monitors standards and improves every child's instruction; ambitious, professionally shared targets rather than politically arbitrary ones; support for school networks where good practices can be exchanged and the strong can help the weak; and recasting parents and communities as actively engaged partners rather than as consumers, recipients, or targets of government strategies and services—these are the international and instructive lessons for education reform if the United States does not want to fall even further behind its international competitors.

Now is the time for U.S. education to learn from other nations about the most productive ways forward. There is no good reason why the wealthiest nation in the world should be ashamed about investing in all of its children and their futures. That is the true challenge that all Americans who care about their nation's future must now face.

ENDNOTES

1. Andy Hargreaves and Dean Fink, *Sustainable Leadership* (San Francisco: Jossey-Bass, 2005).

2. Center on Education Policy, *Choices, Changes, and Challenges: Curriculum and Instruction in the NCLB Era* (Washington, DC: Center on Education Policy, 2007).

3. Jihyun Lee, Wendy S. Grigg, and Gloria S. Dion, *The Nation's Report Card: Mathematics 2007, NCES 2007–494* (Washington, DC: National Center for Education Statistics, Institute of Education Sciences, U.S. Department of Education, 2007).

4. Jean Johnson, Ana Maria Arumi, and Amber Ott, *Issue Number 3: Is Support for Standards and Testing Fading? Reality Check 2006* (New York: Public Agenda, 2006).

5. UNICEF, *Child Poverty in Perspective: An Overview of Child Well-Being in Rich Countries, Innocenti Report Card 7* (Florence: UNICEF Innocenti Research Centre, 2007).

6. Erkki Aho, Kari Pitkänen, & Pasy Sahlberg, *Policy Development and Reform Principles of Basic and Secondary Education in Finland Since 1968, Education Working Paper Series Number 2* (Washington, DC: World Bank, 2006).

7. Manuel Castells and Pekka Himanen, *The Information Society and the Welfare State: The Finnish Model* (New York: Oxford University Press, 2004).

8. W. Norton Grubb, "Dynamic Inequality and Intervention: Lessons from a Small Country," *Phi Delta Kappan,* October 2007, pp. 105–14.

9. Pasi Sahlberg, "Education Reform for Raising Economic Competitiveness," *Journal of Educational Change,* December 2006, pp. 259–87; idem, "Education Policies for Raising Student Learning: The Finnish Approach," *Journal of Education Policy,* March 2007, pp. 147–71; and Aho, Pitkanen, and Sahlberg, op. cit.

10. Andy Hargreaves, *Teaching in the Knowledge Society: Education in the Age of Anxiety* (New York: Teachers College Press, 2003); and Andy Hargreaves and Ivor Goodson, eds., "Change over Time," special issue of *Educational Administration Quarterly,* February 2006.

11. Michael Fullan, *Turnaround Leadership* (San Francisco: Jossey-Bass, 2007); and Land Sharratt and Michael Fullan, "Accomplishing Districtwide Reform," *Journal of School Leadership,* 2006, pp. 583–95.

12. Betty Achinstein and Rodney T. Ogawa, "(In) Fidelity: What the Resistance of New Teachers Reveals About Professional Principles and Prescriptive Educational Policies," *Harvard Educational Review,* Spring 2006, pp. 30–63.

13. Hargreaves and Fink, op. cit.

14. Andy Hargreaves et al., *The Long and Short of School Improvement: Final Evaluation of the Raising Achievement Transforming Learning Programme of the Specialist Schools and Academies Trust* (London: Specialist Schools and Academies Trust, 2007).

15. Clarence N. Stone et al., *Building Civic Capacity: The Politics of Reforming Urban Schools* (Lawrence: University Press of Kansas, 2001).

16. Dennis Shirley, *Community Organizing for Urban School Reform* (Austin: University of Texas Press, 1997).

17. Theda Skocpol, *Diminished Democracy: From Membership to Management in American Civic Life* (Norman: University of Oklahoma Press, 2004).

18. Michael D. Usdan and Larry Cuban, *Powerful Reforms with Shallow Roots: Improving America's Urban Schools* (New York: Teachers College Press, 2003).

19. Academy for Educational Development, *Lead Teacher Report: Second Year Report Submitted to the Community Collaborative to Improve Bronx Schools* (Washington, DC: Academy for Educational Development, 2006).

20. Seema Shah and Kavitha Mediratta, "Negotiating Reform: Young People's Leadership in the Educational Arena," *New Directions in Youth Development,* April 2008, pp. 43–59.

21. Mark R. Warren, "Communities and Schools: A New View of Urban Education Reform," *Harvard Educational Review,* Summer 2005, pp. 133–73.

22. Dennis Shirley, *Community Organizing*; idem, *Valley Interfaith and School Reform: Organizing for Power in South Texas* (Austin: University of Texas Press, 2002); and Dennis Shirley and Michael Evans, "Community Organizing and No Child Left Behind," in Marion Orr, ed., *Transforming the City: Community Organizing and the Challenge of Political Change* (Lawrence: University Press of Kansas, 2007), pp. 109–33.

23. Jeannie Oakes, John Rogers, and Martin Lipton, *Learning Power: Organizing for Education and Justice* (New York: Teachers College Press, 2006).

DISCUSSION QUESTIONS

1. Finland is very different from the United States demographically and geographically. Is it possible to adopt or adapt any of the policies of their educational system? Explain.

2. Which of the different countries' policies do you believe are most practical and feasible for implementation in the United States? Explain.

3. According to the authors, "Americans have endorsed the untested and ideologically driven strategy of more markets, more privatization, and more pupil testing as the path to academic achievement" (p. 298). Do you agree with this statement? Explain.

4. What role do you believe grassroots activism will play in reforming the educational policy in the United States?

5. Using what we know from other countries, how can we recruit and retain quality teachers?

32 Dichotomizing Educational Reform

CARL D. GLICKMAN

FOCUSING QUESTIONS

1. What principles should guide education in the United States?
2. What are some examples of what the author calls ideological absolutes?
3. To what extent does ideological conflict contribute to pedagogical pain?
4. What does it mean to be an educated person in a democracy?
5. Is it possible to find common ground in the issues facing public education today?

I did not lightly take pen in hand (yes, I still use a pen) in writing this chapter. I have devoted my entire professional life to working with colleagues to create, establish, and sustain public schools that are driven by collaboration, personalization, and active and participatory student learning.[1] And I will continue to do so, as I personally believe such is the best way to prepare all students for the intellectual, social, and aesthetic life of a democracy.

Yet, even in the fervor of my beliefs, I still see other concepts of education that generate degrees of uncertainty in me. My memories of my own best teachers are revealing. Most taught in highly interactive ways, but one grand elder taught from behind a podium in a huge auditorium and engaged in little interaction with students. He was perhaps my greatest teacher. Such discrepancies don't change the strength of my own beliefs; they simply remind me that the viable possibilities of educating students well are broad indeed.

Ultimately, an American education must stand on a foundation that is wider than the beliefs of any one individual or any one group. It should encourage, respect, and support any conceptions—no matter how diametrically opposed to one's own—that are willing to be tested openly and freely. Furthermore, it should involve the willing and nondiscriminatory participation of all students, parents, and educators. That is what should be at the core of an American education. But with the "winner take all" wars being fought today, I am seriously concerned about the future of our students and of our public schools and about the vitality of a better democracy.

IDEOLOGICAL ABSOLUTES

The either/or debates about standards versus no standards, intrinsic versus extrinsic motivation, core versus multicultural knowledge, direct instruction versus constructivist learning, and phonics versus whole language are symptomatic of ideologies that attempt to crush one another and leave only one solution standing. Whether the ideology is education anchored in traditional, behaviorist authority or progressive, inquiry-based learning, the stance toward the final outcome is the same. One group possesses the truth, and the other side is demonized as a pack of extremists: scary, evil persons. Articles and books present educators and the public with a forced choice that unfortunately disregards reality and endangers the very concept of an American education.[2]

Let me illustrate the incompleteness of ideological absolutes with one of today's most emotional issues: the relationship of race to socioeconomic achievement. One side of this debate argues that America is the land of opportunity, where freedom rings, where anyone—regardless of race, religion, gender, or class—can work hard and rise to a position of authority, success, and accomplishment. The other side argues that America is a hegemonic system, protecting the ruling class and extant privilege while keeping the poor, the dispossessed, and people of color stifled, oppressed, and marginalized. Well, which side of this debate is correct? The answer to that question has important implications for what our society needs to change in terms of practices, programs, and the targeting of resources. But the truth is that both contradictory realities have compelling evidence and must be used together to figure out what needs to be done next.

Consider the economic component of this debate. Seymour Martin Lipset compares the United States with other Western industrialized nations.[3] Since the post–Civil War era, America has been the wealthiest country, with a steady rise in living standards and unparalleled social and economic advances for the poor and working class. Yet the income of the poorest fifth of this nation continues to *decline* relative to that of other Americans.

The African American scholar Henry Louis Gates, Jr., takes on this same dichotomy in reference to race. He observes that, since 1967, the number of middle-class African American families has quadrupled. Since 1973 the top 100 African American businesses have moved from sales of $473 million to $11.7 billion. In 1970 "only one in ten blacks had attended college; today one in three has." He then goes on to discuss the continuous wrenching poverty of a third of African Americans today and concludes: "We need something we don't have: a way of speaking about black poverty that doesn't falsify the reality of black advancement, a way of speaking about black advancement that doesn't distort the enduring realities of black poverty. I'd venture that a lot depends on whether we get it."[4]

In truth, America has been one of the leading countries of opportunity for disenfranchised persons and, at the same time, a country of the greatest economic stratification between the luxury of the wealthiest and the wretched conditions of the poorest.[5] In essence, the beliefs of Ayn Rand and Pete Seeger are both correct. To speak only of one side and ignore the other is to create disbelief in most ordinary citizens, who know firsthand of counterexamples to any single view. And this is what I believe to be the danger of ideological truth in education. Many educators in classrooms and schools feel that they have become pawns in the reformers' and policy makers' propaganda game that insists there is a single best way to change the system of American schools.

IDEOLOGY IN EDUCATION

The attacks by E. D. Hirsch, Jr., against progressive education and the equally strident attacks by others such as Alfie Kohn against traditional education are wonderful examples of this either/or ideological stance. Hirsch argues that a common core of knowledge is essential for all students, if they are to succeed in mainstream society. Without a common framework of spoken and written English, historical and cultural references, and direct instruction, marginalized and poor children are deprived of the education that wealthier children pick up automatically from their parents and peers. Thus there is the need to rid our schools of the overwhelming "permissive" practices of activity-based education and to use tests of common knowledge to ensure that all children are acquiring the "cultural capital" needed for success in later life. Kohn in turn speaks against standards, core knowledge, and tests and says that children, regardless of their circumstances, are innately curious and that teachers should explore the topics that intrigue them to open up new freedoms and possibilities. Each proponent has his version of "truth." Each sees little validity in any research supporting the methods that oppose his ideology. Again, the reality is that education is composed of many complexities that defeat any singular truth of how the world can and should work.

For example, might it be that both Hirsch and Kohn have valid perspectives? Focusing on core knowledge that students themselves might not choose but that gives them access to a society in which they might possibly change the current balance of power, wealth, and control seems quite reasonable. Using the curiosity of students to learn multiple histories and cultures and to explore a variety of intelligences in an intensely involving way also seems quite reasonable. It is important that schools be joyful and engaging places. Yet is all learning intrinsically or extrinsically motivated? Most would say it's both—we learn for the joy of it, but some of the most useful learning has taken place because others, not we ourselves, demanded that we do it, do it well, and do it until we got it right.

The polemics surrounding standards versus no standards do not account for complex realities. Are external standards bad or good? Might they be both? Might we have state standards and assessments for most (but not all) public schools in the same state? Some states have standards and assessments that have been well received by educators and the public—not seen as heavy-handed, intrusive, or unfair. Many states have standards and assessments that are volatile in makeup, format, pressure, and consequences.

The standards polarization—again, only one side can win—has come about because people have applied the term "standards" to all systems as if they were identical. However, Maine's standards are quite different from Virginia's. Elements of standards systems can be quite good, such as using disaggregated data to focus on the progress of all students, equalizing funding for poor students and communities, and targeting additional resources. Some states grant variances allowing schools and districts to develop their own assessments. And yes, there are cases in which it is good that standards can be used to close and reorganize schools that have done a disservice to students and parents. Standards systems can be demeaning and harmful—when they equate education with narrowly derived assessments and tests. They can also be tremendously positive in challenging schools and communities to leave no student behind.[6] We need to acknowledge simultaneous realities if we are to educate all students better than before.

PEDAGOGICAL PAIN

The "single-truth" wars have created much pain among teachers and school leaders who are swept into the battles. When whole language gained currency as "the" way to teach reading, teachers using phonics were lambasted, swept aside, and made to feel that they were evil, archaic, fascist practitioners of an indefensible method. Recently, the opposing force has "won" in states led by California and Texas. They have blamed whole language and invented spelling for declining literacy in America. Now teachers of whole language are made to feel abandoned and rejected as "feel-good," self-esteem–promoting contributors to the demise of basic skills.

These periodic surges and countersurges occur because one set of believers ignores any possible merits of the other side. Isn't it possible that many highly literate and culturally diverse people—people that you and I both know—were taught how to read mainly by decoding, phonics, and grammatical rules? Isn't it equally obvious that many highly literate and culturally diverse people have learned to read through literacy immersion, writing workshops, and experiential learning? Why is it so difficult to accept that an open mind about possibilities in education should be seen as a virtue rather than a liability?

Cooperative versus competitive learning is another such brawl. Cooperation is a key aspect of how one learns with and from others, and it undergirds much of community, civic, and business life. Research exists that demonstrates the power of structured team activities for academic and social development. Yet humans, as part of the animal kingdom, are also moved to learn by traits that have helped them to survive: dominance, power, and the need to test oneself against others. Cooperation and competition are not different versions of humanity; they are different dimensions of the same humanity. And thus there is evidence that both cooperation and competition bring out high performance in individuals.

The overarching debate about progressive, learner-centered schools versus teacher-centered, direct-instruction schools will be my last venture into the foolishness of single truths. This debate simplifies and silences the cultural and family values that Lisa Delpit so eloquently writes about in *Other People's Children*.[7] Asking students to conform to certain manners, expecting them to learn what adults determine is important for them, being didactic in instruction, and using "call and response" methods have resulted in great success for teachers and leaders such as Marva Collins, Jaime Escalante, and Lorraine Monroe and for a number of school programs.[8] Regardless of what one personally believes about the atmosphere of such classrooms and schools, students and parents in these settings see such didactic methods as expressions of teachers' love, care, and cultural solidarity.[9] The teachers are proud to demand that their students learn, and they go to almost any length to see that their students can compete with other students.

Yet progressive classrooms and schools that are activity- or project-centered and that cultivate imagination, problem solving, responsibility, and a variety of intellectual pursuits have, in the hands of the most dedicated teachers, also attained incredible success for students. Educators such as Eliot Wigginton, Deborah Meier, George Wood, Gloria Ladson-Billings, Sonia Nieto, and Jabari Mahiri have shown the power of inquiry-centered, progressive learning.

My point is *not* that all methods, techniques, curricula, and structures are of equal worth or that the attitude "anything goes" is acceptable. My point is that, when a group of students and parents choose to be with a group of educators dedicated to a particular philosophy and way of learning, the results for students can be awesome. No one group should have the presumption or power to tell another group that only its way is the right way. Instead, in accordance with publicly determined purposes and criteria, we should be seeking, testing, and developing research-based alternative conceptions and practices of successful education. Kenneth Wilson, a Nobel laureate in physics, remarked about the need to test a multitude of educational approaches through longitudinal research and self-correction to find out what works well, what can be adapted, and what should be discarded.[10] The idea is not to prove that one way is the only way but instead to allow for different conceptions of education to flourish in the marketplace of public education.

RELIGION IN AMERICA AND AN EDUCATED AMERICAN

Of all Western nations, America is the country with the highest percentage of citizens actively involved in religious and spiritual practices.[11] Why? Because it has no official state religion and no divine story behind its creation. Those countries that do have histories of such official state religion—a one way to believe for all—tend to have lower percentages of citizen involvement in religious practice. This example suggests why we must avoid a single governmental (local, state, or national) conception of education. The analogy with religion ends at a certain point, as the U.S. government needs to remain neutral and not use public funds to promote any particular set of religious beliefs. But government must use public funds to support a public education consistent with democratic ideals.[12] And the best way for doing so is to create a system of state schools that promote various publicly determined conceptions of an educated American.

Public education can be defined in several overlapping ways. Public education is funded by taxpayers, it is an education for the public, it is open and without cost to students and parents, it is compulsory, it is governed by public authority, it is nonprofit, and it always *should be* nondiscriminatory and nonrepressive of students and parents.[13] It is public because it serves a common good: the education of students to have choices of "life, liberty, and the pursuit of happiness" and to acknowledge those choices for others.

Within these definitions of public, American education is always an experiment—one hopes a thoughtful one—that must constantly test ways to further realize the hopes and aspirations of all the nation's people. Whenever one truth stamps out all others—whether it be through one system of tests, one approach to curriculum, one conception of knowledge, a single method of instruction, or a uniform structure for all public schools—democracy itself and education for a democracy are subverted.

In first proposing the need for common schools, Horace Mann wrote in the 1840s that public schools would be the great equalizers of human conditions, the balance wheel of the social machinery. Poverty would disappear and with it the discord between the haves and the have-nots; life for all people would be longer, better, and happier. The common school would be free, for poor and rich alike, as good as any private school, and nonsectarian. (The common school was not to be a school for common people but rather a school common to all people.) And the pedagogy of the common or free school would stress the "self-discipline of individuals, self-control, and self-governance." The issue for Mann was that the educated person was to have a free, deliberate choice between obedience and anarchy.[14]

Another view of the educated person in a democracy was shaped by the Lockean sympathies of early American thought. The educated person would be the one who renounced self-indulgence, practiced restraint, and saw the virtue of frugality and labor. In this view, one would work not for what one could accumulate but in order to focus the human mind and body.

Jefferson's concept of the educated person was the farmer—a person who lived apart from others; pursued his own curiosity about science, philosophy, and art after a long day of self-sustaining chores; and then determined the times when he should participate in neighborhood and community affairs. The farmer's life was a combination of aloneness, individuality, and self-learning with minimal but significant civic responsibility.

W. E. B. Du Bois, referring to the need for African American children to learn, saw public education as giving "our children the fairness of a start which will equip them with such an array of facts and such an attitude toward truth that they can have a real chance to judge what the world is and what its greater minds have thought it might be."[15]

Education might also be defined as making a good neighbor—one who cares for and respects others, who takes care of his or her own family needs, and who contributes to the welfare of others.[16] Such a person would possess a respect for other people and an understanding of life conditions locally, nationally, and internationally; the ability to communicate with diverse others; analytic and problem-solving skills; and the competence to choose what to do with one's own life in economic, social, recreational, and aesthetic pursuits. Does one need three years of high school or college-level preparatory mathematics to develop these attributes? Does one need to learn French? How about Chinese? What level of mastery does one need in the various disciplines? Is it better to study discrete subjects or an integrated curriculum with applications to the world outside of school? The question here is, "What knowledge, skills, and understandings are needed to be a good neighbor and citizen?"

In a high school curriculum controlled by college admission requirements, there are expected core courses, and good scores on the SAT or ACT have become essential measures of an educated American. Whether going to college or not, most students will not use most of what they are required to learn, whether mathematics or history or language or science. Is it still essential? Again, says who? Dare I ask the unspeakable: Can one be a good neighbor and a wise and productive citizen without going to college?

Is the purpose of public education to train a highly skilled work force to support American corporations? If so, the definition of a well-educated American as a good worker will place a great deal of emphasis on technology. But again, who should determine what is a well-educated person? For example, the Waldorf schools in America have children work with natural materials for the first three to five years of schooling.[17] Children work only with wood, clay, water, and paint, on long, painstaking projects for several years before the technological world becomes a source of their learning—no televisions, no phones, no computers in early childhood and primary classrooms. The prime emphasis is on imagination and work in an all-natural environment. Are these students educated less well than others? According to what criteria?

To be blunt, any single truth or concept of an educated American will be fraught with contradictions. The real danger of any one reform effort, such as a standards movement that relies on a single test, is the promotion of a single definition of the well-educated citizen as a college graduate who is technologically prepared to lead a successful economic life. The idea that an educated citizen might not want to make vast sums of money or work in a corporation but instead might seek success in quietness, resistance, or even detachment from corporate/college-controlled work, has eroded in America. Even to mention the idea that education is not mostly about jobs or money but about choosing how to live one's life among others is to be seen as a romantic, a throwback to another time.

My point is not to convince others of any one definition of a well-educated person but to share the need for varied conceptions of education, conceptions that must be in conformance with "public" criteria and equally based on data about student accomplishments and successes.

WHAT DO WE DO?

As a reformer who advocates the progressive tradition and assists schools in keeping it alive, I do not seek a common ground for public education—an eclectic "all things of equal merit" ground—but instead wish to move beyond that to a higher ground that incorporates complexity and competing conceptions—a higher ground where contradictory truths must be part and parcel of American democracy. We need an education system that supports multiple conceptions of an educated American, that subjects all such conceptions to the scrutiny of research and public accountability, and that fixes all actions of classrooms and schools within the boundaries of equity. American students and schools lose each time one "truth" gains currency and suppresses competing notions of public education.

So let me end by stating that, in my experience with schools, education reformers, policy makers, legislators, corporate persons, community activists, and citizens at large, I have found people of astonishingly good will and passionate intent who labor in the light of controversy about what our schools need or deserve. They are accused by their opponents of being self-indulgent conspirators with sinister motives, but most of them, or at least those that I know, are not. However, many of those who are most influential or powerful are singularly convinced that theirs is the true way to improve education and that all other ways are false, bad, and corrupt.

We need to realize that, most often, life does not contain single truths but instead is about predicaments, competing views, and apparent conflicts. The public school system must value and allow multiple conceptions of education that students, parents, and faculty members can choose from—some purebreds, some hybrids, and some yet to be known, but all devoted to students and their pursuit of the American Dream.

We must fight against any single model, structure, method, or system of education. We must expand the freedom of schools to test new concepts of standards, assessments, and accountability. Ultimately, we must hold every school and district responsible for whether it has provided an education for all children that can be documented to increase choices of "life, liberty, and the pursuit of happiness." *That* is an American education.

ENDNOTES

1. Carl D. Glickman, *Revolutionizing America's Schools* (San Francisco: Jossey–Bass, 1998).

2. See E. D. Hirsch, Jr., *The Schools We Need and Why We Don't Have Them* (New York: Doubleday, 1996); Alfie Kohn, *The Schools Our Children Deserve* (Boston: Houghton Mifflin, 1999); Susan Ohanian, *One Size Fits Few: The Folly of Educational Standards* (Portsmouth, NH: Heinemann, 1999); and I. de Pommereau, "Tougher High School Standards Signal Greater Demands on Students," *Christian Science Monitor*, 16 June 1996, p. 12, 1-C.

3. Seymour Martin Lipset, *American Exceptionalism: A Double-Edged Sword* (New York: Norton, 1996).

4. Henry Louis Gates, Jr., and Cornel West, *The Future of the Race* (New York: Random House, 1996), pp. 19, p. 38.

5. Jim Myers, "Notes on the Murder of Thirty of My Neighbors," *Atlantic*, March 2000, pp. 72–88.

6. Chris Gallagher, "A Seat at the Table: Teachers Reclaiming Assessment Through Rethinking Accountability," *Phi Delta Kappan*, March 2000, pp. 502–7.

7. Lisa Delpit, *Other People's Children: Cultural Conflict in the Classroom* (New York: New Press, 1995).

8. See, for example, such schools as P.S. 161 in New York, KIPP Academies in Texas and New York, and the Frederick Douglass Middle School in New York.

9. Samuel Casey Carter, *No Excuses: Seven Principals of Low-Income Schools Who Set the Standards for High Achievement* (Washington, DC: Heritage Foundation, 1999); and Jacqueline Jordan Irvine, "Seeing with the Cultural Eye: Different Perspectives of African American Teachers and Researchers," DeWitt Wallace–Reader's Digest Distinguished Lecture presented at the annual meeting of the American Educational Research Association, New Orleans, April 2000.

10. Kenneth Wilson and Bennett Daviss, *Redesigning Education* (New York: Teachers College Press, 1994).

11. Lipset, op. cit.; and Warren A. Nord, *Religion and American Education: Rethinking a National Dilemma* (Chapel Hill: University of North Carolina Press, 1995).

12. John Dayton and Carl D. Glickman, "Curriculum Change and Implementation: Democratic Imperatives," *Peabody Journal of Education*, vol. 9, no. 4, 1994, pp. 62–86; Benjamin R. Barber, *An Aristocracy of Everyone: The Politics of Education and the Future of America* (New York: Ballantine, 1992);

and Amy Gutmann, *Democratic Education* (Princeton, NJ: Princeton University Press, 1987).

13. Gutmann, op. cit.

14. Lawrence A. Cremin, *The Transformation of the School: Progressivism in American Education 1876–1957* (New York: Random House, 1964), pp. 3–11.

15. W. E. B. Du Bois, "The Freedom to Learn," in Philip S. Foner, ed., *W. E. B. Du Bois Speaks* (New York: Pathfinder, 1970), pp. 230–31.

16. George H. Wood, *A Time to Learn* (New York: Dutton, 1998).

17. Todd Oppenheimer, "Schooling the Imagination," *Atlantic*, September 1999, pp. 71–83.

DISCUSSION QUESTIONS

1. Does the United States live up to its reputation as the land of opportunity? Does public education live up to its reputation for providing a ladder to success for groups that are not part of the mainstream culture?

2. Are educational decisions made more often on the basis of good intentions, ideology, or results? Which is the criterion that is most appropriate for guiding practice?

3. What essential knowledge and skills should an educated person in a democracy possess?

4. Given the heated debates about education that are prevalent today, is it possible to make decisions about public education in a civil and responsible manner?

5. Would increasing the number of charter schools or the opportunities for school choice have the effect of undermining or reinforcing the principles of democracy?

33 Assessment for Learning Around the World: What Would It Mean to Be Internationally Competitive?

Linda Darling-Hammond
Laura McCloskey

FOCUSING QUESTIONS

1. Compare the curriculum of the United States with those of highly ranked nations.
2. Compare assessment methods in the United States with those of other highly ranked nations.
3. How do curricula and assessment differ based on country size? Explain.
4. Internationally, what role do teachers play in the development of assessments?
5. Compared with the United States, what role do assessments play in school rankings and the development of curriculum worldwide?

High-performing nations integrate curriculum, instruction, and assessment to improve both teaching and learning.

Since the release of *A Nation at Risk*, the United States has launched a set of wide-ranging reforms with the intention of better preparing all children for the higher educational demands of life and work in the twenty-first century. All 50 states have developed standards for learning and tests to evaluate student progress. No Child Left Behind reinforced using test-based accountability to raise achievement, yet the United States has fallen further behind on international assessments of student learning since the law was passed in 2001.

On the Program in International Student Assessment (PISA) tests in 2006, the United States ranked 35th among the top 40 countries in mathematics and 31st in science, a decline in both raw scores and rankings from three years earlier.[1] (Reading scores were not reported, because of editing problems with the U.S. test.) Furthermore, in each disciplinary area tested, U.S. students scored lowest on the problem-solving items. The United States also had a much wider achievement gap than the most highly ranked jurisdictions, such as Finland, Canada, Australia, New Zealand, Hong Kong, Korea, and Japan.

Policy discussions in Washington often refer to these rankings when emphasizing the need to create more "internationally competitive" standards by benchmarking

311

expectations in the United States to those in high-performing nations. Typically, this means looking at topics that are taught at various grade levels in various countries. These analyses reveal that higher-achieving countries teach fewer topics more deeply each year; focus more on reasoning skills and applications of knowledge, rather than mere coverage; and have a more thoughtful sequence of expectations based on developmental learning progressions within and across domains.[2]

However, we must examine how these topics are taught and assessed—so that we understand how other countries' education systems shape what students actually learn and can do. European and Asian nations that have steeply improved student learning have focused explicitly on creating curriculum guidance and assessments that focus on the so-called twenty-first-century skills: the abilities to find and organize information to solve problems, frame and conduct investigations, analyze and synthesize data, apply learning to new situations, self-monitor and improve one's own learning and performance, communicate well in multiple forms, work in teams, and learn independently.

Curriculum differences are reinforced by sharp divergence between the forms of testing used in the United States and those used in higher-achieving countries. Whereas U.S. tests rely primarily on multiple-choice items that evaluate recall and recognition of discrete facts, most high-achieving countries rely largely on open-ended items that require students to analyze, apply knowledge, and write extensively. Furthermore, these nations' growing emphasis on project-based, inquiry-oriented learning has led to an increasing prominence for school-based tasks, which include research projects, science investigations, development of products, and reports or presentations about these efforts. These assessments, which are incorporated into the overall examination scoring system, influence the day-to-day work of teaching and learning, focusing it on the development of higher-order skills and use of knowledge to solve problems.

Smaller countries often have a system of national standards that are sometimes—though not always—accompanied by national tests in the upper grades. Top-ranking Finland uses local assessments almost exclusively in order to evaluate its national standards and manages a voluntary national assessment at only one grade level. Larger nations—like Canada, Australia, and China—have state- or provincial-level standards, and their assessment systems are typically a blend of state and local assessments. Managing assessment at the state rather than the national level, where it remains relatively close to the schools, turns out to be an important way of enabling strong teacher participation and ensuring high-quality local assessments that can be moderated to ensure consistency in scoring.

In many cases, local assessments complement centralized "on-demand" tests, constituting up to 50 percent of the final examination score. Tasks are mapped to the standards or syllabus for the subject and are selected because they represent critical skills, topics, and concepts. They are often outlined in the curriculum guide, but they are generally designed, administered, and scored locally, based on common specifications and evaluation criteria. Whether locally or centrally developed, decisions about when to undertake these tasks are made at the classroom level, so they are used when appropriate for students' learning process and teachers can get information and provide feedback as needed, something that traditional standardized tests cannot do. In addition, as teachers use and evaluate these tasks, they become more knowledgeable about both the standards and how to teach to them and about their students' learning needs. Thus the process improves the quality of teaching and learning.

Like the behind-the-wheel test given for all new drivers in the United States, these performance assessments evaluate what students can actually do, not just what they know. Not only does the road test reveal some important things about drivers' skills, but also preparation for the test helps improve those skills as novice drivers practice to get better. In the same way, performance assessments set a standard toward which everyone must work. The task and the standards are not secret, so teachers and students know what skills they need to develop and how they will need to be demonstrated.

Finally, these countries do not use their examination systems to rank or punish schools or to deny diplomas to students. Following the problems that resulted from the Thatcher government's use of test-based school rankings, which caused a narrowing of the curriculum and widespread exclusions of students from school,[3] several countries enacted legislation precluding the use of test results for school rankings. High school examinations provide information for higher education, vocational training, and employment, and students often choose areas in which they will be examined, as a means of demonstrating their qualifications. Because the systems are focused on using information for curriculum improvement, rather than sanctions, governments can set higher standards and work with schools to achieve them, rather than devising tests and setting cut scores at a minimal level to avoid dysfunctional side effects.

Many states in the United States—including Connecticut, Kentucky, Maine, Nebraska, New Hampshire, New Jersey, New York, Rhode Island, Vermont, and Wyoming—have developed and used state and local performance assessments as part of their testing systems. Indeed, the National Science Foundation provided millions of dollars for states to develop such hands-on science and math assessments as part of its Systemic Initiative in the 1990s, and prototypes exist all over the country. Studies have found that using such assessments has improved teaching quality and increased student achievement, especially on tasks that require complex reasoning and problem solving.[4] However, these assessments have been difficult to sustain, especially under NCLB's annual testing requirements, because the policy community has little understanding about how systems of assessment for learning might be constructed and managed at scale.

The United States can learn a great deal by examining the assessment systems of several high-achieving education systems: two of the highest-achieving Scandinavian nations—Finland and Sweden—plus a group of English-speaking jurisdictions that have some shared approaches to assessment, as well as some interesting variations—Australia, Hong Kong, and the United Kingdom. In particular, we can learn from how assessments in those nations are linked to curriculum and integrated into the instructional process to shape and improve learning for students and teachers alike.

FINLAND AND SWEDEN

Finland has been a poster child for school improvement since it rapidly climbed to the top of international rankings after emerging from the Soviet Union's shadow. Finland now ranks first among all OECD nations on the PISA assessments in mathematics, science, and reading. Finland attributes these gains to intensive investments in teacher education—all teachers receive three years of high-quality graduate-level preparation completely at state expense—plus major overhaul of the curriculum and assessment system. Most teachers now hold master's degrees in both their content and in education, and their preparation is aimed at learning to teach diverse learners—including special needs students—for deep understanding. Preparation includes a strong focus on how to use formative performance assessments in the service of student learning.[5]

Sweden also invests heavily in state-funded graduate teacher education for all teachers and relies on a highly trained teaching force to implement its curriculum and assessment system.

Over 40 years, both Finland and Sweden have shifted from highly centralized systems emphasizing external testing to more localized systems using multiple forms of assessments. Around 1970, Sweden abolished its nationally administered exit exam that ranked upper secondary students and placed them in higher education programs.[6] Finland followed suit, and both nations stopped tracking students into different streams by their test scores, offering a common core curriculum to all students. These changes were intended to equalize educational outcomes and provide more open access to higher education.[7]

Although it may seem counterintuitive to Americans accustomed to external testing as a means of accountability, Finland's leaders point to its use of school-based, student-centered, open-ended tasks embedded in the curriculum as an important reason for the nation's extraordinary success on international exams.[8] Policy makers decided that if they invested in very skillful teachers, they could allow local schools more autonomy to decide what and how to teach—a reaction against the highly centralized system they sought to overhaul. Finland's national core curriculum is a much leaner document, reduced from hundreds of pages of highly specific prescriptions to descriptions of a small number of skills and core concepts each year. (For example, about 10 pages describe the full set of math standards for all grades.) This guides teachers in collectively developing local curricula and assessments that encourage students to be active learners who can find, analyze, and use information to solve problems in novel situations.

Finland has no external standardized tests to rank students or schools. Finnish education authorities periodically evaluate school-level samples of student performance, generally at the end of the second and ninth grades, to inform curriculum decisions and school investments. Local educators design and manage all other assessments. The national core curriculum provides teachers with recommended assessment criteria for specific grades in each subject and for the final assessment of student progress each year.[9] Schools then use those guidelines to craft more detailed learning outcomes and curricula at each school, along with approaches to assessing curriculum benchmarks.

The national standards emphasize that the main purpose of assessing students is to guide and encourage students' own reflection and self-assessment. Consequently, ongoing feedback from the teacher is very important. Teachers give students formative and summative reports both through verbal feedback and on a numerical scale reflecting the students' levels of performance in relation to curriculum objectives. The teachers' reports must be based on multiple forms of assessment, not only exams.

Finland uses assessments to cultivate students' active learning skills by asking open-ended questions and helping students address these problems. In a Finnish classroom, teachers rarely stand at the front of a classroom lecturing students for 50 minutes. Instead, students are generally engaged in independent or group projects, often choosing tasks to work on and setting their own targets with teachers, who serve as coaches.[10] The cultivation of independence and active learning encourages students to develop analytical thinking, problem-solving, and metacognitive skills.

Before attending university, most Finnish students take a voluntary matriculation exam that asks students to apply problem-solving, analytic, and writing skills.[11] Teachers use official guidelines to grade matriculation exams locally, and samples of the grades are re-examined by professional raters hired by the Matriculation Exam Board.

Similarly, Sweden implements its nationally outlined and locally implemented curriculum with multiple assessments managed at the school level. Each school adapts a national curriculum and subject matter syllabi to local conditions.[12] Teachers design and score school-based assessments based on objectives outlined in each syllabus, and they assign grades based on syllabus goals and national assessment criteria. They are expected to meet with every student and parent each term to discuss the student's learning and social development, and they use a number of diagnostic materials to assess students' learning in Swedish, Swedish as a second language, English, and mathematics in relation to goals set by the syllabi.[13]

Schools offer nationally approved examinations in these same subjects in ninth grade and in the upper secondary years, where additional subject exams are available.[14] Teachers work with university faculty to design the tasks and questions, and they weight information from these exams, their own assessments, and classroom work to assign a grade reflecting how well students have met the objectives of the syllabus.[15] Regional education officials and schools provide time for teachers to calibrate their grading practices to minimize variation across the schools and across the region.[16] Toward the end of their upper secondary schooling, Swedish students receive a final grade or "learning certificate" in each area that acts as a compilation of all of these sources of evidence, including projects completed by the student as well as grades awarded for courses.

AUSTRALIA, THE UNITED KINGDOM, AND HONG KONG

Unlike such smaller countries as Finland and Sweden that have national curricula, in the much larger Australia each state has its own curriculum and assessment system. Australia's only national assessment is a periodic, matrix-sample-based assessment, similar to the National Assessment of Educational Progress in the United States. In most Australian states, local school-based performance assessment is a well-developed part of the system. In some cases, states have also centralized assessment with performance components. The two highest-achieving states, Queensland and Victoria, have the most highly developed systems of local performance assessment. Victoria, which uses a blended model of centralized and school-based assessment, also generally performs well on national and international tests.

Queensland, Australia. Queensland has had no external assessment system for 40 years. All assessments became school-based when the traditional "post-colonial" examination system was eliminated in the early 1970s, about the same time as in Finland and Sweden. Teachers develop, administer, and score school-based assessments in relation to the national curriculum guidelines and state syllabi (also developed by teachers). Panels that include teachers from other schools and university professors also moderate the assessments.

The syllabi spell out a few key concepts and skills to be learned in each course and the projects or activities (including minimum assessment requirements) that students should engage in. Each school designs its program to fit the needs and experiences of its own students, choosing specific texts and topics with this in mind. At year's end, teachers use a five-point grading scale to grade each portfolio of student work, which includes specific assessment tasks. To calibrate these grades, teachers assemble a selection of portfolios from each grade level—one from each of the five score levels, plus borderline cases—and send these to a regional panel for moderation. A panel of five teachers rescores the portfolios and confers about whether the grade is warranted. A state panel also looks at portfolios across schools. Based on these moderation processes, the school is instructed to adjust grades so they are comparable to others.

Queensland's "New Basics" and "Rich Tasks" approach to assessment, which began in 2003, offers extended, multidisciplinary tasks developed centrally but used when teachers determine the time is right and they can be integrated with locally oriented curricula. They are "specific activities that students undertake that have real-world value and use, and through which students are able to display their grasp and use of important ideas and skills."[17] Rich Tasks are defined as:

> a culminating performance or demonstration or product that is purposeful and models a life role. It presents substantive, real problems to solve and engages learners in forms of pragmatic social action that have real value in the world. The problems require identification, analysis, and resolution, and require students to analyze, theorize, and engage intellectually with the world. As well as having this connectedness to the world beyond the classroom, the tasks are also rich in their application: they represent an educational outcome of demonstrable and substantial intellectual and educational value. And, to be truly rich, a task must be transdisciplinary. Transdisciplinary learnings draw upon practices and skills across disciplines while retaining the integrity of each individual discipline.

A bank of these tasks now exists across grade levels, along with scoring rubrics and moderation processes by which the quality of the tasks, the student work, and the scoring can be evaluated. Research indicates the system has supported school improvement. Studies have found stronger student engagement in learning in schools using the Rich Tasks. On traditional tests, New Basics students scored about the same as students in the traditional program, but they performed notably better on assessments designed to gauge higher-order thinking.

The Singapore government has employed the developers of the Queensland system to focus its new school improvement strategies on performance assessments. High-scoring Hong Kong has also begun to expand its already ambitious school-based assessment system in collaboration with Queensland assessment developers.

Victoria, Australia. In Victoria, a mixed system of centralized and decentralized assessment combines school-based assessment practices with a set of state exams. Guided by the Victoria Essential Learning Standards, the AIM assessment program indicates how well students' literacy and numeracy skills are developing at grades 3, 5, 7, and 9. Assessment tasks include extended open-ended writing tasks, as well as some multiple-choice responses.

The Victoria Curriculum and Assessment Authority (VCAA) establishes courses in a wide range of studies, develops external examinations, and ensures the quality of the school-assessed component of the Victoria Certification of Education. VCAA conceptualizes assessment as "of," "for," and "as" learning. Teachers, along with university faculty, develop assessments, and all prior year assessments are public in order to make the standards and means of measuring them as transparent as possible. Before students take the external examinations, teachers and academics take the exams themselves, as if they were students. The external subject-specific examinations, given in grades 11 and 12, include written, oral, and performance elements scored by classroom teachers.

In addition, at least 50 percent of the total examination score consists of classroom-based tasks given throughout the school year. Teachers design these required assignments and assessments—lab experiments and investigations on central topics, as well as research papers and presentations. These classroom tasks ensure that students have the kind of learning opportunities that prepare them for assessments, that they are getting feedback to improve, and that they will be prepared to succeed not only on these very challenging tests but in college and in life, where they will have to apply knowledge in these ways.

An example of how this blended assessment system works can be seen in the interplay between an item from the Victoria, Australia, biology test and the classroom-based tasks also evaluated for the examination score. The open-ended item describes a particular virus and how it operates, then asks students to design a drug to kill the virus and explain how the drug operates (the multipage written answer is to include diagrams), and then asks students to design and describe an experiment to test the drug. In preparation for this on-demand test, students taking biology will have been assessed on six pieces of work during the school year covering specific outcomes in the syllabus. For example, they will have conducted "practical tasks," such as using a microscope to study plant and animal cells by preparing slides of cells, staining them, and comparing them in a variety of ways, resulting in a written product with visual elements. They also will have completed and presented a research report on characteristics of pathogenic organisms and mechanisms by which organisms can defend against disease. These tasks link directly to the expectations that students will encounter on the external examination but go well beyond what that examination can measure in terms of how students can apply their knowledge.

The tasks are graded according to criteria set out in the syllabus. The quality of the tasks assigned by teachers, work done by students, and the appropriateness of the grades and feedback given to students are audited through an inspection system, and schools receive feedback on all of these elements. In addition, the VCAA uses statistical moderation to ensure that the same assessment standards are applied to students across schools. External exams are used as the basis for this moderation, which adjusts the level and spread of each school's assessments of its students to match the level and spread of the same students' scores on the common external test score. The result is a rich curriculum for students with extensive teacher participation and a comparable means for examining student learning.

United Kingdom.   As in Victoria, assessments in Great Britain use a combination of external and school-based tasks based on the national curriculum and course syllabi. Throughout the school year, classroom-based tasks scored by teachers are used to evaluate student achievement of curriculum goals. At age 7, students take open-ended, nationally developed assessments in English and math that are scored by teachers in the school; at age 11, similar tests in English, math, and science are marked externally. At age 14, there was once a set of national exams to supplement teacher-created and administered assessments. Those external exams were abolished in October 2008, leaving only the teacher-developed assessments.[18]

While not mandatory, most students take a set of exams at year 11 (age 16) to achieve their General Certificate of Secondary Education (GCSE). Students may take as many single-subject or combined-subject assessments as they like, and they choose which ones they will take based on their interests and areas of expertise. Most GCSE items are essay questions. The math exam includes questions that ask students to show the reasoning behind their answers, and foreign language exams require oral presentations. About 25 percent to 30 percent of the final examination score is based on coursework and assessments developed and graded by teachers. In many subjects, students also complete a project worked on in class that is specified in the syllabus.

Wales and Northern Ireland allow students to participate in the GCSE exams at the high school level on a voluntary basis, but both broke from the more centralized system introduced in England under the Thatcher administration (later modified during the Blair administration as described above) and opted to abolish national exams.[19] Much like Finland and Sweden, Welsh schools during the primary years have a national school curriculum supported by teacher-created, administered, and scored assessments.[20] Northern Ireland, which has recently climbed significantly in international rankings, especially in literacy, is implementing "Assessment for Learning." This approach emphasizes locally developed, administered, and scored assessments and focuses, as in Finland, on students and teachers setting goals and success criteria together, teachers asking open-ended questions and students explaining their reasoning, teachers providing feedback during formative assessment sessions, and students engaging in self-assessment and reflection on their learning. Optional externally graded assessments also focus on how students reason, think, and problem solve.[21]

Hong Kong. In collaboration with educators from Australia, the United Kingdom, and other nations, Hong Kong's assessment system is evolving from a highly centralized examination system to one that increasingly emphasizes school-based, formative assessments that expect students to analyze issues and solve problems. The government has decided to gradually replace the Hong Kong Certificate of Education Examinations, which most students sit for at the end of their five-year secondary education, with a new diploma that will feature school-based assessments. In addition, the Territory-wide System Assessment (TSA), which assesses lower-grade student performance in Chinese, English, and mathematics, is developing an online bank of assessment tasks to enable schools to assess students and receive feedback on their performance on their own timeframes. The formal TSA assessments, which include both written and oral components, occur at primary grades 3 and 6 and secondary grade 3 (the equivalent of ninth grade in the United States).

As outlined in Hong Kong's "Learning to Learn" reform plan, the goal of the reforms is to shape curriculum and instruction around critical thinking, problem solving, self-management skills, and collaboration. A particular concern is to develop metacognitive thinking skills, so that students may themselves identify strengths and areas needing additional work.[22] By 2007, curriculum and assessment guides were published for four core subjects and 20 elective subjects, and assessments in the first two subjects—Chinese language and English language—were revised. These became criterion-referenced, performance-based assessments featuring not only the kinds of essays previously used on the exams, but also new speaking and listening components, the composition of written papers testing integrated skills, and a school-based component that factors into the examination score. Although existing assessments already use open-ended responses, the proportion of such responses will increase in the revised assessments.

As they do with existing assessments, teachers develop the new assessments with the participation of higher education faculty, and teachers who are trained as assessors score them. Tests are allocated randomly to scorers, and essay responses are typically rated by two independent scorers.[23] Results of the new school-based assessments are statistically moderated to ensure comparability within the province. The assessments are internationally benchmarked, through the evaluation of sample student papers, to peg results to those in other countries.

CONCLUSION

The design and use of standards, curricula, and assessments in high-achieving nations around the world are significantly different from the way tests are designed and used in the United States. Most testing in the United States emphasizes externally developed, machine-scored instruments that enter and leave the school in secret, offering little opportunity for teacher engagement with the evaluation of standards and little opportunity for student production of analyses, solutions, or ideas.

By contrast, assessment abroad involves teachers in developing and scoring intellectually challenging performance tasks that are embedded in and guide instruction, providing grist for feedback, student self-evaluation, and learning. The integration of curriculum, assessment, and instruction in a well-developed teaching and learning system creates the foundation for much more equitable and productive outcomes. Teachers and students come to understand the standards deeply, and they work continuously on activities and projects that develop skills as they are applied in the real world, as well as on the examinations themselves.

The tasks common in these assessment systems reflect what people increasingly need to know to succeed in today's knowledge-based economy: the abilities to find, analyze, and use information to solve real problems; to write and speak clearly and persuasively; to defend ideas; and to design and manage projects. While U.S. accountability efforts have focused on achieving higher test scores, they have not yet developed the kind of teaching and learning systems that could develop widespread capacity for significantly greater learning. A new vision for assessment will be critical to this goal—and to the possibilities of success for our children in today's and tomorrow's world.

Linda Darling-Hammond is the Charles E. DuCommun professor of education at Stanford University. Laura McCloskey is a doctoral student in the Stanford University School of Education. © 2008, Linda Darling-Hammond.

SWEDISH ASSESSMENTS

Swedish assessments use open-ended, authentic tasks asking students to demonstrate content knowledge and analytic skills in grappling with real-world problems. This sample question from a fifth-grade exam asks students (age 11–12) to think through a problem that they might have in their own lives:

> Carl bikes home from school at four o'clock; it takes about a quarter of an hour. In the evening, he's going back to school because the class is having a party. The party starts at six o'clock. Before the class party starts, Carl has to eat dinner. When he comes home, his grandmother calls, who is also his neighbor. She wants him to bring in her post before he bikes over to the class party. She also wants him to take her dog for a walk, then to come in and have a chat. What does Carl have time to do before the party begins? Write and describe below how you have reasoned.[1]

Upper secondary exams also frame challenging questions in real-world terms, with the expectation that students will show their work and reasoning. For example:

> In 1976, Lena had a monthly salary of 6,000 kr. By 1984, her salary had risen to 9,000 kr. In current prices, her salary had risen by 50%. How large was the percent change in fixed prices? In 1976, the Consumer Price Index (CPI) was 382; in 1984, it was 818.[2]

Students who experience a steady diet of such challenging assignments, which require thoughtful reasoning and the ability to communicate their thinking, are well-prepared for the kinds of problem solving required in the real world.

[1] Astrid Petterson, *The National Tests and National Assessment in Sweden* (Stockholm: PRIM gruppen, 2008), www.prim.su.se/artiktar/pdf/Sw_test_ICME.pdf.

[2] Max A. Eckstein and Harold J. Noah, *Secondary School Examinations: International Perspectives on Policies and Practice* (New Haven, CT: Yale University Press, 1993), pp. 270–72.

SCIENCE AND ETHICS CONFER

Students must identify, explore, and make judgments about a biotechnological process to which there are ethical dimensions. Students identify scientific techniques used, as well as significant recent contributions to the field. They will also research frameworks of ethical principles for coming to terms with an identified ethical issue or question. Using this information, they prepare preconference materials for an international conference that will feature selected speakers who are leading lights in their respective fields.

In order to do this, students must choose and explore an area of biotechnology where ethical issues are under consideration and undertake laboratory activities that help them understand some of the laboratory practices. This enables them to:

A. Provide a written explanation of the fundamental technological differences in some of the techniques used, or of potential use, in this area (included in the preconference package for delegates who are not necessarily experts in this area).

B. Consider the range of ethical issues raised in regard to this area's purposes and actions, as well as scientific techniques and principles, and present a deep analysis of an ethical issue about which there is a debate in terms of an ethical framework.

C. Select six real-life people who have made relevant contributions to this area and write a 150–200 word précis about each one indicating his or her contribution, as well as a letter of invitation to one of them.

This assessment measures research and analytic skills; laboratory practices; understanding biological and chemical structures and systems, nomenclature, and notations; organizing, arranging, sifting through, and making sense of ideas; communicating using formal correspondence; précis writing with

a purpose; understanding ethical issues and principles; time management; and much more.

ENDNOTES

1. Institute for Education Sciences, *Highlights from PISA 2006: Performance of U.S. 15-Year-Old Students in Science and Mathematics Literacy in an International Context* (Washington, DC: U.S. Department of Education, 2007), http://nces.ed.gov/surveys/pisa/index.asp.

2. See for example, William H. Schmidt, Hsing Chi Wang, and Curtis McKnight, "Curriculum Coherence: An Examination of U.S. Mathematics and Science Content Standards from an International Perspective," *Journal of Curriculum Studies*, vol. 37, 2005, pp. 525–59; Gilbert A. Valverde and William H. Schmidt, "Greater Expectations: Learning from Other Nations in the Quest for 'World-Class Standards' in U.S. School Mathematics and Science," *Journal of Curriculum Studies*, vol. 32, 2000, pp. 651–87; and Peter Fensham, "Progression in School Science Curriculum: A Rational Prospect or a Chimera?" *Research in Science Education*, vol. 24, 1994, pp. 76–82.

3. Elle Rustique-Forrester, "Accountability and the Pressures to Exclude: A Cautionary Tale from England," *Education Policy Analysis Archives*, 2005, http://epaa.asu.edu/epaa/vl3n26/.

4. For a summary, see Linda Darling-Hammond and E. Rustique-Forrester, "The Consequences of Student Testing for Teaching and Teacher Quality," in Joan Herman and Edward Haertel, eds., *The Uses and Misuses of Data in Accountability Testing* (Maiden, MA: Blackwell, 2005), pp. 289–319.

5. Reijo Laukkanen, "Finnish Strategy for High-Level Education for All," in N. C. Soguel and P. Jaccard, eds., *Governance and Performance of Education Systems* (Springer, 2008), p. 319. See also Friedrich Buchberger and Irina Buchberger, "Problem Solving Capacity of a Teacher Education System as a Condition of Success? An Analysis of the 'Finnish Case,'" in F. Buchberger and S. Berghammer, eds., *Education Policy Analysis in a Comparative Perspective* (Linz: Trauner, 2003), pp. 222–37.

6. European Commission, Directorate-General for Education and Culture, *Eurybase: The Information Database on Education Systems in Europe,*

The Education System in Sweden, 2006/2007 (Brussels: Eurydice, 2007).

7. Max A. Eckstein and Harold J. Noah, *Secondary School Examinations: International Perspectives on Policies and Practice* (New Haven, CT: Yale University Press, 1993), p. 84.

8. Finnish National Board of Education, "Background for Finnish PISA Success," 12 November 2007, www.oph.fi/english/SubPage.asp?parxi=447,65535,77331; and Jari Lavonen, "Reasons Behind Finnish Students' Success in the PISA Scientific Literacy Assessment" (Helsinki: University of Helsinki, 2008), www.oph.fi/info/fenlandin-pisastudies/conference2008/science_results_and_reasons.pdf

9. Finnish National Board of Education, "Basic Education," 10 June 2009, www.oph.fi/english/page.asp?path=447,4699,4847.

10. Salla Korpela, "The Finnish School—A Source of Skills and Well-Being: A Day at Stromberg Lower Comprehensive School," December 2004, http://virtual.finland.fi/netacomm/news/showarticle.asp?intNWSAID=30625.

11. The Finnish Matriculation Examination, 2008, www.ylioppilastutkinto.fi/en/index.html.

12. Swedish National Agency for Education, "The Swedish School System: Compulsory School," 2005, www.skolverket.se/sb/d/354/a/959.

13. Eckstein and Noah, op. cit., pp. 83–84; Qualifications and Curriculum Authority, "Sweden: Assessment Arrangements," 2008, www.inca.org.uk/690.html; and Sharon O'Donnell, *International Review of Curriculum and Assessment Framework: Comparative Tables and Factual Summaries, 2004* (London: Qualifications and Curriculum Authority, National Foundation for Educational Research, December 2004), p. 23, www.inca.org.

uk/pdf/comparative.pdf.

14. Swedish National Agency for Education, op. cit.

15. Eckstein and Noah, op. cit.; and O'Donnell, op. cit.

16. Eckstein and Noah, op. cit., p. 230.

17. New Basics Branch, *New Basics: The Why, What, How and When of Rich Tasks* (Brisbane: Queensland Department of Education, 2001), http://education.qld.gov.au/corporate/newbasics/pdis/richtasksbklet.pdf.

18. Qualifications and Curriculum Authority, "England: Assessment Arrangements," 2008, www.inca.org.uk/england-assessment-mainstream.html.

19. Jeff Archer, "Wales Eliminates National Exams for Many Students," *Education Week,* 19 December 2006, www.edweek.org/ew/articles/2006/12/20/16wales.h26.html?qs=Wales.

20. Welsh Assembly Government, "Primary (3–11)," 2008, http://old.accac.org.uk/eng/content.php?cID=5; idem, "Secondary (11–16)," 2008, http://oldaccac.org.uk/eng/content.php?cID=6.

21. Council for the Curriculum Examinations and Assessment, "Curriculum, Key Stage 3, Post-Primary Assessment," 2008, www.ccea.org.uk, search on tide.

22. Jacqueline Kin-Sang Chan, Kerry J. Kennedy, Flora Wai-Ming Yu, and Ping-Kwan Fok, "Assessment Policy in Hong Kong: Implementation Issues for New Forms of Assessment," paper presented at the 32nd annual conference of the International Association for Educational Assessment, Singapore, 2006, www.iaea.info/papers.aspx?id=68.

23. Mark Dowling, "Examining the Exams," no date, www.hkeaa.edu.hk.

DISCUSSION QUESTIONS

1. Curriculum and assessments vary internationally. Why do you believe some nations are more successful in educating their students than others?
2. The authors describe the educational systems of different countries. Which system's methods do you most agree with? Explain.
3. Other high-performing countries use the results of assessments to inform and influence curricular decisions. In the wake of No Child Left Behind and the increased emphasis on accountability, do you believe assessments results should be used punitively to "grade" schools?

4. The United States focuses on multiple choice assessments while other high-achieving countries assess their students using open-ended, school-based tasks, and portfolios. What is the feasibility of adopting these assessment methods in the United States?

5. Some other high-achieving countries such as Finland use local assessments to test their national standards. Do you believe this is an effective way to evaluate student progress? Explain.

34 Perennial Reform: Fixing School Time

LARRY CUBAN

FOCUSING QUESTIONS

1. Compare the different proposals to extend academic learning time over the past quarter century.

2. Why haven't school reform efforts to extend academic learning time been successful?

3. How have the public's goals for education shaped the structure of schools in this country?

4. Compare the views of policy makers and teachers towards school time reform.

5. How has the belief that college is for everyone affected policy makers' attitudes towards school time?

ABSTRACT

Education critics often call for longer school days and years. But there is little research to support such demands and several reasons why little will change.

In the past quarter century, reformers have repeatedly urged schools to fix their use of time, even though it is a solution that is least connected to what happens in classrooms or what Americans want from public schools. Since *A Nation at Risk* in 1983, *Prisoners of Time* in 1994, and the latest blue-ribbon recommendations in *Tough Choices, Tough Times* in 2007, both how much time and how well students spend it in school have been criticized to no end.[1, 2]

Business and civil leaders have been critical because they see U.S. students stuck in the middle ranks on international tests. These leaders believe that the longer school year in Asia and Europe is linked to those foreign students scoring far higher than U.S. students on those tests.

Employers criticize the amount of time students spend in school because they wonder whether the limited days and hours spent in classes are sufficient to produce the skills that employees need to work in a globally competitive economy. Employers also wonder whether our comparatively short school year will teach the essential workplace behaviors of punctuality, regular attendance, meeting deadlines, and following rules.

Parents criticize school schedules because they want schools to be open when they go to work in the morning and to remain open until they pick up their children before dinner.

Professors criticize policy makers for allotting so little time for teachers to gain new knowledge and skills during the school day. Other researchers want both policy makers and practitioners to distinguish between requiring more time in school and academic learning time, academic jargon for those hours and minutes where teachers engage students in learning content and skills or, in more jargon, time on task.[3]

Finally, cyberschool champions criticize school schedules because they think it's quaint to have students sitting at desks in a building with hundreds of other students for 180 days when a revolution in communication devices allows children to learn the formal curriculum in many places, not just in school buildings. Distance learning advocates, joined by those who see cyberschools as the future, want children and youths to spend hardly any time in K–12 schools.[4]

TIME OPTIONS

Presidential commissions, parents, academics, and employers have proposed the same solutions, again and again, for fixing the time students spend in school: Add more days to the annual school calendar. Change to year-round schools. Add instructional time to the daily schedule. Extend the school day.

What has happened to each proposal in the past quarter century?

Longer School Year. Recommendations for a longer school year (from 180 to 220 days) came from *A Nation at Risk* (1983) and *Prisoners of Time* (1994) plus scores of other commissions and experts. In 2008, a generously supported foundation-funded report, *A Stagnant Nation: Why American Students*

Are Still at Risk, found that the 180-day school year was intact across the nation and only Massachusetts had started a pilot program to help districts lengthen the school year. The same report gave a grade of F to states for failing to significantly expand student learning time.[5]

Year-Round Schools. Ending the summer break is another way to maximize student time in school. There is a homespun myth, treated as fact, that the annual school calendar, with three months off for both teachers and students, is based on the rhythm of nineteenth-century farm life, which dictated when school was in session. Thus, planting and harvesting chores accounted for long summer breaks, an artifact of agrarian America. Not so.

Actually, summer vacations grew out of early twentieth-century urban middle-class parents (and later lobbyists for camps and the tourist industry) pressing school boards to release children to be with their families for four to eight weeks or more. By the 1960s, however, policy maker and parent concerns about students losing ground academically during the vacation months—in academic language, "summer loss"—gained support for year-round schooling. Cost savings also attracted those who saw facilities being used 12 months a year rather than being shuttered during the summer.

Nonetheless, although year-round schools were established as early as 1906 in Gary, Indiana, calendar innovations have had a hard time entering most schools. Districts with year-round schools still work within the 180-day year but distribute the time more evenly (e.g., 45 days in session, 15 days off) rather than having a long break between June and September. As of 2006, nearly 3,000 of the nation's 90,000 public schools enrolled more than 2.1 million students on a year-round calendar. That's less than 5 percent of all students attending public schools, and almost half of the year-round schools are in California. In most cases, school boards adopted year-round schools because increased enrollments led to crowded facilities, most often in minority and poor communities—not due to concerns over "summer loss."[6]

Adding Instructional Time to the School Day. Many researchers and reformers have pointed out that the 6½-hour school day has so many interruptions and so many distractions that teachers have less than five hours of genuine instruction time. Advocates for more instructional time have tried to stretch the actual amount of instructional time available to teachers to a 7-hour day (or 5½ hours of time for time-on-task learning) or have tried to redistribute the existing secondary school schedule into 90-minute blocks rather than the traditional 50-minute periods. Since *A Nation at Risk*, this recommendation for more instructional time has resulted only in an anemic 10 more minutes per day when elementary school students study core academic subjects.[7]

Block scheduling in public secondary schools (60- to 90-minute periods for a subject that meets different days of the week) was started in the 1960s to promote instructional innovations. Various modified schedules have spread slowly, except in a few states where block schedules multiplied rapidly. In the past decade, an explosion of interest in small high schools has led many traditional urban comprehensive high schools of 1,500 or more students to convert to smaller high schools of 300 to 400 students, sometimes with all of those smaller schools housed within the original large building, sometimes as separate schools located elsewhere in the district. In many of these small high schools, modified schedules with instructional periods of an hour or more have found a friendly home. Block schedules rearrange existing allotted time for instruction; they do not add instructional time to the school day.[8]

Extended School Day. In the past half century, as the economy has changed and families increasingly have both (or single) parents working, schools have been pressed to take on childcare responsibilities, such as tutoring and homework supervision before and after school. Many elementary schools open at 7 a.m. for parents to drop off children and have after-school programs that close at 6 p.m. PDK/Gallup polls since the early 1980s show increased support for these before-and after-school programs. Instead of the familiar half-day program for 5-year-olds, all-day kindergartens (and pre-kindergartens for 4-year-olds) have spread swiftly in the past two decades, especially in low-income neighborhoods. Innovative urban schools, such as the for-profit Edison Inc. and KIPP (Knowledge Is Power Program), run longer school days. The latter routinely opens at 7:30 a.m. and closes at 5 p.m. and also schedules biweekly Saturday classes and three weeks of school during the summer.[9]

If reformers want a success story in fixing school time, they can look to extending the school day, although it's arguable how many of those changes occurred because of reformers' arguments and actions and how many from economic and social changes in family structure and the desire to chase a higher standard of living.

Cybereducation. And what about those public school haters and cheerleading technological enthusiasts who see fixing time in school as a wasted effort when online schooling and distance learning can replace formal schooling? In the 1960s and 1970s, Ivan Illich and other school critics called for dismantling public schools and ending formal schooling. They argued that schools squelched natural learning, confused school-based education with learning, and turned children into obedient students and adults rather than curious and independent lifelong learners. Communication and instructional technologies were in their infancy then, and thinkers such as Illich had few alternatives to offer families who opted out.[10]

Much of that ire directed at formal public schooling still exists, but now technology has made it possible for students to learn outside school buildings. Sharing common ground in this debate are deeply religious families who want to avoid secular influences in schools, highly educated parents who fear the stifling effects of school rules and text-bound instruction, and rural parents who simply want their children to have access to knowledge unavailable in their local schools. These advocates seek home schooling, distance learning, and cyber schools.[11]

Slight increases in home schooling may occur—say from 1.1 million in 2003 to 2 to 3 million by the end of the decade, with the slight uptick in numbers due to both the availability of technology and a broader menu of choices for parents. Still, this represents less than 3 percent of public school students. Even though cheerleaders for distance learning have predicted wholesale changes in conventional site-based schools for decades, such changes will occur at the periphery, not the center, because most parents will continue to send their children to public schools.[12]

Even the most enthusiastic advocates for cyberschools and distance education recognize that replacing public schools is, at best, unlikely. The foreseeable future will still have 50 million children and youths crossing the schoolhouse door each weekday morning.

THREE REASONS

Reformers have spent decades trotting out the same recipes for fixing the time problem in school. For all the hoopla and all of the endorsements from highly influential business and political elites, their mighty efforts have produced minuscule results. Why is that?

Cost is the usual suspect. Covering additional teacher salaries and other expenses runs high. Minnesota provides one example: shifting from 175 to 200 days of instruction

cost districts an estimated $750 million a year, a large but not insurmountable price to pay.[13] But costs for extending the school day for instruction and childcare are far less onerous.

Even more attractive than adding days to the calendar, however, is the claim that switching to a year-round school will save dollars. So, while there are costs involved in lengthening the school calendar, cost is not the tipping point in explaining why so few proposals to fix school time are successful.

I offer two other reasons why fixing school time is so hard.

Research showing that achievement gains are due to more time in school are sparse. The few studies most often displayed are contested.

Late twentieth-century policy makers seriously underestimated the powerful tug that conservative, noneconomic goals (e.g., citizenship, character formation) have on parents, taxpayers, and voters. When they argued that America needed to add time to the school calendar in order to better prepare workers for global competition, they were out of step with the American public's desires for schools.

SKIMPY RESEARCH

In the past quarter century of tinkering with the school calendar, cultural changes, political decisions, or strong parental concerns trumped research every time. Moreover, the longitudinal and rigorous research on time in school was—and is—skimpy. The studies that exist are challenged repeatedly for being weakly designed. For example, analysts examining research on year-round schools have reported that most of the studies have serious design flaws and, at best, show slight positive gains in student achievement—except for students from low-income families, for whom gains were sturdier. As one report concluded: "[N]o truly trustworthy studies have been done on modified school calendars that can serve as the basis for sound policy decisions." Policy talk about year-round schools has easily outstripped results.[14]

Proving that time in school is the crucial variable in raising academic achievement is difficult because so many other variables must be considered—the local context itself, available resources, teacher quality, administrative leadership, socioeconomic and cultural background of students and their families, and what is taught. But the lack of careful research has seldom stopped reform-driven decision makers from pursuing their agendas.

CONFLICTING SCHOOL GOALS

If the evidence suggests that, at best, a longer school year or day or restructured schedules do not seem to make the key difference in student achievement, then I need to ask: What problem are reformers trying to solve by adding more school time?

The short answer is that for the past quarter century—*A Nation at Risk* (1983) is a suitable marker—policy elites have redefined a national economic problem into an educational problem. Since the late 1970s, influential civic, business, and media leaders have sold Americans the story that lousy schools are the reason why inflation surged, unemployment remained high, incomes seldom rose, and cheaper and better foreign products flooded U.S. stores. Public schools have failed to produce a strong, postindustrial labor force, thus leading to a weaker, less competitive U.S. economy. U.S. policy elites have used lagging scores on international tests as telling evidence that U.S. schools graduate less knowledgeable, less skilled high school graduates—especially those from minority and poor schools who will be heavily represented in the mid-twenty-first-century workforce—than those of competitor nations with lower-paid workforces who produce high-quality products.

Microsoft founder Bill Gates made the same point about U.S. high schools.

> In district after district across the country, wealthy white kids are taught Algebra II, while low-income minority kids are taught how to balance a checkbook. This is an economic disaster. In the international competition to have the best supply of workers who can communicate clearly, analyze information, and solve complex problems, the United States is falling behind. We have one of the highest high school dropout rates in the industrialized world.[15]

And here, in a nutshell, is the second reason why those highly touted reforms aimed at lengthening the school year and instructional day have disappointed policy makers. By blaming schools, contemporary civic and business elites have reduced the multiple goals Americans expect of their public schools to a single one: prepare youths to work in a globally competitive economy. This has been a mistake because Americans historically have expected more from their public schools. Let me explore the geography of this error.

For nearly three decades, influential groups have called for higher academic standards, accountability for student outcomes, more homework, more testing, and, of course, more time in school. Many of their recommendations have been adopted. By 2008, U.S. schools had a federally driven system of state-designed standards anchored in increased testing, results-driven accountability, and demands for students to spend more time in school. After all, reformers reasoned, the students of foreign competitors were attending school more days in the year and longer hours each day, even on weekends, and their test scores ranked them higher than the U.S. students.

Even though this simplistic causal reasoning has been questioned many times by researchers who examined education and work performance in Japan, Korea, Singapore, Germany, and other nations, "common sense" observations by powerful elites swept away such questions. So the United States' declining global economic competitiveness had been spun into a time-in-school problem.[16]

But convincing evidence, drawn from research, that more time in school would lead to a stronger economy, fewer inequalities in family income, and that elusive edge in global competitiveness—much less a higher rank in international tests—remains missing in action.

THE PUBLIC'S GOALS FOR EDUCATION

Business and civic elites have succeeded at least twice in the past century in making the growth of a strong economy the primary aim of U.S. schools, but other goals have had an enormous and enduring impact on schooling, both in the past and now. These goals embrace core American values that have been like second-hand roses, shabby and discarded clothes hidden in the back of the closet and occasionally trotted out for show during graduation. Yet since the origins of tax-supported public schools in the early nineteenth century, these goals have been built into the very structures of schools, so much so that, looking back from 2008, we hardly notice them.[17]

Time-based reforms have had trouble entering schools because other goals have had—and continue to have—clout with parents and taxpayers. Opinion polls, for example, display again and again what parents, voters, and taxpayers want schools to achieve. One recent poll identified the public's goals for public schools. The top five were to:

- Prepare people to become responsible citizens;
- Help people become economically sufficient;
- Ensure a basic level of quality among schools;
- Promote cultural unity among all Americans;
- Improve social conditions for people.

Tied for sixth and seventh were goals to:

- Enhance people's happiness and enrich their lives; and
- Dispel inequities in education among certain schools and certain groups.[18]

To reach those goals, a democratic society expects schools to produce adults who are engaged in their communities, enlightened employers, and hard-working employees who have acquired and practiced particular values that sustain its way of life. Dominant American social, political, and economic values pervade family, school, workplace, and community: Act independently; accept personal responsibility for actions; work hard and complete a job well; and be fair, that is, willing to be judged by standards applied to others as long as the standards are applied equitably.[19]

These norms show up in school rules and classroom practices in every school. School is the one institutional agent between the family, the workplace, and voting booth or jury room responsible for instilling those norms in children's behavior. School is the agent for turning 4-year-olds into respectful students engaged in their communities, a goal that the public perceives as more significant than preparing children and youths for college and the labor market. In elite decision makers' eagerness to link schools to a growing economy, they either overlooked the powerful daily practices of schooling or neglected to consider seriously these other goals. In doing so, they erred. The consequences of that error in judgment can be seen in the fleeting attention that policy recommendations for adding more time in school received before being shelved.

TEACHING IN A DEMOCRACY

Public schools were established before industrialization, and they expanded rapidly as factories and mills spread.

Those times appear foreign to readers today. For example, in the late nineteenth century, calling public schools "factory-like" was not derogatory, unlike the epithet hurled at educators or supporters of public schools in the United States since the 1960s.[20] In fact, describing a public school as an assembly-line factory or a productive cotton mill was considered a compliment to forward-looking educators who sought to make schools modern through greater efficiency in teaching and learning by copying the successes of wealthy industrialists. Progressive reformers praised schools for being like industrial plants in creating large, efficient, age-graded schools that standardized curriculum while absorbing millions of urban migrants and foreign immigrants. As a leading progressive put it:

> Our schools are, in a sense, factories in which the raw products (children) are to be shaped and fashioned into products to meet the various demands of life . . . . It is the business of the school to build its pupils to the specifications [of manufacturers].[21]

Progressive reformers saw mills, factories, and corporations as models for transforming the inefficient one-room schoolhouse in which students of different ages received fitful, incomplete instruction from one teacher into the far more efficient graded school where each teacher taught students a standardized curriculum each year. First established in Boston in 1848 and spreading swiftly in urban districts, by 1900 the graded school became the dominant way of organizing a school. By the 1920s, schools exemplified the height of industrial efficiency because each building had separate classrooms with their own teachers. The principal and teachers expected children of the same age to cover the same content and learn skills by the end of the school year and perform satisfactorily on tests in order to be promoted to the next grade.[22]

Superintendents saw the age-graded school as a modern version of schooling well adapted to an emerging corporate-dominated industrial society where punctuality, dependability, and obedience were prized behaviors. As a St. Louis superintendent said in 1871:

> The first requisite of the school is Order: each pupil must be taught first and foremost to conform his behavior to a general standard. . . . The pupil must have his lessons ready at the appointed time, must rise at the tap of the bell, move to the line, return; in short, go through all of the evolutions with equal precision.

Recognition and fame went to educators who achieved such order in their schools.[23]

But the farm-driven seasonal nature of rural one-room schoolhouses was incompatible with the explosive growth of cities and an emerging industrial society. In the early twentieth century, progressive reformers championed compulsory attendance laws while extending the abbreviated rural-driven short hours and days into a longer school day and year. Reformers wanted to increase the school's influence over children's attitudes and behavior, especially in cities where wave after wave of European immigrants settled. Seeking higher productivity in organization, teaching, and learning at the least cost, reformers broadened the school's mission by providing medical, social, recreational, and psychological services at schools. These progressive reformers believed schools should teach society's norms to both children and their families and also educate the whole child so that the entire government, economy, and society would change for the better. So, when reformers spoke about "factory-like schools" a century ago, they wanted educators to copy models of success; they were not scolding them. That changed, however, by the late twentieth century.

As the United States shifted from a manufacturing-based economy to a post-industrial information-based economy, few policy makers reckoned with this history of schooling.

Few influential decision makers view schools as agents of *both* stability and change. Few educational opinion makers recognize that the conservative public still expects schools to instill in children dominant American norms of being independent and being held accountable for one's actions, doing work well and efficiently, and treating others equitably to ensure that when students graduate they will practice these values as adults. And, yes, the public still expects schools to strengthen the economy by ensuring that graduates have the necessary skills to be productive employees in an ever-changing, highly competitive, and increasingly global workplace. But that is just one of many competing expectations for schools.

Thus far, I have focused mostly on how policy makers and reform-minded civic and business elites have not only defined economic problems as educational ones that can be fixed by more time spent in schools but also neglected the powerful hold that socialization goals have on parents' and taxpayers' expectations. Now, I want to switch from the world of reform-driven policy makers and elites to teachers and students because each group views school time differently from its respective perch. Teacher and student perspectives on time in school have little influence in policy makers' decision making. Although the daily actions of teachers and students don't influence policy makers, they do matter in explaining why reformers have had such paltry results in trying to fix school time.

DIFFERING VIEWS OF TIME IN SCHOOL

For civic and business leaders, media executives, school boards, superintendents, mayors, state legislators, governors, U.S. representatives, and the president (what I call "policy elites"), electoral and budget cycles become the timeframe within which they think and act. Every year, budgets must be prepared and, every two or four years, officials run for office and voters decide who should represent them and whether they should support bond referenda and tax levies. Because appointed and elected policy makers are influential with the media, they need to assure the public during campaigns that slogans and stump speeches were more than talk. Sometimes, words do become action when elected decision makers, for example, convert a comprehensive high school into a cluster of small high schools, initiate 1:1 laptop programs, and extend the school day. This is the world of policy makers.

The primary tools policy makers use to adopt and implement decisions, however, are limited and blunt—closer to a hammer than a scalpel. They use exhortation, press conferences, political bargaining, incentives, and sanctions to formulate and adopt decisions. (Note, however, that policy makers rarely implement decisions; administrators and practitioners put policies into practice.) Policy makers want broad social, political, economic, and organizational goals adopted as policies, and then they want to move educators, through encouragement, incentives, and penalties, to implement those policies in schools and classrooms that they seldom, if ever, enter.

The world of teachers differs from that of policy makers. For teachers, the time-driven budget and electoral cycles that shape policy matter little for their classrooms, except when such policies carry consequences for how and what teachers should teach, such as accountability measures that assume teachers and students are slackers and need to work harder. In these instances, teachers become classroom gatekeepers in deciding how much of a policy they will put into practice and under what conditions.

What matters most to teachers are student responses to daily lessons, weekly tests, monthly units, and the connections they build over time in classrooms, corridors, during lunch, and before and after school. Those personal connections become the compost of learning. Those connections account for former students pointing to particular teachers who made a difference in their lives.

Teacher tools, unlike policy maker tools, are unconnected to organizational power or media influence. Teachers use their personalities, knowledge, experience, and skills in building relationships with groups of students and providing individual help. Teachers believe there is never enough time in the daily schedule to finish a lesson, explain a point, or listen to a student. Administrative intrusions gobble up valuable instructional time that could go to students. In class, then, both teachers and students are clock watchers, albeit for different reasons.[24]

Students view time differently as well. For a fraction of students from middle and low-income families turned off by school requirements and expectations, spending time in classrooms listening to teachers, answering questions, and doing homework is torture; the hands of the clock seldom move fast enough for them. The notion of extending the school day and school year for them—or continuing on to college and four more years of reading texts and sitting in classrooms—is not a reform to be implemented but a punishment to be endured. Such students look for creative shortcuts to skip classes, exit the school as early as they can, and find jobs or enter the military once they graduate.

Most students, however, march from class to class until they hear "Pomp and Circumstance." But a high school diploma, graduates have come to realize, is not enough in the twenty-first-century labor market.

COLLEGE FOR EVERYONE

In the name of equity and being responsive to employers' needs, most urban districts have converted particular comprehensive high schools into clusters of small college-prep academies where low-income minority students take Advanced Placement courses, write research papers, and compete to get into colleges and universities. Here, then, is the quiet, unheralded, and unforeseen victory of reformers bent on fixing time in

school. They have succeeded unintentionally in stretching K–12 into pre-K–16 public schooling, not just for middle- and upper-middle-class students, but for everyone.

As it has been for decades for most suburban middle- and upper-middle-class white and minority families, now it has become a fact, an indisputable truth converted into a sacred mission for upwardly mobile poor families: A high school diploma and a bachelor's degree are passports to high-paying jobs and the American Dream.

For families who already expect their sons and daughters to attend competitive colleges, stress begins early. Getting into the best preschools and elementary and secondary schools and investing in an array of activities to build attractive résumés for college admission officers to evaluate become primary tasks. For such families and children, there is never enough time for homework, Advanced Placement courses, music, soccer, drama, dance, and assorted after-school activities. For high-achieving, stressed-out students already expecting at least four more years of school after high school graduation, reform proposals urging a longer school year and an extended day often strike an unpleasant note. Angst and fretfulness become familiar clothes to don every morning as students grind out 4s and 5s on Advanced Placement exams, play sports, and compile just the right record that will get them into just the right school.[25]

For decades, pressure on students to use every minute of school to prepare for college has been strongest in middle- and upper-middle-class suburbs. What has changed in the past few decades is the spread of the belief that everyone, including low-income minority students, should go to college.

To summarize, for decades, policy elites have disregarded teacher and student perspectives on time in school. Especially now when all students are expected to enter college, children, youths, and teachers experience time in school differently than do policy makers who seek a longer school day and school year. Such varied perceptions about time are heavily influenced by the socialization goals of schooling, age-graded structures, socioeconomic status of families, and historical experience. And policy makers often ignore these perceptions and reveal their tone-deafness and myopia in persistently trying to fix time in schools.

Policy elites need to parse fully this variation in perceptions because extended time in school remains a high priority to reform-driven policy makers and civic and business leaders anxious about U.S. performance on international tests and fearful of falling behind in global economic competitiveness. The crude policy solutions of more days in the year and longer school days do not even begin to touch the deeper truth that what has to improve is the quality of "academic learning time." If policy makers could open their ears and eyes to student and teacher perceptions of time, they would learn that the secular Holy Grail is decreasing interruption of instruction, encouraging richer intellectual and personal connections between teachers and students, and increasing classroom time for ambitious teaching and active, engaged learning. So far, no such luck.

CONCLUSION

These three reasons—cost, lackluster research, and the importance of conservative social goals to U.S. taxpayers and voters—explain why proposals to fix time in U.S. schools have failed to take hold.

Policy elites know research studies proving the worth of year-round schools or lengthened school days are in short supply. Even if an occasional study supported the change, the school year is unlikely to go much beyond 180 days. Policy elites know school goals go far beyond simply preparing graduates for college and for employability in a knowledge-based economy. And policy elites know they must show courage in their

pursuit of improving failing U.S. schools by forcing students to go to school just as long as their peers in India, China, Japan, and Korea. That courage shows up symbolically, playing well in the media and in proposals to fix time in schools, but it seldom alters calendars.

While cost is a factor, it is the stability of schooling structures and the importance of socializing the young into the values of the immediate community and larger society that have defeated policy-driven efforts to alter time in school over the past quarter century. Like the larger public, I am unconvinced that requiring students and teachers to spend more time in school each day and every year will be better for them. How that time is spent in learning before, during, and after school is far more important than decision makers counting the minutes, hours, and days students spend each year getting schooled. That being said, I have little doubt that state and federal blue-ribbon commissions will continue to make proposals about lengthening time in school. Those proposals will make headlines, but they will not result in serious, sustained attention to what really matters—improving the quality of the time that teachers and students spend with one another in and out of classrooms.

ENDNOTES

1. I wish to thank Selma Wassermann for her most helpful comments and suggestions on the penultimate draft and Bruce Smith for inviting me to do this special report.

2. National Commission on Excellence in Education, *A Nation at Risk* (Washington, DC: U.S. Government Printing Office, 1983); National Education Commission on Time and Learning, *Prisoners of Time* (Washington, DC: U.S. Government Printing Office, 1994); New Commission on the Skills of the American Work Force, *Tough Times or Tough Choices* (San Francisco: Jossey-Bass, 2006).

3. David Berliner, "What's All the Fuss About Instructional Time?" in Miriam Ben-Peretz and Rainer Bromme, eds., *The Nature of Time in Schools:*

Theoretical Concepts, Practitioner Perceptions (New York: Teachers College Press, 1990).

4. See, for example, North Central Regional Educational Laboratory, "E-Learning Policy Implications for K-12 Educators and Decision Makers," 2001, www.ncrel.org/policy/pubs/html/pivol11/apr2002d.htm.

5. Strong American Schools, *A Stagnant Nation: Why American Students Are Still at Risk* (Washington, DC, 2008), pp. 3–4.

6. Joel Weiss and Robert Brown, "Telling Tales Over Time: Constructing and Deconstructing the School Calendar," *Teachers College Record,* 2003, pp. 1720–57; Shaun P. Johnson and Terry E. Spradlin, "Alternatives to the Traditional School-Year Calendar," *Education Policy Brief, Center for Evaluation & Education Policy,* Spring 2007, p. 3; for a description of the "Gary Plan" of year-round schooling, see Ronald Cohen, *Children of the Mill: Schooling and Society in Gary, Indiana, 1906–1960* (Bloomington: Indiana University Press, 1990).

7. Strong American Schools, op. cit., p. 4.

8. Robert Canady and Michael Rettig, *Block Scheduling: A Catalyst for Change in High Schools* (Larchmont, NY: Eye on Education, 1995); personal communication from Michael Rettig, April 28, 2008.

9. Lowell C. Rose and Alec M. Gallup, "38th Annual Phi Delta Kappa/Gallup Poll of the Public's Attitudes Toward the Public Schools," *Phi Delta Kappan,* September 2006; Sarah Huyvaert, *Time Is of the Essence: Learning in School* (Boston: Allyn & Bacon, 1998), pp. 59–67; for KIPP, see www.kipp.org/01/whatisakippschool.cfm.

10. Ivan Illich, *Deschooling Society* (New York: Harper & Row, 1971).

11. For a politically conservative view on home schooling and its history, see Isabel Lyman, "Home Schooling: Back to the Future?" *Cato Institute Policy Analysis No. 294,* January 7, 1998, www.cato.org/pubs/pas/pa-294.html. Beginning nearly a decade ago, state- and district-funded cyber schools, such as Florida Virtual School, provide courses for homeschoolers, parents who want more learning options for their children, and students in isolated rural areas who lack access to advanced high school courses. Florida Virtual School served over 50,000 students in 2006-07 and expects to reach 100,000 in 2009. See www.flvs.net.

12. For predictions from the 1990s and current ones for distance learning and students' use of the Internet, see "Predictions Database" in Elon University's "Imagining the Internet," www.elon.edu/predictions/q13.aspx. For an astute analysis of distance learning, see Clayton M. Christensen and Michael B. Horn, "How Do We Transform Our Schools?" *Education Next,* Summer 2008, www.hoover.org/publications/ednext/18575969.html. For the 2003 figure on home-schooled children, see "Fast Facts" from National Center for Education Statistics, http://nces.ed.gov/fastfacts/display.asp?id=65.

13. The Minnesota example comes from Elena Silva, "On the Clock: Rethinking the Way Schools Use Time," *Education Sector Reports,* January 2007, p. 8; for cost savings in year-round schools, see Nasser Daneshvary and Terrence M. Clauretie, "Efficiency and Costs in Education: Year-Round Versus Traditional Schedules," *Economics of Education Review,* 2001, pp. 279–87.

14. Shaun P. Johnson and Terry E. Spradlin, op. cit., p. 5; Harris Cooper, et al., "The Effects of Modified School Calendars on Student Achievement and on School and Community Attitudes," *Review of Educational Research,* Spring 2003, pp. 1–52.

15. Bill Gates, "What Is Wrong with America's High Schools?" *Los Angeles Times,* March 3, 2005, p. B11.

16. One of the better summaries of how schools had become the central problem to the future of the nation in the 1980s can be found in Chester E. Finn, Jr., *We Must Take Charge: Our Schools and Our Future* (New York: Free Press, 1991); also see Diane Ravitch, "The Test of Time," *Education Next,* Spring 2003, www.educationnext.org/20032/32.html; and, in the same issue, see a reprint of Albert Shanker's retrospective (9 May 1993) on the *A Nation at Risk* report. For analyses of other countries compared to the United States, see Norton Grubb and Marvin Lazerson, *The Education Gospel: The Economic Power of Schooling* (Cambridge: Harvard University Press, 2004), pp. 170–72.

17. John Goodlad, *A Place Called School* (New York: McGraw-Hill, 1984); and David Labaree, "Public Goods, Private Goods: The American Struggle over Educational Goals," *American Educational Research Journal,* Spring 1997, pp. 39–81.

18. Lowell C. Rose and Alec M. Gallup, "The 32nd Annual Phi Delta Kappa/Gallup Poll of the

Public's Attitudes Toward the Public Schools," *Phi Delta Kappan,* September 2000, p. 47.

19. There are other personal values, such as honesty, trustworthiness, and others, that are highly prized and reinforced by teachers and school policies, but I will focus on the obvious societal values embedded in the structures and processes of tax-supported schooling. See Robert Dreeben, *On What Is Learned in School* (Reading, MA: Addison-Wesley, 1968); Steven Brint, Mary C. Contreras, and Michael T. Matthews, "Socialization Messages in Primary Schools: An Organizational Analysis," *Sociology of Education,* July 2001, pp. 157–80; and Philip Jackson, *Life in Classrooms* (New York: Holt, Rinehart, and Winston, 1968).

20. For examples of the pejorative use of "factory-like schools," see Samuel Bowles and Herbert Gintis, *Schooling in Capitalist America: Educational Reform and the Contradictions of Economic Life* (New York: Basic Books, 1976); and Joel Spring, "Education as a Form of Social Control," in Clarence Karier, Paul Violas, and Joel Spring, eds., *Roots of Crisis: American Education in the 20th Century* (Chicago: Rand McNally, 1973), pp. 30-39.

21. Quote cited in Raymond Callahan, *Education and the Cult of Efficiency* (Chicago: University of Chicago Press, 1962), p. 152. It comes from Stanford Professor Ellwood P. Cubberley in his textbook, *Public School Administration,* written in 1916.

22. David L. Angus, Jeffrey E. Mirel, and Maris A. Vinovskis, "Historical Development of Age-Stratification in Schooling," *Teachers College Record,* Winter 1988, pp. 211–36.

23. David B. Tyack, *The One Best System: A History of American Urban Education* (Cambridge: Harvard University Press, 1974), p. 43.

24. Marty Swaim and Stephen Swaim, *Teacher Time: Why Teacher Workload and School Management Matter to Each Student in Our Public Schools* (Arlington, VA: Redbud Books, 1999); Claudia Meek, "Classroom Crisis: It's About Time," *Phi Delta Kappan,* April 2003, pp. 592-95; and National Center for Education Statistics, *Time Spent Teaching Core Academic Subjects in Elementary Schools* (Washington, DC: National Center for Education Statistics, 1997).

25. Although aware of anxiety-stressed teenagers, I was surprised by an article that described students in an affluent high school being required to eat lunch because they skipped eating in order to take another Advanced Placement class. See Winnie Hu, "Too Busy to Eat, Students Get a New Required Course: Lunch," *New York Times,* May 24, 2008, pp. A1, A11.

The crude policy solutions of more days in the year and longer school days do not even begin to touch the deeper truth that we have to improve the quality of "academic learning time."

Cost is not the tipping point in explaining why so few proposals to fix school time are successful. Time-based reforms have had trouble entering schools because other goals have had—and continue to have—clout with parents and taxpayers.

DISCUSSION QUESTIONS

1. Do you believe the current school calendar needs to be modified to meet the needs of your students? Explain.

2. Which of the options to extend learning time do you believe is the most practical and suitable? Explain.

3. The author identifies three reasons that have prevented school time reform for gaining any traction: cost, limited research, and powerful, conservative, noneconomic goals. Which of these do you feel best explains why policy makers have been unsuccessful in implementing school time reform?

4. According to the author, there is a disconnect between policy makers and students and teachers in regards to school time reform. What is the best way to bridge this gap? Explain.

5. With the increased emphasis on college access for everyone, what can policy makers and schools do to prepare students for postsecondary education?

CHAPTER

35

Excellence, Equality, and Education

ALLAN C. ORNSTEIN

FOCUSING QUESTIONS

1. How can society distinguish between education and performance?
2. Why are safety nets important for a democratic society? What safety nets do you feel are most important for society?
3. To what extent does education serve as the great equalizer in society? To what extent (or when) is education limited in serving as the great equalizer?
4. How did the common school movement help "assimilate" immigrants?
5. How does the notion of "survival of the fittest" square with safety net programs?
6. What advantages or disadvantages do IQ tests have for testing students?
7. How do noncognitive factors impact learning?
8. How are intelligence and income related?
9. How much education equality should society strive for?

No country has taken the idea of *equality* more seriously than the United States. Politically, the idea is rooted in the Declaration of Independence and the Constitution. We have fought two wars over the definition of equality: the American Revolution and the Civil War. Starting in the 1960s, first with the War on Poverty and then the civil rights movement, the language of progressive thought, and protest became associated with inequality. The concern focused on poor and minority rights, including those of women.

Inequality in today's world deals with the growing gap in income and wealth between the rich and the rest of us, the top 1 to 10 percent and the bottom 90 to 99 percent. The difference in percentages is the function of the authors and what point they are trying to delineate. If the discussion is about a small zip code such as Greenwich, Connecticut; Fisher Island, Florida; or the Hamptons in New York, the discussion can be limited to the top 1 percent. If the discussion focuses on a broader population, then the top 10 percent suffice.

The notion of *excellence* is a recent concept, first introduced by the British sociologist Michael Young in 1958 in his book, *The Rise of the Meritocracy*, in which the process of advancement by merit is outlined. The best and highest-paid positions in society are obtained on the basis of individual performance, rather than positions being allocated at random, by group characteristics such as race or gender, or by political and social networking, patronage, or nepotism. Of course, such a society does not exist, and the book is a utopian concept.

In the United States, John Gardner, the founder of Common Cause, wrote a small pocket-sized book in 1961 called *Excellence: Can We Be Equal Too?* In this book, he points out the need for a democratic society to balance excellence and equality. It must reward people for their abilities, but it also needs to make provision for the less-able person. In both books, the authors remind us that family origins should not count as an advantage or handicap in determining economic outcomes. The key to economic success should be attributable to the person's abilities and education (or training) that should make the person more valuable to society.

DEFINITIONS AND LABELS

Every modern society must deal with the relationship between excellence, equality, and education. When society considers *excellence*, it must deal with the division of labor and what it will pay for certain jobs. When 95 percent of the jobs in the United States pay less than $100,000 per year, we need to ask why certain other jobs pay a million dollars or more—and whether the benefits and importance (or responsibilities) of the high-paying jobs are worth the cost. If merit is defined in terms of performance, we need to distinguish between performance and credentials. (Having the appropriate education credentials does not necessarily guarantee good performance.) We must also work out

definitions or criteria for performance (good, average, poor etc.), test and evaluation procedures in school and in the work place for determining merit and performance—and then what are appropriate rewards.

Society must consider *equality* in terms of power and wealth—which people or groups have more or less political muscle and earn more or less (and how much more or less) than the average income—and why. The more egalitarian or progressive the society, the more safety nets it will provide to help ordinary, slow, unqualified and disabled workers to obtain and pay for essential human goods (such as food and shelter) and services (such as health, education, and transportation). The exact benefits and standards for obtaining the benefits must be worked out politically. Hence, it depends on what political group (liberal or conservative) controls the process. The more benefits available—unemployment insurance, health insurance, pensions, and social security for the poor, disabled, and aged—the more egalitarian the society.

From its birth in 1776 to the turn of the twentieth century, the United States moved from an agrarian to an industrial society. *Education* and training were important but not crucial factors for increasing opportunity. Farm and industrial societies are primarily based on muscle power and not brain power, so a good deal of mobility could be achieved without a high school or college diploma. Apprenticeships, training, and learning on the job were more important than a formal education for the masses to live a descent life.

As society became more complex and bureaucratic, education became more important. With the coming of the information age and knowledge-based society at the mid-twentieth century, formal education took on even greater importance for opportunity and mobility. Brain power now substituted for muscle power as the crucial factor in economic advancement. The female liberation movement, which started in the 1950s, with its demand for more equality, coincides with the coming information/knowledge revolution, and provided a much easier vehicle for women to obtain middle-class jobs, economic independence, and greater equality in just a few decades.

Here it should be noted that the three E-factors—excellence, equality, and education—are impressionistic and idiosyncratic, but these three labels serve as necessary working definitions. Continuing with my assertions, education is the glue or lever that helps balance excellence and equality. And if I may add a touch of poetry, in the language of Dr. Seuss, it's the "Cat in the Hat" that prevents the waste of talent and curbs the vestiges of stratification.

Education, today, is the link between excellence and equality. It is considered essential for promoting a person's opportunity and mobility and for improving the productivity of society. In a society dedicated to the pursuit of social justice, intensive efforts should be devoted to providing the best education for all its citizens and to close the education gaps that exist between the "haves" and "have nots," rich and poor students. It must not write off its disadvantaged populations as "uneducable" or slot them into poorly funded schools and second-rate programs. Our Founding Fathers understood the notion of social justice, although they called it by different names such as "freedom," "liberty," and "natural rights" of man. They wanted the children of the common people to have a fair chance to grow up as equal as possible. Equal opportunity, regardless of parentage, combined with the need for civic responsibility, were the driving forces for schooling in America.

THE EARLY ROLE OF THE SCHOOLS

The origins of American public schools are also demonstrated by the concept of equal opportunity and the notion of universal and free education. Thomas Jefferson understood that the full development of talent among all classes could and should be developed in the New World, and especially among the common class. "Geniuses will be raked from the rubbish," he wrote in his *Notes on the State of Virginia* in 1782. He added that the common people of America had the opportunity and ability for discussing social and political problems denied to them in the Old World.

When Jefferson introduced "the pursuit of happiness" at the end of Locke's famous statement "life, liberty and property," he (like Paine and Rush) was implying that the common man had the natural right for a decent life, for opportunity and success, and to participate in the social progress of the nation. Such an idea stemmed from the humanitarian spirit of the Enlightenment, although it defied 5,000 years of recorded history: Ordinary people had no rights and no expectations to live beyond poverty or subsistence levels. In arguing for human rights (what he called "'natural rights"), Jefferson was implying a legal and moral duty for equality among people, even between the patrician class and plain people. Education was the key to equality.

Writing during the same Revolutionary period, Thomas Paine, an unknown recent arrival from England, began publishing several pamphlets, including the best known *Common Sense* and *The Crisis*. As an anti-monarchical, pro-democratic pamphleteer, Paine lashed out against the vestiges of the property and landholding class and argued that government had the power to abolish poverty and provide social and economic security by introducing policies and programs for the disabled and aged by imposing inheritance taxes and rents on government land. The idea that inequality could be reduced and social programs could be implemented by government was a revolutionary idea—and rooted in Rousseau's notion of a social contract between government and its citizens.

Paine also believed that the farmers, artisans, mechanics, and other plain people had not taken part in the intellectual and artistic life of the colonies (and for that matter in any other previous society) and declared they should have the opportunity for education and culture. He rejected the common notion that education and culture, as well as philosophical and intellectual concepts, were limited to the province of the aristocracy and church.

Benjamin Rush, a well-known Philadelphian physician and signer of the Declaration of Independence, asserted that the role of education was essential if democracy was to succeed. The youth must be trained in civil and patriotic duties and in practical skills in order to retain their political and economic independence as adults. In a short essay, "Of the Mode of Education in a Republic,'" he argued that the "form of government we have assumed has created a new class of duties for every American." Education was the key for preparing young Americans for public service and jobs. In order for the blessings of liberty and equality to spread in the New World, the education system had to "prepare the principles, morals and manners of [its] citizens" for a new form of government and a new pattern of thought.

The American Revolution had opened up a new chapter in human affairs, one that elevated the dignity of the common man and humbled the aristocracy—and all the special privileges that tarnish the dignity and equality of humankind. On trying to elevate the national character, Rush warned about the rise of the banking and finance class and that "a nation debased by the love of money is a spectacle far more awful" than the evils of war.

THE COMMON SCHOOL MOVEMENT

Horace Mann also understood the need for schooling, and argued that education was the chief avenue where "humble and ambitious youth" could expect to rise. The rise of "common school" was spearheaded by Mann in the 1820s. In the words of Columbia University's Lawrence Cremin, in *The Republic and*

the School, Mann envisioned the schools as "the great equalizer of the condition of men—the balance wheel of the social machinery." Mann also saw the schools serving a social need, that is, to assimilate immigrants into the American culture. He skillfully rallied public support for the common school by appealing to various segments of the population. To enlist the business community, Mann sought to demonstrate that "education has a market value" with a yield similar to "common bullion." The "aim of industry . . . and wealth of the country" would be augmented "in proportion to the diffusion of knowledge." Workers would be more diligent and more productive.

Although the pattern for establishing common schools varied among the states, and the quality of education varied as well, the foundation of the American public school was being forged though this system. The schools were common in the sense that they housed youngsters of all socioeconomic and religious backgrounds, from ages 6 to 14 or 15, and were jointly owned, cared for, and used by the local community. Because a variety of subjects was taught to children of all ages, teachers had to plan as many as ten to fifteen different lessons a day. Teachers also had to try to keep their schoolrooms warm in the winter—a responsibility shared by the older boys, who cut and fetched wood—and cool in the summer. Schoolhouses were often in need of considerable repair, and teachers were paid miserably low salaries.

The immigrants and workers saw the schools as a social vehicle for upward mobility, to help their children realize the American dream. Equality of opportunity in this context would not lead to equality of outcomes; this concept did not attempt a classless society. As Stanford Professor David Tyack wrote in *Turning Points in American Educational History,* "For the most part, working men did not seek to pull down the rich"; rather they sought equality of "opportunity for their children, an equal chance at the main chance."

Equality of opportunity in the nineteenth and early twentieth centuries meant an equal start for all children, but the assumption was that some would go farther than others. Differences in backgrounds and abilities, a well as motivation and personality, would create differences in outcomes among individuals, but the school would assure that children born into any class would have the same opportunity to achieve status as persons born into other classes. Implicit in the view was that the schools represented the means of achieving the goal of equal chances of success relative to all children in all strata.

The connection with schooling and society was symbolized by the "little red school house" on the prairie and idealized by the themes in Horatio Alger's sentimental books on the self-made man, vision of the American dream, and power of the individual to rise above his social class. The goal of schooling fit into the popular biographies of Andrew Jackson and Abe Lincoln, who rose from their log cabins on the frontier to become president, and it fit with the words of poet Russell Lowell, that the essence of the American promise was "to lift artificial weights from all shoulders [and] afford all an unfettered start, a fair chance, in the race of life."

In retrospect, the schools did not fully achieve the goal of equal opportunity, because school achievement and economic outcomes are highly related to social class and family background. Had the schools not existed, however, social mobility would have been further reduced. The failure of the common school to provide social mobility raises the question of the role of school in achieving equality—and the question of just what the school can and cannot do to affect cognitive and economic outcomes. Can schooling overcome the effects of class? Such factors as family conditions, peer groups, and community surroundings—are all components of class-influence learning. Just what should the school be expected to accomplish in the few hours each day it has with students who spend more than three-fourths of their time with their family, friends, and community?

Class is a matter of culture—what educators now call "social capital," the kind of family and community resources available to children. The difference in capital leads to a system of inequality in terms of how students perform in schools and what kinds of jobs they eventually obtain. The question of fairness or equity is how we interpret this inequality. Do middle-class children simply "outcompete" their poor and working-class counterparts in school and therefore land better jobs (a conservative perspective), or is it discrimination and exploitation that ensure the latter group performs poorly in school and their parents, who clean up offices or hotels or work in assembly plants, earn significantly less than their bosses (a liberal perspective).

As middle- and upper-class parents jockey for the best schools for their children and hire private tutors and worry about their children's SAT scores, how are less fortunate students supposed to overcome money, power, privilege, and political connections? How is education expected to overcome a system of inequality that leads the rich to pressure the government to reduce their taxes while it cuts services for the poor and provides them with second-rate schools, second-rate healthcare, and second-rate jobs? Given the free-market pundits who wish to reduce inheritance taxes, how do working- and middle-class students compete against those students who were "born on third base" (with tens of millions in net worth)? Education is no longer the great equalizer—not when financial capital, rather than education or human capital, determines outcomes (income and wealth) and creates huge gaps of inequality.

THE CONSERVATIVE PERSPECTIVE

The notion of differences in class and the relationship to heredity have remained in the background in American thought, an idea rooted in the Old World to help explain the success of the property class—and later used by conservative-thinking Americans to explain the rise of the plantation, merchant, and banking class in colonial America, and then the capitalist class in the late nineteenth century during the Gilded Age. By the 1880s, the English philosopher Herbert Spencer maintained that the poor were "unfit" and should be eliminated through competition and the "survival of the fittest." Because the evolutionary process involved long periods of time, according to laws independent of human behavior, education could never serve as an important factor in social and economic progress. The best the schools could do is to provide basic knowledge that enabled people to adapt and survive within their environment. What Spencer failed to grasp is that with an educated mind, the character and speed of evolution for humans change, moving from a traditional and static society to a dynamic and rapid changing society.

From 1873 (when a Kalamazoo, Michigan court decision provided for free public schools) to 1900, questions revolved around the school curriculum: What should be taught at the elementary and secondary school? What courses should comprise the curriculum? How should immigrant children be educated—or assimilated? Who should attend high school? Should there be separate tracks or programs for smart and slow students? Should the same education be available for all students? Should the high school be considered preparatory for college? What curriculum provisions should be made for terminal students? Who should attend college?

At the turn of the twentieth century, the development of mind and nature of academic work in high school were believed to coincide with the so-called "laws of nature," and only a very small percentage of students were expected to succeed in high school or go on to college. Most people accepted this argument, and social and economic improvement for the masses, based on education opportunity, was exasperatingly slow. The outcome is that by 1900, only 11.5 percent of 14- to 17-year-olds were enrolled in high school, 6.5 percent graduated, and 4 percent of 18- to 21-year-olds were enrolled in college. Not too many people were concerned about these figures, because America was still a farm- and factory-based society with plenty of "manly" jobs available for working people—who worked with their hands, not their minds.

During the same period, in his book *The Future of America*, English author H. G. Wells linked peasant immigration to the country with the downfall of America. "I believe that if things go on as they are going, the great mass of them will remain a very low lower class" and the U.S. population "will remain largely illiterate industrial peasants." Today, the debate is couched in terms like "human capital," "brain-drain," and "illegal immigration." Many Americans contend that we are attracting low-wage, low-educated tomato and cabbage pickers, hotel workers, and landscapers while discouraging the foreign-educated students, scientists, and engineers on which the American economy depends.

Ellwood Cubberley, a former school superintendent and professor of education at Stanford University, and one of the most influential education voices at the turn of the twentieth century, feared the arrival of immigrants from Southern and Eastern Europe. In *Changing Conceptions of Education*, he argued they were slow-witted and stupid compared to the Anglo-Teutonic stock of immigrants. The new immigrants were "illiterate, docile, lacking in self-reliance and initiative, and not possessing the Anglo-Teutonic conceptions of law, national stock, and government." Their numbers would "dilute tremendously our national stock and corrupt our civil life." The role of the school was not only to "amalgamate" them, but also to prepare them for vocational pursuits as "common wage concerns." The new immigrant and working-class children had little need for an academic curriculum, according to Cubberley, as they were lacking in mental ability and character; in fact, he insisted the common man demanded vocational training for his children. It was foolhardy to saturate these immigrant and working-class children "with a mass of knowledge that can have little application for their lives."

Although progressive educators were concerned about the education of poor working-class and immigrant children, the fact remains that the great change in school enrollment did not occur until just before and during the Great Depression. Adolescent students were encouraged to attend high school so as not to compete with adults for jobs. By 1930, as many as 50 percent of 14- to 17-year-olds were attending high school, 51 percent of 17-year-olds graduated, and 12 percent of 18- to 21-year-olds were enrolled in college. The concept of mass education was just beginning to take shape—as America moved from a farm-based to an industrial-based country.

IQ TESTING AND SORTING

G. Stanley Hall and E. L. Thorndike, the two most influential psychologists at the turn of the twentieth century, also supported the cult of individual success and the notions that inequality resulting from competition and differences in talent and abilities reflected heredity and that the outcomes and differences in human behavior were rooted in human nature or the gene pool. No one was responsible for this inequality, and there was no reason to penalize intelligent or superior people for their success. This type of relationship—superior and inferior, smart and dumb—is what some might innocently call a "sorting out process" or "tracking system" in school, whereas others would label it as discrimi-

natory and as potential "social dynamite." Nonetheless, this conflict becomes increasingly evident when the economic gap between the upper and lower echelons is continuously widened, and when the lower base comprises an overabundance of people who feel trapped or discriminated against.

For Hall and Thorndike, the main criterion for success or fortune was inherited intelligence. The captains of industry during the Gilded Age (1860s–1920s) had forged their own success and accumulated fortunes because of their unique abilities. Their psychological theories not only fit into the business explanation of wealth, but also the religious explanation of stewardship and charity, including all those who used God and his infinite wisdom to support the business buccaneers and property interests of the wealthy class. Although no adequate tests existed at that period for determining the relationship between heredity and environment, and how these affected human traits or behaviors, their ideas led to the development of intelligence tests in 1908 by Alfred Binet, a French psychologist.

For the next 30 years, the IQ test would be used as an instrument to classify bright and slow students, to classify army recruits into designated assignments, to distinguish between officers and nonofficers, and to justify Anglo-Saxon superiority while stressing the shortcomings of immigrants from Southern and Eastern Europe and later an array of different minority groups. Melded with the idea of Darwinism (biological differences) and later Social Darwinism (social and cultural differences), the IQ test was also used to explain the innate mental superiority of the wealthy and the inferiority of the working class.

Similarly, it was argued that people of limited intelligence, who were suitable for farm and simple rural life, had moved to the cities. Along with the new immigrant arrivals from southern and eastern Europe who settled in urban areas, they were unable to deal with the complexities of city life and unsuitable for urban jobs except the lowest ones. The mass immigration melted the families and streets into an ethnic stew. The peasants and laborers arrived in the cities dazed and stunned, carrying their earthly belongings and bundles. Their fingers were callused and arms muscled by years of toil and drudgery, and their pockets lined with soil, and they had fresh hope of seeking a new life and a new identity, as working men and women of worth and dignity. But they were immediately marked by custom, language, and minimal skills and education. Living in dense areas, and often unemployed, these people of so-called low intelligence were considered responsible for committing crimes and pulling down the general level of American civilization. The difference in their abilities, coupled with their norms and behaviors, only validated the laws of nature, the rise of people with intelligence and drive and the leveling of the masses.

SPUTNIK AND POST-SPUTNIK

Enrollment in high school continued to increase so that by mid-century as many as three-quarters of eligible students were attending high school. During the Sputnik and Cold War era, Harvard University president James Conant wrote two books, *The American High School Today* in 1959 and *Slums and Suburbs* in 1961. In the first book, he argued that in order to stay competitive with the Soviets the schools had to pay special attention to the gifted and talented students as well as the above-average or top 20 percent, and to encourage them to attend college and major in science, math, and foreign languages. The curriculum had to be beefed up with more homework, more testing, and more honor and advanced study courses. An average or below-average student was considered more or less "a postscript" or "nonstudent," someone who could always

get a job and contribute to society as part of the working class.

As for the second book, the civil rights movement was just at its infancy stage and Conant sensed the need for greater education and employment opportunities for minority youth. He warned that "social dynamite" was building in the cities because of massive unemployment among black youth and adults. He compared suburban and city schools, and advocated vocational curriculum for nonacademic students attending slum schools as a method for providing them with future jobs. Although his reform ideas were accepted by the establishment, the minority and reform community in later years condemned his views as racist; it was argued that blacks would be slotted in a second-rate curriculum and be limited to vocational and blue-collar jobs. Conant never responded to his critics.

From the 1950s through the 1990s, conservative psychologists, such as William Shockley, Arthur Jensen, and Richard Herrnstein, placed heavy emphasis on heredity as the main factor for intelligence—and the reason why the poor remained poor from one generation to the next. Although the arguments were written in educational terms, the implications were political and implied class warfare, and, most disturbing, they resulted in a stereotype for explaining mental inferiority among the lower class, especially blacks, thereby explaining the need for vocational programs and putting blacks on the defensive.

According to Richard Hernstein, in *IQ in the Meritocracy*, intelligence tests measure both heritable and socially significant factors. Although the exact percentages are unknown, the genetic factor is estimated to be between 45 and 80 percent, depending on the research cited. But as society succeeds in equalizing opportunity, "the genetic factors likely become relatively more important, simply because the non-genetic factors having been equalized, no longer contribute to the differences among people." To make matters worse, in western societies, where there are no prearranged marriages, and in a democracy, smart people tend to inter-marry—making genetic factors more important and contributing to class differences among future generations. These outcomes, Herrnstein claimed, are "lethal to all forms of egalitarianism." However, he failed to understand that more Americans believe human nature is plastic and capable of improvement through improved social environment and opportunity.

The common purpose of intelligence testing is to predict success in school and suitability for various occupations. The correlation between IQ and school success increases though successive years because the skills called on by conventional intelligence tests (as well as aptitude tests such as the Scholastic Aptitude Test or Miller Analogy Test)—vocabulary, reading comprehension, logic, abstract reasoning, general information—coincide with advanced school work. So long as school and college stress verbal and mathematical skills, IQ tests (and various aptitude tests) are predictive of future academic performance. Children with low IQs usually do poorly in school and children with high IQs cover the range from excellent to poor performance. Here noncognitive factors such as motivation, emotional well-being, and work ethic play a role. High IQ offers merely the potential for academic success and preparation for professional jobs that call for above-average IQs.

Herrnstein talked a great deal about the backlash and name calling he experienced as a result of his publication. To a large extent he is right: Barring drastic egalitarian policies, the gifted and talented will move to the top of the totem pole and earn the most money. Most of us accept this type of mobility and it is the kind of society that leads to the most productivity in today's world. What Herrnstein fails to recognize is that capable people often are held back and prevented from realizing their potential because of discrimination or finances. In fact, throughout the ages societies often have wasted human talent by denying these individuals social and educational opportunities. In today's scientific and technological world, this spells disaster for such a society—and is an important factor why the vast majority of nations remain undeveloped.

Not until post–World War II, with the G.I. bill, were large numbers of capable students attending college. Even then, occupational choices and opportunities did not always reflect IQ potential—rather, social circumstances and family and personal expectations. Nevertheless, by the year 2000, more than 15.3 million students were enrolled in degree-granting institutions of higher teaching. Ten years later, the number totaled 21 million, illustrating the current need for a college education in order to economically succeed. The fact is, mass education is a major reason for why the United States is the leading economic engine of the world.

However, one might also make the argument, which some conservative educators do, that half of all children are statistically below average in IQ and basic achievement, and many just do not belong in college. Writing for the *Wall Street Journal*, Charles Murray, the co-author of *The Bell Curve*, states "if you don't have a lot of g," that is, general intelligence, "when you enter kindergarten, you are never going to have a lot of it. No change in the educational system will change that hard fact." Now that is a tough pill to swallow, especially in a society that prides itself in being egalitarian or among school people who are reform oriented and believe in the power of education and the opportunities that go along with it.

For Murray, the top 25 percent of high school graduates have the abilities to make good use of a college education, and the remaining youth would do better in vocational training. Combine those who are unqualified and those who are qualified but unmotivated, and the majority of college students today are putting a false premium on attending college and looking for something that college was not designed to provide. Few working- and middle-class parents, who are spending tens of thousands of dollars a year on their child's college education, want to hear this analysis—or, even worse, that perhaps their children should become plumbers or electricians.

Now, it may also be too frightening for the rich and well-born to suppose that the reason for their fortunes has little to do with intelligence, but in a longitudinal study of 7,400 Americans between 1979 and 2004, Ohio State's Professor Jay Zagorsky found no meaningful correlation between wealth and high IQ scores: "Those with low intelligence should not believe they are handicapped and those with high intelligence should not believe they have an advantage." There was a slight correlation between IQ scores and income; each point in IQ scores was associated with about $400 of income a year. Assuming a 10-point spread in IQ and 40 years of work, the difference is only $160,000, which can evaporate in one or two bad financial decisions. The IQ link breaks down with wealth—that is, the accumulation of assets—because smart people are just as likely as others to make bad financial choices over their lifetime. One very bad decision can wipe out a lifetime of savings. (Investors in the Madoff ponzi scheme certainly learned this fact of life the hard way.) More important, wealth often takes generations to accumulate and to pass from one generation to the next.

What all this seems to mean is that the relationship between IQ, education, and economic outcomes is not easy to separate out or pigeon-hole into neat predictions. Not only do Americans have multiple chances to succeed, but also you don't have to be an intellectual whiz-kid or a college graduate to succeed. Michael Dell, Bill Gates, Steve Jobs, Evan Williams (of Twitter), and Mark Zuckerberg (of Facebook) never finished college; neither did Alex Rodriguez, Willie Nelson, or Lady Gaga. We would like to think that the American education system is designed, at least in theory, to enable every youngster to fulfill his human potential, regardless of race, ethnicity, gender, or class and regardless of intelligence or creativity. But education, although important, is only one factor to consider in explaining economic mobility and social stratification.

EDUCATIONAL AND ECONOMIC OPPORTUNITY

The modern view of educational equality, which also emerged in the 1950s, goes much further than the old view that was concerned with equal opportunity. In light of this, James Coleman, erstwhile professor of education at Johns Hopkins University, outlined in the *Harvard Educational Review* five views of inequality of educational opportunity, paralleling liberal philosophy: (1) inequality defined by the same curriculum for all children, with the intent that school facilities be equal; (2) inequality defined in terms of social or racial composition of the schools; (3) inequality defined in terms of such intangible characteristics as teacher morale and teacher expectation of students; (4) inequality based on school consequences or outcomes for students with equal backgrounds and abilities; and (5) inequality based on school consequences for students with unequal backgrounds and abilities.

The first two definitions deal with race and social class; the next definition deals with concepts that are hard to define and hard to change; the fourth definition deals with school finances and expenditures. The fifth definition is an extreme revisionist interpretation: Equality is reached only when the outcomes of schooling are similar for all students—those who are lower class and minority as well as middle class and majority.

All these definitions and nuances may be hard for the reader to follow, so let me sum up. The easiest and most explicit way is to rely on the *New York Times* Op writer David Brooks' ditty: "Liberals emphasize inequality... Conservatives believe inequality is acceptable so long as there is opportunity." Now let me advance one step further. Most communities in the United States are stratified by income, and public schooling cannot compensate for tremendous variations in wealth and status. But within the community, the people spend about the same amount of money on each student and are inclined to let the best student go to Harvard or Yale and the best person win in economic matters.

When great economic divides exist, the solutions are unclear and open to more debate. New York City, for example, with 8 million people has roughly 700,000 residents worth a million dollars or more and another 1.5 million residents living in poverty. How can education, or for that matter any policy short of redistribution of wealth, rectify this gap, the inequality between the rich and the poor? The public generally accepts wide discrepancies in achievement and reward, partially because of the notion of the "self-made man" and the American Dream. Nonetheless, it should be opposed to excess or extremes at both ends of the scales—and without critics stifling debate by using labels such as "socialist" or "redistribution" in a derogatory and divisive way.

When inequality is defined in terms of unequal outcomes (both cognitive and economic), we start comparing racial, ethnic, and religious groups. In a heterogeneous society like ours, this results in some hotly debated issues, including how much to invest in human capital, how to determine the cost effectiveness of social and educational programs, who should be taxed and how much, to what extent we are to handicap our brightest and most talented minds (the swift runners) to enable those who are slow to catch up, and whether affirmative action policies lead to reverse discrimination.

Indeed, we cannot treat these issues lightly, because they affect most of us in one way or another and lead to questions over which wars have been fought in the past.

In a more homogeneous society, such as Japan, South Korea, Norway, or Germany, the discussion of race, ethnicity, or religion would not deserve special attention nor require judicial measures. Although it is doubtful whether increased spending in big-city schools (where poor and minority students are concentrated) would dramatically effect educational outcomes, poor and minority students still deserve the same education spending—better-paid teachers, small class sizes, high-tech resources, new textbooks, and clean bathrooms—as those in affluent suburbs where expenditures often are twice or more the amount in adjacent cities.

Students deserve equality of expenditures simply on the basis that schools are public institutions, not private. In a democracy, citizens and their children are entitled to similar treatment, especially because intellectual capital is a national concern, not designed for the benefit of one class or group of students nor the exclusion of another group. It can also be argued that the poor are entitled to special treatment because in the long run the health and vitality of the nation are at stake. Sadly, in comparison to other industrialized nations, the United States enrolls the largest percentage of poor students, approximately 24 to 25 percent. Because school performance reflects the social and economic system, this high percentage of poverty explains why, among other factors, U.S. students on international tests score consistently behind their industrialized counterparts.

THE HAZARDS OF MERIT

There is no question that other factors that prevent equal school spending are not simply symptoms of racism or class prejudice. These deal with notions of social and moral values and the rights of people: the preservation of neighborhood schools, concern about big government and state-imposed policies directed at the local level, fear of increased taxation and why someone should have to pay for someone else's child's education, and the inability of politicians to curtail well-to-do parents from supporting their own neighborhood schools and property values. The question is how much education equality should we strive for? We can have greater equality by lowering standards or by pulling down bright students. We can have more equality by handicapping bright students (as in affirmative action) or by providing an enormous amount of additional resources for low-performing students (as in compensatory funding). But eventually we come to a slippery slope and ask: How much money? Who is to pay for it?

If we stop and meditate a little on how both sides of the political aisle embrace the vision of America and how the "meritocrats" and "egalitarians" of society phrase their words in the public arena, we can get a better feel for how divided the American people are on the issue of mobility and opportunity. The Republicans during the Bush administration cut the tax rates of the rich at the same time when they were amassing huge fortunes and while the gap between wealthy and working people was widening. The Democrats during the Obama administration tried to protect safety nets and entitlements, despite the fact there were insufficient revenues to meet these obligations. In addition, the Democrats seem married to a system of affirmative action that judges people on the basis of race—not merit—and are less inclined to embrace standardized tests for schools and colleges that result in connecting decisions based on performance. The assumption is that more people would be willing to accept some kind of affirmative action program based on income and thus widen the idea of equality for more Americans. Of course, self-help is

crucial; the goal is not to bury test scores nor provide a free ride for incompetents.

While consideration for efficiency and objectivity are good reasons for relying on standardized tests, they should not be allowed to distort or limit our notion of talent. There are many different forms of talent—creative, artistic, athletic, and others—that don't rely on heavy academic emphasis, nor are they measured by standardized tests. The demand for talent is crucial in a bureaucratic and complex society, but the importance of formal education is not always paramount for higher-order and special kinds of talent.

Not only are there talented physicians and engineers to nurture, but we need also to recognize talented plumbers and talented chefs. While we need to reward different forms and types of talents, society needs to be realistic and discourage negative talents like the ability to pick pockets or deemphasize esoteric talents such as the ability to stand on your head. A democratic society must recognize multiple talents, and not only talents based on academic or cognitive intelligence. That is the genius of a progressive and democratic society.

CONCLUSION

Allow me to throw one more factor into the mix. The question of talent and rewards goes hand-in-hand and leads to results related to inequality—and the values of society. What rewards should highly talented individuals earn? In 2010, the median salary for American wage earners was approximately $36,000—about the same as it was in 1980, after considering inflation. When someone is paid tens of millions of dollars because of a special talent related to entrepreneurial risk, acting, or sports, we need to consider how these earnings contribute to inequality, as well as the emotional consequences felt by middle-income and professional people who are highly skilled or have college degrees and play by the book and can barely keep up with payment of their bills. We need to consider whether the rewards, especially if excessive, contribute to the common good and needs of society, to what extent these extraordinary salaries or earnings lead to inequality, and how they affect the standard of living of ordinary working people that comprise the foundation of American democracy. Because services and goods are limited, people with vast amounts of income drive up the prices of homes, autos, college tuition, and even baseball tickets.

For example, today, the average cost for attending a baseball game for a family of four, including sandwiches and sodas, parking, and tickets in the second tier between third base and left field, is now between $500 and $600. This amount is more than the weekly take-home pay of the average worker in America. Of course, Yankee Stadium has history and is located in the "Big Apple," where prices often are sky-high. A box seat at the stadium runs $2,500—available only for Wall Street players and global high-flying capitalists—perceived now by 99 percent as the *bastards* and *plunderers* of the world, but for blue bloods and aspiring MBAs *heroes* and *superstars* to emulate. (You might want to know that Madoff's season box seats were auctioned off).

The point is, essential good services—housing, education, health, and so on (as well as leisure activities such as watching a baseball game)—have increased far more than the median wages of workers ($36,000 annually) or household incomes ($50,050) as of 2012. Now, both spouses must work in order to live a "middle class" life style, when 50 years ago, it took one spouse working to live a similar life style—as portrayed in *Ozzie and Harriet*, *Father Knows Best*, and *I Love Lucy*. The same house that cost $100,000 in 1980 now costs $400,000 and it takes two breadwinners' income to support the mortgage.

To be sure, the 2008 recession was partially caused by the housing bubble—inflated home prices and mortgage payments that wages could not keep up with. Similarly, it now costs over $50,000 per year for private college tuition, room, and board. In 1980, the total cost was approximately $10,000. That said, wages have not increased four- or five-fold to keep up with housing prices and college tuition costs. Wages, in fact, have remained flat in real dollars for the last 30 years. The result is, the middle class is shrinking! Even worse, trapped in the context of our times—no matter how talented, smart, or educated a person might be, opportunity is limited. Despite increased education levels among our student populace, the American Dream is becoming a fable for future generations.

DISCUSSION QUESTIONS

1. How would you define excellence? Equality?
2. Can a society strive for both excellence and equality? How?
3. Why is education more important in a knowledge-based society than in a farm-based or industrial society?
4. How would you distinguish among opportunity, entitlements, and affirmative action?
5. How would you compare the post-Sputnik era with today's emphases on standards and high-stake testing?

Should parental choice be a major consideration in determining where students attend school?

PRO	CON
1. The public school system is a monolithic structure that fosters middle-class conformity.	1. School choice will promote a dual-class educational system— schools for the rich and schools for the poor.
2. Public schooling perpetuates the existing power structure, including the subordinating effects of class, caste, and gender.	2. Parental choice will breed intolerance for diversity and will further religious, racial, and socioeconomic isolation.
3. The reduced quality of public education necessitates that parents be given options in order to locate better learning environments.	3. Transporting students out of neighborhoods is costly for school districts and is time-consuming for students.
4. Increasing choices means expanding educational opportunities for low-income and minority students.	4. Choice may not increase equity. In fact, it may lead to further segregation of low-income and minority students.
5. Competitive schools should stimulate statewide efforts to implement school reform.	5. Choice is not a solution for securing adequate funding, upgrading teachers' pedagogical skills, or reforming education.

School Board Debates Bilingual Education Program

"There can be no debate," demanded school board member Ricardo Del Rotberg. "Public education monies should be used for educating students in English only. Bilingual education is poor use of the community's tax dollars." Following this fiery opening statement, people in the gallery sat momentarily stunned. The entire community knew that this school year was sure to be contentious. No one doubted that the school board members were deeply divided over the issue of providing bilingual education to immigrant children.

After a long silence, board member Evita Ellmano moved toward the microphone. She reminded the board that the number of immigrant children attending district schools was increasing dramatically each year. She cited research showing that children who were given several years of instruction in their native language learned English faster and were successful academically. Ellmano also read results from the district's test scores, which demonstrated that students for whom English was not the dominant language lagged significantly behind other students academically. Del Rotberg retorted that it was his belief that multilingual education is an ill-founded practice that seeks to instill pride in students with low self-esteem. He also suggested that the school board lobby for legislation declaring English to be the nation's official language.

School board president Sarah Turner could no longer remain silent. She reminded board members that schools are obligated to help all students live up to their fullest potential and to provide an education in their native language. Turner remarked that schools must embrace and value the traditions and cultures of all students. Moreover, she commented that bilingual education had become a target for people who opposed immigration. Finally, she stated that all teachers should be competent enough to teach their subject matter in at least one foreign language. Immediately, the teachers in the audience roared with protest. Turner pounded her gavel for nearly 8 minutes to restore order. Meanwhile, several security personnel came to the meeting room to encourage calmness.

Consider the following questions:

1. What information should be obtained to clarify the facts reflective of both positions?

2. What members of the community should become involved in discussions related to bilingual education programs?
3. Should teachers be expected to retool their pedagogical skills and learn to teach their subject matter in a foreign language? Why? Why not?
4. Are there programmatic alternatives to providing bilingual education to immigrant children?
5. Do schools have a responsibility to maintain the ethnic culture of immigrant children?

CREDITS

Name Index

Note: Page numbers followed by *n* represent endnotes.

Subject Index